Analysis of
Tonal Music:
A Schenkerian
Approach

Allen Cadwallader
and David Gagné

New York   Oxford
OXFORD UNIVERSITY PRESS
1998

Oxford University Press

Oxford   New York
Athens   Auckland   Bangkok   Bogota
Bombay   Buenos Aires   Calcutta   Cape Town
Dar es Salaam   Delhi   Florence   Hong Kong   Istanbul
Karachi   Kuala Lumpur   Madras   Madrid
Melbourne   Mexico City   Nairobi   Paris
Singapore   Taipei   Tokyo   Toronto   Warsaw

and associated companies in
Berlin   Ibadan

Published by Oxford University Press, Inc.
198 Madison Avenue, New York, New York 10016

Oxford is a registered trademark of Oxford University Press

Library of Congress Cataloging-in-Publication Data
Cadwallader, Allen Clayton.
Analysis of tonal music : a Schenkerian approach / Allen
Cadwallader and David Gagné.
p. cm.
Includes bibliographical references and index.
ISBN 0-19-510232-0
1. Schenkerian analysis.   I. Gagné, David.   II. Title.
MT6.C12A53 1998 781—dc21
97-5752

3   5   7   9   8   6   4   2

Printed in the United States of America
on acid-free paper

Contents

Part 2. *Analytical Applications*   196

Preface

Scholar, critic, practical musician, theorist, analyst, and pedagogue—Heinrich Schenker led a musical life of remarkable diversity. Born in Galicia (now the western region of Ukraine) in 1868, Schenker showed remarkable talent for the piano from an early age. In the late 1880s he studied at the Conservatory in Vienna, and also earned a doctoral degree in jurisprudence at the University. He was active early in his career as a pianist, a conductor, an editor, and a composer. His compositions gained the favorable notice of Brahms and Busoni, and his essays in musical criticism appeared in a variety of periodicals. But it is his insights into the character and structure of tonal music that have made him one of the most important music theorists of this or any century, profoundly influencing the pedagogy and scholarship of music theory, both in the United States and abroad.

Dissatisfied with the state of musical thought and music theory pedagogy in his time, Schenker began work on a series of original theoretical works entitled *Neue musikalische Theorien und Phantasien (New Musical Theories and Fantasies)*. The first part of this series, *Harmonielehre (Harmony)*, appeared in 1906. Part II, *Kontrapunkt (Counterpoint)*, was published in two volumes (1910 and 1922). Though Schenker originally began work on *Der freie Satz (Free Composition)* with the idea that it would form the conclusion of *Kontrapunkt*, it continued to grow in scope through the remainder of his life, and was published after his death in 1935. (For a complete listing of Schenker's published theoretical works and available translations, see the Bibliography.)

Our book is intended as an introduction to Schenker's work. It therefore assumes no prior knowledge of the subject and does not cover all aspects of this vast field of study. We assume our audience will consist of upper-class undergraduates and first- or second-year graduate students. The book can be used over the span of one or two semesters, depending on how much emphasis is given to the early chapters, the quantity of assignments and works covered, and the degree to which additional readings are assigned for study from the Bibliography.

The study of Schenkerian analysis requires knowledge of tonal harmony, which typically is studied during the first four semesters in many college and university music programs. Counterpoint—especially the principles exemplified in species counterpoint—is fundamental to Schenker's approach. Furthermore, familiarity with the conventional categories of musical forms (binary, ternary, etc.) will further facilitate the study of Schenkerian analysis.

Schenkerian theory is a theory of tonal music. Some scholars have explored music of the Middle Ages, Renaissance, and twentieth century from a modified Schenkerian perspective. While interesting and rewarding, these studies are beyond the scope of an introductory text. Schenker's ideas have also been used by recent scholars to explore in greater detail the nature of rhythm and form. Much of this research has been motivated by Schenker's own ideas on these subjects, which are sometimes more preliminary and limited in scope than his concepts of harmonic and contrapuntal structure. Although the latter part of our book is organized by formal categories, we deal with form and rhythm as separate topics only to a limited extent. Our goal is to present the most essential principles of the harmonic and contrapuntal dimensions of tonal music.

Schenkerian analysis has traditionally been taught through a "hands-on" approach: learning by doing many analyses. Schenker himself discovered his most profound theoretical postulates after many years of analysis. We follow this approach and begin with a series of chapters devoted to basic principles, which set the stage for the analyses of phrases, phrases in combination, and finally complete movements. The well-known precepts of Schenkerian theory are therefore developed and explained through the analysis of specific pieces, an approach that parallels the evolution of Schenker's work.

Despite its great importance, Schenker's final work, *Free Composition*, presents many difficulties of style and content for the beginning student. Many commentators have noted that, while theoretically sound, the organization of Schenker's treatise—from background to middleground to foreground—does not represent the most appropriate conceptual and pedagogical sequence for the beginner. We recommend that the instructor select appropriate passages from *Free Composition* that correspond to the subject or technique under discussion. These may be given as assignments or read and explained in class. Though *Free Composition* can be obscure at times, and is often difficult to understand for those not familiar with Schenker's earlier writings, this great theoretical treatise nonetheless offers valuable insights into tonal music for those who patiently study its contents.

We believe that the ideal literature for introductory work is from the high Classical period, though we have included examples from the Baroque and Romantic eras. We have attempted to provide as much of the actual music as is possible with the graphs, though this procedure has not been feasible for the later chapters. It is essential to point out, both to instructors and students, that the score should *always* be consulted when studying a graphic analysis. We recommend that readers seek out *Urtext* editions, which are usually accessible in most music libraries. For the Beethoven piano sonatas, we recommend

Schenker's edition, which is reproduced by Dover Publications. Mozart's piano sonatas appear in an edition by Theodore Presser (edited by Nathan Broder), which was prepared from the autographs and earliest printed sources. Some of our examples can be found in Charles Burkhart's excellent *Anthology for Musical Analysis* (4th and 5th editions); all of the examples in his anthology faithfully reproduce the composers' works.

Exercises of graded difficulty are provided for Chapters 2–11. We recommend that students play or listen to each example or exercise before proceeding. Any analysis of a musical work should not be based solely on a visual interpretation of the score—it should be based on the *sound* of the piece. It may initially be played on a piano or listened to on a recording, but it should ideally be memorized and heard in one's *inner ear.*

Edward Laufer has stated that "analysis becomes not an end in itself, but a means to a richer and clearer understanding of the music, essential for performance."* A Schenkerian voice-leading analysis primarily depicts the harmonic/contrapuntal structure of a composition, but such an analysis is not intended to be complete. Aspects of rhythm, texture, and form should also be considered in a more comprehensive view of a piece; a graphic analysis can provide the basis for the elaboration of these other dimensions of tonal music. This holistic approach enhances a student's ability to recognize musical structure and design on the immediate level of the musical surface, and to become more aware of the nature and interrelationships of larger structural units. (Higher levels of structure may not be immediately perceptible; like deeper structures in language and literature, they serve rather to guide and shape the music as heard.) We assume no knowledge of graphic notation. In the early chapters we introduce some notation gradually and somewhat informally, reserving a more complete discussion of graphic symbols until the beginning of Chapter 5.

A NOTE ON TERMINOLOGY AND SYMBOLS

1. Some of Schenker's original German terms have remained in use. English terminology, however, is becoming increasingly commonplace, especially since the English translation of *Free Composition* appeared in 1979. In general we use English terms in this book, with the corresponding German term given at its first appearance. Some terms have become so familiar in the theoretical literature that we use the English and German forms interchangeably:

scale step	*Stufe*
fundamental line	*Urlinie*
fundamental structure	*Ursatz*
composing-out	*Auskomponierung*

*Edward Laufer, review of Schenker's *Free Composition*, *Music Theory Spectrum* 3 (1981), p. 159.

2.   Schenker used a caret-like symbol (∧) to designate tones of the *Urlinie* (the fundamental line of an entire composition). In Chapters 5–7 we will modify Schenker's usage and use carets also for main upper-voice tones of a line that governs a segment (the excerpts in these chapters are generally brief and self-contained). In Chapters 8–12, we follow Schenker's usage more closely; the conventions we adopt for these chapters are described in the introduction to Part II.

3.   The system of registral designation used in this book is in common use, and was employed by Schenker in his published analyses:

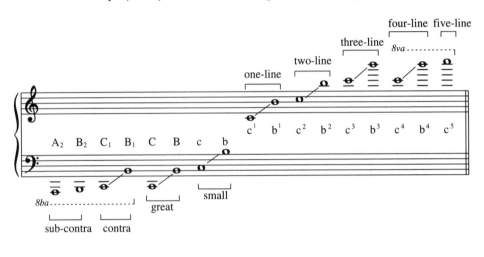

ACKNOWLEDGMENTS

We owe many people a debt of gratitude for their assistance with this book. First, we extend our heartfelt appreciation to Carl Schachter, who has been a source of inspiration for both authors over many years. In a sense he has been a guiding spirit for our work and it is to him we dedicate this book. We also express our thanks to another special musician, Charles Burkhart, who read the manuscript in various stages and provided detailed and extensive commentary. His great enthusiasm for the text provided us impetus and fresh insights during the long hours we spent in writing its many drafts. Special thanks are extended to Carl Schachter and to William Rothstein, who as reviewers for Oxford University Press offered many fine suggestions for the final draft. In addition, David Loeb, Saul Novack, William Rothstein, Hedi Siegel, Severine Neff, and Richard Randall gave generously of their time and expertise. We are grateful to Maribeth Anderson Payne and to the Oxford staff for their guidance through the various production stages of this book; a special note of thanks is extended to Natalie Bowen, who read the manuscript with great care and provided expert manuscript editing. Finally we thank the students of our classes at the Oberlin College Conservatory of Music, Queens College and the Graduate Center, CUNY, and the Eastman School of Music for their suggestions.

Analysis of Tonal Music

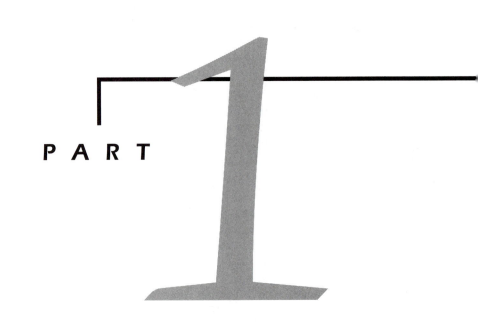

PART 1

Basic
Principles

Introduction

During the latter part of the twentieth century, many principles and ways of thinking that were first introduced by Heinrich Schenker have become an integral part of musical discourse. Concepts such as *prolongation* and *structural level* are now frequently taught to music students, and analytical graphs are commonplace in theory journals.

Notions about Schenker and his work differ greatly. For some, Schenker's legacy is associated with broad, general ideas that pertain to the essential nature of tonality, while for others his approach is a way of revealing the individual and intricate features of specific compositions. His work, in fact, embodies both characteristics. Schenker's theoretical ideas developed from the analysis of a very large number of individual compositions, where he focused on the details of melody, counterpoint, harmony, and form. It was not until relatively late in his life that he formulated the theoretical principles that are now widely associated with his work.

Many of Schenker's writings are now available in excellent English translations, which are listed in the Bibliography.[1] His mature theory is presented in *Free Composition*, which was published after his death in 1935. Despite its great importance, this work is not suitable for use as an introductory text: it is organized as a treatise rather than a textbook, and is written in a compressed manner with language that is often difficult to understand.[2] Once you know more about Schenkerian theory, with the aid of this book you will be able to read *Free Composition* and to understand Schenker's ideas, as well as the analyses that he published.

Schenker's approach is sometimes seen as rational and detached from perceptual experience; however, it is grounded in the fundamental principles of harmony and counterpoint, and requires solid musicianship and a developed musical ear. Schenker began his musical career as a pianist, composer, and music critic. He also was a pioneer in the study of autograph manuscripts and the use of autographs to prepare musical editions.[3] His interest in theory and analysis grew naturally out of these activities, since he believed the theoretical understanding and teaching methods of the time to be inadequate. Schenker always valued performance and practical musicianship, and saw himself as both a theorist and an artist.[4]

It is our goal in this book to present Schenkerian analysis in this light: not just as a theory, but as a comprehensive way of understanding a musical work. Though a Schenkerian graph focuses on elements of harmony and counterpoint, analytical decisions involve consideration of all aspects of the work. In the discussion of principles and analyses, we seek also to convey the spirit and process of this approach.

Schenkerian analysis provides a comprehensive view of a work in all dimensions from the small to the large. As such it is a great asset to hearing, understanding, and performance. A Schenkerian graph uses noteheads and various rhythmic notations, not in the usual ways, but to represent various kinds of analytical interpretation. The graph is not an end in itself, but a means by which the analysis may be expressed and understood. In the early chapters of this book you will learn the basic principles that underlie Schenkerian analysis, and then we shall proceed to analyses first of phrases and then of complete pieces. In Schenker's approach, the analysis is not imposed on the music. Rather, you will learn how to evaluate a musical context based on your hearing and perception of all aspects of that context.[5]

Schenkerian analysis often reveals connections among tones that are not readily apparent. When a configuration of tones recurs in identical or similar form, whether in immediate succession or over a broader span of music, such a recurring pattern is called a *motive*. Schenker's extended concept of motive is one of his most profound and far-reaching contributions to the understanding of music.

As an introduction to the Schenkerian approach, we will explore some motivic aspects of the first movement of Beethoven's Piano Sonata, Op. 2, No. 1. Before you read further, play or listen to the entire movement. Notice the large sections of the form, and the key areas associated with them. Although we shall focus primarily on motivic aspects of this movement, we shall do so in relation to the form.[6] Our discussion is based on an analysis by Schenker, but one that was done prior to the mature work for which he is best known. After you have read this book, you may wish to return to this piece and study Schenker's original analysis.[7]

BEETHOVEN, PIANO SONATA, OP. 2, NO. 1, I

Example 1.1 presents bars 1–8 of the exposition. If you play or listen to these bars, you will notice a propulsive energy created by the rapid arpeggiated ascent in the right hand that reaches $a\flat^2$ in bar 2 and $b\flat^2$ in bar 4. These

EXAMPLE 1.1:

Beethoven, Piano Sonata, Op. 2, No. 1, I, bars 1–8

tones are emphasized not only as goals of the ascents, but also because the left-hand supporting chords enter only after they are reached.

The figures of bars 2 and 4 are repeated in bars 5 and 6, now in rapid succession because the preceding arpeggiated figure is absent. This represents a type of thematic development that both delays (through repetition) and intensifies (through contraction) the forward motion to a subsequent goal.

Though not the conclusion of the phrase, the I^6 chord in bar 7 supports the tone c^3, the goal of the repeated ab^2–bb^2 motion and the highest melodic point. This tone is highlighted not only by the high register, but also through the dynamics of the phrase. Notice also the rolled chord that supports the climax. It is a version—rhythmically contracted—of the arpeggio figure in bars 1–2, which is restated in bars 3–4, and echoed in the ascending leaps from the grace notes in bars 5–6. In bars 7–8, as the dynamic level decreases to *piano*, C falls a sixth to E♮. This sixth is highlighted in our musical example with beamed stems. The falling sixth is a pattern or figure that recurs in various guises throughout the movement. As such, it is a kind of motivic "seed" that appears, more fully developed, as the piece progresses. For convenience, this figure is identified in the examples as motive *a*.

Consider now Example 1.2, which presents the end of the first theme, the transition section (bars 9–20), and the beginning of the second theme.[8] Following a restatement of the first-theme arpeggio figure in C minor (V), the transition section is permeated with different expressions of the falling sixth (beamed in the music). In accordance with the section's modulatory function, the sixth is *transposed* to begin on E♭.

EXAMPLE 1.2:

Beethoven, Piano Sonata, Op. 2, No. 1, I, bars 6–21 with analytical interpretation

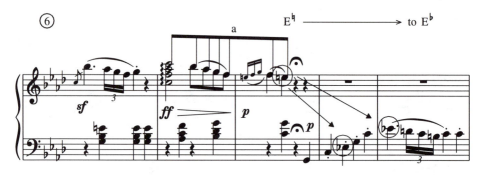

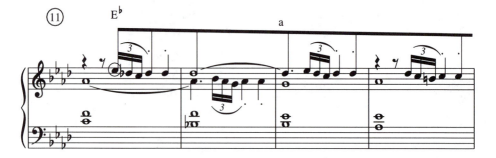

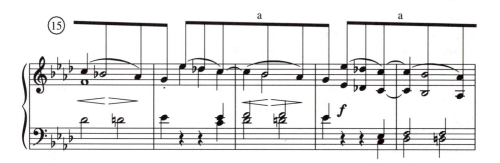

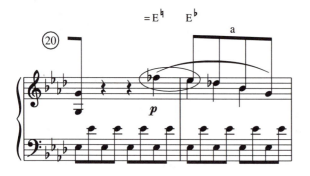

Note also that the first repetition of the motive (bars 11–16) is an *enlarged* form of the original sixth. The subsequent sixths appear in quicker note values, producing a composed rhythmic accelerando before the transition concludes in bar 20.

Consider again the end of the first theme and the beginning of the transition section. The first phrase ends with a half cadence and E♮ as the uppermost pitch in the right hand. After the fermata, the transition section begins with a recurrence (an octave lower) of the first theme in C minor, thereby producing a juxtaposition of E♮ and E♭. As we show in Example 1.2, E♭ occurs twice in the lower register (left hand); it then appears (bar 11) in the *same register* as the E♮ in bar 8. Beethoven thus associates E♭ and E♮ through registral position in the same octave, even though other tones intervene in the lower register. This larger connection is revealed notationally in the score by the visual space created by the rests in the right hand.

Chromatic relationships of this kind often have a larger meaning in tonal music. Before exploring the implications of this relationship, let us first consider the second theme. Although the second key area is the mediant (A♭), the second theme begins over a dominant pedal; an authentic cadence in A♭ major does not occur until the theme concludes in bars 40–41. Notice also that the second theme initially expresses both A♭ major and A♭ minor before the major form emerges more definitively in bars 26ff. Thus Beethoven incorporates a prominent element of the A♭-minor scale: the use of F♭, which falls to E♭ in bars 20–21. This preparation, as it turns out, has been foreshadowed earlier: F♭/E♭ is an enharmonically respelled version of the chromatic juxtaposition E♮/E♭ that links the first theme and transition section.[9] Notice (in the music) that this relationship is echoed by the f♭^{3} in bars 29 and 30—the highest note in the piece so far, which is left registrally unresolved—and the e♭^{3} in bars 32–33 that later resolves this tone in its register.

We shall now consider a different, and extraordinary, expression of motive *a* in the development section of the movement. The development begins with a statement of the first theme (bars 49–54), followed by a rather lengthy passage based on the second theme. Listen again to this section, noting the quasi-cadential patterns that suggest fleeting key areas. For instance, bars 55–62 imply B♭ minor, followed by a passage in C minor (beginning in bar 63). The patterns are "quasi-cadential" because the V–I motion associated with the bass of an authentic cadence is presented in the right hand over the dominant *pedals* of the respective key areas: compare the leap of an ascending fourth F-B♭ in bars 57, 59 and G–C in bars 65, 67.

In bar 69 this pattern changes, signaling an important event in the course of the development section. Here, the second theme shifts to the left hand (beginning in bar 67) and the cadential motion occurs in the bass: we hear V^7–I in C minor (the bass now carries the leap of a fourth). Example 1.3 is a chordal simplification of bars 69–81. As the example indicates, cadential soprano motions occur frequently. In the overall descent of the soprano line, most of the circled notes achieve local stability through support by the fleeting tonics, or tonicizations.[10] The rhythmic patterning established by the cadential motions also relates those tones that are circled.

EXAMPLE 1.3:

Beethoven, Piano Sonata, Op. 2, No. 1, I, bars 69–81, analytical interpretation

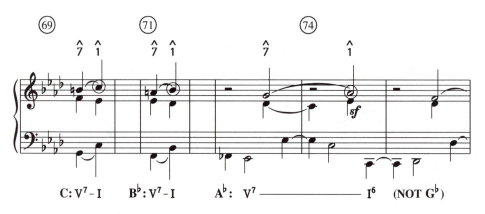

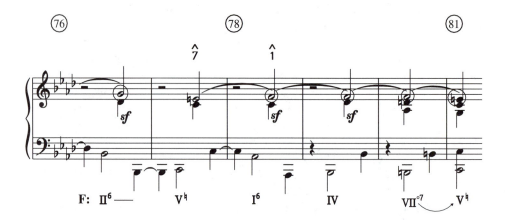

What occurs in these bars is truly remarkable. Beethoven has recomposed the *untransposed* falling sixth from bars 7–8, C to E♮, over the span of 13 bars in the development section. (Here and throughout this book, the word "span" refers to either a specified portion of a composition, or the length and scope of a specific motion or gesture within a work such as the falling sixth referred to here.) In other words, a large portion of the development section incorporates an *enlarged* version of a motive from the very beginning of the piece! Beethoven also uses dynamics to emphasize the prominence of these right-hand tones; notice the sforzando markings in bars 74–79, which, in conjunction with the broadening of the harmonic rhythm, highlight the tones A♭, G, and F of the original falling sixth.[11]

Before proceeding to the recapitulation, we will point out one additional passage influenced by this seminal motive. Example 1.4 is a sketch that illustrates the final bars of the development section and the first bar of the recapitulation. This passage is the retransition, which links V of F minor, the

EXAMPLE 1.4:

Beethoven, Piano Sonata, Op. 2, No. 1, I, bars 93–101, analytical interpretation

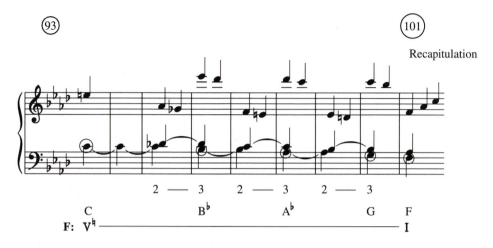

harmonic goal of the development, with the harmony at the beginning of the recapitulation. The circled notes on the music reveal a motion from C down to F, five notes of the original falling sixth. The motive is abbreviated since the goal of the bass descent is F, the root of tonic harmony. Such a bass motion is not particularly unusual at the end of a retransition section; in this particular sonata, however, it assumes motivic significance because of its prominence throughout the movement. Beethoven thus presents another enlarged version of the motive just a few bars before the original form appears in the first phrase of the recapitulation.

In the recapitulation, many of the motivic associations we discussed in the exposition recur in the course of the repetition inherent in the sonata form's broad compositional plan. There are, however, differences between the exposition and recapitulation that can be related to the conventions of large-scale harmonic structure. In many minor-mode sonata movements, for example, the second theme is first heard in the exposition in the major mediant area, and recurs in the recapitulation (down a third) in the minor tonic. In this exposition, Beethoven prepared us early on for the minor-mode version of the second theme (of the recapitulation) by incorporating a prominent element of the A♭-minor scale, the note F♭.

We will conclude our discussion with some observations of how the motive of a falling sixth exerts its influence on the concluding section of this movement. Example 1.5 shows the beginning of the second theme. The F♭/E♭ (E♮/E♭) relation is not present, because the second theme appears in the tonic. Consider, however, bars 120 and 122 of the second theme. The falling sixth from C to E♮ is now compressed into single measures; in this case we are illuminating a relationship between the motive and the *span* of the original motive–the minor sixth. (Because of the arpeggiated character of the second

EXAMPLE 1.5:

Beethoven, Piano Sonata, Op. 2, No. 1, I, bars 119–124 with analytical interpretation

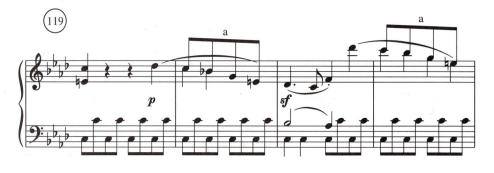

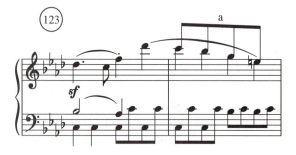

theme, two notes of the original, stepwise motive are omitted.) Perhaps the most fascinating aspect of this restatement in a new context is that Beethoven uses the *untransposed* span from bars 7–8.[12] Could this unifying relationship occur under any set of circumstances?

We know from Beethoven's sketches that the overall character and compositional plan of his works were strongly influenced by their themes and motives. We mentioned above that one of the characteristics of the sonata's second theme is that it begins over a dominant pedal. Another possibility, perhaps the more typical one, is for the second theme to begin with its local tonic harmony. Imagine this passage beginning with an F-minor chord; you will quickly realize that a sustained tonic will not support the literal repetition of C falling to E♮. We might say that this motivic recollection has been prepared, in the exposition, by the nontonic beginning of the second theme. In other words, the dominant pedal of F minor provides the necessary tonal context for the untransposed form of the falling sixth in the recapitulation.

Example 1.6 presents the coda, a section that typically affirms the tonic of the piece and is often characterized by the recollection of motives stated throughout the composition. Another succession of tones has been circled on the music: A♭–G–F–E♮–F. Notice that the final tone F does not follow immediately after E♮, but is delayed by the leap to the C; the resolution of the leading tone E♮ to F has simply been delayed by the consonant skip to C. Does this

EXAMPLE 1.6:

Beethoven, Piano Sonata, Op. 2, No. 1, I, bars 140–152 with analytical interpretation

tone succession represent another version of the falling sixth? It is perhaps possible to suggest such a connection. One might view the falling part of this line (A♭ to E♮) as an incomplete version of the descent from C to E♮. There is, as it turns out, a more literal reference. Take a moment and examine the right-hand part in bars 1–2 (Example 1.1). The opening of Beethoven's first theme comprises an upward arpeggiation followed by a change of direction and a figure in a dotted-quarter/sixteenth-triplet/quarter-note rhythm. In bar 2 this figure literally describes the notes A♭–G–F–E♮–F. In the coda, therefore, Beethoven recalls (in enlarged form) another important motive of the piece.

Our final observation about the falling-sixth motive focuses on the concluding seven bars (Example 1.6, bars 146–152). In a virtuosic passage that brings this exciting movement to a close, Beethoven once again traces the path of C descending to E♮ in the *original register of bars 7–8*. The closing tonic harmony then allows the falling-sixth motive to achieve closure on F, the first degree of the F-minor scale.[13] As in the development section, almost every tone of the motive is highlighted with a dynamic marking; notice in addition that the sforzandos (bars 149–150) accent weak beats in these bars, further emphasizing the tones of the falling sixth.

In this introductory discussion we have traced a single motive in its many transformations through the first movement of a Beethoven sonata. The study of motives is only one aspect of Schenkerian analysis, but it illustrates ways in which this approach can illuminate works by revealing connections and relationships that are not immediately apparent. The deeper understanding thereby gained can be beneficial both to our appreciation of a piece and to its performance. Schenker's approach is remarkable in its ability to inform us about what is unique about a composition, as well as what that composition shares with other pieces in the tonal repertoire.

We have, of course, only begun to scratch the surface of this remarkable movement. We could easily devote many more pages to the examination of harmony, rhythm, form, and other motivic associations. Our purpose in this first chapter, however, is to offer a preview of what Schenker's approach can reveal about a tonal composition. The remainder of this book is intended to provide you with a greater understanding of Schenker's work and to guide you in the development of skills that will allow you to return to this sonata and discover more of its extraordinary attributes.

Many musicians are familiar with certain theoretical aspects of Schenker's work. Yet you may have noticed in this chapter that we have not dealt with the broad similarities that relate this piece to other tonal compositions, but have focused instead on motivic features, on *specific* characteristics that make this movement a truly unique work of art. Analysis has as its first and central goal the understanding of a piece on its own terms. But the recognition of general principles is also fundamental. Schenker's motto, "Always the same, but not in the same way," reminds us of what his lifelong work with tonal music revealed: that general principles of harmony and counterpoint underlie a vast and varied repertoire.[14]

In this book we will explore Schenker's theoretical ideas through the analysis of complete works and excerpted passages. For example, in addition to illuminating motivic associations in Beethoven's sonata, we also mentioned that it begins in I and progresses to III before the end of the exposition, after which the development progresses toward its goal, V in F minor. If you think about the bass tones of the harmonic progression I–III–V, you will see that the large-scale harmonic plan of the exposition and development is based on the motion F–A♭–C, an expanded arpeggiation of the tonic triad! This is the sort of global principle Schenker's approach can reveal with great clarity.

Before we begin to study Schenkerian analysis in detail, a few closing remarks about repertoire and Schenker's philosophy are in order. Schenker himself dealt almost exclusively with music of the Baroque, Classic, and Romantic eras. Later scholars have investigated music of earlier and later periods using Schenkerian techniques, though not without some controversy. Some aspects of the approach, particularly the focus on the linear nature of music, are undoubtedly relevant to at least some pre-Baroque and twentieth-century repertoires. Schenker's theory itself, however, is based on harmonic tonality of the eighteenth and nineteenth centuries. We have therefore followed this approach and have chosen examples from this period.

Another aspect of Schenker's work that has aroused some controversy is his philosophical and cultural perspective. Like many Germans and Austrians in his era, Schenker believed in the superiority of German culture, and German music in particular. (This was at a time when writers in other countries, such as France, were often equally nationalistic.) Schenker's beliefs and preferences, which are obvious in his writings, may at times seem odd and even repellent from our perspective many decades later. Yet the value and importance of Schenker's approach clearly transcends such beliefs. Like Plato and many later medieval and Renaissance philosophers and scholars, Schenker also saw music as an ideal combination of nature and art with extraordinary power to touch the human soul.

Other recent studies have explored the philosophical aspects of Schenker's work.[15] The scholarship that deals with the metaphysical aspects of Schenker's thought, such as the philosophical implications of the *Ursatz*, may seem irrelevant to some students of Schenker's theories, but will engage the imagination of others. Although it is enlightening to view Schenker's ideas in the context of his cultural milieu, the fact that his opinions were conditioned by that milieu does not diminish the importance of his analytical insights for our own time. The great importance of Schenker lies in his extraordinary theoretical and analytical contributions, which have transformed the way that music is taught and understood. It is his approach to analysis, rather than his philosophy and its origins, that is the subject of this book.

CHAPTER 2

Melody and Counterpoint

Schenkerian analysis examines the interrelationships among melody, counterpoint, and harmony in the *structure* of tonal music. "Structure" in this sense may refer to the makeup and character of one aspect of a composition—such as melody—or to the complete fabric of the composition as established by melody, counterpoint, and harmony in combination.

In this chapter, we shall examine aspects of single-line melody in relation to major and minor keys, and summarize some basic principles associated with the combination of two or more melodic lines as illustrated in species counterpoint. In Chapter 3 we will consider bass lines and harmonic structures, and harmonic prolongation. These chapters will put familiar material in a new perspective and will introduce a variety of Schenkerian analytical concepts.

MELODY

The literature of tonal music contains an extraordinary variety and diversity of melodies. Yet each has been influenced and shaped in various ways by inherent characteristics of the tonal system. We shall begin by considering the ways in which essential features of the major and minor modes govern selected melodies from the literature.

Example 2.1 presents the first three phrases from a setting of the chorale melody "O Ewigkeit, du Donnerwort" by J. S. Bach. In the opening phrase,

EXAMPLE 2.1:

J. S. Bach, "O Ewigkeit, du Donnerwort," bars 1–6

the melody outlines an F-major scale which is highlighted by the regular rhythm and chordal support.

Although the soprano melody in this phrase is entirely stepwise, the tones are related to one another in a dynamic manner. Between the tonic notes that begin and end the scale, the other tones of the tonic triad are emphasized by metrical position (A and C) and repetition (C). In the upbeat figure, scale degree $\hat{2}$ (G) connects $\hat{1}$ and $\hat{3}$ as a nonharmonic passing tone.[1] The relative instability of this tone enhances the forward movement to A. Scale degree $\hat{4}$ (B♭) likewise connects $\hat{3}$ and $\hat{5}$ and is harmonized by VII^6, which is less stable than the tonic chords it connects. In bar 2, the final three soprano notes of the first phrase are strongly directed to the tonic, with the half step between $\hat{7}$ and $\hat{8}$ creating a definitive arrival on the tonic note in conjunction with the supporting cadential motion in the bass.

In purely melodic terms, the major scale is a configuration of tones where each note is in unique relation to the other notes in the scale because of the characteristic pattern of whole and half steps. (In this sense it is fundamentally different in nature from the chromatic and whole-tone scales, where all the notes of the scale are equidistant.) The tones of the major scale thus exist in dynamic relation to one another. Scale degrees $\hat{1}$, $\hat{3}$, $\hat{5}$, and $\hat{8}$, tones belonging to the tonic triad, tend to sound relatively stable compared to the other notes of the scale. The half step between $\hat{7}$ and $\hat{8}$ gives the leading tone its strong tendency to move to the tonic. Scale degree $\hat{2}$, though a whole step above the tonic, may also be active in the direction of the tonic, and is sometimes called the *descending leading tone*. The tritone (the augmented fourth or the diminished fifth) formed by the combination of $\hat{4}$ and $\hat{7}$ is often called a "key-defining" interval, since any particular augmented fourth or diminished fifth occurs in only one major key, and its resolution by half steps to $\hat{1}$ and $\hat{3}$ clearly identifies the tonic of that major key. Thus you can see how the major scale embodies a diverse network of potential relationships.[2]

The second phrase of the chorale melody begins like the first, though it is harmonized differently. After outlining the tonic triad and reaching scale degree $\hat{5}$ the melody changes direction and descends to $\hat{2}$. Approached from above and supported by V of a half cadence, the supertonic note is active in the direction of the tonic and does not sound conclusive. Consequently the listener is left with an expectation that the melody will later resolve to $\hat{1}$.

Scale degree $\hat{2}$, therefore, may be active in the direction of $\hat{3}$, or it may function as the descending leading tone, strongly directed to the tonic even though the interval between the two tones is a whole step. The tendency of this tone is, of course, determined by the context.

Notice that the melody in Example 2.1 comprises mostly stepwise motion. In both vocal and instrumental tonal music, stepwise motion provides the greatest possible continuity in a melody. Schenker used the term *melodic fluency* to describe the balance and poise that a stepwise line can provide. A melody consisting entirely of stepwise motion, however, could quickly become dull and monotonous. The judicious use of leaps therefore becomes necessary to provide variety.[3]

In contrast to the stepwise motion of the first two phrases, the third phrase contains two leaps before a stepwise descent to the tonic. The initial descending leap from A to F provides the expected tonic note. It is, however, supported by VI and consequently does not resolve the melodic (and harmonic) tension of the previous half cadence. The second leap ascends from F to B♭, creating the space of a fourth that is then filled in by descending motion. The descending and ascending leaps and subsequent stepwise motion create a balanced effect, combining melodic variety and continuity.

The final four notes of the melody also complete the descent left unfulfilled in the previous phrase, and provide local closure to this portion of the chorale melody. Notice how the descending motion contrasts with the rising motion of the opening bars. In tonal melodies, falling motion is typically associated with a release of tension and with closure, while rising motion conveys a sense of growing intensity, as if in opposition to gravity. Supported by both II$^6_5$ and V in the cadence, the descending leading tone is expanded to a half note—the only half note in the example. The greater length emphasizes the tone, and provides one final element of delay before the tonic note appears at the cadence.

The opening of Chopin's Etude, Op. 10, No. 3, is presented in Example 2.2. The shape of this beautiful melody outlines a symmetrical arch from the E at the beginning (with the preceding upbeat) to the E at the end. Certain tones stand out within this overall pattern because of length, rhythmic position, and other factors. In bars 1–2 the tones E, F♯, and G♯ are heard as

EXAMPLE 2.2:

Chopin, Etude, Op. 10, No. 3, bars 1–5 with analytical interpretation

primary, with neighbor figures decorating but not fundamentally altering this stepwise ascent. Notice that the extended tones F♯ and G♯ occur on the second beat and are tied over to the following downbeat, creating a syncopation reinforced by the notated accents. (These syncopations highlight the tones in conjunction with the supporting harmonies, which are also syncopated.)

In bar 2, the G♯ neighbor note on the first beat anticipates the longer G♯ on the second beat. Accordingly, when the neighbor figure recurs a step higher on the first beat of bar 3, the neighbor tone A suggests that this tone will again follow on the second beat. Instead, the gradual, serene progression of the melody is altered: a leap to C♯ occurs in place of the expected A, shifting it (as an accented passing tone) to the downbeat of bar 4. In bar 4, A is followed by G♯. The stepwise motion of the large-scale melodic arch, however, is interrupted by a descending leap of a fourth to D♯, which balances the ascending fourth G♯–C♯ in bar 3. The tones F♯ and E in bars 4–5, emphasized through duration as in bars 1–2, conclude the essentially stepwise melodic arch.

This melody thus combines continuity and variety in an extraordinary way, by outlining the tonic triad. Beginning with the upbeat tone B, the mel-

ody moves through E to G♯, ultimately returning to E. The third motions E–
G♯ and G♯–E are filled in with F♯ so that stepwise motion is introduced into
the line. This continuity is interrupted by the leap to C♯: the resulting gap in
the melody is filled in by the following sixteenth-note passage that cascades
from the melody's high point. Both the melodic and harmonic motion are
accelerated at this climactic moment, augmenting the rhythmic irregularity of
this five-bar phrase.[4]

In contrast to the consonant support of F♯ in bar 1 and G♯ in bar 2, C♯
(bar 3) functions as an appoggiatura, resolving to B over the V^7 chord. Thus
Chopin further intensifies the climactic tone by setting it as a dissonance. In a
beautiful motivic relationship, this C♯ and the B that follows create a rhythmic
augmentation of the preceding neighbor figures G♯–F♯ (bar 2) and A–G♯ (bar
3) as indicated by brackets. The C♯ is also associated with F♯ in bar 1 and G♯
in bar 2 by its position in the bar, and by its relatively long duration.

Beginning with the figure E–D♯–E in bar 1, we have seen that neighbor
motions elaborate the principal tones of the melody. We may consequently
distinguish between two aspects: the accented and harmonically supported
principal tones, and the embellishing figures. (For example, notice that the
melody in bar 4, first beat, echoes the neighbor figures in bars 3 and 1.) This
line therefore embodies both consistency and variety as it unfolds. The tones
of the tonic triad serve as the melodic framework, with the arrival on the
tonic in bar 5 creating a definitive goal of the melodic motion.

Chopin's melody will serve to illustrate the meaning of the term *structural
level.* The melody as heard, note for note, represents what we may call the
musical surface (or *surface level*). By distinguishing between those tones on
the musical surface that are primary, and between those that are tones of
figuration, we have established a new level of melodic coherence distinct from
the surface. That is, we have observed connections among tones that are not
immediately consecutive (such as the motion E–F♯–G♯ in bars 1–2). Two structural levels are thereby distinguished: the surface level that contains all tones,
and a second, more *reduced* level that includes the principal tones only, without embellishing figuration. As we shall see, such connections can also occur
over broader spans of music, on various *levels of structure.*[5]

The striking melody that begins the third movement of Beethoven's
String Quartet, Op. 59, No. 1, illustrates some of the ways in which melodies
in the minor mode may differ from those in major (Example 2.3). Following
the initial C in the first violin, the leap to E♭ and descent to D♭ suggest that
downward motion will follow—as it does with the descent to F and E♮.[6]

Beethoven's setting of this part of the melody creates a dramatic, almost
eerie effect. Following the solo C in the second violin on the upbeat, the C in
the first violin enters an octave higher, with the Cs forming an open fifth with
the viola. Both the subsequent tones E♭ and D♭ are heard as dissonant
with the open fifth below; the melody then leaps to F, another dissonant tone,
before moving to E natural (the consonant third of the dominant chord).

This poignant melodic and harmonic tension is resolved in the second
bar. The tones F and C resolve the preceding E♮ and D♭, respectively. In other
words, the D♭, left "hanging" in bar 1, resolves to C in the proper register

EXAMPLE 2.3:

Beethoven, String Quartet, Op. 59, No. 1, III, bars 1–2 with analytical interpretation

only in bar 2. The tendency of flat $\hat{6}$ to resolve to $\hat{5}$ is strong; the listener will expect to hear a resolution even after several intervening notes. The leap from F to C, and the subsequent leaps that converge on A♭, balance the melodic disjunction of bar 1. During the course of the contracting leaps, two distinct melodic strands are formed in bar 2, both converging on A♭: C–B♭–A♭ and F–G–A♭ (the added beams in the example clarify these relation--ships).

In our discussion of melodic fluency we noted that leaps are typically combined with stepwise motion for the sake of variety. This is particularly true of melodies conceived for instruments such as the violin, which can perform many leaps with little difficulty. Yet, as Beethoven's passage illustrates, a series of leaps may be related through underlying stepwise patterns.

The centrality of the mediant, A♭, as the concluding focal point of this melody highlights this most characteristic tone of the minor mode. The three scale degrees that differ between the major and natural minor scales—$\hat{3}$, $\hat{6}$, and $\hat{7}$—create many dissimilarities between the major and minor modes. The quality (major or minor) of the third between tonic and mediant—and the resulting quality of the tonic triad—is of course the most striking, and invariable, difference. Many other contrasts between major and minor will be explored as we proceed.[7]

Example 2.4 presents the last two phrases from Bach's harmonization of the chorale melody "Gib dich zufrieden und sei stille." In the first two bars of the excerpt, the soprano line employs chromatic alterations that are customary in minor, using raised $\hat{7}$ to return to the tonic in the neighbor figure E–D♯–E, and reverting to natural $\hat{7}$ in the stepwise descent from the tonic (E–A). In the descent that follows (bar 9), however, the tones D♯ and C♯ are used

EXAMPLE 2.4:

J. S. Bach, "Gib dich zufrieden und sei stille," bars 8–12

before the goal tone B. The reason for this form of the scale becomes clear when the harmonic support is considered. Both D♯ and B are supported by dominant chords in the half cadence; consequently, the tones of the descent from F♯ must be in agreement with the forthcoming B-major triad.

The tension of the half cadence is not resolved by the subsequent E-major chord; complete resolution occurs only with the tonic chord of the perfect authentic cadence. During this final phrase the melody descends through an octave (embellished with leaps), now with the natural forms of 7̂ (as an appoggiatura) and 6̂. Notice that between the tonic notes that begin and end the phrase, scale degree 5̂ (B) is emphasized through repetition, through metric placement (beat 3), and by the leap away from B (beat 3), while 3̂ (G) is highlighted on the downbeat of the final bar. Once again, the leaps do not disrupt the overall stepwise motion of the descending line. For example, the leap in bar 11 isolates B momentarily, but this detour merely postpones the unifying, stepwise relationship to A on the final eighth of the bar.

The structural association of tones that are not immediately adjacent can also be seen in Example 2.5. In this fugue subject by Bach, an initial leap of a fifth from D♯ to A♯ creates melodic tension that is balanced by subsequent motion in the opposite direction. Before the descent takes place, however, A♯ is decorated by its upper neighbor B and by a descending and an ascending motion that returns to A♯. These intervening figures expand and embellish, but do not fundamentally interrupt, the overall shape of the melody indicated by the stems placed on the music. When a tone (like the A♯ in bars 1–2)

EXAMPLE 2.5:

J. S. Bach, Fugue in D# minor (*WTC* I), subject, bars 1–3 with analytical interpretation

remains active in its context, even though other tones may intervene, that tone is said to be *prolonged*. The broken slur in the example indicates this *melodic prolongation*. Chords can be expanded in similar ways: *chord prolongation* will be discussed in the next chapter.

Example 2.6 presents another fugue subject from Bach's *Well-Tempered Clavier.* The first part of the subject circles around C ($\hat{5}$), which is decorated by upper and lower neighbor figures. The subsequent leap to $\hat{7}$ creates a temporary gap in the line that is filled by the subsequent rising stepwise motion. This motion reaches $\hat{4}$ on the next downbeat, a tone which is highlighted both by its longer duration relative to the sixteenth notes before and after it, and by its accented metrical position. A final group of sixteenth notes begins on C (an upper neighbor to B♭) and leads to A at the conclusion of the subject. Once more a melodically fluent line—C–B♭–A, expanded by the neighbor tone D—forms the "backbone" or structural foundation of the melody and provides overall coherence and direction.

The dynamic quality of this subject is enhanced by an additional, more subtle element: the rising motion from E to B♭ ($\hat{7}$ to $\hat{4}$) in bars 2–3 outlines the interval of the diminished fifth. (The notes that begin and end motions

EXAMPLE 2.6:

J. S. Bach, Fugue in F major (*WTC* I), subject, bars 1–4 with analytical interpretation

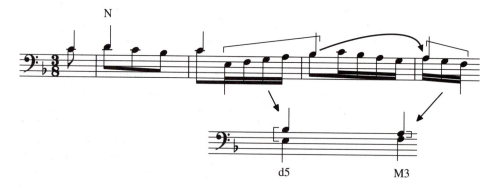

frequently stand out more than the tones in between.) The tension created by this interval is not released until bar 4, where the expected resolution of the diminished fifth to a major third is provided by the tones A and F at the end of the subject. (The subject proper ends on A, with F forming part of the countersubject that follows.) In a sense two "voices" may be perceived in this apparent single-line subject. As indicated in the second part of Example 2.6, the progression of a diminished fifth to a major third is embedded in the melodic flow. A melody that articulates two or more distinct voices, such as this fugue subject, is called a *polyphonic melody*. Frequently the alternation of two or more voices may become a primary compositional idea, as in the familiar tune "Greensleeves" (Example 2.7).

The melody begins with an arpeggiated ascent, partly filled in, through the notes of the tonic triad D–F–A. The climax tone A (embellished with an upper neighbor) initiates a stepwise top-voice descent, as indicated by the long stems and connecting beam. Each of these principal melodic notes is embellished in various ways, often through additional arpeggiations. If each arpeggiation were played as a block chord, the lower notes would be heard as inner tones, or voices, of the chord. Because the melody is written so that it can be sung by one person or played by a single-line melodic instrument, the chords or harmonies it suggests are incorporated into the melodic line itself.

EXAMPLE 2.7:

"Greensleeves" with analytical interpretation

Once again we see a polyphonic melody, where distinct voices are incorporated into a single melodic line. The partial structural descent in bars 1–4 (A–G–F–E), and the complete descent to the tonic in bars 5–8 indicated by the beams, provide large-scale continuity and direction, as in the fugue subjects.

In bar 7 the tone F is not followed by E (in the descent of the "framework"), but by the leading tone C♯ (on beat 2). The effect of melodic fluency is so strong that Schenker regarded the leading tone in contexts such as this a *substitute* for scale degree $\hat{2}$, which would, if actually present, produce a completely stepwise descending line. In the first phrase of the melody, the motion A–G–F did in fact lead to E, supported by V. In this second phrase E is still suggested—in part *because of* the substitution of C♯—as the simplest and most usual connection between the F and the D, and by analogy with the preceding phrase. Parentheses, as in bar 7 of the example, are used by Schenkerian analysts to indicate suggested or "implied" notes.[8]

A single line can unite different voices that are widely separated, as in Example 2.8, the opening of the Prelude from J. S. Bach's Suite No. 1 for unaccompanied cello. In this work the degree of separation is extreme, as it is in much of Bach's music for unaccompanied instruments. However, melodic partitions of this type occur frequently—especially in music for solo instruments, where a single line may outline two, three, or more independent polyphonic lines. Having considered some basic characteristics of single melodic lines, we shall now explore further aspects of melody as revealed in the combination of two or more parts in species counterpoint.

EXAMPLE 2.8:

J. S. Bach, Suite No. 1 for Unaccompanied Cello, Prelude, bars 1–4 with harmonic representation

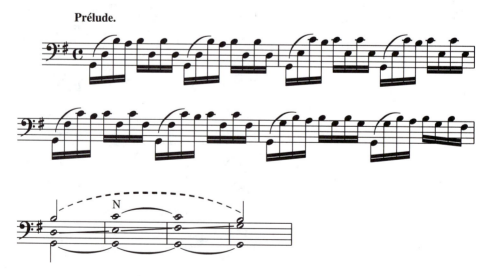

COUNTERPOINT

In tonal music, counterpoint exists wherever there is the presence or the suggestion (as in Example 2.8) of two or more voices moving simultaneously. It is a fundamental musical element that is in no way restricted to inventions, canons, fugues, and similar genres.

For hundreds of years composers considered training in the discipline of counterpoint to be essential for the development of compositional technique. This concern with elaborating the ways in which lines are combined is easy to understand if we realize that in Western music contrapuntal principles were the earliest means by which polyphonic musical compositions were organized, and that the compositional use of harmonic principles developed gradually during later centuries.[9]

Schenker believed in the value of contrapuntal studies, and in fact was partly responsible for a renewed emphasis on counterpoint as a pedagogical discipline. He considered the study of counterpoint to be invaluable, not only as a necessary preparation for composition, but as a way to hear and to understand many fundamental principles of polyphonic tonal structures. He also believed that harmony and counterpoint are separate but closely related dimensions of tonal compositions, each with its own laws and characteristics and each working interactively with the other. Consequently, Schenker undertook the great task of explaining separately and abstractly the principles of harmony and counterpoint, which he believed would lead him to a profound understanding of the techniques of actual composition (which he referred to as "free composition").

In 1906, near the beginning of his career as a music theorist, Schenker published his study of harmony.[10] Four years later, in 1910, he published the first volume of a comprehensive treatise on species counterpoint; the second volume did not appear until 1922. This treatise reflects Schenker's growing awareness that the most ornate and complex melodies are shaped by simpler, underlying guiding lines that tend to resemble the lines of strict (species) counterpoint, as he demonstrated with a series of examples from the literature of tonal music. In other words, Schenker discovered that the principles of melodic organization in tonal music are partly an outgrowth, or more elaborated version, of the linear techniques presented in the study of counterpoint.

We therefore continue our study of melody by turning to the five species of strict counterpoint, a framework ideally suited to the examination of voice-leading principles and dissonance treatment. Species counterpoint involves the addition of one or more lines to a *cantus firmus,* which is a simple melody, traditionally given in alto clef. A comprehensive discussion of the principles of species counterpoint is beyond the scope of this book, but we will consider the essential characteristics of each species. In so doing we retrace some of the steps taken by Schenker in the development of his ideas. For through this approach we shall also begin to discover how the ornate melodies of musical compositions are related to the simple lines of strict counterpoint. Our minds and ears will thereby become more sensitive to the role played by the linear dimension of tonal music, which is largely responsible for creating the sense of flow and directed motion we associate with music as a dynamic art.

First Species

In first species, a counterpoint is added to a preexisting cantus firmus in the same note values (whole notes), thereby creating a note-against-note texture. Example 2.9 presents a first species exercise in which a counterpoint is added above a cantus firmus. Note that all of the intervals are either perfect or imperfect consonances, which are the only vertical intervals used in first species.[11] The ability to comprehend more complex textures in which dissonances embellish and connect consonances over broader spans of music depends upon the initial understanding of such simple but coherent musical structures based solely on consonances.

Notice that the exercise begins and ends with perfect intervals (indicated in boxes): these intervals embody maximum stability and repose. On the other hand, the more fluid imperfect consonances are most appropriate for the body of the exercise. In fact, the sense of motion or "flow" that most persons associate with tonal music is produced in part by imperfect consonances leading to and from stable points defined by the perfect consonances. If you play the example on the piano you will probably notice immediately the marked difference in stability between the perfect and imperfect consonances.

Observe also the differences among the four types of relative motion: *parallel* (same direction, same interval maintained between the parts), *similar* (same direction, different interval), *contrary* (opposite direction), and *oblique* (one part moves, the other remains stationary). Among the types of relative motion, contrary and oblique motion most directly promote independence between two lines: in this context, the stability of the perfect intervals in the middle of the exercise is considerably softened by contrary motion (bar 3) and oblique motion (bar 5), and by the predominance of imperfect consonances in the flow of the counterpoint from the second bar to the cadence.

EXAMPLE 2.9:

First species counterpoint

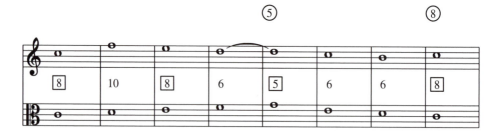

The upper-voice counterpoint begins with an upward leap of a fourth, which produces some tension in the line (leaps generally are associated with tension), and it also opens up more musical "space" between the voices. After the leap, however, the line changes direction and proceeds by step, a strategy that lends variety and shape to the line, and also begins to dissipate some of the tension created by the initial leap (stepwise motion in the opposite direction after a leap generally balances the effects of the leap). The counterpoint then continues down by step to the cadence.

A question might now occur to the reader: Is the counterpoint monotonous and undifferentiated because of the predominance of stepwise motion? Although unrelieved melodic motion in the same direction can produce a line without shape and profile, it does not do so in this case for two reasons. First, the line begins with a leap, after which the E and D in bars 3–5 fill in the gap produced by the leap. Second, the tied D creates oblique motion; the pause in the line counterbalances the still rising cantus firmus and also allows both voices simultaneously to begin a descending approach to the cadence. Descending motion is associated with release of tension; here, the relatively long descent of the counterpoint from its climax fully dissipates the tension of the initial leap.

Hence the counterpoint nicely contrasts, and therefore complements, the cantus firmus through the blend of parallel, similar, contrary, and oblique motion it fosters. Furthermore, considering that the exercise is only eight bars long, the counterpoint itself is a convincing and coherent line because it comprises a balance of disjunct and conjunct motion, with the latter predominating. Here, as in the examples discussed earlier, we see the characteristics of *melodic fluency,* a principle that will continue to be of concern to us throughout this book. Another aspect that contributes to the fluency of this line is the way it achieves a high point (a climax) and then descends purposefully toward the cadence. As mentioned above, descending motion relates to the release of tension; the descending stepwise motion to the cadence contributes to the sense of stability and finality (closure) we experience at the conclusion of the exercise.

We now consider an excerpt from a work by Handel, the theme of the Chaconne from *Trois Leçons,* bars 1–4 (Example 2.10a). A traditional harmonic analysis might represent the phrase as I–V^6–VI–V^{7}of V–V, as shown in the chordal reduction of Example 2.10b. A deeper understanding of this passage, however, arises from the realization that this succession of "chords" results as much from contrapuntal factors as from harmonic ones. As illustrated by the reductions of Example 2.10b, the phrase is framed by the harmonic progression from I to V. An essential part of this motion is the contrapuntal relationship between the outer voices, which can be represented in first species terms (see the second part of Example 2.10b). The top and bottom voices form the intervallic pattern 5–6–10–10, a contrapuntal pattern that provides the framework for the motion from I to V. The intervals, however, are realized harmonically as triads, and the applied dominant chord in bar 3 conclusively establishes the dominant as the goal of the phrase.[12]

This passage illustrates the interactive roles of harmony and counterpoint

EXAMPLE 2.10:

(a) Handel, *Trois Leçons,* Chaconne, bars 1–4; (b) harmonic and first species representations

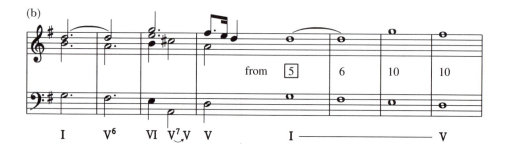

in music, which is a temporal art. Musicians have long used physical metaphors such as "motion," "tension," and "flow" to describe how music is expressed in time. Since we often conceive of time metaphorically in horizontal terms, we might say that counterpoint, the linear dimension of music, provides the kinetic impulses by which harmony, the vertical dimension of music, is expressed in time. The passage is organized harmonically by the motion from I to V, one of the most fundamental means of harmonic organization in tonal music. But as we shall see, the ways in which harmony organizes different spans of music are dependent upon the prolonging effects of counterpoint.

Second Species

In second species, a counterpoint in half notes is set against the whole notes of the cantus firmus (two notes against one). The differentiation between the lines is enhanced by the quicker motion of the counterpoint, which leads to an enlivened musical texture more complex than that of first species.

Consider first that the two half notes of the counterpoint create metrical organization within the bar, a downbeat and an upbeat. The downbeat, the strong part of the bar, corresponds exactly to the beginning of a bar in first species. Therefore, consonance must occur on all downbeats in second species. The upbeat, or weak part of a bar, is different. Its purpose is to provide rhythmic momentum to the line and to connect the consonances on successive downbeats. Because of its subordinate rhythmic status, the second beat is evaluated in respect to the consonant downbeats it connects. Our purpose now is to determine the ways in which the second half note can function in a musical texture still regulated, as in first species, by the progression of consonances.

Example 2.11 shows a second species exercise in which we can explore the role of the second half note. The most important use of the second half note occurs in bar 2. The F on the second beat (species counterpoint assumes two beats per bar) connects the consonances on the downbeats of bars 2 and 3, and represents straightforward *melodic progression*. This F, of course, is an instance of the very familar tone of figuration, the *passing tone*.

Moreover, because the F forms the interval of a fourth with the cantus firmus, an interval which is categorized as dissonant in two parts, it is a disso-

EXAMPLE 2.11:

Second species counterpoint

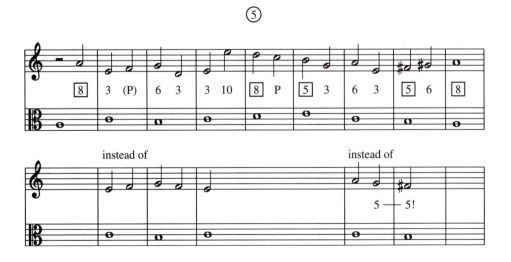

nant passing tone. This dissonant tone is correct in second species because it occurs on the second beat and is approached and left by step as described above. Notice that the note C in bar 5 is also a dissonant passing tone, and fulfills the same conditions. The passing tone is the first dissonance to be introduced in species counterpoint and is the most fundamental type of dissonance in tonal music since it embodies directed motion to a goal. Stepwise motion to and from a dissonance has been regarded by composers throughout most of music history as one of the essential principles of voice leading.

While dissonant passing tones are the most characteristic feature of second species, consonant passing motion is also possible. The motions "5–6" or "6–5" above a cantus firmus will produce consonant passing tones; this is the only relationship where two consonances form a stepwise melodic line, whatever the melodic configuration may be.

In the limited context of second species counterpoint, the passing tone (on the second beat) connects two different consonances (on the preceding and following downbeats)—or, considered only horizontally, two different tones. When we begin to examine actual compositions, this observation will acquire additional significance. In those more elaborate contexts we will be able to amplify our statement to say that in connecting two different tones, passing tones will often connect two different registers or *voices* (such as a soprano and an alto voice). Although strict counterpoint per se is not concerned with such issues, we find in second species a foreshadowing of an important technique that figures prominently in the realm of prolonged harmony and counterpoint.

Another function of the second half note can be seen in the third bar of our example. Here, the leap in the counterpoint, which is possible only because both intervals in bar 3 are consonant, creates the familiar technique of the *consonant skip*. A leap from consonance to consonance is often desirable, because a line consisting entirely of passing tones would be scalar and would lack sufficient variety and differentiation. In this case, the skip to D substitutes for F, which already occurred as a passing tone in the previous bar (compare the two parts of the example). Hence the leap helps to avoid monotony in the line and substitutes for direct melodic progression. We will discover that *melodic substitution* can serve various compositional functions (as in the substitution of C♯ for E in bar 7 of "Greensleeves," Example 2.7). Bear in mind, however, that this technique elaborates but does not alter the continuity of underlying, melodically fluent stepwise progression. In this case, the ear still follows the motion from the G on the downbeat of bar 3 to the E on the downbeat of the following bar.

Substitution is also evident in bar 7. On the second half of that bar, E is a virtual necessity. A leap to any other tone would lead either to a forbidden vertical interval (such as a fourth, F over C) or a *dissonant* melodic interval in approaching the F♯ in the next bar (a diminished or augmented interval such as C to F♯). On the other hand, a stepwise continuation from a G on beat 2 would create parallel fifths in approaching the following downbeat, as indicated in the example. Substitution, therefore, can serve to improve voice leading through the avoidance of forbidden progressions or intervals.

Another use of a leap can be seen in bar 4, from E up to E, which does not so much substitute for another tone as it effects a *transfer of register.* At this point in the exercise, the counterpoint is (and has been) relatively close to the rising cantus firmus. The change of register opens up some additional space between the voices, establishes the climax of the phrase, and allows the upper voice to descend gradually, proceeding primarily in contrary and oblique motion to the cantus firmus before the cadence. Later in this book we will see how transfer of register can be a valuable compositional technique in free composition, where it makes possible richly polyphonic melodies and the integration of contrasting registers.

We now examine another passage, the opening two bars of Brahms's Intermezzo in A minor, Op. 76, No. 7 (Example 2.12a). As with the theme from Handel's Chaconne discussed above, this passage is best understood in terms of a combination of harmonic and contrapuntal principles. In the upper voice, the tone E is embellished first by a consonant skip to A, an embellishing tone (compare Example 2.12b). The line then proceeds by step back to E, through a G and a passing tone F. The E is consequently embellished and sustained—that is, *prolonged*—by a five-note figure. This figure develops within a harmonic motion from I to III. The chord supported by the second tone in the bass could be labeled a VII⁶ (or V⁶ of III), but may also be de-

EXAMPLE 2.12:

(a) Brahms, Intermezzo, Op. 76, No. 7, bars 1–2; (b) second species representation

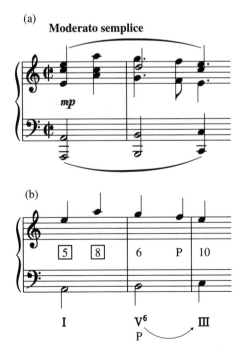

scribed as a "passing chord" because the B, in the characteristic fashion of a passing tone, connects the A and C in the bass: correspondingly the $^6_3$ chord itself passes between I and III.

This last observation illustrates that basic contrapuntal patterns must be further evaluated in contexts shaped also by harmonic principles. In our simplification, the B in the bass resembles a tone in a cantus firmus, the tones of which are neutral and are not generally associated with a specific contrapuntal function (such as is implied by the designation "passing tone"). In the music, however, the B supports a chord that connects tonic and mediant harmonies. Thus, influenced also by harmonic principles, the B is a form of passing tone (supporting a passing chord), but one of a higher structural order than the F in the upper voice, which serves a more local purpose. This distinction between two different types of passing tones is significant, and foreshadows the notion of structural levels, one of Schenker's most profound ideas that will be continually explored and refined throughout this book.

In our discussion of second species counterpoint, we have illustrated straightforward melodic progression, which is achieved primarily by the dissonant passing tone that connects one tone with another. Another type of stepwise melodic embellishment, the *neighbor note*, decorates a single tone with the note immediately above or below. In second species counterpoint the consonant neighbor-note configuration is possible (resulting from a fifth moving to a sixth or the reverse), though it is usually employed sparingly, because in the rather slow moving half-note rhythm of second species a series of neighbor notes can produce a sluggish and static line.

Third Species

Third species counterpoint employs four quarter notes against the whole note in the cantus firmus (Example 2.13). This faster rhythm permits the use of rapid stepwise embellishment (including dissonant neighbor notes) to enliven the musical texture.

Third species melodies combine scalar motion with passages in which embellishing tones prolong a note or otherwise retard the movement of a line. In bars 2–4 of the example, the octave ascent from d^1 to d^2 is filled in with stepwise motion, quickly reaching a new, higher register. In bars 4–5, the overall development of line seems slower by comparison, primarily because of the leaps and changes in direction. Following the climax tone f^2 on the downbeat of bar 6, the descending leap of a sixth to a^1 creates a "gap" in the line that is balanced by the concluding stepwise motion.

Third species melodies may sometimes be related to first and second species counterpoint, as shown below bars 8 and 9. Neighbor notes retard motion by prolonging a tone: thus, the dissonant neighbor f^1 in bar 8 prolongs g^1, thereby creating an underlying motion in the bar (g^1–a^1) that is similar to a second species figure. In bar 9, the leading tone b^1 is prolonged throughout the measure by upper and lower neighbors; its motion to the cadence there-

EXAMPLE 2.13:

Third species counterpoint

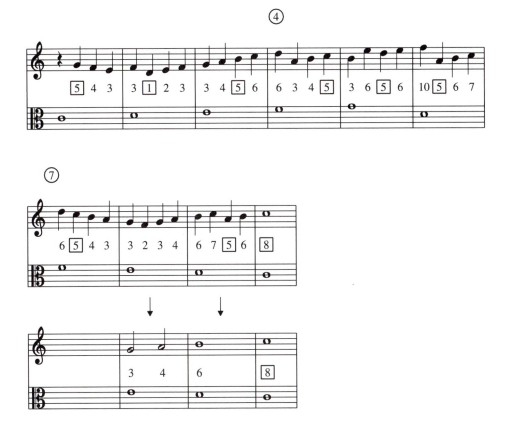

fore simulates a first species progression. This prolonging figure, incidentally, commonly termed the *double neighbor,* has been used in composition since the Middle Ages. Though the neighbor notes appear to be incomplete, because of the leap from the dissonant C to A, both tones may be understood as complete neighbors of the first and last tones of the measure. This indirect relationship of notes illustrates that the ear can perceive relationships of tones over spans of varying lengths, even when other notes intervene.[13]

Neighbor tones, whether complete or incomplete, dissonant or consonant, are an essential aspect of tonal music, and it is important to learn to recognize them in different contexts. In Example 2.2, elaborated neighbor motion delays the forward motion of the line. The neighbor tones are dissonant against the supporting chords, and therefore represent surface figuration. By contrast, the highest melody tones in Example 1.1, Ab–Bb–Ab–Bb–C (bars 2–7), are all supported harmonically. Nevertheless the Bb in bar 4, and the supporting tone E natural in the bass, function as neighbors to the tones Ab and F, respectively in the progression I–V$_5^6$–I (bars 2–5). When Bb returns in bar 6, it functions as a passing tone to C in the motion I-VII⁶-I⁶ (bars 5–7). (We will discuss more relations between counterpoint and harmony in Chapter 3.)

Fourth Species

The dissonant passing tone and neighbor note both arise through the addition of new notes to a melody, and thus may be described as *melodic* dissonances. Fourth species introduces a second category, *rhythmic* dissonance, which is created through rhythmic displacement rather than through the addition of new melodic tones. In this species the counterpoint consists primarily of tied half notes, producing a rhythm closely related to the whole notes of first species. The tones, however, do not coincide with those of the cantus firmus, but are shifted to the second (weak) part of the bar. Example 2.14 shows the relationship between the whole notes of first species and the syncopation of fourth species.

This rhythmic displacement creates the characteristic type of dissonance in fourth species: the *suspension*. The initial note of the suspension, or *tone of preparation,* occurs on the second beat and must be consonant. The second part of the tied note, on the downbeat, is called the *suspension*. A dissonant suspended tone must resolve downward and by step on the following (second) beat, to the *tone of resolution*. If the tied note is consonant with the cantus firmus, resolution is not an issue (there is no requirement for descending motion by step). Example 2.15 presents a complete fourth species exercise. Notice that the rhythmically displaced counterpoint is otherwise similar to those of first and second species. Because the suspension occurs on the strong part of the bar, it has the strongest effect of the three fundamental dissonances.

The obligatory downward resolution of dissonant suspensions limits the possibilities for melodic development; in other words, a series of dissonant suspensions can lead only to a descending, stepwise line. There are, however, "expedients" that allow one to shape and balance the line more fully. In Example 2.15, for instance, the counterpoint reverts to the untied half notes of second species (bars 4–5 and 7–8). This technique, known as "breaking the

EXAMPLE 2.14:

Relationship between first and second species counterpoint

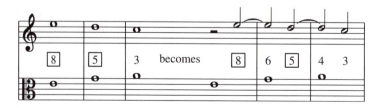

EXAMPLE 2.15:

Fourth species counterpoint

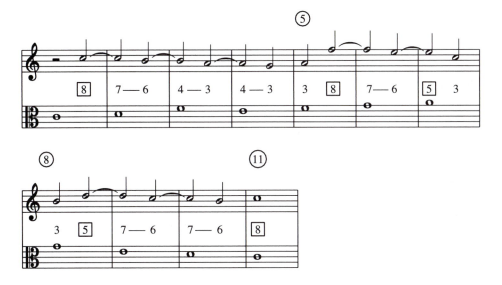

species," provides opportunities for leaps and changes in direction, both of which help to create a balanced and varied line.

Notice that the tone that forms the consonance with the cantus firmus, what one might call the "main" tone, occurs on the second part of the bar in a metrically weak position. Thus fourth species provides us with a clear example of an important principle: the structural weight or significance of a tone does not necessarily coincide with its metrical position. In free composition, where more complex contrapuntal, harmonic, and rhythmic techniques come into play, this realization will figure significantly when we attempt to determine the function of a tone or harmony. The principles of rhythm (including meter) work in conjunction with, but somewhat independently of, the principles of harmony and counterpoint. Rhythmic factors can support or reinforce the structural function of a tone, but just as frequently they can conflict with harmonic and contrapuntal factors, thereby raising questions about structural function. In analyzing tonal music, one must always weigh carefully the interplay of harmonic, contrapuntal, and rhythmic factors that work interactively to achieve the development—the unfolding—of a musical composition.

We now return to Handel's Chaconne, to the ninth variation of the theme (Example 2.16a). In sets of variations the techniques of elaboration include increased rhythmic and melodic figuration, which transform and provide contrast to the theme. The ancient principle of variation is not restricted to pieces called "variations" (or "chaconnes" or "passacaglias"), but is a powerful means of organization in many different kinds of musical compositions. The principles and techniques presented in this book will enable you to better understand and recognize variation processes as they occur in tonal music.

EXAMPLE 2.16:

(a) Handel, Chaconne, Variation 9, bars 1–4; (b) fourth species representation

A brief comparison of the first four bars of the theme (Example 2.10) with the corresponding part of the ninth variation reveals that the constant, the common denominator that unifies the varied presentations of the theme, is the descending "ground" bass from G to D. (Note that the use of the minor mode is another way of achieving varied repetition.) In the variation, however, the tenor voice is rhythmically displaced: a 5–6 shift above the bass prepares the first of a series of two 7–6 suspensions (Example 2.16b). The first phrase of the variation therefore retains the initial harmonic framework of the theme, but the suspensions provide a forward-moving impulse that intensifies the motion from I to V. The suspensions illustrated in fourth species counterpoint occur in compositions of many different styles, enlivening and transforming the note-against-note texture of underlying first species progressions.

Fifth Species

We have seen how second, third, and fourth species introduce various types of melodic and rhythmic elaboration in the contrapuntal line. In fifth species, the procedures of the previous species are combined, with pairs of eighth notes added as an additional resource. The use of mixed note values naturally affords the line considerably more possibilities for variety and complexity. We shall now examine some of the idiomatic patterns of fifth species in relation to the suspensions of fourth species, enabling us to understand how smaller note values can decorate but not disrupt the continuity of underlying stepwise progressions, the essential characteristic of melodic fluency (Example 2.17).

Example 2.17a shows a first species motion to a cadence in parallel sixths; in 2.17b the upper voice has been rhythmically displaced, resulting in a series of 7–6 suspensions. Example 2.17c illustrates some ways in which this fourth species progression can be elaborated in fifth species with quarter- and eighth-note embellishments. The first suspension is decorated by a leap to consonance from the suspension, to the lower neighbor of the tone of resolution; the second suspension is decorated by a leap to and from a consonant embellishing tone; the third is embellished by the upper neighbor of the suspension; and the fourth is embellished by a pair of eighths that pass from the suspension to the lower neighbor of the tone of resolution. The point is that the stepwise progression of the fourth species line is still the guiding force of a line that now exhibits leaps and detours; the resolution of the suspensions is so powerful that the ear retains the stepwise connections *through* the intervening notes.

This technique of embellishment (in free composition) has traditionally been referred to as *diminution,* because the embellishing tones are usually smaller note values. Another use of the term is to refer to the repetition of a line in smaller note values; this often happens in fugues, where, for example, a subject originally presented in half notes is then repeated in quarter notes. But just as frequently diminution is associated with the embellishment of an underlying guiding line that shapes the course of an upper voice.

The line is often presented first in unadorned fashion, as in sets of variations on a chorale or folk tune; but an initial statement of a preexisting mel-

EXAMPLE 2.17:

Embellishment of suspensions in fifth species counterpoint

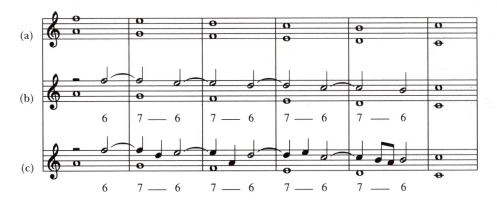

ody is not a necessary condition for diminution. We shall see that simple, melodically fluent lines lie beneath the surface of elaborate, freely composed melodies in virtually all styles of tonal compositions. And like the embellished progression in our fifth species example, the more direct stepwise progressions are perceived by the ear even as the texture is enlivened through the basic elements of diminution: passing tones, neighbor tones, consonant skips, and suspensions.

A SAMPLE ANALYSIS

We have seen several excerpts from the literature in which the fundamental voice-leading principles of species counterpoint function in the tonal fabric. Excerpts from Mozart's set of variations on the folk tune "Ah! Vous dirai-je, Maman" will provide another example of the role of contrapuntal motion in a tonal composition. In our examination of part of the theme and one of the variations, it will become apparent that melodically fluent lines similar to those encountered in strict counterpoint can establish the framework and provide the coherence for the most disjunct and wide-ranging melodies in free composition.

Example 2.18a presents the first phrase of the theme. Before examining the relationship between specific elements of diminution and the folk tune, we will begin with a general overview of the phrase. The harmonic and contrapuntal framework of the two-part setting is indicated in Example 2.18b: the tonic governs the first part of the phrase, after which an arpeggiation leads through VI to the II^6-V-I cadential pattern. (The N indicates a neighbor note, the dotted tie indicates a retained or prolonged note, and the solid slur or beam indicates tonal motion from one point to another.)

The characteristics of this tune are remarkably similar to the upper voice of our first species counterpoint exercise (Example 2.9). Both begin with a rather large leap (a fourth in the exercise, a fifth in the folk tune), followed by stepwise motion to the cadence. (In "Ah! Vous dirai-je, Maman," the incomplete neighbor e^2 in bar 7 decorates but does not interrupt the stepwise descent.) In other words, the initial leaps in both melodies create gaps in the lines and a degree of musical tension that are subsequently dissipated by the change in direction and the descending stepwise motion to the cadence.

In conjunction with the expansion of tonic harmony in the opening bars, the tones on the downbeats of bars 2–6 form a succession of parallel tenths between the two voices (Example 2.18b). In bars 2–4, these notes in the left-hand part can be described as a "tenor" voice (again illustrating the principle of polyphonic melody). In bar 3, the tenor F functions similarly to the A in the soprano: it is a neighbor note that decorates and prolongs the tenor Es (of tonic harmony) on the downbeats of bars 2 and 4; in bar 5, the tenor D is a passing tone that leads from E to C.

Just as tonic harmony governs much of the bass, so many of the notes of

EXAMPLE 2.18:

(a) Mozart, Variations on "Ah, vous dirai-je, Maman," K. 265, bars 1–8 (Theme); (b) graphic representation

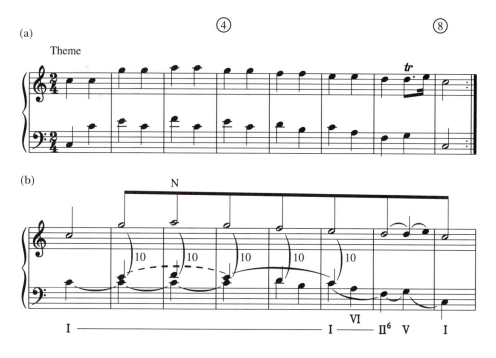

the upper voice express the tones of the tonic triad, C-E-G. The line begins with a leap from the root to the fifth of tonic harmony, scale degree $\hat{5}$, which is decorated and prolonged by an upper neighbor A. The line then passes through F to E, the third of tonic harmony. It concludes with D and C ($\hat{2}$ moving to $\hat{1}$), tones supported by the II⁶-V-I cadential pattern. Hence this well-known melody, in its characteristics of voice leading and melodic fluency, resembles in striking fashion a line of first species counterpoint.

We now turn to the opening phrases of the first variation (Example 2.19) and third variation (Example 2.20). For clarity we have circled and beamed together the tones in each measure that correspond to the tones of the folk tune (compare with Example 2.18). What becomes immediately apparent is that Mozart has presented the tune within various kinds of figurations (or embellishments) that allow performers to display not only their technical skills, but also the capabilities and idiomatic aspects of the piano. (Sets of variations were often composed as vehicles for virtuosic display on a particular instrument.)

In the first variation, upper and lower neighbor motion embellishes C and G in bars 1 and 2 respectively: because the neighbor motion is dissonant with the bass and the underlying chord, its role as figuration is clear. In bars 27–30 scalar motion occurs, also clearly an embellishment of the underlying

EXAMPLE 2.19:

Mozart, Variations on "Ah, vous dirai-je, Maman," K. 265, bars 25–32 (Variation 1) with analytical interpretation

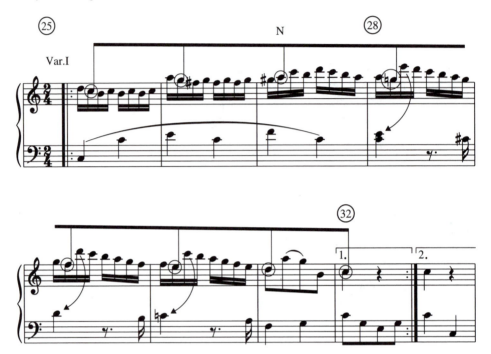

line. The high notes initiating the scales in bars 28–30 (E–D–C) are chord tones that add an additional strand of voice leading to the right-hand part, making it polyphonic. Notice, however, that these tones do not form an *independent* line, but double notes in the left-hand part. Note also that each of the first six bars of the variation begins with an accented figuration tone, so that the chord tone is delayed. As we said earlier, it is important to bear in mind that metrical position and structural value do not always coincide, as this variation illustrates.

Chordal skips and arpeggiation predominate in the third variation (Example 2.20). In the first bar, the tone C of the melody is embedded within a rapid, wide-ranging arpeggiation that employs the skill of the performer's right hand. The arpeggiation, moreover, confirms our *reading*—that is, our interpretation—of the theme, that a C major triad, tonic harmony, is expressed in bar 1. In bar 74, the second tone of the melody, G, appears on the second eighth (after a chordal skip from C) and initiates a stepwise line that descends through the passing tones F and D to the tonic note C. The passing tones fill in the intervals between the fifth, third, and root of tonic harmony outlined in the arpeggiation of the first bar.

In bar 75, the A is decorated first with a chromatic lower neighbor and

EXAMPLE 2–20:

Mozart, Variations on "Ah, vous dirai-je, Maman," K. 265, bars 73–80 (Variation 3) with analytical interpretation

then by a consonant skip to C, followed by a passing tone back to A. The way in which the melody tone G appears in bar 76 is especially interesting: the A on the downbeat is a suspension of the melody note from the previous bar (suspensions are not always tied in free composition). The resolution of the suspension, however, is further decorated by F♯, an incomplete chromatic lower neighbor to G, the tone of resolution. We observed similar decorated suspensions in the fifth species (Example 2.17): in the present example the suspension and the decoration of its resolution shift the main tone to the third eighth, the weakest part of the first beat. This variation again illustrates that metric position does not necessarily correspond to structural "importance": sometimes, as here, harmonically and structurally prominent tones may occur in metrically weak positions.

On the second beat of bar 4 Mozart shifts the line upward through arpeggiation, creating a climax in the phrase through the establishment of a new register. The main melody notes of bars 5–7 are each preceded with the rather large leap of a descending seventh. The notes in the higher register (as in bars 28–30 of Example 2.19) are notes from an inner voice of the texture that have been shifted above the main melody tones. (Note that the high notes appear as "fourth species" suspensions.) Clearly the decoration of an underlying line is not always accomplished by means of stepwise motion or small leaps. Instruments can perform large leaps and change registers much more easily than the human voice: such highly disjunct embellishments frequently characterize instrumental music.

Through our discussion of this example we have seen how Mozart has transformed the simple, melodically fluent folk tune into a line of remarkable variety and complexity. Despite the detours produced by the leaps, arpeggiations, and passing tones, the stepwise character of the theme is present, behind the scenes as it were, in the upper voice of the variation; the theme, in effect, has become an underlying guiding line for the variation. We can now better understand how significant was Schenker's discovery: that melodically fluent lines, similar to those encountered in the five species of counterpoint, lie beneath the most complex and ornate melodies of actual compositions.

Exercises

Exercise 1. Study the theme from Beethoven's set of variations on "God Save the King," WoO 78

a.   Provide a roman numeral analysis of the entire theme, noting in particular the cadential patterns in bars 5–6 and 13–14.

b.   Examine and discuss the theme with the following questions in mind:
  1.   Is it melodically fluent? That is, does the melodic line move in a predominantly stepwise manner, with skips carefully treated?
  2.   Is there a purposeful motion to a melodic highpoint (a climax), followed by a second motion that leads to the cadence?

Exercise 2. Examine the upper voice of Variation 1 of the above work.

a.   Identify the tone or tones in each measure that correspond to the notes of the theme.

b.   Describe how the theme is elaborated. That is, identify and label the four basic types of embellishing tones—passing tones, neighbor tones, suspensions, and consonant skips—used to elaborate the theme.

Exercise 3. Study the upper voice of Variation 5 of the above work.

a.   Examine bars 1–6 and 12–14 in the same manner. If appropriate, you may write on the music for this exercise.

b.   *Circle* each of the notes that correspond to notes in the theme and use the following symbols as shorthand for the tones of figuration: N = neighbor; CN = chromatic neighbor; IN = incomplete neighbor; P = passing tone; CP = chromatic passing tone; SUS = suspension, and so forth.

Exercise 4.

a. Beethoven, Six Easy Variations (G major), WoO 77
  1. Analyze the theme in the manner described in Exercise 1.
  2. Compare Variation 1 with the theme as described in Exercise 2.
b. Mozart, Nine Variations on a Minuet by Duport, K.573. Analyze the theme; compare with Variations 1, 6, and 8. What elements of the theme are retained in each variation, and when does each variation depart from it?

Exercise 5. Bellini, "Casta Diva" from *Norma,* bars 16–23

a. Provide a roman numeral analysis of the excerpt.
b. Identify the figuration tones in the melody, using the symbols N, P, etc. as specified above.
c. Put long stems on those notes in the melody that you think are primary in a structural sense (as opposed to decorative or figuration tones). Consider the harmony: a structural melodic tone is usually consonant with the supporting chord.

Exercise 6. Below is a list of several polyphonic melodies or melodic passages from the tonal literature. Analyze each of the melodies as follows:

a. Put long stems on structural tones. In cases where top and inner voices are clearly distinguished, use ascending and descending stems respectively (as in Example 2.6). Be sure to consider harmonic support.
b. Identify figuration tones (P, N, etc.). This is not a "formal" structural analysis; the objective is to distinguish structual and figuration tones, and to obtain a general sense of melodic shape and motion.
  1. Schubert, *Die schöne Müllerin,* No. 13, "Mit dem grünen Lautenbande" (complete vocal melody)
  2. Brahms, Ballade in B major, Op. 10, No. 4, bars 1–46
  3. Mozart, Fantasia in C minor, K. 475, bars 1–4
  4. Wolf, *Mörike-Lieder* No. 7, "Das verlassene Mägdlein," bars 5–12 (vocal melody)
  5. Beethoven, Piano Sonata, Op. 22, III, bars 1–18
  6. Chopin, Nocturne in B major, Op. 32, No. 1, bars 1–8
  7. Bach, Suite for Unaccompanied Cello in D minor, Prelude (bars 1–13); Menuet 1 (complete)

Bass Lines and Harmonic Structure

In Chapter 2 we examined aspects of upper-voice melody; in this chapter we shall consider the nature of the lowest voice, and its relationship to harmonic structure. The bass differs from other voices because of the particular role it plays in supporting and defining harmonic motion. It does so at levels ranging from immediate, chord-by-chord events to the larger harmonic organization of a entire work. As we study various bass lines we shall also explore related aspects of harmonic and voice-leading structure.

In your studies of harmony and voice leading, you learned to identify different chords and to understand how they can function in the context of a key. Roman numerals and figured-bass symbols were used to facilitate the identification of chords and tonal functions. Such labeling techniques can be an important and necessary first step in analysis. But the use of roman numerals and associated arabic figures do not constitute a complete analysis, since any chord—such as IV, V^6, or I—can function in many different ways depending upon the context in which it occurs. As we investigate bass lines and harmonic structure, we will begin to see how such contextual differences arise.

Prolonging Tonic Harmony

The opening of the second movement from Mozart's Piano Sonata K. 545 (Example 3.1a) illustrates various kinds of chord functions. Tonic harmony influences a large portion of the phrase, from bar 1 to bar 6. The V^4_3 on the third beat of bar 1 provides harmonic variety, yet it also serves to expand (or prolong) the initial tonic harmony. Melodically the bass note A (beat 3) is a neighbor; hence the contrapuntal neighbor motion G–A–G supports the (local) harmonic progression I–V$^4_3$–I (bars 1–2).

In Chapter 2 we saw ways in which a tone can be prolonged or extended by means of other tones. Here we see the prolongation of tonic harmony by means of a different chord. The stepwise voice leading and neighbor motion in the bass minimize harmonic contrast, and reinforce the continuity of the harmonic progression. Consider the difference in effect between the inverted V^7 in bar 1 and the root-position V that occurs in the cadence at the end of the phrase (bar 8). This V serves as the goal of the preceding harmonic motion, and is elaborated by a cadential $^6_4$ on the first beat. Thus the dominant chords in bars 1 and 8 have markedly different functions that are determined by the context in which they occur.

Like the V$^4_3$ in bar 1, the chords in bar 3 also embellish tonic harmony. They do so through double-neighbor motions, as shown by lines connecting the tones D–E–C#–D and B–C–A#–B in the inner voices (Example 3.1b). These linear motions create a neighboring $^6_4$ and a common-tone diminished

EXAMPLE 3.1:

(a) Mozart, Piano Sonata, K. 545, II, bars 1–16; (b) analytical interpretation, bars 1–8

EXAMPLE 3.1 (*continued*)

EXAMPLE 3.1 (*continued*)

(b)

seventh chord over a stationary bass. Chords formed through either passing motion or, as in Example 3.1, through neighboring motion (including the use of *incomplete* neighbors) are called *contrapuntal* chords. The contrapuntal chords in bars 1 and 3 serve to prolong tonic harmony; contrapuntal chords can also form part of a motion from one harmony to another.

The return to I in bar 6 (after another neighboring V_3^4) is followed by a descent in the bass through E to B, supporting VI and I^6.[1] As indicated in Example 3.2, this descending sixth inverts the rising third that would typically support a motion from I to I^6. The larger descending interval is subdivided into two smaller leaps by the tone E, which supports VI. Here, the prolonga-

EXAMPLE 3.2:

Expansion of tonic harmony through interval inversion

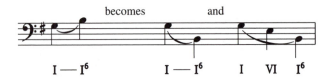

tion of tonic harmony ($I–I^6$) involves leaps, in contrast to the stepwise bass line of bars 1–5.

Tonic harmony, therefore, is prolonged in the first six bars of the Andante. Other chords provide variety in various ways, but function within this governing harmony or harmonic "space." Integration of the related chords with the primary harmony is achieved through contrapuntal motion and close harmonic relationships, such as that of dominant and tonic, or the common-tone association of I and VI. These chords function in a more "local" way than does the tonic harmony that governs bars 1–6.

The prolongation of tonic harmony is followed by a motion to the dominant in bars 7–8. In the bass, the motion to B (bar 6) is followed by the tones C and D, supporting the IV and V chords. (As shown in Example 3.1b, the leap to E on the third beat of bar 7 is a local detour that does not disrupt the stepwise motion from IV to V.) Example 3.3 represents the bass and harmonic structure of the phrase in two stages: I–IV–V becomes $I–I^6$–IV–V. In other words, tonic harmony is prolonged for a sixth bar by motion through a descending sixth before the cadential IV–V closes the phrase in bars 7–8.

We observed above that the $^6_4$ chord on the downbeat of bar 8 is a contrapuntal chord that serves to elaborate dominant harmony. The cadential $^6_4$ chord typically intensifies (through suspensions or accented passing tones) the dominant to which it resolves. For this reason cadential $^6_4$ chords will be represented by the symbol V^6_4, instead of the more literal $I^{6\,2}_4$. In general, roman numerals serve to indicate harmonic functions in Schenkerian analysis, rather than to identify the spelling of individual chords. They are used sparingly in graphs, as will be seen in later chapters.

This type of cadence—a semicadence or half cadence—exhibits a kind of dual nature: it achieves a certain degree of repose, but also embodies a sense of continuation. The dominant note in the bass usually strives for resolution; a forward melodic impulse (directed toward the tonic note) is also inherent in the second scale degree in the soprano and the leading tone in the alto. This need is fulfilled at the *conclusion of the second phrase,* where the melody completes the descent to $\hat{1}$ (G). Thus the V of the semicadence does not "resolve" to the tonic that immediately follows, which is not a goal but the beginning of the second phrase. In other words, the ultimate resolution of the V in bar 8 is achieved by the authentic cadence of the consequent phrase.[3]

Minor changes occur in the consequent phrase, such as the use of II^6

EXAMPLE 3.3:

Mozart, Piano Sonata, K. 545, II, bars 1–8:
bass and harmonic structure

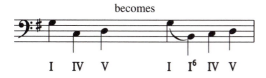

becomes

I IV V   I I^6 IV V

instead of IV over the bass C in bar 15; furthermore, the cadential $^6_4$, interme-diate II^6, and dominant harmonies are compressed into one bar (compare bars 7–8 with bar 15). This recomposition ensures that the tonic will arrive in bar 16, thereby maintaining two symmetrical eight-bar phrases. Fundamen-tally, however, the motions $I–(I^6)–IV–V$ and $I–(I^6)–II^6–V–I$ represent parallel harmonic progressions with different but complementary cadences.

Reflect for a moment on your own experiences playing and listening to tonal music. Have you felt a sense of motion and progression, both within individual phrases and in complete works? If so, have you thought about what creates that movement? Like literature and drama, Western music has tradi-tionally incorporated some kind of progression (melodic and harmonic) from a point of depature to a goal. In this case, the phrase moves from the initial tonic to the perfect authentic cadence in bar 16. The bass line characteristi-cally plays an integral role in harmonic motion, forming the basis and support for the succession of chords and the larger harmonic framework they create.

In simplest terms, the motion I–V–I illustrated in Example 3.4 forms the structural harmonic framework that other chords serve to expand and elabo-rate. One reason why the I–V–I relationship is so essential in tonal structure is that the dominant tone is the first independent pitch (after the octave) in an overtone series above a given note. Moreover, the dominant tone—the root of the V chord—is also the fifth of the tonic chord. Thus the bass of I–V–I can be regarded as an *arpeggiation* of the root and fifth of the tonic (no-tice how the *vertical* triad is expressed as an arpeggiation in Example 3.4). Just as melodic continuity is based on stepwise motion, so the disjunct motion I–V–I forms the most fundamental harmonic motion of tonal music.

The bass line is the support and organizing influence for a succession of chords, and is therefore fundamentally different in character from the types of melodic lines discussed in Chapter 2. In most compositions, however, this "foundation" bass is elaborated, which makes it more melodic in character. In other words, as we move from the framing I–V–I closer to the musical "sur-face" (or the moment-to-moment events), we may observe a series of stages THat successively embellish this essential harmonic progression.

Example 3.5a presents the bass and soprano lines for the first phrase of the chorale "O Ewigkeit, du Donnerwort." (The complete phrase is given in Example 2.1.) Like Example 3.1, the chorale begins with a prolongation of I. Here the VII^6 (bar 1, beat 2) is used as a passing chord between I and I^6: notice that passing motion occurs in both soprano and bass, which move in

EXAMPLE 3–4:

Linear expansion of vertical triad

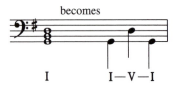

I   I—V—I

EXAMPLE 3.5:

(a) J. S. Bach, Chorale, "O Ewigkeit, du Donnerwort," bars 1–2, bass
and soprano lines; (b) harmonic structure

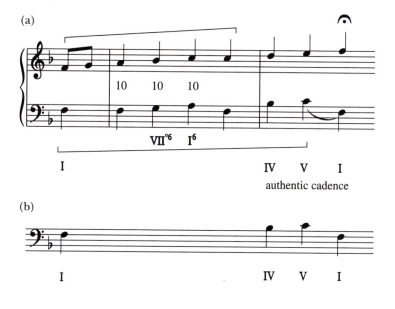

parallel tenths from the first to the third beat of the first complete bar. The
prolongation of tonic harmony continues with a return to a root-position I
on the fourth beat of the bar.

Intermediate Harmonies

The IV chord on the next downbeat functions as part of the authentic cadence (IV–V–I) that ends the phrase. Like the IV chord in bar 7 of Example
3.1, this subdominant chord connects the initial tonic prolongation with the
dominant. Chords that connect the initial tonic (prolonged or otherwise)
with the structural dominant are called *intermediate* (or *pre-dominant*) *harmonies*. (In Example 3.1, both the IV in bar 7 and the II^6 in bar 15 are intermediate harmonies.) Among the many chords that can function in this manner
are II, IV, VI, and III (the II and IV chords often appear also in inversion).
Intermediate harmonies are perhaps the most frequently encountered elaborations of the structural harmonic motion I–V–I. Because they appear with
such great frequency in structural bass-line patterns throughout the tonal literature, we can, for the sake of convenience, consider intermediate harmonies as part of the structural harmonic pattern itself: *tonic–intermediate harmony–
dominant–tonic,* as indicated in Example 3.5b.[4]

The leap of a fourth in the bass from the initial I to the IV of the cadence
is filled in (compare Examples 3.5a and 3.5b), resulting in a motion that

leads mainly by step to the V of the cadence. (The return to F on the fourth beat is a consonant skip that embellishes the stepwise motion of the bass.) Notice that the designations "VII^6" and "I^6" appear on a separate level beneath the staff, indicating that they occur within the expanded root-position tonic harmony. We will sometimes use different levels of roman numerals to distinguish contrapuntal and prolonging chords from the more fundamental chords of the harmonic structure. The brackets, incidentally, point out a beautiful motivic relationship between the outer voices: the broader ascent from F to C in the bass is anticipated in the soprano (and highlighted by the repetition of C) as part of its octave ascent. These symbols, called *motivic brackets,* are often used in Schenkerian graphs to indicate various kinds of motivic relationships.

Example 3.6 presents the first phrase of the chorale "Wach' auf, mein Herz." While the large-scale harmonic structure in this phrase is similar to

EXAMPLE 3.6:

(a) J. S. Bach, Chorale, "Wach' auf, mein Herz," bars 1–4; (b–d) levels of bass structure

those in some of the previous examples, differences in its elaboration and, consequently, in the bass melody begin to illustrate the almost limitless number of ways in which the fundamental tonal pattern *tonic–intermediate harmony–dominant–tonic* can be varied.

The framing harmonic pattern I–V–I, including the intermediate harmony, is shown in Example 3.6b. Even though the bass descends in the music, in the graph (reductions *b* and *c*) we have represented the initial tonic note in two registers to clarify the role of the expanded tonic and its relationship to the intermediate harmony before the cadence. (The "understood" low B♭, like the E at the end of Example 2.7, "Greensleeves," is shown in parentheses.)

The primary elaboration of this progression is achieved through a prolongation of the initial tonic that extends to the I^6 on the third beat of bar 2 (Example 3.6c). It is significant that the bass note of this chord and the intermediate II^6_5 almost completely fill in the melodic space between scale degrees $\hat{1}$ and $\hat{5}$ (B♭–D–E♭–F): it is for this reason that the implied low register has been suggested for the initial B♭.

The next step in understanding the role of the progression $I–II^6_5–V–I$ as the structural bass pattern is to clarify how the initial tonic is prolonged. By so doing we will continue to discover how different passages, with different chord successions, may be based on similar underlying bass-line patterns.

Like the tonic prolongation in bar 6 of Example 3.1, the overall motion is from I *down* to I^6 (the final beat of bar 2). Levels *a* and *d* of Example 3.6, however, show many more intervening chords than in bar 6 of Mozart's sonata. In Bach's chorale, the initial tonic B♭ moves through G to D, which supports a mediant chord. (The mediant triad shares two common tones with the tonic and can substitute for a I^6 in a prolongation of the tonic.) The bass then rises to E♭ on the next downbeat before D, the bass of I^6, enters in bar 2. As indicated in level *d*, therefore, the bass motion within the prolonged tonic consists of two descending thirds, B♭–G–E♭, followed by a step to D (bar 2).[5]

When IV is first heard in bar 2, it might initially be perceived as the intermediate harmony of the harmonic progression. But scale degree $\hat{4}$ is held over as a suspension, and the IV moves to an inverted dominant seventh (V^4_2) on the second beat. Because the seventh is in the bass, the tendency of this chord to resolve is very strong; its resolution highlights the I^6 shown in Example 3.6d. With the stepwise resolution to the inverted tonic chord, the structural cadence has been avoided.

The IV in bar 2, therefore, is not the intermediate harmony of the fundamental bass-line structure. Such an internal progression that appears to lead toward a cadence and then "backs off," often through the motion $V^4_2–I^6$, is called an *avoided cadence,* and is one way in which a phrase can be extended. The avoided cadence also explains why we must regard the II^6_5, and not the IV, as the principal intermediate harmony: the II^6_5 leads to a *root-position* V in an authentic cadence that achieves closure (finality) in the harmonic progression of the phrase, with the characteristic leap from dominant to tonic in the bass.[6]

Dominant Harmony and Cadences

The motion I–V–I can be expanded with an almost limitless variety of bass-line patterns. Example 3.7, the beginning of the second movement of Beethoven's Piano Sonata, Op. 13 ("Pathetique"), begins with tonic harmony prolonged from bar 1 to the downbeat of bar 3. The elaboration of the tonic can be understood on two levels, which are illustrated in Example 3.8. The primary motion is I–I⁶–I, which is expanded by two inverted dominant seventh chords. We have seen that the function of a contrapuntal chord is often determined by the role of its bass note as a melodic (contrapuntal) element. Here, the bass tones D♭ and G are incomplete neighbor tones to C and A♭, respectively. The V_2^4 and V_5^6 chords, consequently, are neighbor chords (more specifically, *incomplete* neighbor chords).

Now focus on the contrapuntal relationship between the bass and soprano (bars 1–3) in the chordal reduction of Example 3.9. As the numbers above the soprano indicate, the intervals between the two voices alternate between tenths and sixths. In general, the relationship between the outer voices constitutes a primary element of tonal structure; here, the predominance of imperfect consonances produces a fluid motion within the initial tonic region.

We have seen that a single harmony can be prolonged with other chords. Similarly, a motion from one harmony to another can be expanded by one

EXAMPLE 3.7:

Beethoven, Piano Sonata, Op. 13, II, bars 1–8

EXAMPLE 3.8:

Beethoven, Piano Sonata, Op. 13, II: expansion of initial tonic

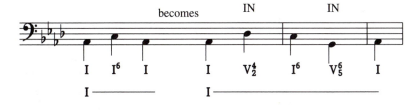

EXAMPLE 3.9:

Beethoven, Piano Sonata, Op. 13, II, bars 1–8: chordal reduction

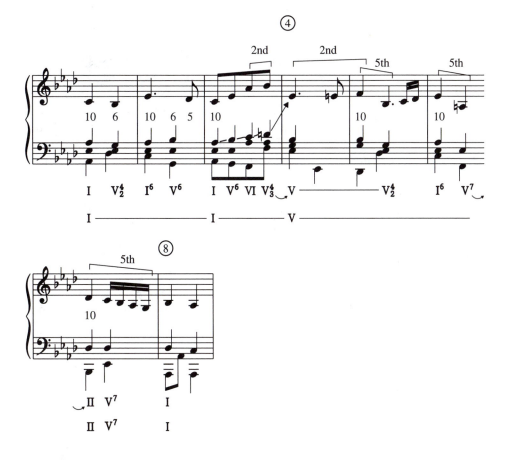

EXAMPLE 3.10:

Beethoven, Piano Sonata, Op. 13, II, bars 1–8: structural bass motion

or more intervening chords. In the motion from I to V (bars 3–4) indicated in Example 3.9, the bass notes G and F (bar 3) support chords that connect A♭ (I) and E♭ (V). Since G and F are passing tones, the chords are referred to as passing chords. The last of these, however, is altered chromatically, and functions as V_3^4 of V. Notice the manner in which the leading tone is introduced in the applied dominant chord: an inner-voice passing motion leads from A♭ to E♭ (bars 3–4). The resolution of the leading tone does not occur in the same voice, but is transferred to the soprano line. This contrapuntal motion, in conjunction with the falling bass line and the rapidly rising soprano in the first part of the bar, intensifies the progression to the dominant chord in bar 4. The passage also illustrates the primary importance of the leading tone, both as a melodic element and as an agent of directed harmonic motion.

The remainder of the passage is based on motion from V (bar 4) to the authentic cadence in bars 7–8. The bass initially descends by step to a I⁶ chord in bar 6.[7] Subsequently, the stepwise motion of the bass gives way to falling fifths, with the tones F, B♭, E♭ and A♭ supporting root-position chords (with one of the fifths expressed as an ascending fourth to remain within an appropriate range in the bass). A series of chords related through falling fifths is the most basic type of harmonic motion, and may therefore be contrasted with contrapuntal motion, which, as we have seen, is fundamentally stepwise. The combination of "harmonic" leaps with "contrapuntal" stepwise motion gives the bass line its distinctive melodic character.

Example 3.10 illustrates that the bass line of this excerpt traces stepwise motion through an octave. The octave is subdivided by the arrival on E♭ in bar 4, a division that creates strong coherence in the passage. Variety is achieved through changes of register (such as the octave leaps) and by the descending fifths at the cadence (bars 6–8).[8] Intervallic relationships with the soprano (for instance, the parallel tenths indicated in Example 3.9 on the downbeats of bars 5, 6, and 7) reinforce the integration of the outer voices both motivically and contrapuntally.[9]

LARGER CONTEXTS

Our next example, Bach's figured-bass chorale "Ihr Gestirn, Ihr hohen Lüfte" (Example 3.11), illustrates some distinctive qualities of the minor mode.[10] Bach's setting of the chorale melody uses various techniques of prolongation, many of which we have already seen in earlier examples. Bars 1–8 are summarized below (compare with the outer-voice reduction in Example 3.12):

1. Bars 1–2 (tonic prolongation): Two root-position tonic chords are connected by a dominant chord in root position. In other words, the prolonged I is elaborated by an octave leap, which is subdivided by A, the root of the dominant chord, into two smaller descending leaps, a

EXAMPLE 3.11:

J. S. Bach, Chorale melody with figured bass, "Ihr Gestirn, ihr hohen Lüfte"

fourth and a fifth. Note that the bass leaps, plus the soprano's ascending third, fully outline the tonic triad.[11]

2. Bars 2–3 (continued tonic prolongation): Return to original octave in the bass; motion from I to I^6 via a passing VII^6.

3. Bar 3 (continued tonic prolongation): Return from I^6 to I by means of a V$^4_3$. (Though the figure implies a VII^6 chord, A is sustained in the top voice, so that a V$^4_3$ chord is actually heard. In figured-bass settings, a "6" is frequently realized as a $^4_3$.)

4. Bars 3–4: Motion away from prolonged tonic harmony to dominant harmony. Compare the function of the V chord in bar 1 to that in bar 4: the former appears on a weak beat between two tonic chords, and supports a passing tone in the soprano. In contrast, the V chord in bar 4 occurs on the downbeat, and its bass and soprano notes are melodically prominent. However, the chord is not entirely stable: its soprano

EXAMPLE 3.12:

(a) J. S. Bach, "Ihr Gestirn, ihr hohen Lüfte": melodic and harmonic interpretation;
(b) transformation of III

(a)

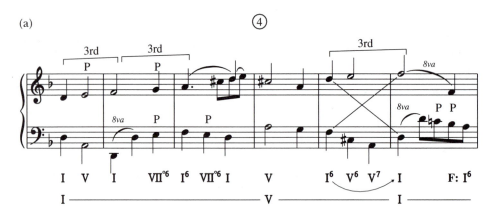

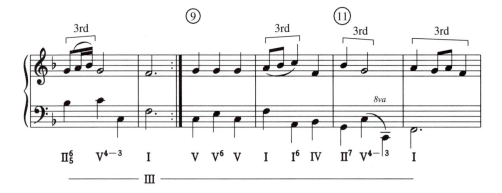

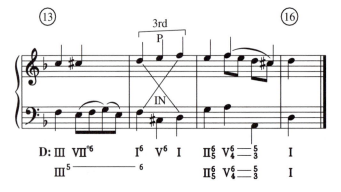

EXAMPLE 3.12 (*continued*)

(b)   ⑬

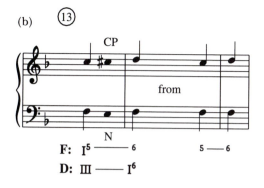

F: I⁵ ———— 6   5 —— 6
D: III ——— I⁶

note is the leading tone, and the subsequent continuation V_2^4–I^6 connects bars 1–4 with bars 5–8.

5. Bars 4–6: Return to I; notice the combination of stepwise motion and leaps in the bass. After the stepwise descent A–G–F (V to I^6), a continued stepwise motion through E to D might have been expected. Instead, the bass leaps to C♯ and A, both of which belong to dominant harmony. These tones substitute for the expected E (which would probably support a VII^6 or V_3^4 chord).

   The crossed lines in bars 5–6 indicate a *voice exchange:* the upper and lower voices exchange the tones D and F in the motion from I^6 to I. This exchange of tones associates the I^6 and I_3^5 chords; however, because of the intervening dominant chords, the return to tonic harmony is not fully established until bar 6. In essence, the I^6 chord "looks ahead to" or anticipates the associated root-position tonic chord in bar 6, as indicated by the arrow in the example.[12]

   In the soprano, notice the broad ascent through an octave from d^1 in bar 1 to d^2 in bar 5, followed by a continuation to f^2 in bar 6. This stepwise ascent lacks only scale degree $\hat{6}$ (bar 3) to be completely stepwise: this tone is replaced by the elaborated motion up to D in that bar. The goal of the ascent, f^2, occurs as tonic harmony returns in bar 6.

6. Bars 6–8: Modulation to III. In contrast to the brief tonicizations that we observed in earlier examples, F is established as a key area in its own right. The soprano tone f^1 in bar 8 serves as the melodic goal of the phrase, and also initiates a new melodic ascent in the next phrase.

Modulation creates a temporary change of key center, in which a new pitch is heard as the tonic. Accordingly, it is often said that the piece "changes key." This is true in a sense, but it is not a sufficient explanation. For example, a modulation to the dominant in a sonata-allegro movement creates a dynamic opposition to the tonic not only because of the contrast of tonality, but also because of the potential of the new "tonic" to function as a dominant again, as it eventually does. In a larger sense, therefore, it remains the dominant, even though it is treated like a tonic for a period of time. Because of this dual characteristic, Schenker described modulation as motion to an "illusory key." That is, the impression of a new key is ultimately perceived as illusory when viewed from the perspective of the global (or home) tonic.

In listening to the individual phrases of "Ihr Gestirn," one may perceive a modulation from D minor to F major. In a larger sense, however, F represents III in D minor, and is part of a broader harmonic motion that will continue after the double bar. From this perspective, the modulation can be seen as an extended tonicization of III, an intermediate harmony in the global tonic of D minor. Indeed, from a broad perspective, *every* modulation can be understood as a tonicization within the home key (in a tonal work that begins and ends in the same key).

We have seen the importance of the octave in the bass (as in bars 1–2, 6, and 7). This interval permeates the work, becoming a kind of motive and occurring in a variety of different ways. In the soprano (bars 1–6), a long-range ascent from d^1 to f^2 unfolds essentially through an octave, which is extended to a tenth by the repetition of the opening D–E–F figure from bars 1–2 (see the brackets in Example 3.12). The octave relationship between these two figures is then echoed by the descending leap from f^2 to f^1 in bar 6. Two different registers are thus compositionally related, a technique that we shall encounter frequently.

The motion to III may be regarded as a modulation in part because of the continued prolongation of the mediant key area after the double bar. The bass line employs many leaps in this passage, arpeggiations and harmonic (V–I) motions that enhance the stability of the new key area. Notice also that the final bass motion of the cadence in bars 7–8, C–C–F, is echoed an octave lower in bars 11–12, reaching the lowest bass note of the piece.

In bars 13–14 the I chord in F is transformed into a I^6 chord in D; the transformation is shown in Example 3.12b. Such a motion over a chord in $\frac{5}{3}$ position to one in $\frac{6}{3}$ position over a common bass note (or, in figured bass terms, simply "5–6") is very common and is called the *5–6 technique*.[13] By means of this motion, Bach leads from the prolonged key area of the mediant back to the tonic key. Through the raising of the natural seventh degree, which had been employed throughout the prolongation of the mediant, the leading tone of the home tonic is reestablished.

A motion from I^6 to I in bar 14 begins to highlight the return to the home tonic of the piece (note the voice exchange between the outer voices); the definitive confirmation of tonic harmony, however, occurs only at the cadence in bars 15–16. Example 3.13 shows the large-scale bass and harmonic structure for the work: I–III–II$^6_5$–V–I. The use of the mediant as a secondary key area is characteristic of pieces in minor.

Our next composition is also by Bach, the well-known C-major Prelude from the *Well-Tempered Clavier,* Book I (Example 3.14). The complete work will be studied later; at this point we shall consider the bass line and harmonic structure.[14]

EXAMPLE 3.13:

J. S. Bach, Chorale, "Ihr Gestirn, ihr hohen Lüfte":
structural bass

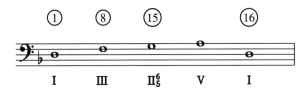

The consistent figuration and rhythm create a continuum of motion from the beginning of the prelude until its end. The work has the quality of an improvisation in which no major sectional divisions occur. Internal articulations are created by the bass and harmonic structure and are reinforced by subtle changes in the arpeggiated patterns. (The nature of the upper voices will be explored in Chapter 8.) For most of the piece a single chord is arpeggiated in each bar, a feature that is closely related to improvisation. It will be useful to represent the chords in block form (Example 3.15).

A four-bar progression establishes the tonic at the beginning of the work. In this quasi-cadential progression all voices move by step or retain common tones; both the II^4_2 and V^6_5 chords function as contrapuntal chords. The dissonances formed by the left hand in bar 2 (C–D) and the diminished fifth between the outer voices in bar 3 (B–F) create tension that is resolved by the return to I in bar 4.

In tonal music continuity and change are often combined, particularly at points of transition. This happens in bars 4–5, where the tonic is transformed,

EXAMPLE 3.14:

J. S. Bach, Prelude in C major (*WTC* I)

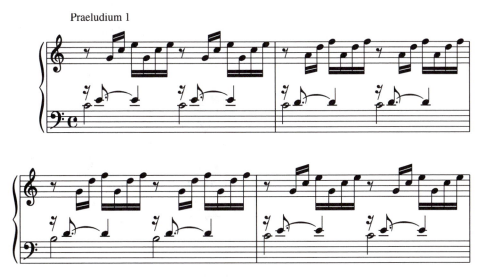

EXAMPLE 3.14 (*continued*)

EXAMPLE 3.14 (*continued*)

⑰

㉑

EXAMPLE 3.14 (*continued*)

through a 5–6 motion, into an A-minor $\frac{6}{3}$. Two chords related by a 5–6 motion are closely associated: the A-minor $\frac{6}{3}$ chord of bar 6 is related to tonic harmony through two common tones (note that the bass note C is a common bass tone; in other words, the $\frac{6}{3}$ chord of bar 5 is an outgrowth of the root-position tonic chord).[15] This contrapuntal motion "destabilizes" the tonic of bar 4, and the resulting $\frac{6}{3}$ chord initiates the descending-fifth sequence in bars 5–8 (which occurs in the variant form $\frac{6}{3}$–$\frac{4}{2}$–$\frac{6}{3}$, etc.). This sequence leads to V, which is established as an intermediate goal by the cadential pattern II^7–V^7–I in G (bars 9–11).

Another sequence begins after the tonicized V, one similar in structure but more chromatic than the sequential pattern in bars 5–8 (the pattern changes from $\frac{4}{2}$–$\frac{6}{3}$ to $^{o}\frac{4}{3}$–$\frac{6}{3}$). This second sequence leads to a cadence in the tonic (bars 17–19) that parallels, in transposed form, the cadential motion of bars 9–11.

Bars 1–19, therefore, comprise two broad motions, the first leading to V, the second returning to I. As shown in Example 3.16, the bass descends a fourth from I to V (bar 11) and then continues to I (bar 19). (Compare this division of the octave with the similar division in Example 3.10.)[16]

The bass thus descends through an octave, which is subdivided by the arrival on G in bar 11. When tonic harmony returns in bar 19, the upper voices are in the same position as in bars 1 and 4 (E over C), but an octave lower. The association of the tonic chords (bars 1, 4, and 19), produced in part by the stepwise descent in the bass and the parallel cadences, represents a prolongation of tonic harmony in bars 1–19. (Compare this prolongation with bars 1–2 in Examples 3.11 and 3.12, where the octave descent is much more rapid, and therefore only a dominant chord intervenes.) Within this harmonic space a variety of different types of chords and motions occur that are unified by the descending bass and the framing tonic chords.

Bach's C-major Prelude contains several large-scale harmonic prolongations, the first of which, the prolonged tonic of bars 1–19, we have examined in detail. For the sake of context, we will also point out that a three-bar prolonged subdominant is followed by an eight-bar prolonged dominant; a four-bar prolonged tonic then concludes the prelude (these bars unfold over a pedal; the appearance of the structural tonic triad is delayed until the final bar). Because of the consistency of figuration and rhythm, clearly delineated phrases and marked sectional divisions do not occur. Rather, harmonic and melodic motions establish the prelude's shape and form. The harmonic prolongations, which we will examine in greater detail in Chapter 8, create the sectional boundaries within the composition.

The structural harmonic progression I–IV–V–I thus serves as the foundation of Bach's prelude; it is truly remarkable that such a motion can serve as a cadential pattern, the basis of a phrase, or, as in this case, the underpinning of an entire piece (Example 3.17). Schenker referred to such structural harmonic "pillars" as *Stufen* (the English translation is "scale steps"). In essence, a *Stufe* is a triad that serves in the harmonic foundation of a passage or composition; it may or may not be prolonged, depending on the context.[17] In Bach's prelude, I–IV–V–I are scale steps. Notice that Schenkerians identify

EXAMPLE 3.15:

J. S. Bach, Prelude in C major (*WTC* I): chordal simplification

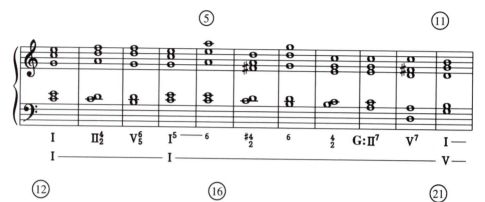

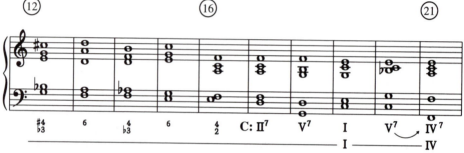

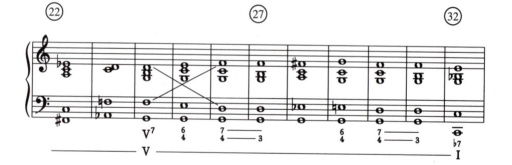

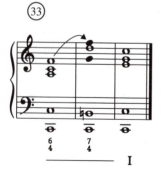

EXAMPLE 3.16:

J. S. Bach, Prelude in C major (*WTC* I), bars
1–19 bass structure

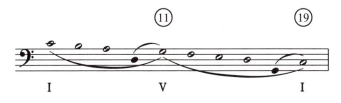

scale steps with roman numerals (which refer in the usual manner to the *root* of the harmony). Other chords, such as passing and neighboring sonorities, may also be assigned roman numerals for identification or other purposes. But in principle, such elaborating chords serve to expand or connect other harmonies, and are not themselves scale steps.

You should notice that we use block chords and figured-bass symbols extensively in Example 3.15, which can be considered a "continuo" realization of the prelude. Bear in mind that the thoroughbass tradition—so prevalent in the eighteenth century—continued to influence approaches to composition well into the nineteenth century, even when a continuo part was not an aspect of performance. In other words, it is usually possible to construct an "imaginary continuo" for a tonal composition. This procedure can be a valuable first step in analysis. As we proceed to more advanced techniques of composition, the imaginary continuo will help you, for instance, in making decisions between local melodic detail and broader, structural associations among tones.[18]

CHORD PROLONGATION: SUMMARY

In this chapter we have discussed the notion of *chord prolongation:* that is, the expansion of a chord (or scale step) by means of one or more other chords.

EXAMPLE 3.17:

J. S. Bach, Prelude in C major (*WTC* I): harmonic structure

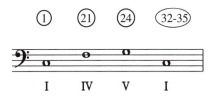

We have also seen that, just as a single chord can be prolonged, so the motion between two different chords can be expanded.

Chord prolongation occurs in a variety of different ways. Typically the melodic and contrapuntal motion of one or more voices forms the basis of the prolongation. A variety of different types of prolongation is illustrated in Example 3.18; the patterns are drawn from previous examples studied in this chapter.

EXAMPLE 3.18:

A.   *Bass arpeggiation expanding a triad by moving from one inversion to another* (Example 3.11, bars 9–10; see also Example 3.1, bar 7; Example 3.5, bar 1, beats 3 and 4)

B.   *Neighbor motion*
    1.   In the bass (Example 3.1, bars 1–2; Example 3.7, bars 1–3)

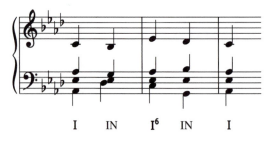

2. In the inner voices (Example 3.1, bars 2–4)

IN   IN

I $^6_4$ $^{\circ 4}_2$ I

3. Alternating in upper voices and bass (Example 3.14, bars 1–4)

N

N

I $^4_2$ $^6_5$ I

C. *Passing motion*
  1. In the bass (Example 3.11, bars 3–4)

P

I^6 ———— I   V

2. In the upper voices (Example 3.14, bars 24–27)

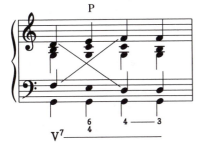

P

$^6_4$ 4 —— 3

V^7————————

3. Parallel tenths (Example 3.5, bar 1)

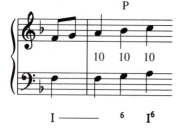

D. *Voice exchange between the outer voices* (Example 3.11, bar 14)

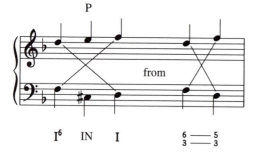

E. *Applied dominant chord* (Example 3.7, bars 6–7)

F. *Leaps in bass* (Example 3.1, bar 6). In this example the bass motion from I to I^6 is inverted from an ascending third to a descending sixth. The resulting sixth is subdivided by E into two descending leaps of a third and a fourth. A typical example of this type of prolongation is motion in descending thirds; I–VI–IV, for instance, can prolong the motion from I to IV.

I —————— 6

G. *Prolongation through transformation* (Example 3.14, bars 19–21). The prolongation includes the addition of ♭7, which transforms the initial prolonged tonic triad into V^7 of IV. This type of prolongation also includes 5–6 motions (Examples 3.14 and 3.15, bars 4–5).[19]

I ——— ♭7   IV

H. *Elaboration of a chord* (Example 3.1, bars 8–9; Example 3.14, bars 31–35)

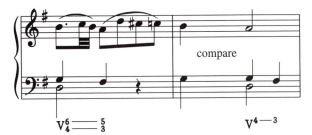

compare

V^6_4 ═══ $^5_3$ V^4 — 3

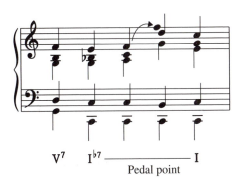

V^7 $I^{♭7}$ ——————— I
Pedal point

I.   *Elaborating motions between two chords* (Example 3.9, bars 3–4: passing motion in the bass). Other types of elaborating motions may include chordally supported passing motion in an upper voice. See Example 3.6, bars 1–2: I–VI–IV becomes I–VI–(III)–IV, where III supports the tone A in the upper voice. Consider also motion in thirds, as in the progression I–(VI)–(IV)–II.

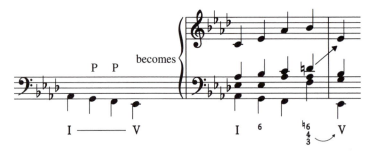

Like the examination of melody and voice leading presented in Chapter 2, this investigation into the nature of bass lines and harmonic structure should be regarded as an introduction. Detailed analysis requires that all aspects of the music be considered, and our understanding of one facet of a passage will often be influenced by other features. Thus melody, harmony, and rhythm, as well as such compositional elements as texture and instrumental setting play a role in what Schenker called *composing-out* (*Auskomponierung*), or the expansion of a structure through prolongations and motions of various kinds. Through the diminutions which develop from level to level, "All the manifold experiences of the lines—which are none other than our experiences—are transformed into song . . . [and] music itself organically lives, sings, and speaks."[20]

In later chapters we will learn to examine works in a comprehensive way, and to relate the concepts that you have learned in these introductory discussions. We will initially examine excerpts from longer compositions (occasionally interspersed with some complete works). We shall then undertake the analysis of whole movements and compositions.

Exercises

Exercise 1. Bach Chorale No. 269 (G minor), first phrase, fourth phrase (bars 8–10; analyze in B♭ major), and last phrase only. Focus on the harmonic structure.

a.   Some distance below the bass line, write in the roman numerals for each chord.

b.   Below that, write the roman numerals for those harmonies that function on a higher level of structure. (What are the main scale steps in the bass-line framework of each phrase?)

Exercise 2. Beethoven, Variations on "God Save the King," WoO 78

a.   Theme: Analyze the *bass-line* structure only. Identify the primary scale-step progression (the "main" harmonies; think in terms of tonic–intermediate–dominant–tonic) of both phrases. Don't be overly concerned with graphing symbols; use the analyses in this chapter as your guide.

b.   Variation 5: Analyze bars 1–6 and 11–14.

1.   Focus first on the harmonic structure (along the lines of the theme). Identify the main harmonic "framework" (two phrases) and explain the harmonic "areas" (expansions) that elaborate the scale steps of the frameworks.

2.   Then, align the tones of the melody above the corresponding bass pitches.

Exercise 3. Explain the harmonic and bass-line structure in the passages listed below. Indicate the following:

a.   *All local chords,* using roman numerals and figures (or simply figures) as appropriate.

b.   *Contrapuntal and other prolonging chords* (N for neighbor chord, P for passing chord, etc.).

c.   The main elements of the bass-line structure: tonic–intermediate–dominant–tonic areas. Be able to explain how each is prolonged (if applicable).

d.   On a lower level of the page, indicate with roman numerals those harmonies that are primary in each phrase. Use lines to indicate prolongations (as in Examples 3.6 and 3.9).

e.   (optional) Using slurs, indicate associated motions and prolongations in the bass melody itself (as in Examples 3.6 and 3.10).

1.   Mozart, Piano Sonata, K. 570, II, bars 1–4
2.   Beethoven, Piano Sonata, Op. 10, No. 2, I, bars 1–12
3.   Beethoven, Piano Sonata, Op. 14, No. 2, I, bars 1–8
4.   Brahms, Waltz, Op. 39, No. 2 (complete)
5.   Beethoven, Piano Sonata, Op. 10, No. 3, II, bars 1–9
6.   Mozart, Piano Sonata, K. 333, III, bars 1–16
7.   Beethoven, Piano Sonata, Op. 14, No. 2, II, bars 1–20
8.   Bach, *St. Matthew Passion,* Aria, "Erbarme dich," bars 1–8
9.   Beethoven, Piano Sonata, Op. 26, III, bars 1–21
10.   Schumann, *Album for the Young,* Op. 68, Little Study, bars 1–17

11. Beethoven, Piano Sonata, Op. 2, No. 3, III, Trio (bars 1–24)
12. Handel, Keyboard Suite No. 7 in G minor, Sarabande (complete)
13. Beethoven, Piano Sonata, Op. 2, No. 1, III, Menuetto (bars 1–40)
14. Bach, French Suite in E major, Sarabande (complete)

4

Linear Techniques

The melodic and harmonic dimensions of tonal music may be considered independently, yet they are closely interrelated. How do they work together? We shall begin to answer this question by considering ways in which melody may interrelate with harmony to form *linear progressions*.

LINEAR PROGRESSIONS

Example 4.1 shows the opening of a work by Bach, one of his grand Preludes for Organ. The piece begins with an ascending line in the right hand, a line that is essentially a C-major scale. The same gesture is immediately imitated by the left hand in the next bar. In fact, you will notice that most of the other lines in this brief passage are similar to the melody of the first measure: they are portions of the C-major scale that acquire a life of their own as they participate in a rhythmically animated texture that develops, by bar 5, into a three-part polyphonic fabric.

You may also notice that we refer to the scale in bar 1 as a "melody"; a scale passage can be, in many respects, one of the purest manifestations of melody. In this respect, you may find it useful to recall the discussion of melodic and contrapuntal principles in Chapter 2. The scale passage has a definite beginning and end, defined by occurrences of the tonic note in different registers; most importantly, however, *it proceeds entirely by step*. The scale that begins this Prelude—one of the most characteristic features of the piece—is a melodically fluent line that resembles the formations we encountered in our discussion of strict counterpoint.

Consider for a moment that compositional practice, particularly during

EXAMPLE 4.1:

(a) J. S. Bach, Organ Prelude in C Major, bars 1–5 with foreground interpretation; (b) arpeggiation of triad

the Baroque and Classical periods, sought to establish the key definitively at the beginning of the piece. And if you sing the beginning of the prelude up to the downbeat of bar 2, the scale passage leaves you with little doubt that the work is in C major: it needs no harmonization, no accompanying second voice; the scale passage by itself establishes the key. A closer look will reveal something more than pure melody: consider that a diatonic scale (with the first note repeated an octave higher) comprises eight pitches. Bach's scale, on the other hand, contains ten notes. By repeating the mediant and dominant tones, Bach expands the scale and creates groups within the passage.

This grouping leads us to hear the first, third, and fifth degrees more prominently than the others. In other words, as Example 4.1b illustrates, one can describe the passage as based on an *arpeggiation* of the C-major triad, with rhythmically weak passing tones filling in the *intervals* of the triad, thereby creating the melodically fluent scale. This passage portrays with great clarity how closely harmony and melody are interrelated.

Now look beyond bar 1 of Example 4.1a. You will soon discover that the harmonic basis of the entire excerpt is the C-major tonic chord, which is being expressed and expanded through linear means. In other words, the intervals of the C-major triad (represented schematically in Example 4.1b) are being expressed horizontally either with stepwise lines or arpeggiations (consonant skips). For instance, the top voice of bar 4 to the downbeat of bar 5 is explicitly an arpeggiation of the C-major triad. Try mentally inserting passing tones between the strong part of each beat and you will recognize the relationship between bars 1 and 4: the top voice of bar 4 is a "variation" of bar 1 transferred up an octave, an arpeggiation of the tonic triad minus the passing tones.

Now examine the top voice of bar 2. The consonant skips *within* each beat create disjunct motion, in contrast to the scale passage of bar 1. Yet there is a "hidden" stepwise relationship that unifies bars 1 and 2. Focus on the notes on the strong part of each beat in bar 2 to the downbeat of bar 3. You will notice that these notes form the line C–C–D–E (see the circled notes in Example 4.1a). Not only do we see another instance of a nonadjacent stepwise relationship between tones, but in this case we realize also that the upper voice from the downbeat of bar 2 to the next downbeat is an expanded repetition of the first three notes of the piece—C–D–E! This motion through the lower third of the tonic triad—C–D–E—can be said to be repeated on two different "levels," because each occupies a different span of tonal space.[1] Moreover, because of this relationship we perceive the opening melody to the downbeat of bar 3 as an *integrated* melodic gesture.

This elegant beginning to Bach's prelude concisely illustrates a fundamental principle of tonal music: melodically fluent lines, which have their own melodic identity and character, often participate in the vertical dimension of chord and harmony. That is, they may serve to *expand* a chord into the horizontal dimension by "linearizing" the intervals of the chord, which may then be filled in with passing tones, the basic ingredient of melodic fluency.

Consider the vertical representation of the C-major triad shown in Example 4.1b. From the bottom up, the triad comprises two thirds plus a fourth. These groupings correspond to bar 1 of Bach's prelude, where repeated notes articulate the third-third-fourth segmentation. (One certainly does not hear the B as the final note of the last segment; the tendency of the leading tone propels the line upward to the C.) In bar 3 (see the slur above the top voice), the motion from C up to G is not divided into a third plus a third as it is in bar 1, but appears as a continuous motion through the interval of a fifth.

This motion delineates the boundary—the first and last notes—of the triad, the basic structural element of tonal music. The outer interval of a triad, however, may be expressed not only as a fifth—as in a three-note chord in close position—but also as an octave in a four-voice texture (Example 4.1b).

The initial scale passage completely traverses this octave: our ears perceive both the smaller chordal intervals within the bar and the larger interval that spans the downbeats of bars 1 and 2. In general, the intervals of the triad may serve as the basis for melodic motions associated with the expansion of triads: the third, fifth, octave; fourth (as the inversion of the fifth), and sixth (as the inversion of the third).

Similar instances of the linear expression of harmonic intervals are shown in Example 4.2, which presents bars 1–4 from Mozart's setting of "Lison dormait." The top voice from bar 1 to the downbeat of bar 2 ascends from C to G, outlining the fifth of tonic harmony in stepwise motion. In this respect the opening is similar to that of Bach's prelude: the linearized interval of the tonic triad is expressed in immediate succession, with no elaborating tones.

In bars 2–4 another linear motion occurs, but in a manner slightly different from the opening. As the beamed notes indicate in Example 4.2, the final note of the initial ascending motion, G, becomes the first note of a descending motion through the third G–F–E, which is elaborated by repeated and nonadjacent tones. Note also that the tones of this descending third receive

EXAMPLE 4.2:

Mozart, Variations on "Lison dormait," K. 264, bars 1–8 with foreground interpretation

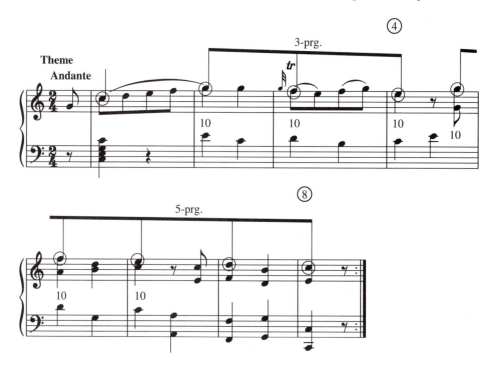

more substantive bass support than the rapidly ascending line in bar 1. The corresponding bass tones E–D–C are highlighted through their placement on the downbeat of each bar and move in parallel tenths with the top voice, outlining the triadic interval E–C. This outer-voice motion expands tonic harmony, leading from the I^6 of bar 2 back to root-position tonic harmony in bar 4. Finally, as if to answer the rapid initial ascending fifth, the last part of the phrase is based on a more expansive descending fifth from G to C. This line is supported by a bass motion that again begins with parallel tenths between the outer voices and concludes with the cadence in bars 7–8 (II^6–V–I).

Scalar motions such as those indicated in the example—stepwise motions (in one direction) that form part of the harmonic and melodic structure—are called *linear progressions*. Linear progressions most frequently move within the triadic intervals of the third, fourth, fifth, sixth, and octave. They are referred to by the interval they span (third-progression, fifth-progression) and by the direction of motion (ascending or descending). They may prolong a single chord, or form a motion that connects two different chords.[2]

Some characteristic types of linear progressions are illustrated in Example 4.3. In Example 4.3a, the third and the root of the tonic triad form the boundaries of a descending progression that is filled in by the dissonant passing tone D. The second progression ascends from the third to the fifth of the triad, a span of a third that is also filled in with a single passing tone. Both progressions extend, or prolong, a harmony in musical space by connecting the initial and the goal tones with stepwise motion.

Example 4.3c illustrates a descending progression from the fifth to the root of the triad. It therefore horizontalizes the complete triad, transforming it (with two passing tones) from a vertical configuration to a horizontal motion. We see here a broader melodic span that may be harmonized by a variety of intervening chords, as in the progression shown in the second part of the example. Always bear in mind, however, that the line ultimately represents an expression of tonic harmony, delineated in this case by the motion from the fifth of tonic harmony to the tonic note.

Linear progressions can also expand the motion between two different harmonies. In Example 4.3d, the motion ascends from the fifth of tonic harmony to the third of dominant harmony. In this case G is a common tone between both chords. Also significant is that the first and last tones are both related to dominant harmony, the *goal* of the progression. The descending

EXAMPLE 4.3:

Characteristic linear progressions

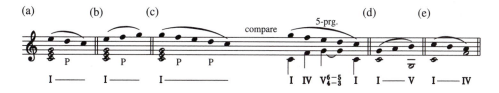

third-progression illustrated in Example 4.3e likewise elaborates the motion from one harmony to another. Here, also, the interval outlined by the linear progression (C–A) belongs to the goal of the chord progression (IV).

Our next example presents the beginning of one of Bach's many settings of the chorale melody "Jesu, meine Freude" (Example 4.4a). In this opening phrase, the upper voice begins with B ($\hat{5}$) and proceeds down by step to E ($\hat{1}$). The soprano melody thus forms a fifth-progression, a line that fills in the E-minor tonic triad (see Example 4.4b).

Like the opening of Bach's organ prelude in Example 4.1, the upper voice of this phrase represents an extension of tonic harmony. However its bass and harmonic structure are more complex: a succession of intervening chords connects the initial tonic to the closing tonic that marks the conclusion of the phrase. Because linear progressions are usually harmonized in some fashion, a more complete picture of the tonal framework will emerge if we evaluate the outer-voice structure and its relation to the harmonic context.

The essential harmonic structure of the phrase is shown in stages (Example 4.4b). Over the span of this two-bar phrase, the bass arpeggiates the tonic triad by moving from its root to its fifth and back again: E–B–E. The II$^6_5$ chord on the downbeat of bar 2 is an intermediate harmony, and we indicate its close relationship to the dominant with an eighth-note flag. The bass motion

EXAMPLE 4.4:

(a) J. S. Bach, Chorale, "Jesu, meine Freude," bars 1–2, (b) linear expression of vertical triad

is further elaborated with passing tones that traverse a descending fifth from
I to II_5^6.[3] In contrast to the bass motion E–A, the top-voice descending fifth
E–B moves more slowly, embracing the entire phrase. Consequently, when the
bass has descended a fifth to A on the downbeat of bar 2, the soprano has
descended through only four tones of its descending fifth. The fourth and
fifth tones (F#–E) are supported by the complete cadential progression that
concludes the phrase.[4]

We saw in Example 4.3 that a linear progression can either prolong a
single chord or move from one chord to another. This example illustrates
both functions: the bass descent from E to A progresses from I to II_5^6. The
top-voice descent from B to E, on the other hand, completely linearizes the
tonic triad; the first, last, and intervening tones work within one chord—
the E-minor tonic triad (the A and F# are passing tones). Much of the remainder of our discussion of linear techniques will focus on similar processes of
prolongation and motion.

In Chapter 3 we made a general distinction between "chord" and "harmony," a distinction we will continue to refine as we examine larger spans of
music. For now, think of harmonies in one sense as chords (because they are
indeed vertical entities), but also in a larger sense as scale steps (*Stufen*).[5]
Harmonic scale steps are structural "pillars" that shape the *vertical* (harmonic)
dimension of tonal compositions over broader spans. A harmonic frame work
generally consists of a series of *Stufen,* frequently an initial tonic and a concluding V–I cadence; the V is often preceded by an intermediate harmony.
(The framework will end with a V if a half cadence concludes the passage.)[6]

Example 4.5 presents the opening bars from the Trio of Beethoven's Piano Sonata, Op. 2, No. 1. In Example 4.5b, various elements of graphic notation are employed: broken lines and slurs indicate the retention of a single
tone over a longer span, while solid slurs indicate motions among different
tones.[7] A notehead without a stem signifies a tone of lesser priority. Among
stemmed notes, stem length corresponds to relative structural priority, with
the longest stems showing greatest priority. Again, the letter P indicates passing function and N, neighbor function; neighbor function may also be shown
with a flag.[8]

If you sing the melody of the right hand, you will notice that the upper
voice is a stepwise, melodically fluent line that moves up to a high point in
bar 3 and back down in bar 4. As the reduction in Example 4.5b shows,
another melodically fluent line lies beneath the eighth notes—A–B♭–C–B♭–A
(sing this "hidden" melody and you should easily perceive the relationship to
the surface version). What, precisely, is the reason that leads us to distinguish
this deeper "guiding" line beneath the surface of the music?

To answer this question we will need to consider the left-hand part as
well. The motions to and from the bass and tenor registers define two separate stepwise lines, the lower of which defines the harmonic structure. The F
(supporting tonic harmony) on the downbeats of bars 1 and 4 is prolonged
by its upper and lower neighbors G and E, which support the II and V^6
chords, respectively. Thus each bar contains one principal chord, each contributing a primary bass and top-voice tone in what is essentially a note-

EXAMPLE 4–5:

(a) Beethoven, Piano Sonata, Op. 2, No.1, III (Trio), bars 1–4; (b) analytical reduction;
(c) outer voice reduction

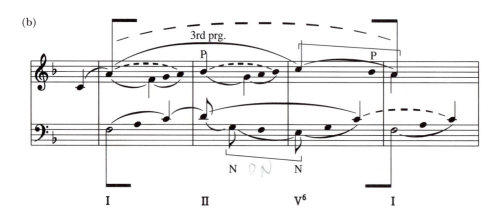

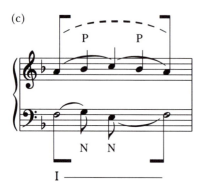

against-note framework (the bass G in bar 2 is delayed by the arpeggiation in the left hand; compare Examples 4.5b and c). Hence our analysis of the "guiding" line of the upper voice is made *in conjunction with* a similar analysis of the bass line. Now we can determine with even greater clarity that the upper voice incorporates *third-progressions* that lead from A to C and back again, moving through the upper third of the F-major tonic triad; this motion prolongs A throughout bars 1–4.[9]

We have now observed several levels of structure in the top voice: (1) the prolongation of A, (2) the linear progressions rising to C and returning to A, and (3) the tones of figuration (neighbor notes, passing tones, and consonant skips) that further embellish these third-progressions. There are, moreover, other relationships among these levels: note the smaller third-progressions (indicated on the music) that foreshadow the larger third-progression A–B♭–C (bar 1 to the downbeat of bar 3). Also significant is the embellished A–F–A figure of bar 1, which is a smaller (and inverted) version of the A–C–A motion that spans the entire four-bar segment.[10]

Finally, consider the brackets in bars 2–4 of Example 4.5b. The concluding passing motion in the upper voice "answers" a similar passing motion in the bass. That is, G–F–E in the bass is followed by the more deeply embedded C–B♭–A in the upper voice, creating a concealed imitative relationship between the outer voices. This statement-answer pattern is called a *motivic parallelism* (these descending figures are also related to the *ascending* thirds F–G–A and G–A–B♭ in bars 1–2). We will see the unifying effects of parallelisms again in different contexts.[11]

Our next excerpt illustrates a more elaborated form of a linear progression that prolongs an underlying chord. Example 4.6 presents bars 8–12 of the exposition from one of Clementi's sonatinas.[12] An examination of the bass reveals the progression I–V⁶–I–V⁴₃–I⁶, which supports the ascending fifth-progression G–A–B–C–D. The melodic span from G to D is a perfect fifth,

EXAMPLE 4.6:

(a) Clementi, Sonatina, Op. 36, No. 1, bars 8–12 with analytical interpretation;
(b) outer voice reduction

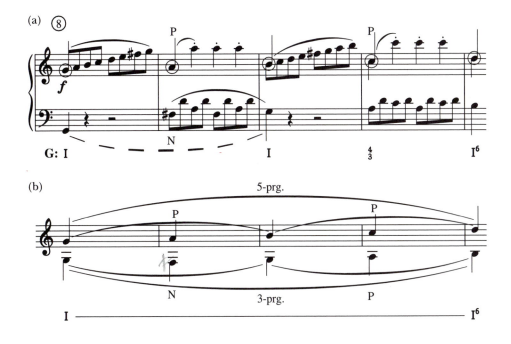

the boundary interval of the G-major harmony that governs this passage. This is a particularly clear example of how a triad, an element of the vertical dimension of musical structure, may be expressed in the horizontal-temporal dimension with passing tones. Our analysis would be insufficient if we concluded here, however, because we have said little about the details of the musical surface that give this passage its own unique character and that distinguish it from countless other passages based upon fifth-progressions.

Notice that each note of the linear progression (except for the final D) is transferred up an octave within each measure. The linking of two different octaves is one of several procedures used by composers to integrate the different registers of a composition. The integration of the two registers in this case is accomplished alternately with a scale passage that connects the registers in stepwise motion, followed by a direct leap up an octave. The alternation provides variety and creates an interplay between the left and right hands that enlivens the musical texture. When the right hand is rhythmically the most active, the bass is essentially silent; silence can be a way of "punctuating" musical space. When the bass then imitates the eighth-note rhythm in the following bar, the right hand reverts to quarter notes. This alternation directs our attention first to the right hand, then to the left, and so forth.

A related but different type of registral shift occurs in the left hand. The first G appears in the lower register, the lower neighbor F♯ and the G appear in the higher register. Here we see how a motion of a descending second, in this case from G to F♯, is inverted to an ascending seventh (G up to F♯). This technique is called *interval inversion* and is particularly common in instrumental music.

The ascending fifth-progression in the upper voice, therefore, is supported by a bass motion from I to I⁶ (G to B). Within this prolongation of tonic harmony, there is also an element of progression. The motion between the two positions of the tonic triad involves two different bass notes: G to B is a third-progression, a motion through the lower third of the tonic triad. Thus, the harmonic expansion in this excerpt is achieved by the melodic progression between two tones of the same chord.[13]

The opening of the Air from Bach's Partita No. 6 in E minor (Example 4.7) illustrates a descending fourth-progression in the bass that was especially

EXAMPLE 4.7:

J. S. Bach, Partita No. 6, Air, bars 1–2 with analytical interpretation

common in music of the seventeenth and early eighteenth centuries.[14] In the harmonic progression from I to V, the intervening V^6 and IV^6 chords are contrapuntal chords, built on the passing tones D and C. The descending fourth in this context functions as an inversion of the rising perfect fifth. In other words, this *descending* progression provides another path from I to V, another resource for the shaping of musical space and the expansion of this fundamental harmonic motion.[15]

Example 4.8, from the Courante of Handel's F-minor Suite, is similar to the previous example in that the fourth-progression in the bass expands the musical space between tonic and dominant harmonies, but in this case the motion is reversed, proceeding from dominant to tonic. This particular chromatic progression combines aspects of the major and minor modes, incorporating both forms of scale degrees $\hat{6}$ and $\hat{7}$. The motion to the tonic is intensified by the integration of the half steps into the fourth-progression.

Example 4.9 illustrates the elaboration of a single chord, but of a different type than we have previously considered. In this passage from Beethoven's Bagatelle, Op. 119, No. 1, the particular expansion involves the unfolding of a *dissonant* span, the seventh of a dominant seventh chord. As the left hand sustains the vertical seventh from Bb up to Ab, the upper voice "linearizes" the same interval with descending passing tones. This combination of a sustained, vertical chord with its "linearization" clearly illustrates how the prolongation of a harmony, which is essentially a vertical entity, is expressed (or projected) into the horizontal dimension of tonal music.[16]

This example also illustrates another common procedure related to linear progressions, particularly those that involve a dissonance. It is clear in the left hand alone that the dominant seventh chord is sustained for four bars and that its seventh, Ab, resolves to the third of tonic harmony in the fifth bar of the example. Because the upper voice is a horizontal expression of the same chord, the high Ab functions in the same way: it does not resolve within the bar, but rather to the high G of tonic harmony. In other words, the resolution of the 7th in the upper voice is *delayed* (through intervening tones) until V^7 resolves to I.[17] This delay is produced by the passing tones of the linear pro-

EXAMPLE 4.8:

Handel, Keyboard Suite No. 8, Courante, bars 43–46 with analytical interpretation

EXAMPLE 4.9:

(a) Beethoven, Bagatelle, Op. 119, No. 1, bars 25–29 with analytical interpretation;
(b) linear expression of V[7]

(a)

(b)

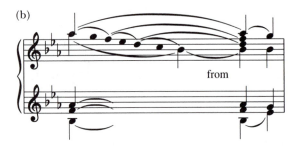

gression, which serve to unfold the chord and retain the presence of A♭. In so doing they lead from an "upper" voice to an "inner" voice of the underlying dominant seventh chord. We will discuss this technique (called "motion into an inner voice") more thoroughly in Chapter 6.

Example 4.9b also shows that the passing tones form groups of thirds. Because all of the chord tones are either stated or implied at the outset, we certainly perceive this grouping with the dominant seventh chord. Notice, however, that the dissonant passing tones G, E♭, and C are *accented* passing tones (Example 4.9a). Because the chordal context is so clearly established by the left hand and boundaries of the motion, the melodic function of these tones within the chord is clear, even though they occupy relatively strong rhythmic positions.

Near the beginning of this chapter we mentioned that linear progressions normally involve the consonant intervals of major and minor triads, the primary vertical sonorities of tonal music. However, certain dissonant chords— among them the dominant seventh, diminished seventh, and augmented sixth chords—were incorporated by composers into the language of tonal music. Species counterpoint demonstrates the principle that dissonances function subordinately in a context defined by consonances. Likewise, dissonant chords are secondary relative to the consonant triads to which they resolve. Thus, we may designate the linear motions that expand dissonant harmonies as "secondary" linear progressions.[18]

LINEAR INTERVALLIC PATTERNS

Harmonic sequences are often characterized by a repeated interval pattern between a pair of voices; these are known as *linear intervallic patterns.*[19] Sequences and their associated linear intervallic patterns frequently participate in harmonic prolongations and define larger structural connections. Like linear progressions, linear intervallic patterns may move within (prolong) a chord or lead from one chord to another.

Handel's keyboard Passacaille in G minor provides a fine example of the varied voice-leading patterns that can be associated with a single sequence type. This work employs the descending-fifth sequence. Example 4.10 shows the sequence in its basic form, the complete circle of fifths with every chord in root position.

Consider the linear characteristics of this sequence. The interval pattern repeated by the outer voices is 5–10, an alternation of a perfect with an imperfect consonance. Note that we are not focusing here on a single-line linear progression, but on a recurring pattern that involves two voices moving in a complementary manner.[20] In textures of more than two voices, chords naturally arise in conjunction with the repeated pattern, thereby forming chordal sequences. The chords in the pattern, like the linear chords discussed in Chapter 3, therefore result from contrapuntal motion.

Roman numeral analysis can be helpful in identifying the type of sequence with which the pattern is associated, and in specifying the function of the initial, final, and other principal chords. We have mentioned that linear intervallic patterns, like linear progressions, either expand a single chord or lead from one chord to another. In a descending-fifth sequence in which every chord occurs in root position, it is sometimes difficult to make a decision about the precise function of the linear intervallic pattern. Does the progression connect the initial tonic directly with the V–I cadence, or should the II sonority that precedes the V be considered a structural chord (the intermediate harmony), and consequently the goal of the motion? The decision is difficult because the bass line is undifferentiated; every step in the sequence involves a descending fifth (or its inversion, an ascending fourth).

In evaluating this passage, consider that the bass of a descending-fifth sequence pattern typically incorporates two intertwined, stepwise lines. In Example 4.10b, compare the line G–F–E♭–D, formed by the bass notes on the downbeats, with the line C–B♭–A–G, formed by the notes in the second part of each bar. The upper line—which begins on the tonic and receives greater rhythmic emphasis—seems primary, while the lower line appears to follow. Consequently, the linear intervallic pattern expands the motion from I to V in the overall motion I–V–I. The chords in the second part of each bar break

EXAMPLE 4.10:

(a) Handel, Passacaille, bars 5–8; (b) outer voice reduction

(a)

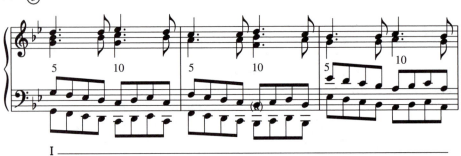

up the parallel fifths and octaves that would otherwise occur between the chords on the downbeats.

The next example presents the beginning of Handel's Passacaille, the theme of the variations (Example 4.11). Here we see a variant form of the descending-fifth sequence: the outer-voice framework is shaped by the succession 5–8, an alternation of two perfect consonances. Notice, however, that in bar 2 the pattern is 5–10 instead of 5–8. Changes like these, even if apparently incidental, can often clarify aspects of the structural framework.

EXAMPLE 4.11:

(a) Handel, Passacaille, bars 1–4; (b) outer voice reduction

In the previous example (the first variation) we saw that it was initially difficult to make decisions about chordal functions within the linear intervallic pattern, because the bass consists of motion by fifths. In Example 4.11 the situation is different. The sequence is a variant of the descending-fifth progression in which root-position chords alternate with six-three chords. In bar 2, however, the pattern is 5–10 (instead of 5–8). This "exception" allows the Bb-major chord to appear in root position (the bass is the lowest note heard thus far), producing stability *in the midst* of the sequence that highlights the function of the Bb chord as a *scale step* in the progression I–III–II⁶–V–I. Remember that III frequently proceeds to a IV or a II⁶ before moving to V. (Although the mediant is often a secondary chord in a descending-fifth progression, here it becomes a higher-ranking component of the harmonic structure.) Thus an apparently insignificant change in surface detail—the change in the intervallic pattern—can significantly influence the analytical interpretation of the passage.

Example 4.12, a passage from Mozart's Piano Sonata in C major, K. 545, is also organized by a descending-fifth sequence in which root-position chords alternate with six-three chords. Many of the roman numerals have been enclosed in parentheses, differentiating these fleeting chords (produced locally through contrapuntal motion) from the broader context of the harmonic prolongation in which they function.

The first part of Example 4.12b shows the pattern 10–10, which is repeated before the intermediate II^6 appears. In this case, the sequential pattern leads from I^6 to I, expanding tonic harmony. In the second part of the example, we have "normalized" the register. Much of the charm of this excerpt results from the interplay of two different registers in the right hand, resulting from the elaboration of this pattern through interval inversion. If you compare the two parts of Example 4.12b, you will discover that the seconds inherent in the upper voice of the basic pattern are realized as descending sevenths in the actual music. Nevertheless, the framework based on a series of tenths is not undermined by the contrasting registers; in fact, the pattern serves to unify these registers.

Example 4.13, from Handel's Passacaille, illustrates the common linear

EXAMPLE 4.12:

(a) Mozart, Piano Sonata, K. 545, I, bars 18–22; (b) outer voice reduction

EXAMPLE 4.12 (*continued*)

intervallic pattern 8–10. In contrast to the 5–10 pattern of Example 4.10, the upper-voice tone remains constant throughout each bar, traversing a fourth-progression from G to D. (As we have seen, linear progressions are often associated with linear intervallic patterns.)

The rapid sixteenth-note scale passages, which are characteristic of virtuosic writing for keyboard instruments, prolong each tone of the fourth-progression by the technique called *transfer of register.* In other words, the right hand consists of scalar figuration that leads from the high to the middle register of the keyboard. Note also that were it not for the tenths in the second part of each bar, the bass and upper voice would proceed in parallel octaves. In intervallic patterns involving a perfect consonance (such as 5–10 and 8–10), the alternating interval improves the voice leading between adjacent chords.

Example 4.14, our last excerpt from Handel's Passacaille, shows another situation in which the note in the upper voice is sustained in each statement of the pattern. This is the first example we have encountered in which one of the voices is dissonant with the other (10–7). The seventh between the outer voices in the second half of each bar is prepared as a common tone by the preceding tenth; the dissonance then resolves to the tenth on the downbeat of the next bar (which prepares the following seventh, and so forth). These local seventh chords intensify the triads on the downbeats. Consequently, we

EXAMPLE 4.13:

(a) Handel, Passacaille, bars 33–36; (b) outer voice reduction

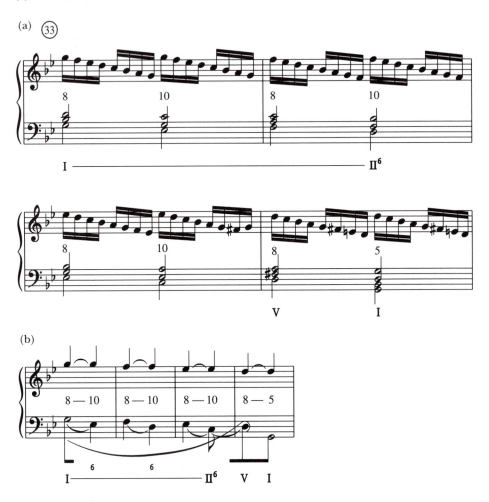

regard the function of this linear intervallic pattern as leading from the tonic at the beginning of the phrase to the dominant in the cadential measure; the chords in the second half of each bar mitigate the parallels between the triads on the successive downbeats.

In the excerpts we have examined thus far, we have only shown linear intervallic patterns associated with the descending-fifth sequence. We shall conclude this section with patterns that work in conjunction with other sequence types.

Compare the passage in Example 4.15 with its reduction. In the music, chordal skips animate (and somewhat conceal) a stepwise linear intervallic pattern. The 5–6 contrapuntal motion creates the alternating $\frac{5}{3}$ and $\frac{6}{3}$ chords of the *ascending 5–6 sequence*. In this pattern, the 5–6 motion breaks up the

EXAMPLE 4.14:

(a) Handel, Passacaille, bars 41–44; (b) outer voice reduction

parallel fifths that would otherwise occur in a series of rising root-position triads.

Because of the repeated leaps in the soprano melody, we must look to the tenor voice to understand the continuity of the upper voice shown in the reduction (notice that we have placed the implied tones in parentheses). In other words, the intervals of the fifth and sixth above the bass occur alternately between two voices (soprano and tenor). The polyphonic skips in the soprano serve to *elaborate* the underlying stepwise line inherent in this sequence.[21] This rising series of 5–6 motions therefore prolongs tonic harmony (I⁶–I). Through the rising fourths in the soprano, the dialogue between the soprano and the lower voices, and the rhythmic animation of the complemen-

EXAMPLE 4.15:

(a) Dowland, "Come Again, Sweet Love," bars 15–20; (b) linear reduction

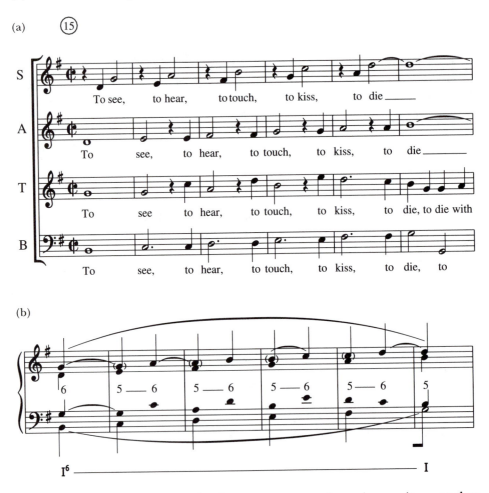

tary quarter-note motion, Dowland creates a sense of growing excitement that perfectly suits the emotional intensity of the text.

In Example 4.16, the 5–6 motion is enhanced through the use of chromatic passing tones. As a result the $\frac{6}{3}$ chords not only intervene between the root-position chords, but also (bars 12 and 13) function as applied dominant chords. In the upper voice, the chromatic passing tones G♯ in bar 11 and C♯ in bar 14 similarly intensify the motion to the following chords. As Example 4.16b shows, a chromatic passing motion occurs in every bar of the example beginning with the motion from III to VI, the chord that begins the sequence. The sequence moves from VI to I⁶, with the bass rising a fifth overall. Notice that the outer voices proceed in parallel tenths. A succession of tenths very often accompanies the 5–6 motion of this sequence type.[22]

Our next example, the opening bars of the last movement from Beethoven's Piano Sonata, Op. 79 (Example 4.17), is based on the descending 5–6 sequence (sometimes called the *falling thirds* sequence). It beautifully illus-

EXAMPLE 4.16:

(a) Mendelssohn, *Song Without Words,* Op. 62, No. 1, bars 10–15; (b) linear reduction

(a)

(b)

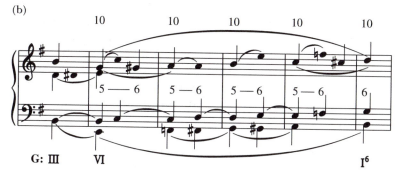

EXAMPLE 4.17:

(a) Beethoven, Piano Sonata, Op. 79, III, bars 1–4; (b) linear reduction

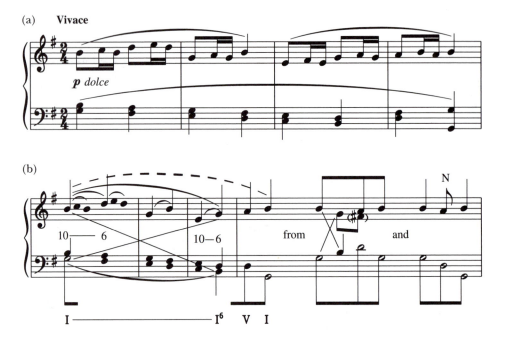

trates how a linear intervallic pattern can expand a single harmonic scale step over a broader span, in this case from I to I^6.

A comparison of the bass and the main notes of the upper voice reveals a 10–6 pattern that continues through the end of bar 3, where the bass changes direction and proceeds by leap to the V. This change in direction suggests that the I^6 in bar 3 is an intermediate goal in the phrase (Example 4.17b). Notice that the bass of the linear intervallic pattern traverses a descending sixth-progression. It is important to bear in mind that linear progressions are usually part of linear intervallic patterns.

This example also provides a clear illustration of the distinction between "chord" and "harmony." As we described above, intervening chords in sequences arise through the contrapuntal motion between a pair of voices; individually they do not represent harmonies. Here only the prolonged I and I^6, the tonic chords that begin and end the sequence, represent harmonies in a structural sense (as do the concluding V and I chords).[23]

The fact that the expansion of tonic harmony largely shapes the organization of the phrase is evident not only from the linear progression in the bass. If you compare the notes between the outer voices at the beginning and end of the linear intervallic pattern, you will discover a voice exchange (Example 4.17b). Remember that a voice exchange expands a chord through an arpeggiation of its tones between two voices. In this case, B to G in the upper voice is accompanied by G to B in the lower (the ascending third from I to I^6 is expressed as a descending sixth in the music). The voice exchange frames the linear intervallic pattern and clarifies further how the initial tonic is expanded through contrapuntal means.[24]

Our final example of a linear intervallic pattern comes from Mozart's Piano Sonata in G major, K. 283, and shows a technique from fourth species counterpoint—a series of 7–6 suspensions. The passage presented in Example 4.18 is from the second part of the exposition; at this point Mozart has conclusively established the secondary key of D major.

Note that we have indicated an implied A in the upper voice in Examples 4.18b and c. A 5–6 motion typically produces the initial preparation in the first of a series of 7–6 suspensions, but it is not for this reason alone that we read the continued presence of this note in the analysis. Prior to the quoted

EXAMPLE 4.18:

(a) Mozart, Piano Sonata, K. 283, I, bars 43–51; (b–c) outer voice reductions, bars 45–48

EXAMPLE 4.18 (*continued*)

passage, throughout the entire second theme, high A is quite prominent. Here its presence is implied as part of the D major triad and the f#² on the downbeat is understood as an inner-voice tone.

Like the phrase from Beethoven's piano sonata (Example 4.17), the bass outlines a descending sixth-progression that expands the motion from I to I⁶. At this point in the phrase the chain of suspensions ends and the bass changes direction, features that highlight II⁶ as the intermediate harmony in the structural progression I–II⁶–V⁷–I. In our discussion of fourth species counterpoint we explained that suspensions arise through rhythmic displacement. Example 4.18c realigns the notes of the suspension series and shows the relationship of the outer voices to first species counterpoint (this is sometimes referred to as "normalizing" a passage with suspensions). With the normalization, we can see the succession of parallel $\frac{6}{3}$ chords on which the 7–6 linear intervallic pattern is based and the two linear progressions embodied in the pattern. You should now be able to recognize the same 7–6 series in bars 48–49, which is an altered repetition, a decorated version, of bars 45–46.

THE NEIGHBOR NOTE

We have begun to discover ways in which harmony and counterpoint can interact in the formation of linear progressions and intervallic patterns. In this final section we will explore briefly another type of contrapuntal formation that may serve to expand tonal structure on various levels: the neighbor note. Schenker, of course, was not the first to write about neighbor notes, but he was the first to recognize their full significance at different levels of tonal structure; consequently, he gave them special attention in his work. Neighbor notes can serve many purposes in tonal music: for now, we will consider two representative examples.

In the opening bars of Brahms's Waltz in A♭, Op. 39, No. 15 (Example 4.19), tonic harmony is prolonged throughout the phrase and supports C as the main tone in the upper voice in bars 1, 2, and 4. Although A♭ also occurs in the bass on the downbeat of bar 3, the chord in that bar is a neighboring $^6_4$, which supports D♭ in the upper voice as a neighbor to C.

Pay special attention to bar 3: the upper neighbor D♭ *does not* resolve to C on the second beat. This C is a passing tone within the line D♭–C–B♭, a motion that sustains the neighbor D♭ for the duration of the bar (the D♭ in the bass and tenor on beat 2 helps to confirm this point). The resolution of D♭ to C occurs *across* the bar, and corresponds with the restatement of root-position tonic harmony. Thus scale degree $\hat{3}$ is prolonged in the upper voice by the tone succession C–D♭–C. The different functions of c^2 in bars 3 and 4 provide further clarification that repeated tones may embody different meanings.

Example 4.20 shows another instance of the prolonging function of a neighbor note; here, it occurs within a linear progression in the first movement of Beethoven's "Moonlight" Sonata. After four bars of introduction, the main part of the movement begins. As the reduction shows, the upper voice traverses a third-progression, G♯–F♯–E, which is supported by the harmonic progression from I to III. This third-progression is elaborated and *expanded* by A, the upper neighbor to G♯ (note that tonic harmony is also expanded by

EXAMPLE 4.19:

Brahms, Waltz, Op. 39, No. 15, bars 1–4

EXAMPLE 4.20:

(a) Beethoven, Piano Sonata, Op. 27, No. 2, I, bars 5–9; (b) linear reduction

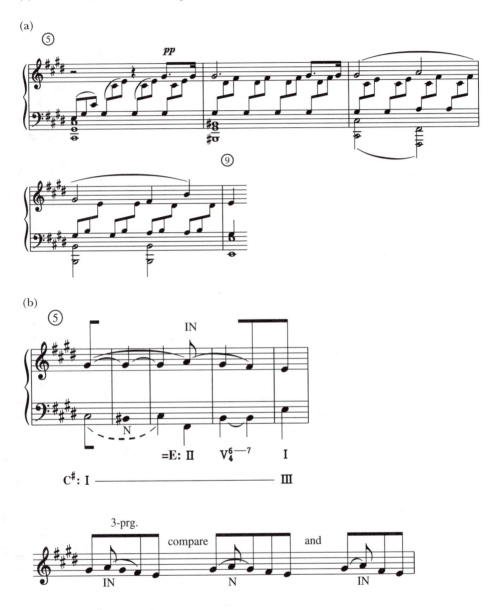

a lower neighbor B♯ in the bass before the phrase begins to move toward E major).

You will see in the reduction that we interpret the A as an *incomplete* upper neighbor (IN). In other words, it relates as a neighbor only to the first G♯. The second G♯ is supported by the cadential six-four of the cadence and therefore is an *accented passing tone* that resolves to F♯, the second tone of the linear progression (the sixth and fourth of a cadential six-four usually enter either as suspensions or accented passing tones). The elaboration of a linear progression with an incomplete upper neighbor figure is very common in tonal music. Incidentally, you will notice that we have represented the neighbor note in the reduction with an eighth-note flag, a notation commonly used in Schenkerian graphs to indicate neighbor notes; the bass tones of intermediate harmonies are also indicated in this manner.[25]

Exercises

Examine the following passages; identify linear progressions and linear intervallic patterns as indicated. Be able to explain the *function* of each: that is, whether the linear progression or intervallic pattern expands a single harmony or leads from one harmony to another. Identify any sequences.

Linear progressions only

1. Mozart, Piano Sonata K. 280, III, bars 1–5
2. Bach, Chorale No. 244, bars 1–2 (upper voice)
3. Bach, Little Prelude in F major, BWV 927, bars 1–8
4. Bach, Prelude in B major (*Well-Tempered Clavier* I), bars 1–2 (upper voice)
5. Mozart, Rondo in A minor, K. 511, bars 1–5 (upper voice)
6. Schumann, *Album for the Young*, Op. 68, "Trällerliedchen," bars 1–8
7. Bach, Prelude in D major (*Well-Tempered Clavier* I), bars, 1–3
8. Mozart, Piano Sonata, K. 284, III, Variation 7, bars 1–4
9. Schubert, *Die Winterreise*, No. 10, "Rast," bars 6–10
10. Brahms, Waltz, Op. 39, No. 5, bars 1–8
11. Chopin, Prelude in E major, Op. 28, No. 9, bars 9–12
12. Beethoven, Piano Sonata, Op. 10, No. 2, I, bars 1–12 (bass)
13. Bach, Partita No. 1 in B♭ major, Praeludium, bars 1–3 (upper voice)
14. Handel, Keyboard Suite No. 8 in F minor, Praeludium, bars 1–8 (bass)

Linear progressions and linear intervallic patterns

1. Mozart, Piano Sonata, K. 545, I, bars 63–66
2. Beethoven, Piano Sonata, Op. 28, Rondo, bars 17–28
3. Mozart, Piano Sonata, K. 280, III, bars 20–37
4. Bach, Little Prelude in C major, BWV 943, bars 29–36 (linear intervallic pattern begins in bar 30)
5. Mozart, Piano Sonata, K.533/494, III, bars 95–98
6. Chopin, Etude, Op. 25, No. 9, bars 1–4

7. Bach, Little Fugue in A minor for organ, BWV 559, bars 13–25 and 35–end (linear intervallic pattern: two forms)

8. Beethoven, Piano Sonata, Op. 53 ("Waldstein"), I, bars 1–13 (linear intervallic pattern and linear progression)

9. Bach, Prelude in E minor *(Well-Tempered Clavier* I), bars 1–4 (linear progression) and 4–9 (linear intervallic pattern)

10. Corelli, Trio Sonata, Op. 1, No. 4, Allegro, bars 16–20

11. Handel, Keyboard Suite No. 8 in F minor, Courante, bars 7–11

12. Mozart, Piano Sonata, K. 310, I, bars 22–31 (linear intervallic pattern begins in bar 28)

13. Bach, French Suite in E major, Gavotte, bars 1–4 (linear intervallic pattern)

14. Corelli, Trio Sonata, Op. 2, No. 11, Allemande, bars 16–18 (linear intervallic pattern)

CHAPTER 5

Tonal Structure

All musical elements considered thus far—melody, bass line and harmonic structure, and linear motions—are essential considerations of Schenkerian analysis. As a first step, it can be beneficial to focus on a single element, such as melodic structure, but it is crucial to remember that these aspects are not independent but are dynamically interrelated. In analysis, all facets of the harmonic (vertical) and contrapuntal (horizontal) dimensions should be examined together.

In this chapter we will begin to explore how these dimensions work interactively to form tonal structure in its broadest sense. We will also learn how to use graphic symbols to represent a structural analysis. Graphic notation employs various symbols, including slurs and symbols from rhythmic notation; these acquire new meanings in graphs, as you have seen in some of the previous examples. You may have also noticed that many of the analyses in this book do not, for instance, indicate aspects of rhythm and dynamics. A Schenkerian graph illustrates (for the most part) the interrelationships among harmony and counterpoint over various structural levels of a composition. (The concept of *structural levels* will be discussed more fully below.) [1]

NOTATIONAL SYMBOLS

The following notational symbols are commonly used in Schenkerian graphs: [2]

1. *Unstemmed filled noteheads* indicate notes that form part of the immediate musical context, but are not part of the larger framework.

2. *Stems* added to black noteheads designate a broader structural significance. The relative length of the stem may further distinguish various

levels of structure. For instance, noteheads with long stems belong together and form part of a higher level of structure than noteheads with shorter stems.[3]

3. *Half notes* are normally used to indicate those tones that are on the highest level of the structure.

4. *Parentheses* around a note indicate a tone that is implied by a specific context, but is not actually present. Occasionally parentheses may be used to isolate a sounding tone or series of tones that are functionally independent from the surrounding context.

5. *Beams* and *slurs* group related tones, such as arpeggiations, linear progressions, and neighboring motions, and show unified spans on all levels of structure.

6. *Broken slurs (or ties)* indicate the retention of a single pitch over a broader span, usually after the intervention of other tones. *Broken beams* are similarly used by some analysts.[4]

7. *Arrowheads* are sometimes added to slurs or lines indicating the direction of a motion.

8. *Roman numerals* denote primary structural harmonies.

Some of these symbols appear in Example 5.1b, which depicts the voice-leading structure of the opening phrase of the aria "Addio del passato" from Verdi's opera *La Traviata*. The example contains a number of features characteristic of graphic analyses:

1. The first bass note is written as a half note to indicate that the influence of tonic harmony extends over the span of the entire phrase. In other words, from the perspective of the entire aria, the opening bars represent a prolonged tonic harmony.

2. The initial tonic relates also to the V^7–I that defines the end of the phrase. This relationship is shown by stemming all of the notes in the bass and by filling in the noteheads; observe also the use of slurs, which indicate the associations among these tones.

3. In the upper voices, upward stems normally indicate top-voice tones, while downward stems denote tones of inner voices. This notation is analogous to the notation of four-part writing, but can also (as here) represent two polyphonically interwoven voices.

4. *Unstemmed notes* can have several meanings. They may indicate melodic tones that are not part of the underlying harmony, such as the dissonant passing tone b^1 in bar 1; repetitions of previously heard tones of identical function, such as the final c^2 and a^1 of bar 1; or, inner-voice tones that complete a chord, such as the e^1 on the downbeats of bars 3 and 4.

5. Repeated notes are often shown only once, as with the repeated c^2 in bar 1. If a measure is repeated with no significant change, it may be represented with a repeat sign (bar 2).

EXAMPLE 5–1:

(a) Verdi, "Addio del passato" (from *La Traviata,* Act III), bars 3–8; (b) analytical reduction

A distinctive element of this melody is the interval of the third, which becomes motivic. Following the initial rise of a sixth from the inner voice, much of the melody employs leaps of a third or motions through thirds, as indicated by the slurs within each measure.[5] Notice that the stemmed upper tones of the polyphonic melody, C–B–A, consist of the same notes as in bar 1. Yet the tones of this third are not heard in immediate succession. Rather, they are nonadjacent, occurring over a broader span as the initial notes of bars 1, 3, and 4. If you sing or play just these tones, you will hear that they help to establish the overall shape of the phrase.

Because the third-motive in "Addio del passato" occurs both in immediate succession and over a longer span, we may say that it occurs on more than one level of structure. This happens in many compositions: the repetition of motives is one of the most remarkable resources in tonal music. Motives create variety through varied expression, and unity through their underlying identity. In general, repetition—whether of motives, phrases, or formal sections—is a basic aspect of musical coherence that has profound implications for analysis.

Example 5.2 illustrates the combination of two almost identical phrases at the beginning of a theme used by Beethoven for a series of variations. In the top voice (bars 1–4), the phrase begins with the elaboration of the initial tone C by motions to and from inner-voice tones, before continuing by step to the supertonic note g^2 (over V).

The second phrase (bars 5–8) begins as before, but concludes with a perfect authentic cadence in bar 8. Such a grouping of phrases is called an *antecedent/consequent* construction. In this case the upper voice of the consequent phrase completes the descent left unfinished by the antecedent phrase, and the harmonic motion of the consequent completes the motion left incomplete at the half cadence in bar 4. Together these paired phrases form a complete musical segment, or *period*.

Having considered the essential top-voice structure of this passage, we shall now examine the ways in which it is expanded and elaborated in the composition. First of all, notice that the right-hand part begins alone on an upbeat. In many cases initial upbeats are anticipatory, and do not form part of the principal structure of a phrase. Contextual factors, however, should always be considered in analysis. Here the upbeat is a quarter note in length, and is marked sforzando. It is followed by eighth notes in bar 1, with a return to C on the last eighth; the top-voice tones B♭ and A follow as quarters in bar 2. The ear will naturally associate the longer note values (C–B♭–A) in this passage, particularly with the sforzando emphasis of the upbeat and the return to C at the end of bar 1. Compositional features, therefore, support the reading of the upbeat as the first tone of the underlying, stepwise line.[6] Notice that C is heard before the bass note of the chord to which it belongs. Such a relationship is called a *displacement*, and is indicated in a graph by a diagonal line (Example 5.2b).

The initial C is elaborated with arpeggiation, motions to and from inner voices that outline the tonic triad. Following the return to C at the end of bar 1, the descent continues without further melodic elaboration until bar 3. Here another motion to the inner voice occurs, but this motion is filled in

EXAMPLE 5.2:

(a) Beethoven, Seven Variations on a Theme by P. Winter, WoO 75, Theme, bars 1–8;
(b) analytical interpretation

(a)

(b)

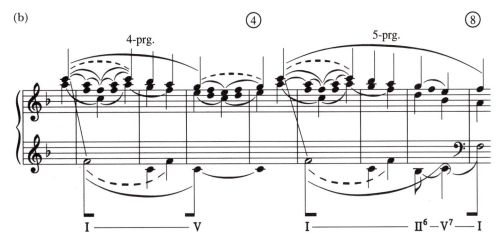

with passing tones (in contrast to the unfilled chordal skips in bar 1). In the graph, slurs group the unstemmed passing tones within the motion from G to the inner-voice tone E and back to G.

The bass line and harmonic structure are straightforward in these bars. Notice, however, the difference in function between the dominant chords in bars 2 and 4. The broken slur connecting the bass note F in bar 1 with the F in bar 2 indicates that the first V^7 chord, which supports the top-voice passing tone B♭, occurs within the larger tonic prolongation. It thus functions locally, and is not given a roman numeral. The dominant chord bars 3–4, on the other hand, is the cadential goal of the first phrase, and as such is an independent structural harmony. We have seen that two identical melody notes may differ in function; in like manner, two similar chords may function differently.

In the consequent phrase a significant harmonic change occurs: in bar 7, II⁶–V both appear in the penultimate bar (V lasts only one beat because of the need to conclude on I in the final bar of the phrase). The addition of the intermediate II⁶, the first chord that we have heard other than I and V, intensifies the authentic cadence. In conjunction with this harmonic change a new bass note is introduced: B♭, the lowest bass tone that we have heard in the high bass line. The phrase concludes with a still lower bass tone, F in bar 8. A change of register is often employed by composers to highlight the end of a phrase or section.

The authentic cadence of the consequent phrase also produces a change in the upper voice, because a *complete* descent to F is necessary to conclude the upper voice of the phrase (bar 8). Compare bars 3–4 with bar 7. The two third-motions from bars 3–4 are compressed into a single third in bar 7. Also note that F recurs, but as a grace note. While ornaments generally embellish other tones, they can play an integral role in the melody. In bar 7, F completely fills in the G–E motion, in a rhythmically altered version of the motion in bar 3. Both the ornament and the sixteenth-note motion are additional elements that intensify the motion to $\hat{1}$ over I.

Finally, notice that the top-voice tone G is supported by the II⁶ intermediate harmony, not by the dominant as it was in the previous phrase. In Chapter 2 we observed that in two-part, first species counterpoint, the measure before the final tonic contains both scale degrees $\hat{2}$ and $\hat{7}$. Because of their stepwise relationship to the tonic, these are the tones with the greatest melodic tendency to move to and therefore establish the tonic.[7] In free composition, $\hat{2}$ and $\hat{7}$ are often combined into a characteristic harmonic idiom. Scale degree $\hat{2}$ belongs to the intermediate supertonic harmonies: II, II⁶, II⁶₅; *both* scale degrees $\hat{2}$ and $\hat{7}$ belong to the dominant and dominant seventh chords. Hence the harmonic progression from an intermediate II to a V provided composers with the opportunity to present both leading tones at the cadence. You can see from the reduction in Example 5.2b that the succession 2–7 represents motion into an inner voice, like the similar motion in bar 4. The motion to $\hat{7}$ is thus a brief detour; we say that the leading tone momentarily "substitutes" for scale degree $\hat{2}$.

Example 5.3, a chordal representation of the consequent phrase (a good example of an *imaginary continuo*), shows the structural prominence and aural retention of G; we place it in parentheses and connect it with a broken slur to the G that actually appears over the II⁶. This procedure, where the leading tone extends the influence and thus implies the continued presence of scale degree $\hat{2}$, can be described as the *implied retention of a tone* (similar in principle to the retention of C in bar 1). We will learn about various ways in which tones may be implied by a particular context. One usual condition for reading

EXAMPLE 5.3:

Combinations of $\hat{2}$ and $\hat{7}$ at cadences

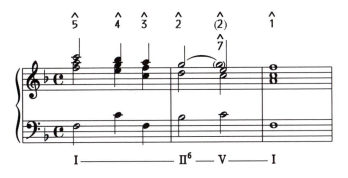

implied tones is that they must belong (explicitly or implicitly) to the underlying harmony (to the imaginary continuo). The replacement of $\hat{2}$ by $\hat{7}$ at a structural cadence (or the combination of both in succession), as also occurs in "Greensleeves" (Example 2.7), is one of the most frequently encountered idioms in the tonal literature.[8]

Before leaving this piece, we refer you back to Example 5.2b and offer a final comment about its notation. Schenker uses two slurs in the bass at the authentic cadence to show multiple meanings in the function of chords leading to V (in a half or authentic cadence). The first slur leads from I to V and curls around the II^6, indicating that the essential harmonic motion is I–V. The second slur shows that II^6 is subordinate but is associated with and leads to V. Both slurs are optional and are used when an intermediate harmony occurs in the I–V structural progression.

The corresponding bars of the first variation are given in Example 5.4. If you compare Example 5.4b with Example 5.2b, you will see that the open thirds in bar 1 of the theme have now been filled in with passing tones in the first bar of the variation. And, while stepwise motion has replaced arpeggia-

EXAMPLE 5.4:

(a) Beethoven, *Seven Variations on a Theme by P. Winter*, WoO 75, Variation 1 bars 1–8;
(b) analytical interpretation

(a)

EXAMPLE 5.4 (*continued*)

(b)

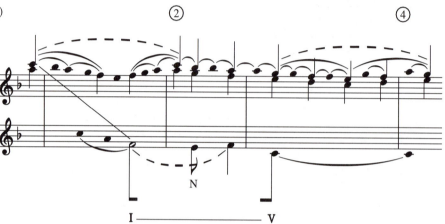

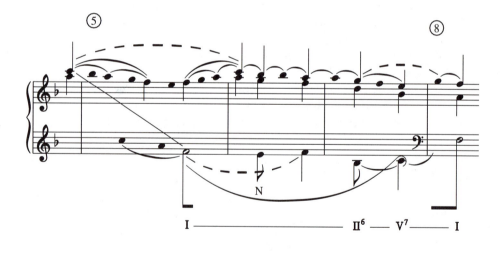

tion in the top voice, the bass line now assumes the role of arpeggiating the tonic triad. Note also that arpeggiation delays the tonic note in the bass so that the C in the top voice and F in the bass are even more displaced than in the theme, as indicated by the longer line on the graph.

The new sixteenth-note pattern in the right hand delays the return of c^2 until the downbeat of bar 2, where it functions as a suspension over the V_5^6 chord implied by the three-voice texture (compare Examples 5.4a and 5.4b).[9] This descending-second figure becomes a new thematic element in the remaining bars of the phrase. A comparison of Examples 5.4b and 5.2b will reveal that, despite all of the surface changes, the essential structural motions of the first phrase in the variation remain the same as in bars 1–4 of the theme.

Finally, the accented tones of figuration of this variation raise an important point. As we saw in Chapter 2, suspensions displace one or more notes in relation to the underlying rhythm. When analyzing passages that involve one or more suspensions, it is important to clarify the underlying context. Consider, for instance, bar 2 of the first variation. The rate of chord change is the same as in bar 2 of the theme, where the V and I chords each occupy one beat. In the variation, however, the I chord is not literally present until the last eighth note because of the rest in the left hand and the suspension in the right hand. Likewise, in bar 8 of the variation, tonic harmony governs the *entire* bar, even though it is postponed until the second eighth by the tone of figuration. Contextual factors must be carefully evaluated to determine the actual position of a harmony in musical space.[10]

TONAL STRUCTURE AND THE *URSATZ*

One of Schenker's most far-reaching discoveries was the realization that the types of harmonic progression and voice-leading patterns that occur within a single phrase or section of a musical work can also serve as the basis for longer sections or, indeed, whole compositions. Our next example is another nonmodulating phrase that is a self-contained tonal structure, the first phrase from one of Haydn's piano sonatas (Example 5.5). We will use this phrase to introduce some of the essential features of Schenker's notion of the *Ursatz*, or *fundamental structure*.[11] We will use the two terms interchangeably in this book.

We shall examine first some of the broader aspects of the harmonic and melodic structure of this excerpt. The phrase begins with a two-bar prolongation of tonic harmony, and concludes in its final two bars with a perfect authentic cadence; hence, the structural bass-line pattern, as we have seen before, is I–II^6–V–I. The qualifier "perfect" in the name of the cadence also tells us something about the melodic structure, that during the course of the development of the phrase the upper voice has descended to the tonic.

As we show on the music, the initial anacrusis in the right hand leads from inner-voice tones to the top-voice tone G through an arpeggiation across

EXAMPLE 5.5:

Haydn, Piano Sonata, Hob. XVI/35, I, bars 1–8 with analytical interpretation

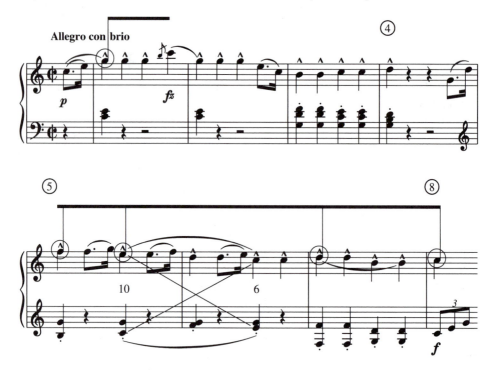

the bar line. The rhythmic position of this figure highlights the prominence of G on the first downbeat; note that this tone is further emphasized by the tones of the left hand that complete the tonic chord. After it is established, G initiates a motion that descends, over the span of the entire phrase, to 1̂ in bar 8.

It is often a good strategy—as we have done here—to begin by drawing a few conclusions about the broader structural "markers" that may stand out at first glance, especially in the first and last portions of a passage. But it is also important to bear in mind that such initial impressions and assumptions may need to be reevaluated as the analysis proceeds. One should not be reluctant to abandon first impressions if further investigation reveals other conclusions and ideas that better describe a passage or section.

We shall now consider the phrase in greater detail, and in particular how the upper voice traverses the space from 5̂ to 1̂ as the bass harmonic progression moves away from the tonic toward the cadence in bars 7–8. If the details of the upper and lower voices *together* lead us full circle back to our initial ideas—that is, if the upper and lower voices mutually confirm our basic ideas—then we have probably arrived at a viable interpretation of the harmonic and contrapuntal properties of this brief tonal pattern.

Example 5.6 presents a graphic representation of the phrase. (Don't

EXAMPLE 5.6:

Haydn, Piano Sonata, Hob. XVI/35, I, bars 1–8: analytical reduction

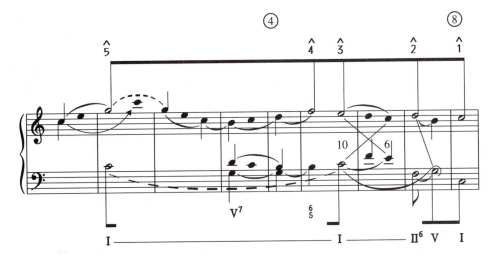

worry if some of the symbols appear foreign to you; their meaning will become clearer as we continue to discuss the phrase.) Perhaps the best place to
begin is the bass, which is the most straightforward part of this harmonic/
contrapuntal framework. Note that only tonic and dominant harmonies appear in bars 1–6. At the beginning of bar 7 a significant event occurs: the bass
leaps from the E at the end of bar 6 *down a major seventh* to the F that supports
the II^6 at the beginning of bar 7. This leap highlights the F as the lowest note
of the phrase up to this point, in contrast to the prevalent high register of
the bass voice in the bars immediately preceding the low F. In other words,
the leap throws the II^6 into sharp relief compared to all preceding chords
except the beginning tonic; it emphasizes the bass note F and the II^6 chord
as an intermediate harmony leading into the cadence. But how do we interpret the preceding dominant chords?

This example shows that the beginning tonic leads to a half cadence in
bar 4 that articulates the phrase into two *subphrases*. One should also note
that the internal "breath" of this phrase is related to the rests on beats 2 and
3 of bar 4, and the anacrusis on beat 4 that parallels the anacrusis at the
beginning of the phrase. Although there is a pause in bar 4, a point of articulation within the phrase, there is also a tendency to move forward. As we
noted in Chapter 3, the half cadence is one of the more subtle aspects of
tonal music. On the one hand, a V can signal a goal, because it is one of the
two principal structural harmonies in tonal music (I and V). On the other
hand, it contains the tones $\hat{7}$ and $\hat{2}$, which embody the tendency for further
motion. The dominant at a half cadence is consequently poised between rest
and continuation; ultimately, this tension will be resolved by a more conclusive tonic.

The I–V motion, therefore, continues into bar 5, where the dominant $\frac{6}{5}$

leads back to a root-position tonic.[12] The influence of tonic harmony, however, continues beyond this chord; note the voice exchange between the outer voices that continues to prolong the tonic. Also significant are the cessation of the dotted-rhythm motive and the return to quarter notes in the upper voice, which highlight the end of the tonic prolongation and the subsequent II^6.

The broken slur connecting the bass C in bar 1 with the C in bar 5 indicates a larger connection. The return of tonic harmony in bars 5–6 represents a continuation—a prolongation—of the *initial* tonic through bar 6. In this prolongation the influence of the tonic is kept active not only by the presence of the tonic itself, but also by the dominant seventh chord and its inversions. These chords are not truly independent of the tonic, but function as part of its prolongation. Tonic harmony thus governs the phrase until the cadential pattern II^6–V–I in bars 7–8. The pivotal importance of the II^6 chord illustrates an important principle: a strong II or IV often represents both a new harmonic realm, a move away from tonic harmony, and also the preparation for the dominant of the structural cadence.

Thus far we have focused on the bass in conjunction with our initial interpretation and ideas. The next and final step will be to examine the upper voice to discover if the subsidiary motions and detours that lead this voice from $\hat{5}$, at the beginning of the phrase, to $\hat{1}$, at its conclusion, corroborate our reading of the bass structure.[13]

We have noted the prominence of G in bars 1–2—that it was established through an arpeggiation on the anacrusis of the phrase. We shall now explore what happens to the G, both within its obvious retention in bars 1–2 and in the subsequent bars of the phrase, where it no longer seems to be an active element of the melodic structure. The interpretation of bars 1–2 is fairly straightforward: the high C on the fourth beat of bar 1 is an embellishing tone, a consonant skip that decorates G and recalls the first pitch of the phrase an octave higher. Bear in mind that because G serves as the uppermost or initial main tone of the upper voice, the C, both at the beginning and in the higher register, conceptually belongs to an inner voice of the arpeggiated C major tonic triad, as indicated by the arrow in Example 5.6. The technique of placing an inner-voice tone above a main tone of the upper voice is called *superposition*.[14]

The next stage in our analysis of the upper voice involves a more sophisticated concept. We learned from our examination of basic principles in Chapters 2 and 4 that lines in free compositions are often based on melodically fluent, stepwise motions exemplified in the study of strict counterpoint. We discovered that such motions can lie beneath the surface of even the wide-ranging, disjunct lines characteristic of instrumental music. Such is the case here. After the G is repeated in bars 1–2, the upper voice retraces the arpeggiation of the anacrusis and moves back into the inner voice. This technique is known as *motion to an inner voice* (in the reduction, we have indicated the inner-voice tones with downward stems). From this point the right-hand part remains in the inner voice until bar 5, as shown in Example 5.6.

Does this detour, the motion to and from the inner voice, mean that a more fundamental stepwise continuation from G has been avoided? The answer is no: the continuation has been *delayed*. The notes of the arpeggiation after G and the third-progression B–D belong to the inner voices of a polyphonically conceived melody; they create a "gap" in the main upper voice, a detour that extends until the F appears in bar 5 over the dominant $^6_5$, in the original register of the main upper voice. (We have indicated the stepwise association of G with F by a slur that arches over the inner-voice tones.) In short, this is a good example of a *nonadjacent* relationship of two tones: the detour, the motion into an inner voice, temporarily postpones the motion of a step from G to F.

The longer-range influence of G from bars 1–4 illustrates what Schenker called the "mental retention" of a tone: in this case, the conceptual retention of a structural top-voice note as a melody moves into the inner voices of a polyphonic texture. While the inner voices are active, the initiating tone is still conceptually present, but at a *higher level* that is temporarily static, that is, literally without activity and motion. To use Schenker's words, the G on the downbeat of bar 1 "combines within itself a mental retention . . . a motionless state and an actual motion." In the case of our Haydn phrase, the actual motion is the arpeggiation to the inner voice.

This principle has far-reaching ramifications. A motion into an inner voice can create detours and delays for the upper voice, prolonging a higher-ranking tone and retarding what would otherwise be a direct stepwise motion: in effect, the steps of the upper voice are "spread out" over a greater span of music. Although Schenker discussed this principle in connection with the first structural tone of an upper voice, we will see that other structural tones can be prolonged in similar fashion.

The continuation from F in bars 5–8 is more straightforward. The tendency of scale degree $\hat{4}$ is often to move *down*: because it forms a diminished fifth with the B in the bass of the V^6_5, this tendency is intensified. The F, first decorated by its incomplete upper neighbor, moves to E over the reestablished tonic harmony in bar 5. Hence the main melodic and harmonic motions thus far are G–F–E over I–V^7–I; together they confirm our first impression that the initial tonic harmony has been prolonged from bar 1 to at least bar 5 (Example 5.6).

After this point our ears are in a sense misled: we hear a stepwise motion to C, scale degree $\hat{1}$, which *melodically* suggests closure. However, *harmonically* we do not feel that a definitive ending has been established, because a I^6 supports scale degree $\hat{1}$. In general, an *authentic* cadence (with the leap of a fifth in the bass from V to I) provides the most conclusive ending for any tonal structure, regardless of length. Another reason why our ears do not hear the D–C motion as structurally conclusive is that $\hat{1}$ over I^6 produces a sixth between the outer voices (C over E); as we mentioned in our discussion of counterpoint, the octave (or unison) is the interval that most strongly signals closure. Moreover, the overall rhythm and continuity of the phrase support the sense of I^6 as a momentary point of arrival, not as a goal.

The motion E–D–C in bars 5–6, therefore, does not represent a continuation of the main line from high G. As Example 5.6 shows, this motion should be interpreted instead as another motion into an inner voice. The third-progression E–D–C descends over a local motion from I to I^6, produced by the 10–6 voice exchange. Voice exchanges often participate in the prolongation of a chord. And since we are considering also the relative structural "weight" of upper-voice tones, we can generalize further and say that a voice exchange usually extends the influence of either the first or last tones of the motion. In this case, E (melodically) and I (harmonically) are extended by the voice exchange.

What Haydn has accomplished through this interesting "deception" is to foreshadow the ultimate and highest-ranking continuation of the main upper-voice line from G to C. The D reappears over the registrally (and rhythmically) highlighted II^6 in bar 7, confirming our interpretation that the previous motion to C functions as a detour within the larger descent. Notice that d^2 in bars 6 and 7 both appear over F in the bass, but the low F in bar 7 supports a stable II^6, in contrast to the unstable V$^4_2$ in bar 6. Thus the d^2 in bar 7 is clearly the higher-ranking of the two statements of that pitch.

This passage illustrates a principle that can be suggested as a rule of thumb regarding the *intermediate harmonies of structural harmonic progressions:* when they lead away from (rather than prolong) beginning tonics, they often support correspondingly high-ranking tones of the upper voice. In this case, the II^6 supports the $\hat{2}$ that eventually will lead to $\hat{1}$ at the end of the phrase.

Example 5.7 illustrates the essential features of the structure and clarifies the melodic motion at the cadence. Scale degree $\hat{2}$ does not lead directly to C ($\hat{1}$), but moves to B ($\hat{7}$) before the cadence is completed on the downbeat of bar 8. The motion $\hat{2}$–$\hat{7}$ is more than a common melodic idiom of the tonal system; in this phrase it can be considered an aspect of the phrase's unique motivic structure. The motion from D to B, a descending third, answers the previous descending third E–D–C that foreshadows the conclusion of the main upper voice. In other words, E–D–C in bars 5–6 is echoed by the abbreviated D–B motion in bar 7. This internal repetition is a *motivic*

EXAMPLE 5.7:

Haydn, Piano Sonata, Hob. XVI/35, I, bars 1–8: analytical reduction

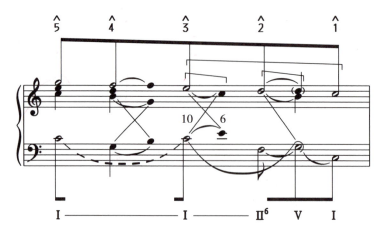

parallelism, which is a technique that can create melodic coherence.[15] We highlight this procedure by placing brackets—called *motivic brackets*—above or below these repetitions to isolate them visually and indicate their association.

We may now begin to form some general theoretical observations about tonal structure. We have considered Haydn's phrase as if it were a complete piece for ease of illustration and discussion, not because it could actually stand alone as an autonomous composition. Nevertheless the tonally complete, nonmodulating phrase displays in microcosm many of the same characteristics that shape much longer spans of music, including complete pieces. We have chosen the phrase as our point of departure because a phrase that ends with a perfect authentic cadence is often the smallest complete tonal structure found in compositions.

Example 5.8 presents the last in our series of illustrations of Haydn's phrase; considered collectively, they constitute a multilevel *voice-leading graph* (*Urlinie-Tafel*). Such depictions illustrate in graphic form the voice leading of the harmonic and contrapuntal structure of a passage or piece. And by showing various stages of reduction, where the detours, prolongations, and tones of figuration are gradually removed, we can arrive at a representation of the most fundamental structure of the phrase. Notice, for instance, that in our final level of reduction (Example 5.8) we have removed the bass note of the dominant chord in bars 3–4, because it serves to expand a larger tonic area indicated in the graph by the two Cs connected by a broken slur.

As Schenker's ideas developed, he began to realize that such a fundamental structure underlies phrases, sections, and entire compositions. As a theoretical construct, the *Ursatz* symbolizes the most essential melodic and harmonic components of a tonal composition and consequently has far-reaching ramifications for the ways in which musicians understand the general principles of tonality. We shall, therefore, examine the characteristics of the *Ursatz* in some detail.

EXAMPLE 5.8:

Haydn, Piano Sonata, Hob. XVI/35, I, bars 1–8: analytical reduction

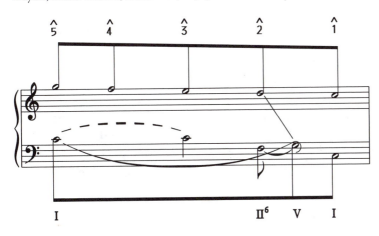

EXAMPLE 5.9:

The *Ursatz* forms

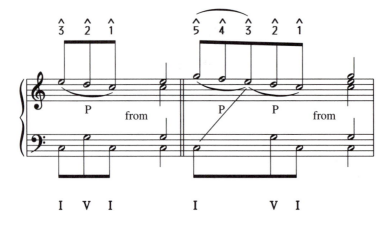

The Bass Arpeggiation (Bassbrechung)

Example 5.9 shows schematically two of the *Ursatz* patterns that arise in tonal composition. Notice that the bass motions are the same for both patterns. As we noted in Chapter 3, the primary harmonic progression in tonal music is I–V–I; the bass "linearizes" the tonic triad through a disjunct arpeggiation, by moving from the root to the upper fifth and back again. Schenker referred to this motion as the *bass arpeggiation (Bassbrechung)*. In *Free Composition* Schenker initially represents the *Ursatz* without an intermediate harmony, although in later examples he shows how they may function in relation to I and V. The occurrence of certain intermediate harmonies—as in the case of IV moving to V—introduces stepwise motion in the disjunct bass arpeggiation (I–V–I). In fact, the introduction of melodic motion *intensifies* the motion toward the dominant. Ultimately, however, Schenker regarded intermediate harmonies as subsidiary to the tonic and dominant scale steps.

The Fundamental Line (Urlinie)

Schenker used the term *Urlinie* (*fundamental line*) to refer to the descending, stepwise upper voice of the *Ursatz*. If we focus our attention momentarily on the first pattern, the descent from $\hat{3}$, we can sharpen our understanding of what the *Urlinie* signifies. The motion from $\hat{3}$ to $\hat{1}$ linearizes ("horizontalizes") the lower interval of the tonic triad: compare the *Ursatz* pattern to its vertical, chordal representation. Scale degree $\hat{2}$, then, is a passing tone, made *consonant* by the leap to the dominant tone in the bass. The *Urlinie* thus abstractly represents the *melodic* dimension of tonal music; it is a linear manifestation of tonic harmony, a linear progression in which the intervals of the tonic triad are filled in by passing tones. Indeed, the *Urlinie* is the highest-level linear progression of an entire piece or movement.

The second part of Example 5.9 shows an *Urlinie* that begins on the fifth of tonic harmony (note the correspondence with the final reduction of our Haydn phrase). This *Urlinie* traverses the entire span of the tonic triad: the tones $\hat{5}$–$\hat{3}$–$\hat{1}$, representing an arpeggiation of tonic harmony, are filled in with the passing tones $\hat{4}$ and $\hat{2}$. The "5-line" can be a more problematic musical construct than a "3-line," at least theoretically, because of complications in the support of one or more of its tones. We will address this issue, and what is termed the *unsupported stretch,* in Chapter 12.[16]

It is important at this point to underscore a characteristic of the *Urlinie:* the fundamental line *descends* from the initial tone to the final $\hat{1}$. The reason for this aspect of Schenker's theory is that he considered the first tone of the *Urlinie*—the *primary tone*—as an "image" or representation of the overtone in an overtone series of which the tonic note is the fundamental.[17] He therefore considered the descending motion to be the most direct path for this "overtone" to return to its fundamental, a direction that also corresponds to a release of musical tension (Schenker made a distinction between ascending and descending motion in his writings on counterpoint). In Western music since the Middle Ages, and in the music of many other cultures as well, falling melodic motion has been characteristic of cadences and endings. This may reflect an innate sense of a correspondence of musical motion with physical motion, and with the force of gravity (and the essential fact that things on earth fall *down,* not up). Thus we can see why it is theoretically feasible for an *Urlinie* to begin from an upper tone of the tonic triad, *but not from $\hat{1}$* (which is conceptually a point of rest).[18]

The fundamental structure therefore consists of two components, the fundamental line and the bass arpeggiation. The fundamental line is a *stepwise, horizontal expression* of tonic harmony: in the Haydn phrase, the tones $\hat{5}$–$\hat{3}$–$\hat{1}$ of the tonic triad are filled in by passing tones ($\hat{4}$ and $\hat{2}$). The only other theoretical possibilities for the fundamental line are $\hat{3}$–$\hat{2}$–$\hat{1}$ ($\hat{3}$–$\hat{1}$ filled in by one passing tone) and the much less frequently encountered $\hat{8}$–$\hat{7}$–$\hat{6}$–$\hat{5}$–$\hat{4}$–$\hat{3}$–$\hat{2}$–$\hat{1}$ ($\hat{8}$–$\hat{5}$–$\hat{3}$–$\hat{1}$ filled in by four passing tones). The bass arpeggiation also expresses the tonic triad in the horizontal dimension, but through a *disjunct* arpeggiation from the root to the upper fifth (dominant) and back again.

STRUCTURAL LEVELS

We have seen that not every association in tonal music occurs between adjacent pitches. Schenker came to this realization gradually, as he discovered ways in which the principles of melodic fluency and harmonic organization operate beneath the surface of musical compositions. In the 1920s, when his theoretical ideas were developing into their final form, he eventually recognized that tonal compositions consist of a continuum of interrelated structural levels: *each is based on and is related to the others through similar harmonic and contrapuntal procedures.* The theory of structural levels has revolutionized the way many theorists and musicians understand music, and it is perhaps Schenker's greatest discovery.

The structural level we examined in theoretical detail was the *Ursatz,* which emerged as the final reduction in our analysis of Haydn's phrase (Example 5.8). Examples 5.6–5.8 collectively illustrate the three basic "realms" of structural levels commonly associated with Schenker's theory of tonal structure. If we continue to regard Haydn's phrase as a complete piece (remembering that this analogy is intended only for purposes of explanation), the graph of Example 5.6, which shows most of the notes in the original music and some of the simpler nonadjacent tonal associations, represents the *surface* and *foreground* levels. The graph of Example 5.8, however, depicts only the fundamental line and bass arpeggiation (with an intermediate harmony). We have already identified this representation as the *Ursatz,* but when considered the final step in a series of successive reductions, it is also referred to as the *background* level. In the middle is, quite literally, the *middleground* level (Example 5.7), illuminating the broader harmonic and contrapuntal motions that reside between the foreground and background.

Bear in mind that we are not suggesting that every musical composition consists of three clearly delineated structural levels. Schenker explicitly states in *Free Composition* that "it is impossible to generalize regarding the number of structural levels."[19] Rather, it is more appropriate to speak of three interrelated *types* of level (the foreground and middleground in particular are pluralistic in nature), which are distinguished by the amount of detail they contain. The more detail, the lower the level, and the "closer" its relationship to the musical surface. In this book we use the adjectives "lower" and "higher" to distinguish relatively among structural levels. A lower level is one closer to the surface and foreground than a higher level, which is closer to the background. These words capture the visual impression of many of Schenker's published examples.[20]

Schenker like most theorists today, used the terms *fundamental structure, fundamental line,* and *bass arpeggiation* in the most general sense to describe the basic structure of an *entire piece.* In this chapter we departed from this usage for clarity of discussion. As you may recall, the later excerpts are brief but self-contained tonal structures, and we used the term *Urlinie,* for instance, to refer to the main upper-voice line of the passage. One often finds in tonal music patterns that replicate or "parallel" in miniature the patterns that serve as fundamental structures *(Ursätze),* for entire pieces; some theorists refer to such patterns as "*Ursatz* parallelisms."[21] In Chapters 6 and 7, we will for convenience retain this informal usage of these terms (in Chapter 7 we examine *Ursatz* parallelisms in considerable detail). In the complete analyses of Part II (Chapters 8–12), we will follow Schenker's usage more closely and will provide additional conventions (in the text and in the examples) to distinguish the *Ursatz* and *Urlinie* of a complete piece from versions at more immediate structural levels.

Exercises

Examine and graph the miniature fundamental structures in the following excerpts (refer to the examples in this chapter for help in preparing your graphs):

1. Bach, *Notebook for Anna Magdalina Bach* (1725) BWV Anh. 114, IV, "Menuet" in G major, bars 9–16.

2. Mozart, *Don Giovanni*, Duet, "Là ci darem la mano," bars 5–8

3. Brahms, *Variations on a Theme by Haydn* (two-piano reduction), bars 19–23

4. Mozart, *Six Variations on Salve tu, Domine*, K. 398, Theme, bars 1–12

5. Schumann, *Album for the Young*, "Melodie," bars 17–20

6. Mozart, *Eine kleine Nachtmusik*, K. 525, III, Trio, bars 1–8

7. Brahms, Op. 76, No. 7, Intermezzo, bars 1–8

8. Beethoven, Piano Sonata, Op. 7, II, bars 1–8

9. Schumann, *Album for the Young*, "Armes Waisenkind," bars 4–8

6

Techniques of Melodic Prolongation

A fundamental structure consists of the most essential harmonic and voice-leading elements in a passage or piece of music. In this sense it may be compared to the skeleton that supports the human body and provides its shape. But for Schenker the essence of composition lay in the process of *composing-out* (*Auskomponierung*), or expansion of the fundamental structure in various ways and on different levels. The techniques discussed in this chapter include some of the most common ways in which tonal structures may be expanded, varied, and transformed. Since the role and meaning of these techniques can only be fully understood in specific contexts, every technique is defined in conjunction with the discussion of one or more musical examples.

THE INITIAL ASCENT

As we have seen, Schenker regarded the *Urlinie*—the top voice of the *Ursatz*—as a descending line. On the middleground and foreground levels, however, both ascending and descending linear progressions are common. Rising linear progressions may occur in a variety of contexts; one important possibility is a motion, usually beginning on the tonic note, that leads to the first or *primary* tone of the fundamental line. This type of linear progression, which Schenker termed an *initial ascent* (*Anstieg*), rises through the tones of the tonic triad from the root to the third or fifth. Because it postpones the arrival of the first tone of the *Urlinie*, an initial ascent represents a delay of that tone. The delay may be brief, or it may extend over a considerable span of a work.

123

The beginning of Schubert's Impromptu in A♭ is presented in Example 6.1a. As indicated in the graphs (6.1b and c), the initial ascent rises from A♭ in bar 1 (which is introduced with an ascending leap from E♭ on the anacrusis) to B♭ in bar 3 and C in bar 4 (C is then prolonged through bar 8). Because the *initial ascent* leads to and therefore delays the first tone of the fundamental structure, this C embodies a twofold function—the culmination of the ascent itself, and, on the background level of structure, the beginning of the *Urlinie*.

EXAMPLE 6.1:

(a) Schubert, Impromptu, Op. 142, No. 2, bars 1–8; (b) foreground reduction; (c) initial ascent

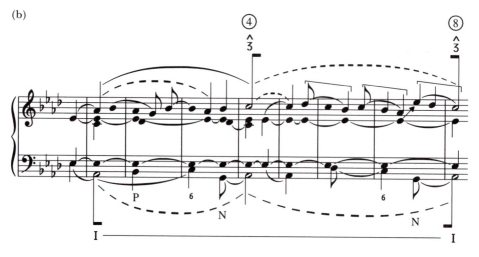

EXAMPLE 6.1 (*continued*)

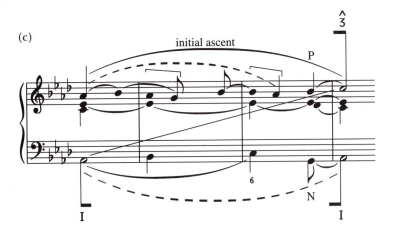

(c)

The term "initial ascent," by definition, always implies a motion to the *first* tone of the *Urlinie*. Linear progressions that lead to other tones of the *Urlinie* are defined in different ways, as this chapter will describe.

The graph also indicates a number of other features that are related to the initial ascent. Before the ascent to 3̂, a double neighbor figure prolongs the top-voice A♭ in bars 1–3. Notice that b♭¹, which functions as a dissonant neighbor in bar 1, recurs twice thereafter, each time on a different level of structure: as a consonant upper neighbor in bar 2, resolving to A♭ in bar 3, and as a passing tone to C (bar 4). Because the function of each B♭ is different, the many repetitions of this tone do not produce monotony in the upper voice.

As indicated in Example 6.1c, the accented dissonances and their resolutions in bars 2 and 3 are "marked for consciousness" as descending seconds, even though the A♭ in bar 2 is an accented passing tone in the descending third B♭–G. The association of these two descending figures is highlighted by their position on the downbeat, and by the sarabande-like rhythms of the opening theme. (Accented passing and neighbor tones are often related to suspensions, because in each case the dissonance is accented and the resolution unaccented.)

THE ARPEGGIATED ASCENT

Another way in which the appearance of the primary tone may be delayed is through an *arpeggiated ascent*. This technique is similar to an initial ascent, but instead of a stepwise linear progression, an arpeggiation through the tones of the tonic triad leads to the first tone of the fundamental line. The specific length and nature of the arpeggiation may vary, depending upon the tone on which it begins, and on whether 3̂ or 5̂ is the goal.

EXAMPLE 6.2:

(a) Mozart, Piano Sonata, K. 309, I, bars 1–8; (b) foreground reduction

Example 6.2 shows an arpeggiated ascent through the tones of the tonic triad to the initial tone G ($\hat{5}$), followed by a stepwise descent to the tonic note at the end of the phrase. The unison texture in bars 1–2 recalls the opening tutti passages that characterize many Classical symphonies (such as Mozart's "Haffner" Symphony). Notice a beautiful compositional detail, the initial grace note figure that anticipates the arpeggiated ascent of the melody. Schenker's student Oswald Jonas remarked about this passage: "How marvel-

ous the arpeggiation in the right hand's grace-note figure, which finds its continuation as though in a great arc!"[1]

The orchestral quality of this phrase is also reflected in the contrast of registers that develops in the bass from I to I^6 in bars 1–3 (from the "small" to the "one-line octave" in the left hand). The return to the lower register in bar 7 articulates the beginning of the cadence, and frames the phrase through its association with the opening bass register. Notice also that the descending third-motion in bar 2 (E–D–C) is echoed on a higher structural level in bars 3–5 (G–F–E); thirds recur prominently in the elaboration of the descending line in bars 5–7.

Another work by Mozart (Example 6.3) incorporates both arpeggiated and stepwise motion in approaching the first structural tone. (The techniques

EXAMPLE 6.3:

(a) Mozart, Piano Concerto, K. 453, III, bars 1–8 (strings only); (b) foreground reduction; (c) middleground reduction

EXAMPLE 6.3 (*continued*)

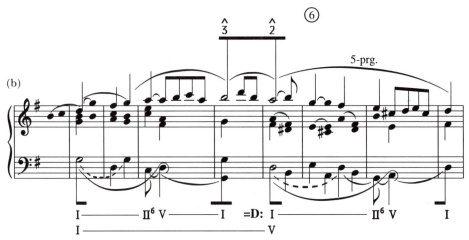

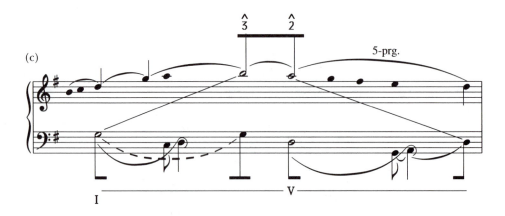

of initial ascent and arpeggiated ascent are frequently combined.) An arpeggiation from D to G leads to the structural tone B ($\hat{3}$); the third between G and B is filled in with the passing tone A, which creates a stepwise motion from $\hat{1}$ to $\hat{3}$ within the larger arpeggiation. The arrival on the first tone of the *Urlinie* is followed immediately by a motion to A, which is the beginning of a descending fifth-progression to D ($\hat{5}$–$\hat{1}$ in the key of the dominant).

Example 6.3c shows the structure of the period in simplified form. It is divided into two symmetrical four-bar phrases, the first establishing I, and the second prolonging a tonicized V. Each concludes with a similar cadence, in the tonic and dominant key areas respectively. This reduced example clearly shows the archlike shape of the melody, in which the arpeggiated ascent to B ($\hat{3}$) is balanced by the descending fifth-progression.[2]

UNFOLDING

In polyphonic melodies, two or more voices may be related through stepwise motion, leaps, or both in combination. One distinct type of motion between two voices is termed *unfolding*. This technique, which generally linearizes a pair of intervals, offers rich compositional possibilities (Example 6.4).

EXAMPLE 6.4:

(a) Schubert, Impromptu, Op. 142, No. 3, bars 1–4; (b) foreground reduction; (c) middleground reduction

(a)   **THEME**
      Andante

EXAMPLE 6.4 (*continued*)

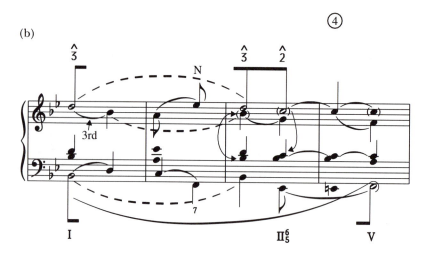

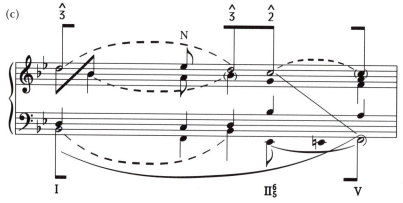

In bars 1–4 the melody in the right hand outlines two voices (compare Examples 6.4b and c). In bars 1–2, the pattern "top-inner, inner-top" emerges (D–Bb is followed by A–Eb). Notice also that the bass has a complementary unfolding pattern: Bb–D followed by C–F. In bars 3–4 a different unfolding pattern occurs in the right hand: "top-inner, top-inner" (D–G, C–F). Though the type of unfolding that occurs in bars 1–2 is a characteristic form of this technique, various other patterns can occur, either between tones of the same chord (as in bars 1 and 2) or between tones of different chords (as in bars 3 and 4). Regardless of the specific pattern, however, unfolding always involves a change of direction.[3]

When the unfolding is associated with more than one chord, melodic and harmonic ambiguities can occur. In bar 3, the top-voice tone D is repeated over the bass note Eb before the leap to G, suggesting that the resulting chord may be IV[7]. Yet the uppermost part of the left-hand accompaniment (the "tenor" voice), which doubles the top-voice D at the beginning of the bar, moves to C over the bass E♭. Since the accompaniment specifically establishes each chord of the harmonic succession, it clarifies the role of d^2 in the right hand as a dissonant suspension against the underlying II$_5^6$ chord (Example 6.4b). The tone of resolution that would normally follow—C in the two-line octave—does not occur immediately because of the unfolded leap to G (though it is present in the left hand). The upper voice supplies this tone at the beginning of bar 4 in the appropriate register as a kind of delayed resolution: the c^2, in effect, has been displaced by the unfolding.

Many such interrelationships occur in the passage between the right-hand melody and the left-hand accompaniment. In the graph, the associations between tones that are implied in the right hand (but not expressed because of the unfolding or harmonic movement) and the left-hand doublings that actually contain these tones are indicated with arrows. Ties connect the Cs that are implied over the II$_5^6$ and V chords with the unfolded C at the beginning of bar 3. Finally, a diagonal line connects the F bass note of the V with the c^2 in bar 3, indicating the underlying association of these tones despite the displacement in the foreground.

Example 6.5 illustrates several other characteristic types of unfolding. As indicated in Example 6.5a, a descending motion in parallel thirds might be integrated into a single line as "top-inner, inner-top" or "inner-top-top-inner." Example 6.5b illustrates similar alternative possibilities with a pair of voices

EXAMPLE 6.5:

Unfolding patterns

(a)

(b)

(c)

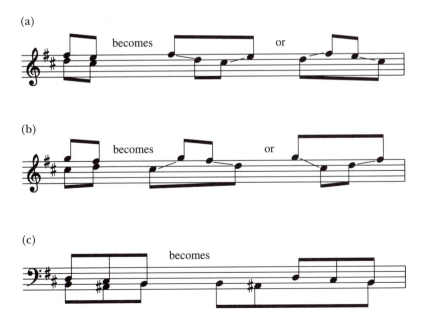

moving in contrary motion from a diminished fifth to a major third. Finally, the two voices in Example 6.5c alternate in pairs of notes before converging onto a unison.[4]

MOTION INTO AN INNER VOICE

A melody can incorporate two or more voices in various ways: sometimes this will happen with leaps (as in an unfolding), and sometimes the voices will be connected with stepwise motion. Frequently the melody will move from an established top-voice tone into an inner voice through a linear progression, a technique that is referred to as *motion into an inner voice*. This is one of the most frequent of all compositional techniques used to expand a top voice; it is also common in the bass voice, where rising linear progressions can move from the structural bass line into the tenor register. This technique can occur on various levels of structure, and frequently serves to create an independent section within a larger form.

Example 6.6 presents bars 1–4 of Schubert's G♭-major Impromptu, Op. 90, No. 3. The lyricism of this composition is established in part by the rich polyphony in the upper voice. Following the leap from the initial B♭ to G♭ in bar 2, A♭ is prolonged in bar 3 through motion into an inner voice (a descending fifth-progression) before it moves to G♭ in bar 4. On a higher level,

EXAMPLE 6.6:

(a) Schubert, Impromptu, Op. 90, No. 3, bars 1–4; (b) foreground reduction; (c) middleground reductions

(a)

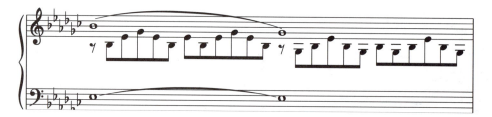

EXAMPLE 6.6 (*continued*)

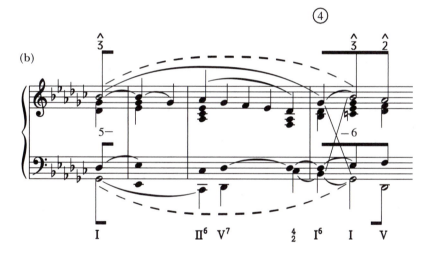

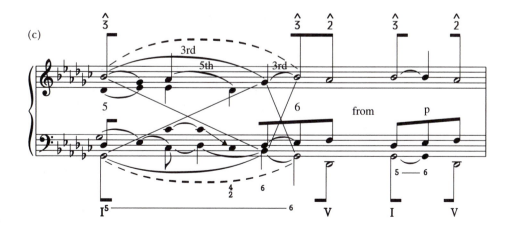

the descending third B♭–A♭–G♭ participates in a voice exchange with the bass, in a motion from I to I^6 (see Example 6.6c).

The local harmonic motions in bars 2 and 3, therefore, occur within an embracing tonic prolongation. The third-progression B♭–A♭–G♭ moves from the third to the root of tonic harmony in the upper voice of bars 1–4. (Notice that the tones of the descent echo in expanded form the descending-third leap B♭–G♭ of bar 2.) This four-bar motion into the inner voice (B♭–A♭–G♭) and its elaborations as discussed above form much of the content of the phrase.

Bear in mind that this example illustrates *two* motions into an inner voice, which occur on different structural levels. The first is more local and moves from A♭ to D♭ in bar 3, from the fifth to the root of the V^7 chord; at a higher level of structure, the descending third B♭–A♭–G♭ spans bars 1–4, supported by the motion from I to I^6 that prolongs the tonic. We will see many examples of this technique as we proceed, and will explore its implications for structure and form in later chapters.

MOTION FROM AN INNER VOICE

In contrast to motion into an inner voice, melodies also frequently move from an inner voice to regain a structural top-voice tone by means of a rising linear progression.

Example 6.7 presents the beginning of the Allegro section from one of Beethoven's piano sonatas. The beginning is striking in that it begins, not with a tonic chord, but with IV^6. This "nontonic" beginning is related to the preceding slow introduction, which ends with the same chord, thus creating a smooth transition between the Adagio and Allegro sections. In the example we see a motion from IV^6 to V^7–I at the cadence in bar 21.

Also retained from the Adagio is the A♭ in the upper voice. As Example 6.7b indicates, the chromatic bass descent and the chordal skips in the upper voice elaborate a descending motion in parallel sixths. With the arrival on V$^4_3$ (bar 19) the pattern changes: the bass descends without further chromaticism to B♭, the root of the V^7 chord. The upper voice changes direction and ascends by step to A♭, which now functions as the seventh of V^7. The ascent continues one step further to B♭; however in view of the prominence of A♭ at the beginning of the Allegro, and its harmonic importance as the seventh of V^7, the B♭ is understood as an incomplete neighbor that elaborates the seventh before it resolves to G.[5]

The top-voice motion from D to A♭ and the complementary bass motion from F to B♭ occur within prolonged dominant harmony (bars 19–21). While the bass descends from the fifth to the root of the V^7, the upper voice ascends a diminished fifth from the third to the seventh. Considered from a middleground perspective, D and F (of the V$^4_3$) are inner voices, and A♭ and B♭

EXAMPLE 6.7:

(a) Beethoven, Piano Sonata, Op. 81a, I, bars 17–21; (b) foreground reduction; (c) middleground reductions

(a)

(b)

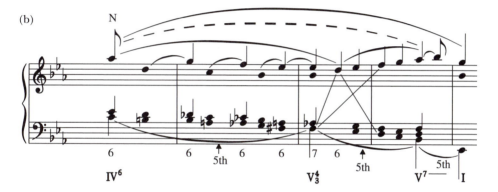

(c)

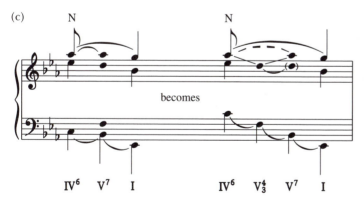

are outer voices, of the dominant seventh harmony (compare Example 6.7b and c). Thus the top voice ascends by step from the inner voice to regain the top-voice tone A♭, a motion that signals the prolongation ("mental retention") of A♭ from bar 17 (Example 6.7b). A linear progression from an inner-voice tone to a structural top-voice tone is called *motion from an inner voice.*[6]

VOICE EXCHANGE

Voice exchange is a common technique we have already seen in several examples, including bars 5–6 and 14 of Example 3.12, and bars 1–3 of Example 4.17. Beethoven's Piano Sonata, Op. 110, begins with a series of voice exchanges that expand the tonic and intermediate harmonies in bars 1–3 (Example 6.8). Perhaps the most characteristic type of voice exchange occurs in bars 1 and 2, where the soprano and bass exchange two tones within the same chord. In bar 3, the voice exchange occurs between two intermediate harmonies, II⁴₃ and IV. Notice that this motion is filled in with passing tones (Example 6.8b). The complementary thirds of a voice exchange are often

EXAMPLE 6.8:

(a) Beethoven, Piano Sonata, Op. 110, I, bars 1–5; (b) foreground reduction; (c) middleground reduction

EXAMPLE 6.8 (*continued*)

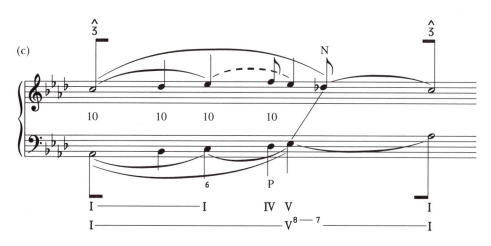

elaborated with passing tones, which (as here) may support a passing chord.

As in the expansion of tonics and dominants, two (or more) intermediate chords will often function to expand a single intermediate harmony. Most frequently the first chord of the pair will be the "main" harmony; sometimes, however, circumstances will suggest that the second chord of the expansion will be primary. As indicated in Example 6.8b and c, the deeper outer-voice motion consists of ascending parallel tenths until the arrival on V in bar 4. Because of the way in which this pattern shapes and guides this progression, we hear the harmonic organization of the phrase as an expansion of I (I–I^6), followed by a motion to V. The most direct (stepwise) connection of the outer voices, from the I^6 to the V, is through the IV (note the neighbor F in the top voice and the passing tone D♭ in the bass). The $\frac{4}{3}$ chord is therefore a "detour" that expands the motion from I^6 to IV (compare Examples 6.8b and c).

The large-scale harmonic motion I–V–I, and the associated top-voice motion C–D♭–C, are indicated by the lower line of roman numerals and the large slur in Example 6.8c. It might seem more appropriate to regard E♭ as the principal top-voice tone over V. The strongly dissonant D♭ (the seventh of V^7), however, is highlighted by the fermata, trill, and dynamic marking. Once again we see a seventh that is decorated from above. At a deeper level of structure, the D♭ is an upper neighbor to C of bar 1 (Example 6.8c).

In Example 6.8 the voice exchanges involve diatonic pitches. One or both tones in a voice exchange, however, may be altered chromatically, forming a *chromaticized* voice exchange. In Example 6.9, the essential harmonic structure is I–IV–V in F minor. At the cadence (bars 41–42), the motion to V is intensified through its leading tone, B♮, in the upper voice, and through its upper neighbor, D♭, in the bass. The augmented sixth chord that contains these tones is associated with a chromaticized voice exchange that prolongs the intermediate IV of the deeper bass progression.[7] Chromaticized voice exchanges often signal an important point of arrival in a passage or section of a composition.

EXAMPLE 6.9:

(a) Haydn, String Quartet, Op. 64, No. 3, I, bars 37–42; (b) foreground reduction; (c) middleground reduction

(a)

SHIFT OF REGISTER

Some of the most common types of elaboration and transformation of a structural line involve motion to a higher or a lower register. This can occur in various ways, among which are octave displacement, the inversion of an interval (such as the inversion of a falling second to a rising seventh), or a

EXAMPLE 6.9 (*continued*)

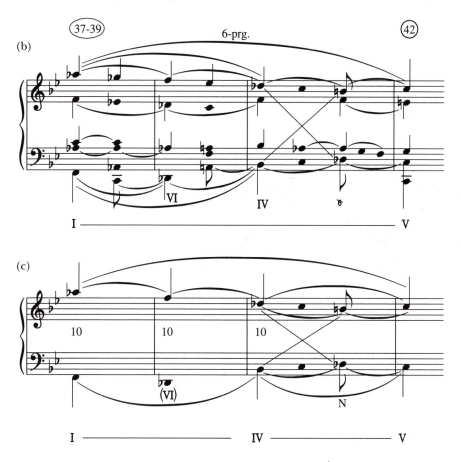

change in the relative position of two voices. We shall consider several techniques that involve such shifts of register.

Descending and Ascending Register Transfer

Example 6.10 presents bars 7–11 of Schubert's song "Gute Nacht" from *Winterreise*. You will notice that the vocal melody is represented as the principal top-voice line: in listening to an accompanied song, our attention is usually given primarily to the vocal melody. As a rule, therefore, the vocal line will be heard as the principal melody, even if the accompaniment is actually in a higher register than the voice.

EXAMPLE 6.10:

(a) Schubert, "Gute Nacht" (No. 1 from *Winterreise*, Op. 89), bars 7–11; (b) foreground reduction

The vocal line in Example 6.10 begins in the two-line register (on f^2), then descends an octave through a combination of stepwise and arpeggiated motion before pausing briefly on e^1 in bar 9 (a ninth below the starting note f^2).[8] The second subphrase returns to d^2 (which has been sustained in the piano accompaniment), initiating another arpeggiation that leads again to f^1 and, finally, to d^1 in bar 11. A change of register that is accomplished by a descent through an octave, as in the descents from f^2 to f^1 in this example, is called a *descending register transfer*.

The play of register in this passage gives the melody much of its character: the principal line F–E–F–E–D is elaborated by means of registral shifts, which are in turn composed out through a combination of arpeggiated and stepwise

motion. The association of the two registers is reinforced by the motivic association between the notes F–E–D in bars 7–8 (bracketed in the example) and
the more expanded descent through these tones in the lower register at the
cadence (bars 10–11). The connection of the two registers is also prepared by
the ascending leap from d^1 to d^2 in the piano (bar 7). Thus a register transfer may occur by means of a single leap through an interval (like the ascending octave in bar 7), or it may involve an elaborated motion through an
interval (as with the arpeggiations in the vocal melody in this example). Although Schenker describes motions through the interval of an octave as the

EXAMPLE 6.11:

Mozart, Variations on "Lison dormait": (a) Theme, bars 1–4; (b) Variation 2, bars 1–4;
(c) foreground reduction

basis of the concept of register transfer, the technique is not limited to this interval alone, as the next examples will demonstrate.[9]

The technique of register transfer is freqeuntly associated with the inversion of an interval. In Example 6.11, compare the opening of the theme of Mozart's Variations on "Lison dormait" with bars 1–4 of the second variation. The theme begins with a rise to the tone g^2, followed by an elaborated descending third to e^2 (g^2–f^2–e^2). In the variation the descending second from g^2 to f^2 has been inverted to a rising seventh (g^2–f^3), which is filled in with passing tones.[10] The original descent is then completed with the arrival on e^3 in the newly gained register.

The examples we have seen so far illustrate what Schenker calls a "direct" transfer of register, expressed either as an unfilled leap, or composed-out through figuration (arpeggiation, passing tones, and so forth).[11] Schenker discusses a second type of register transfer that is "indirect," occurring over a longer span of time with intervening motions. We shall see examples of more extended uses of direct and indirect register transfers later in this book.

Coupling

The technique of register transfer often involves the composing-out of a linear progression between two different registers. In Example 6.11, Mozart transforms the line g^2–f^2–e^2 into g^2–f^3–e^3 (the initial interval of a second becomes a seventh), a process that activates two registers in the musical texture. The next technique that we shall consider, *coupling*, is related to register transfer, but is generally associated with the interval of the octave.

Coupling occurs when a single pitch, such as the primary tone of the *Urlinie*, is transferred between different registers an octave apart. The transfer of register in coupling usually occurs more than once, and embraces connective motions within the octave transfers. This process consequently establishes an *alternation* of registers: one becomes "primary," the other plays a supportive role (Schenker referred to the latter as the reinforcing, "coupled" octave). This technique, therefore, differs from "simple" register transfer in that it utilizes differentiation of register in a more structural manner. It may occur on various levels, and sometimes forms an essential aspect of the compositional plan for an entire work.

Portions of the Alla Turca movement from Mozart's Piano Sonata, K.311, are shown in Example 6.12a. As may be readily observed in the music and the graph, the movement begins with an arpeggiation from c^2 to c^3 over tonic harmony. (The initial motion on the upbeat is a consonant skip that decorates c^2.) Scale degree $\hat{2}$ over V follows in bar 5, and the phrase concludes with closure in the dominant; notice the fifth-progression from b^2 to e^2 ($\hat{5}$–$\hat{1}$ in E minor) that helps to establish the tonicized dominant region. In the concluding parallel phrase (bars 16–24), the coupling involves the transference of the primary tone twice between two registers: c^2 leads to c^3 (bar 20), followed by a return to c^2 (bar 23). Melodic closure for this section of the piece (b^1–a^1) occurs in the lower register before the double bar.[12]

As we have seen, the purpose of a coupling is to connect two registers. Bear in mind, however, that this technique necessarily involves a composing-out of the connective passage, and that a fleeting association between octaves does not represent a coupling.

In the Mozart the juxtaposition of the two registers becomes a significant aspect of the composition. The arpeggiated ascent to the higher register in

EXAMPLE 6.12:

(a) Mozart, Piano Sonata, K. 311, III, bars 1–8 and 17–24; (b) middleground reduction

(a)

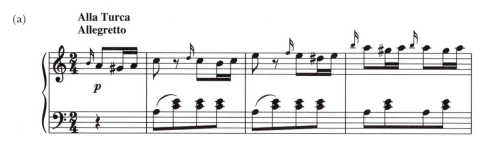

EXAMPLE 6.12 (*continued*)

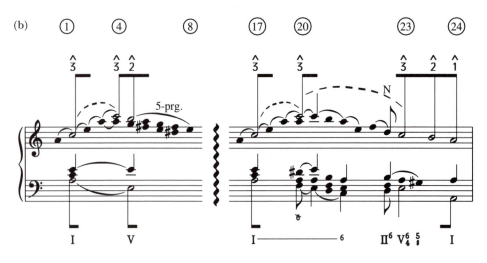

bars 1–4 opens a registral space (or span) in which the connective motions occur throughout the passage. In addition, the return to the initial register in bars 22–24 provides a sense of completeness and closure, because this section ends in the same register in which it began.

Schenker believed that, although a structural line may be disposed in different registers, a single register will usually be primary. He called this primary structural register the *obligatory register* (*obligate Lage*). In Example 6.12, the upper voice concludes in the lower register, which emerges as primary.

Superposition

Another compositional technique that incorporates elaboration and transformation of a structural line through transfer of register is *superposition,* in which one or more inner-voice tones are shifted above the principal top-voice line.[13]

The opening of Mozart's Piano Sonata, K.332, is presented in Example 6.13. The right-hand melody unfolds with remarkable freedom, soaring upward in register in bars 3–4, only to return through a series of leaps in bars 5–7. This ascending and descending motion is then echoed in the final bars of the phrase. Also notice that the texture changes frequently in these opening bars, creating a quasi-orchestral quality that enhances the dramatic effectiveness of the passage.

The right hand begins (bars 1–2) by arpeggiating the tonic triad, F–A–C, which is answered in bars 3–4 with the motion B♭–G–E (notice the change of direction in this arpeggiation!). Example 6.13c simplifies the register and reveals a series of *unfolded* harmonic intervals: F/C, B♭/E, F/A; the "main" notes of this series form the third-progression C–B♭–A (Example 6.13c). Because of the interplay of register, however, the *inner-voice* tones E and F (circled on the graph) appear in the higher register; they are *superposed* above the guiding third-progression C–B♭–A in this polyphonic texture. Notice also that the final unfolded interval is expressed as f² *down* to a¹, a motion that reestablishes the original register and completes the third-progression C–B♭–A (Example 6.13c).[14]

Reaching Over

Reaching over (*Uebergreifen*) is related to the technique of superposition in that it involves, in a general sense, the transfer of inner-voice tones to a higher position. Reaching over, however, typically involves a specific melodic pattern, which is illustrated in Example 6.14. In bar 1, the inner-voice tone C "reaches over" the top-voice tone A♭, then descends to the neighbor tone B♭. A similar pattern recurs in bar 3, where the tenor D♭ reaches over B♭. In both cases,

EXAMPLE 6.13:

(a) Mozart, Piano Sonata, K. 332, I, bars 1–12; (b) foreground reduction; (c) unfolded harmonic intervals

(a)

EXAMPLE 6.13 (*continued*)

(b)

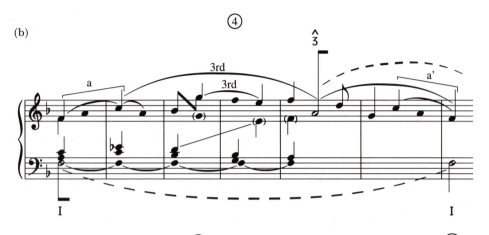

(c)

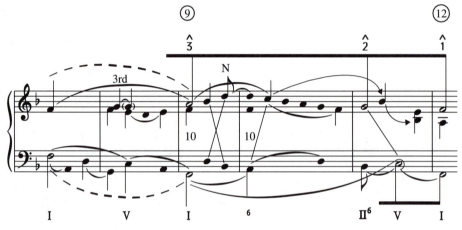

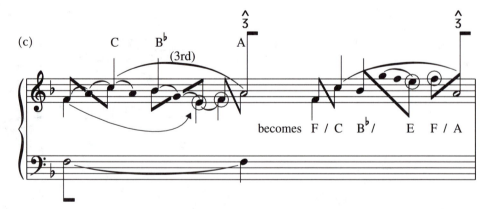

EXAMPLE 6.14:

(a) Beethoven, Piano Sonata, Op. 10, No. 1, II, bars 1–5; (b) foreground reduction

the incomplete neighbor (appoggiatura) produced by the reaching-over procedure resolves downward to a chordally supported neighbor tone, which in turn resolves to the original tones (A♭ and B♭, respectively). The broader point to bear in mind is that the technique of reaching over decorates an underlying ascent (note the *initial ascent* to C) with local *descending* motion. Here, the appoggiaturas (to the upper neighbor notes) subtly participate in the ascending motion by preparing the listener for the tones that follow (A♭–C in bar 1 foreshadows A–C of the initial ascent in bars 1–5).[15]

A more complex instance of reaching over appears in the opening of Bach's Little Prelude in C major, from the Wilhelm Friedemann Bach *Klavier-büchlein* (Example 6.15). In the ascending-fifth sequence of bars 1–3, the chords are grouped in pairs: I–V, II–VI. The broader function of the sequence is to lead from I to III. The chords on the downbeats support a series of parallel tenths between the outer voices: E–F–G in the upper voice over C–D–E in the bass.

The chords on the downbeats unquestionably would not appear in direct succession, because of the octaves and fifths that would result. The intervening chords prevent the faulty voice leading, and also allow the tones of the

EXAMPLE 6.15:

(a) J. S. Bach, Little Prelude in C major, bars 1–3; (b) and (c) foreground reductions

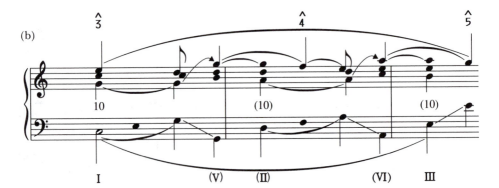

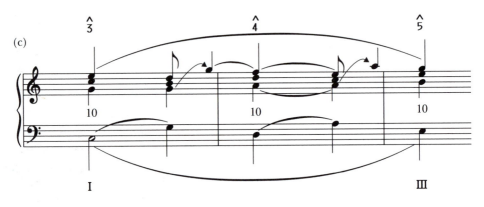

main line (E–F–G) to be decorated from above. In this process the top voice falls a step before leaping to the higher position (in bar 1, E down to D, then up to G). As indicated in Example 6.15c, the leaps in bars 1 and 2 result from the transfer of inner-voice tones to a higher register (through ascending register transfer); these tones then resolve to the next tone of the underlying ascending line. Example 6.15b indicates the further embellishment of the reaching-over motions through suspensions on the downbeats of bars 2 and 3.[16]

In general, therefore, the technique of reaching over involves an inner voice that reaches over, or across, the top voice, and then resolves *downward* to a higher top-voice tone. In Example 6.14, the higher tone is an upper neighbor note; in Example 6.15 it is the next principal tone of the structural line. Reaching over frequently, though not always, includes a descent through two or more tones as part of a broader ascent. That a descent can occur in a broader ascending motion is perhaps the most essential characteristic of reaching over, one that Schenker was careful to point out in describing this technique.[17]

Cover Tone

A *cover tone* is an inner-voice tone which is superposed above the principal top-voice line; it remains for a period of time, in the manner of a *discant* tone.

The final bars of Schubert's Moment Musical, Op. 94, No. 2, are presented in Example 6.16. This section follows the final cadence and the arrival of the *Urlinie* on $\hat{1}$ (bar 82), and serves as a coda for the work. Bars 82–85 recall the opening theme, and return to $\hat{1}$ over I in bar 86. At this point the inner-voice tone E♭, which has been prominent throughout the piece, shifts above the top-voice A♭. The E♭—a cover tone—then remains poised in the higher register, struck occasionally like a bell, while more active voice leading continues underneath. Despite its relative independence, a cover tone will often be related to other aspects of the voice leading: notice, for example, that the final statement of $\hat{1}$, now in the two-line octave (a♭²), is attained through an arpeggiation from the cover tone (bars 89–90).

Substitution

Composers frequently choose (for reasons pertaining to variety or voice leading) to substitute one tone for another that would normally be expected in a given context. This technique, called *substitution,* occurs in situations where the absent tone is clearly implied by the context.

Example 6.17a is a passage from a string quartet by Haydn. In the cadence which concludes the passage, the resolution of the cadential $^6_4$ chord in bar 88 is delayed by the cadenzalike figuration in the first violin. After it reaches the final note of this cadenza passage (e⁴ in bar 90), the first violin makes an astonishing leap downward to b¹ (over V⁷) followed by c² (over I, bar 21).

Example 6.17b illustrates the voice leading that forms the basis of this passage. Just as the high register of e⁴ is left unresolved (in this passage), the tone D—which would typically follow E in the resolution of the cadential $^6_4$)— does not appear in the first violin part. Instead, the inner-voice tone B ($\hat{7}$) appears, enhancing the dramatic quality of the passage at this point. The "detour" does not nullify the descending nature of the line; the leading tone

EXAMPLE 6.16:

(a) Schubert, Moment Musical, Op. 94, No. 2, bars 82–90; (b) foreground reduction

(a)

(b)

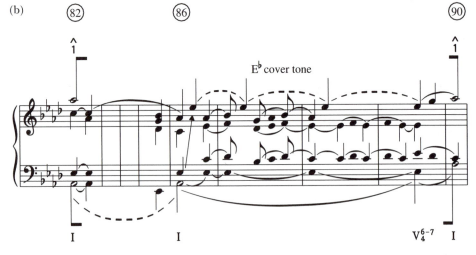

EXAMPLE 6.17:

(a) Haydn, String Quartet, Op. 76, No. 1, II, bars 86–91; (b) foreground reduction

(a)

(b)

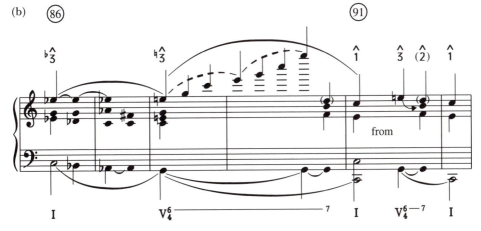

simply *substitutes* for scale degree $\hat{2}$, which is shown in parentheses to indicate both its role in the descent and its literal absence from the violin line. Note that the tone D does appear an octave lower in the viola part, in the tenor register, in Example 6.17a; when a substitution occurs, the absent tone will frequently appear in another voice. Bear in mind that the implied tone and the tone literally stated normally belong to the same chord. Thus thinking in terms of the underlying (or "imaginary") continuo part can help you to recognize tones that are expected, but not literally stated.[18]

THE PHRYGIAN $\hat{2}$

The use of chromatic tones—whether through modal mixture or other types of chromaticism—for melodic prolongation is a multifaceted subject. One chromatic chord with particular importance for voice leading on higher levels of structure is primarily associated with the minor mode: the Neapolitan sixth chord, which contains flat $\hat{2}$ (or *Phrygian* $\hat{2}$). (This chord is also known as the *Phrygian II* chord, because of the association of flat $\hat{2}$ with the Phrygian mode.) This chord will serve as a representative example of the replacement of a diatonic scale degree with a chromaticlaly altered form of the same scale degree, a frequent compositional technique.[19]

The Neapolitan sixth is an expressive sonority that has many compositional uses. It often sounds unexpected and—despite its major quality—can sound strikingly dark and somber, particularly in the minor mode. An altered form of II^6 (which sometimes appears in $^5_3$ or $^6_4$ position), it frequently occurs as an intensifying element in cadences. One of its voice-leading characteristics is the tendency of flat $\hat{2}$ to descend a diminished third to the leading tone, and not to ascend directly to the diatonic form of $\hat{2}$ (a direct chromatic succession that tends to sound awkward).

Schenker states that the Neapolitan sixth chord is "an event that originates only in voice leading."[20] As Example 6.18a shows, the diminished third is often filled in with a passing tone before diatonic $\hat{2}$ appears over the dominant. Another important possibility, shown in Example 6.18b, is for flat $\hat{2}$ to move to the leading tone without natural $\hat{2}$ appearing in the upper voice. In both cases, the motion to the leading tone represents motion into an inner voice; in the second situation natural $\hat{2}$ is understood by implication in the upper voice, although in composition it typically appears in an inner voice (such as the tenor) when the dominant appears.

The Neapolitan sixth may appear on any structural level, from the deep middleground to a foreground progression. Because it is an intermediate harmony, it is also possible for the chord to prepare the structural dominant of the *Ursatz* and consequently to inflect $\hat{2}$ of the fundamental line (remember that II^6, the diatonic counterpart of the Neapolitan sixth, often supports structural $\hat{2}$ before V enters). In *Free Composition* Schenker clearly shows that he does not regard the Phrygian $\hat{2}$ (or other elements of mixture) to form an

EXAMPLE 6.18:

Phrygian $\hat{2}$ in the fundamental line

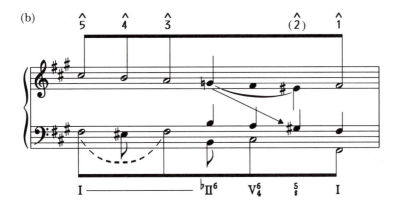

actual part of the fundamental structure, which is ultimately diatonic. Rather it enters (conceptually) as a transformation on the first level of the middleground. It will inevitably revert to the diatonic form of $\hat{2}$, which is the only possibility at the background level itself.

Exercises

For centuries composers and other musicians have copied scores, not only to obtain a personal copy, but also as a way of learning the music thoroughly. This practice continued long after scores were commercially available. Similarly, Schenker would ask students to copy a graph so as to understand better both its notation and its meaning. It is an excellent way to improve both your understanding of graphs and your ability to create them.

Copy some or all of the graphs in this chapter. As you copy a foreground graph and then a subsequent middleground graph, think carefully about the relationship of the two: what is retained, and what is left out; how the notation changes on higher levels; what is shown about the overall structure of the phrase. Be prepared to discuss each graph in detail, and the technique it illustrates.

CHAPTER 7

Some Basic Elaborations of Fundamental Structures

In Chapter 5 we examined Schenker's idea of a fundamental structure (*Ursatz*), which comprises the interrelated components of the fundamental line (*Urlinie*) and bass arpeggiation (*Bassbrechung*). Then, in Chapter 6, we examined separately some of the basic compositional techniques associated with musical development that create content and variety in a musical composition.

In this chapter we will continue to explore the nature of fundamental structures, and the ways in which they may be elaborated. In particular, we will examine in more detail the interrelationships between specific compositional techniques and general principles of tonal organization exemplified in the *Ursatz*. We will also introduce a new compositional technique, *interruption,* which is one of the most significant and far-reaching of all tonal procedures. The framework we develop here will enable us to proceed to an examination of complete tonal structures and musical forms in subsequent chapters.

As we focus on the expression of various techniques in actual compositions, we will also consider ways to develop strategies for analysis. The study of Schenkerian analysis involves more than learning to recognize tonal patterns and compositional procedures on different levels of structure. It is also a process of developing musical understanding that leads to the discovery of what is unique in a composition. An analysis should investigate general tonal procedures and techniques, common to many pieces, but it should also reveal those aspects that define any composition as a unique work of art. For theories and generalizations are, in the long run, useful only to the extent they enable us to understand better the individual pieces we perform and listen to.

This chapter will therefore present complete phrases that exemplify some of the essential principles associated with Schenker's work. We will initially discuss the analyses in some detail. As we proceed, and as you become more familiar with techniques, terminology, and graphic symbols, we will explain less in words and allow more details of the music to be conveyed graphically. It was Schenker's intention that his method of graphic analysis could make this possible.

MOZART, PIANO SONATA, K. 283, I, BARS 1–16

Example 7.1 presents bars 1–16 of the first movement of Mozart's Piano Sonata in G major, K. 283. In large forms, such as sonata-allegro movements, individual sections are often relatively self-contained. Like the Haydn passage in Chapter 5 (Example 5.1), this phrase is tonally complete in that it presents in microcosm the essential structural characteristics of an entire piece. The phrase structure, however, is asymmetrical: the main body of the phrase comprises ten bars, with a six–bar extension in bars 11–16 that results from a slightly modified repetition of bars 5–10. Because the repetition is nearly exact (with registral variation in bars 11–12), we show only bars 1–10 in Example 7.3. We will discuss the features that lead to the asymmetry of bars 1–10 in connection with the voice-leading structure of the passage.

As a first step in analyzing bars 1–10, consider the prominence of G-major tonic harmony throughout, in bars 1, 4, 6, 8 and, finally, in bar 10, as the last chord of the perfect authentic cadence that concludes the phrase. Clearly, tonic harmony is prolonged for much of the phrase. The initial tonic note in the bass is decorated via an upper and lower neighbor figure in bars 1–4, G–A–F♯–G (see the circled notes in Example 7.1), supporting inversions of V^7 that serve as contrapuntal (neighbor) chords prolonging I. In bars 5–6, IV leads back to I^6 on two successive downbeats. Finally, a rhythmically strong root-position tonic in bar 10 concludes the phrase.

In conjunction with our initial consideration of the harmonic structure, notice the internal divisions of the phrase that result from its rhythmic articulation: bars 1–4 form a rhythmically regular opening statement that, while complete in its own terms, requires continuation. Bars 5–7 form another rhythmic unit, but one that is asymmetrical, two bars plus one. The final part of the phrase, bars 8–10, is also rhythmically asymmetrical. Mozart achieves this effect by introducing hemiola, in conjunction with more rapid right-hand figuration. The hemiola accelerates the harmonic rhythm, "driving through" the chords of the structural cadence: $I–IV^6–V^6_4–V^7–I$, as illustrated in Example 7.1.[1]

EXAMPLE 7.1:

Mozart, Piano Sonata K. 283, I, bars 1–16

Consider the upper voice at the beginning of the phrase (the anacrusis and bar 1), in bar 6 (as part of the I^6 chord), and over the tonic that coincides with the beginning of the hemiola in bar 8. Based on its overall prominence, a good preliminary assumption is that D is the primary tone of the melodic structure. Now that we have made some initial observations about the melodic and harmonic structure, how can we proceed to a more comprehensive view of the tonal structure? As a next step, we can take a closer look at the top voice.[2]

Like tonic harmony, the D in the upper voice is clearly present for a good deal of the phrase. Furthermore, to consider scale degree $\hat{5}$ as the principal tone during much of the phrase is consistent with other aspects of the music, especially its support by the rhythmically strong, recurring tonics that we have observed. But what subsequently happens to D beginning in bar 8, where marked changes in design—the sixteenth notes and the beginning of the hemiola—signal the motion to the cadence?[3] To answer this question we will consider the path of the upper voice in relation to the harmonic progression in bars 8–10. The D is not a member of the IV^6 chord: hence the voice leading (shown in Example 7.2) suggests that the top voice begins to *descend* from D as the bass progression begins its movement away from the initial tonic toward the structural cadence.

Example 7.2 shows that the fifth-progression D-C-B-A-G guides the upper voice in these bars. The D, however, is first transferred upward by the scale passage, so that C is introduced in a higher register before it is transferred down by another scale passage. The ascending and descending register transfers in turn create tonal spaces for the scalar figuration. Thus three "levels" may be discerned in this passage: (1) the linear progression itself, (2) its elaboration through register transfer, (3) the filling in of the resulting octave

EXAMPLE 7.2:

Mozart, Piano Sonata, K. 283, I, bars 8–10: reductions

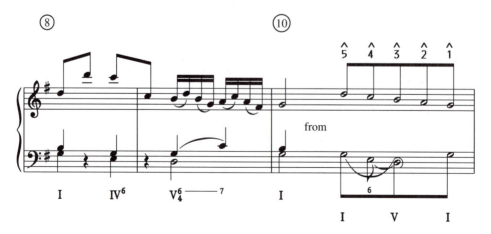

leaps with scalar figuration. This figuration and the associated hemiola intensify the rhythmic impulse to the tonic of the cadence, the harmonic and rhythmic goal of the phrase.

The sixteenth notes in beats 2 and 3 of bar 9 might seem to suggest more than one possible interpretation of the notes in the upper voice; however, the rhythmic position of B and A on the strong parts of beats 2 and 3, and their repetition within each beat, suggest that the arpeggiated figures elaborate part of an underlying stepwise line: D-C-B-A-G. We have observed that tones of figuration may often occur above the structural line they decorate. In bar 9, as the main line is drawing to a close, the skips to d^2 and c^2 on beats 2 and 3 echo the motion from D to C that occurred immediately before in bars 7–8 (see the music).[4] Such a recollection of previously stated tones so as to summarize the path of the upper voice occurs in many tonal compositions. Frequently, motivic associations are created as well. We will see more instances of this type of melodic integration in successive examples.

We mentioned above that this excerpt represents a self-contained musical structure, one that can be viewed "as if" it were a complete work. Such small-scale, closed structures occur in tonal music with great frequency. One of Schenker's most far-reaching insights is the realization that *Ursatz* patterns are replicated on both middleground and foreground levels of structure.

Example 7.2 illustrates this point with a reduction of bars 8–10 in the second part of the example. Note that, in the bass, the dominant note (D) is approached from above (E), with the E supporting a IV^6 chord. This inverted subdominant chord is lighter and more fluid in effect than a root-position subdominant chord.

Example 7.3 is a comprehensive graphic analysis that puts the cadence illustrated in Example 7.2 into the broader context of the complete phrase. The graph clarifies the role of associated tones and chords in the prolongation of tonic harmony and $\hat{5}$ through bar 8, where the motion to the structural cadence begins (compare with Example 7.2). Example 7.3 clearly reveals that the initial tonic governs much of the phrase, as frequently occurs in music composed during the Classical era. This broad observation reveals much about the phrase, but leaves many interesting and beautiful features still to be considered.

The graph shows that a foreground line D-C-B shapes the path of the upper voice in bars 1–4, foreshadowing the later descent to the tonic. By examining the three levels of the graph *backward* (compare levels *c*, *b*, and *a*, in that order), you can progressively discover how the three notes of the third-progression D-C-B are decorated and consequently expanded over four bars. Note especially the following:

1.   The right-hand melody moves between an outer and an inner voice in a polyphonic framework. Consider first of all the unfolded intervals D–G and F♯–C. The initial D belongs to the outer voice; G, F♯, and A are inner-voice tones, with F♯ and A changing positions through a voice exchange with the bass (level *b*) before C resumes the upper voice and moves to B.

EXAMPLE 7.3:

Mozart, Piano Sonata, K. 283, I, bars 1–10: (a) foreground reduction; (b) and (c) middleground reductions

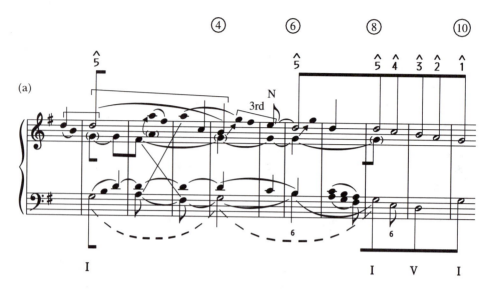

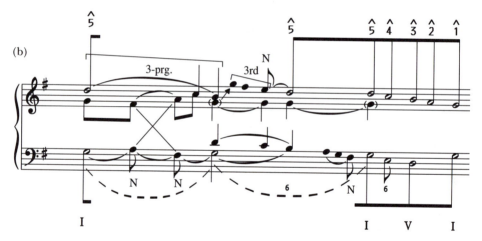

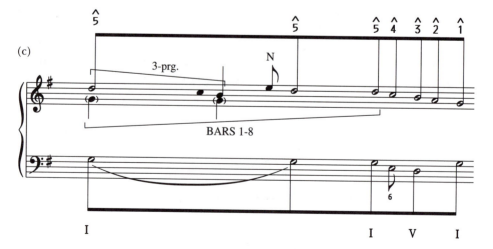

2.   Mozart masterfully juxtaposes different registers, creating registral associations of tones throughout the passage. The A in bar 2—the final tone of the voice exchange—occurs in the higher register, superposed above the main line (level *a*). In so doing Mozart creates a sonoric association with g^2 in bars 4 and 6, and anticipates the motion to d^3 in bar 8. Such associations of tones through register is an important compositional resource that does not necessarily form part of the principal top-voice line, but can provide an independent type of long-range continuity and integration.[5]

3.   Another unifying interrelationship in the upper voice is indicated by the motivic brackets in Example 7.3 (compare in particular levels *a* and *b*): the third-progression D–C–B of bars 1–4 is motivically related to the opening consonant skip D–B–D in the right hand, the ensuing A–F♯–A in the higher register (bars 2–3), and, finally, the motion G–F♯–E in bars 4–5, which is a miniature, transposed repetition of the line D–C–B. Thus the third-motive appears at different structural levels, unifying the music as it develops.

An especially interesting aspect of the phrase involves the third-motive G–F♯–E in bars 4–5 (shown in Examples 7.3a and b). As we noted, the foreground line of bars 1–4 has descended from D through C to B. Suddenly the third-motive G–F♯–E occurs in the higher register in bars 4–5, leading to E over IV, which in turn moves to D over I^6 in bar 6 (note the *fp* markings in the music at these points). This rapid motivic echo effectively precludes any further descent of the upper voice: it leads to E ($\hat{6}$) as upper neighbor to the primary tone d^2 ($\hat{5}$), which is then reinstated in bar 6.

To better understand this process, compare levels *a* and *b* of the graph in Example 7.3. The g^2 of bar 4 is structurally an inner-voice tone that is shifted or *superposed* above the foreground line. The technique of superposition in this case leads to e^2 in bar 5 and reestablishes the higher register of the primary tone $\hat{5}$ established at the beginning of the phrase.

Consequently, the passage embraces two "guiding" lines, both of which share the same first pitch. These lines in effect shape the course of the upper voice. As illustrated in Example 7.3c, the first descent is a motion into an inner voice that expands (and elaborates) the *Urlinie* of this passage, delaying its full descent to the tonic until the final bars of the phrase. To be sure, the role of the first descent only becomes clear after the *entire* phrase is put into perspective. In this sense analysis—like listening itself—is partly retrospective: we comprehend a musical event in terms of both preceding and successive events, just as our view of a literary character may evolve and change in the unfolding of a play or a novel.

Bars 11–16 are not shown in the graph: they repeat bars 4–10, with some variation of register (compare the music with Example 7.3). The absence of this phrase extension from Examples 7.2 and 7.3 is not meant to suggest that it is in any sense nonessential. Considering the first group as a whole they are *very* important, for they establish overall symmetry (a total length of 16 bars) following the asymmetrical phrase of ten bars that begins the movement.

Without bars 11–16, the first group would sound brief and incomplete; the varied repetition provides a necessary and satisfying continuation in this section of the movement.[6]

Finally, we might consider that, from an analytical perspective, repetition may have different functions or purposes. A simple repetition of part or all of a phrase or section, as here, adds length but normally does not change the nature of what has already happened in any fundamental way, except to articulate and reinforce it. We will, however, see in later examples that other repetitions—particularly within a phrase—can vary or change the nature of what is being repeated, or otherwise transform its meaning.[7]

BEETHOVEN, PIANO SONATA, OP. 14, NO. 1, II, BARS 1–16

Example 7.4a shows a passage by Beethoven, comparable in length to the previous example by Mozart. We observed that, after $\hat{1}$ over I concludes the main phrase in bar 10, Mozart repeats the final six bars as an extension to create the 16-bar length of the first theme group. In the present example, also 16 bars in length, Beethoven establishes a different—and more symmetrical—kind of internal division with an antecedent/consequent phrase construction. The antecedent phrase is articulated by the half cadence in bars 7–8, and the consequent phrase by the subsequent full cadence in bars 15–16.[8]

As indicated in the reductions of Example 7.4, the harmonic organization of the passage is fairly straightforward. The tonic is prolonged through the initial six bars of the phrase by means of a descending register transfer of the tonic note in the bass (e to E), followed by the motion to V in bars 7–8 that concludes the antecedent phrase. Once again, we see that the prolongation of an initial tonic is a technique composers frequently use to create musical content before leading to the structural cadence of the phrase or section.

As we focus more specifically on the individual chords in the foreground of the phrase, one potentially confusing question emerges: How should we interpret the diminished seventh chord in bar 3, which Beethoven highlights through duration and dynamic emphasis? The roman numeral designation, vii°[7] of V, suggests a chromaticized intermediate harmony (that is, an altered IV[7]) that tonicizes and leads to V; in the bass, A♯ is expected to resolve to B. Instead, the vii°[7] of V moves directly to vii°$^4_3$, which serves very often as a functional equivalent to V$^4_2$. (The G in the upper voice on the first beat of bar 4 is a suspension.) Consequently, the expected root-position V chord is bypassed altogether.

Example 7.5 clarifies this harmonic motion in two stages. In stage A, the "normal" progression, the vii°[7] of V chord resolves as it normally would to V in root position; the vii°$^4_3$ then enters as a passing harmony, connecting V with I[6] (the suspended G has been omitted in stage A to represent clearly the normalization). Stage B restores the suspension and eliminates the V (the

EXAMPLE 7.4:

(a) Beethoven, Piano Sonata, Op. 14, No. 1, II, bars 1–16; (b) and (c) foreground reductions

(a)

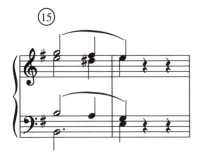

EXAMPLE 7.4 (*continued*)

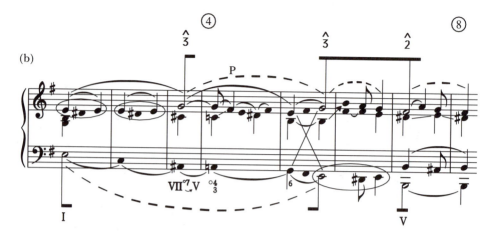

(b)

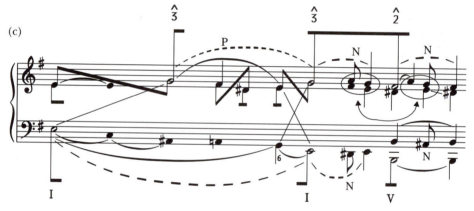

(c)

EXAMPLE 7.5:

Beethoven, Piano Sonata, Op. 14, No. 1, II: comparative reductions of bars 1–5

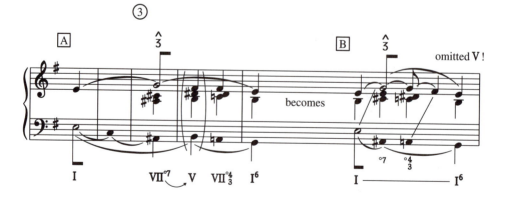

understood resolution of the vii°⁷ of V), leading us back to the actual progression. We see here a characteristic example of harmonic and contrapuntal *elision*; the expected resolution to the dominant, and of sharp $\hat{4}$ to $\hat{5}$ in the bass, is omitted. Therefore, we can now understand the bass in bar 3 to the downbeat of bar 5, A♯–A♮–G, as a *contracted* (or elided) form of A♯–(B)–A♮–G. From this point the vii°⁴₃ resolves to the I⁶ and then to I in root position through a voice exchange (see Example 7.4c).

The upper voice of this passage presents us with a situation that we have not previously encountered in a replicated *Urlinie* pattern. In the opening bars, $\hat{1}$ is twice elaborated by its lower neighbor D♯ (note the repetition of the E–D♯–E motive in the bass in bars 5–6, circled in Example 7.4b). We have learned from our study of *Ursatz* patterns that an *Urlinie* does not begin with $\hat{1}$; rather, this tone serves as the *goal* of the descending fundamental line. In Chapter 6, however, we discovered that $\hat{1}$ may serve as an initial tone in a different way: it can initiate a motion to the first *Urlinie* tone, either through a stepwise ascent (*Anstieg*) or through an arpeggiation to the primary tone. In other words, we learned that the appearance of the primary tone can be delayed. The most common scenario is one in which such a delayed primary tone enters over a prolonged tonic harmony, a situation that harmonically reinforces the function of the primary tone as an upper tone of the tonic triad, despite its late appearance; Example 7.6 (from Schenker, *Free Composition*) shows this situation.

The most noteworthy feature of this passage, however, is that the primary tone $\hat{3}$ is not only delayed, but appears over a *nontonic* harmony, after the bass has moved downward from the initial tonic. In Example 7.4c, the g¹ of bar 3 is connected with the bass e of bar 1: the diagonal line indicates that, although these outer voice tones are displaced in the foreground, they are structurally associated. As the primary tone, g¹ is the upper third of the opening tonic harmony. But this tone is delayed by the initial e¹; when it enters in bar 3, it is supported in the foreground by the diminished seventh chord on sharp $\hat{4}$ in the bass. Because G is a member of both the tonic chord and the diminished seventh chord, the common-tone relationship permits this nontonic support of the primary tone at the surface of the music. (Bear in mind that the primary tone G has already been stated indirectly as a member of

EXAMPLE 7.6:

Delayed appearance of primary tone supported by tonic harmony (from Schenker, *Free Composition*)

(10)

tonic harmony, in the inner voice of the right hand in bar 1). This excerpt suggests one of the many possibilities for the realization of a fundamental structure in composition.

The remaining features of the upper voice will become apparent through study of the reductions in Example 7.4. In the final reduction, note especially the unfoldings by third that shape the rising and falling motions to and from the inner voice, beginning with e^1 to g^1. Also significant is the enlargement of the initial E–D♯–E motive in bars 4–5 (indicated between the staves in Example 7.4c). Finally, notice the "reaching over" that appears in bar 6 (Example 7.4b). At the end of bar 5, the primary tone G is restated (now over tonic harmony!). It is followed by a leap to b^1 in the next bar, and then a descent back to g^1 through a^1, the upper neighbor to the primary tone $\hat{3}$. In other words, the stepwise elaboration of the primary tone, G-A-G ($\hat{3}$–$\hat{4}$–$\hat{3}$), is decorated at the surface by the skip to b^1, which comes from the "alto" voice of tonic harmony in bar 5. After this motion, the primary tone G ($\hat{3}$) moves to F♯ ($\hat{2}$) over the half cadence of the phrase.[9]

Now that we have examined some aspects of the first phrase, we can turn our attention to a general feature of the entire passage that many pieces share. You may have noticed that the second phrase is virtually identical to the first, except for the change in register, and different cadences: as mentioned above, the first phrase ends with a half cadence, the second with a perfect authentic cadence. Because the phrases are otherwise alike, we can forgo a detailed graph of the second phrase and proceed to an illustration that shows the essential structural features of each phrase as well as the different cadences. Example 7.7 illustrates.

The graph in Example 7.7, which we might describe as a *schema,* or basic tonal pattern, represents abstractly the most essential features of the tonal structure: the path of the *Urlinie* $\hat{3}$–$\hat{1}$ and unfolding of the bass arpeggiation I-V-I. In some respects, particularly the degree of abstraction, this graph resembles an *Ursatz*. An *Ursatz*, however, is fundamentally a representation of a singular, undivided tonal structure. The two parts of Example 7.7, which

EXAMPLE 7.7:

Beethoven, Piano Sonata, Op. 14, No. 1, II, middleground interruption from $\hat{3}$

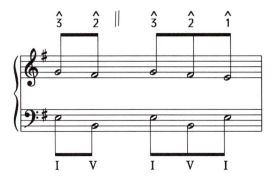

correspond to the two phrases, illustrate a harmonic and melodic process that begins from $\hat{3}$ over I and continues to $\hat{2}$ over V, where the tonal motion ceases. At this point the processes are interrupted, resulting in a divided structure. Immediately thereafter, the same motions begin again and this time achieve the goal, $\hat{1}$ over I, that was expected but denied in the first motion.

It is important to stress that the sense of completion is fulfilled only after the structure begins again, that is, after the second phrase retraces its path from $\hat{3}$ over I, moves through $\hat{2}$ over V, and this time attains the $\hat{1}$ over I that is the goal of an *Urlinie* and bass arpeggiation. In short, the second part of an interrupted structure resolves the tensions created by the interruption of the first part.

This procedure, called *interruption,* plays a significant role in shaping tonal structures, and appears in different guises and over various spans of music. Example 7.8 shows an interrupted structure from $\hat{5}$, the other divided *Ursatz* pattern that is frequently encountered.[10] For purposes of generalized discussion, the example shows only the most essential harmonies, I and V. Intermediate harmonies and other elaborations and prolongations of the harmonic motion from I to V typically occur in ways comparable to those that we have already seen in previous examples.

Schenker referred to the two parts of this tonal process as the two *branches* of the interruption. Note that the goal of the first branch is V, supporting $\hat{2}$ in the upper voice. A dominant chord that serves as the goal of a structural motion in this manner, without a resolution to tonic harmony at the conclusion of the motion, is frequently referred to as a *divider* (*Teiler*) or *dividing dominant.* Because V contains the leading tone, which embodies a strong tendency to *ascend* to $\hat{1}$, while $\hat{2}$ in the upper voice tends to *descend* to $\hat{1}$, it is easy to understand why so much tension is accumulated when the bass and melodic motions are interrupted at this point. The second branch of the interruption consequently begins again, retraces the path of the first motion, and, as we noted above, finally achieves closure and dissipates the tension of the incomplete first branch with the arrival of $\hat{1}$ over I.

EXAMPLE 7.8:

Middleground interruption from $\hat{5}$

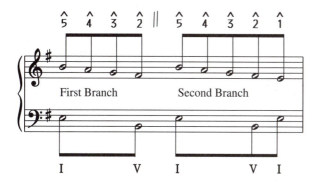

In the example by Beethoven it should be noted that the second branch (the second phrase) begins almost immediately; less than a full measure separates the end of the first phrase from the beginning of the second. We will see in some instances that the end of the first branch—the "point" of interruption—can be extended; that is, $\hat{2}$ over V can be prolonged, sometimes over large spans of music. Such an extension can be used by composers as a means of creating form, for the prolongation itself may become a discrete section within the overall form. We will see this procedure especially in rounded binary and sonata forms.

It is not always easy to determine whether an interruption has occurred in a specific instance: not every half cadence, for example, necessarily indicates an interrupted structure. In many cases the second branch of the interruption, whether it be a phrase or larger section, will begin identically or similarly to the first branch—both melodically and harmonically—creating the impression that the second branch "answers" the first. In this sense there is a relationship between the two branches of the interruption and the conventional notion of a *parallel period*—an antecedent phrase followed by a thematically similar consequent—which is the form of the initial 16 bars of Example 7.4.

BEETHOVEN, PIANO SONATA, OP. 2, NO. 1, II, BARS 1–8

The opening of the Adagio of Beethoven's Piano Sonata, Op. 2, No. 1, is similar in structure to the passage by Beethoven we examined in the previous section. In general terms, the passage consists of two phrases (in this case, two four-bar phrases) that are articulated by half and perfect authentic cadences, respectively. Notice also the thematic and harmonic similarities in the way each phrase begins (bars 1 and 5). This preliminary view of the thematic beginnings and the harmonic goals of each phrase suggests that, as with the previous example, the two parallel phrases may be related through the principle of interruption.

Unlike the previous example, however, the continuations of the phrases differ in some significant respects. We shall begin by considering those local and particular features that are unique to this work, and proceed to the identification of various structural characteristics. And we shall see that two passages which seem quite different may in fact be based upon similar or identical deep middleground structures.

Example 7.9 presents the music and a realization of the upper voice in bar 1; we have written out the turn, which foreshadows on a small scale many of the details and melodic shape of the upper voice of the entire phrase. Note first the leap from the anacrusis to the downbeat of the bar, a motion that rhythmically emphasizes a^1 over tonic harmony. The turn itself, of course,

EXAMPLE 7.9:

(a) Beethoven, Piano Sonata, Op. 2, No. 1, II, bars 1–8; (b) foreground reduction of melody, bar 1

decorates a^1 with its upper and lower neighbors. There is, however, a more deeply embedded decoration of a^1. The second part of the example illustrates a leap from a^1 to c^2 (the grace note), followed by a stepwise descent back to a^1 and then to f^1. The figure A–C–B♭–A is another instance of reaching over, one almost identical to that described in the previous section (Example 7.4b): a tone is elaborated first by a consonant skip, which leads from above to the upper neighbor of the main tone. This interpretation implies, of course, that a^1 is the main or primary tone, which is further decorated and prolonged by the motion into an inner voice, A–G–F, that occurs at the end of the bar. The hierarchical relationships of these tones are put into sharper focus in the last part of the example.

The reductions of Example 7.10 place this beginning in the context of the complete first phrase. The prominence of a^1 ($\hat{3}$) in bar 1 has been noted; now look carefully in bars 3–4, where a^1 returns over tonic harmony and then is suspended into bar 4 before moving to $\hat{2}$ over V, the harmonic goal of the phrase. Scale degree 3, therefore, is both a prominent point of departure, and a point to which the line returns before establishing $\hat{2}$ over V as the goal of the phrase.

The broad overarching line in the upper voice, A–C–B♭–A, shown in all parts of Example 7.10, emerges when one understands how tonic harmony shapes bars 1–3 of the phrase. The tonic is initially prolonged by the motion I–I^6 before V$^6_5$ (built on an incomplete lower neighbor) returns to I at the end of bar 3. The bass notes of this progression correspond to and consequently emphasize the foreground tone succession A–C–B♭–A; furthermore, the leap from f^1 to c^2 in bar 3 highlights the c^2 and signals the return of a register that has not been active since bar 1. This reading illuminates a remarkable feature of the phrase: the shape of the upper voice before the half cadence mirrors exactly the underlying path of the upper voice in bar 1 (compare Examples 7.9b and 7.10). In other words, over the span of bars 1–3, the primary tone A reaches over to C before B♭, the upper neighbor to $\hat{3}$, leads back to A, a figure that occurred in bar 1 and is now enlarged. This is a good example of why Schenker often used organic metaphors to describe the processes of tonal music: the shape of the upper voice seems to "grow" from bar 1, which we might metaphorically regard as a musical "seed."

Our reading shows that the primary tone a^1 is prolonged from bar 1 to bar 3. What, however, "happens" to the a^1 for almost seven beats—that is, how is it prolonged? Comparing the music with Example 7.10a, one can clearly see the descent from a^1 into the inner voice tone f^1 and to the leading tone e^1 in bar 2, followed by a motion from c^1 back to f^1 on the downbeat of bar 3 (labeled y in Example 7.10a). The second f^1 (over I^6 in bar 3) is pivotal in the phrase not only because it initiates the leap that reestablishes the upper voice, but because it completes a voice exchange with the $\hat{3}$ over I from bar 1, marking the boundary of the first part of the tonic prolongation (see Example 7.10b). Thus, the third-motion from a^1 in bar 1 to the inner-voice tone f^1 in bar 3 occurs within the space of prolonged tonic harmony, and consequently prolongs $\hat{3}$ as the associated upper voice of the tonic chord.

Less clear in the music are the two levels of motion into the inner voice. The first level involves the surface motions discussed above, which are shown in levels a and b of Example 7.10 (the descent from $\hat{3}$ to $\hat{7}$, and the Y motion). The voice leading of the progression I-V in bars 1–2, however, suggests another strand or level of melodic motion: the foreground step of a second from a to g (which is supported by the dominant in bar 2 that articulates or "divides" the space between I and I^6). As the second level illustrates, the e^1

EXAMPLE 7.10:

Beethoven, Piano Sonata, Op. 2, No. 1, II, bars 1–4: (a) and (b) foreground reductions; (c) middleground reduction

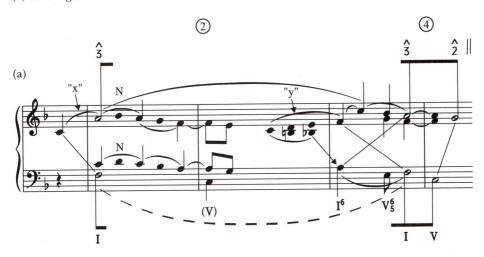

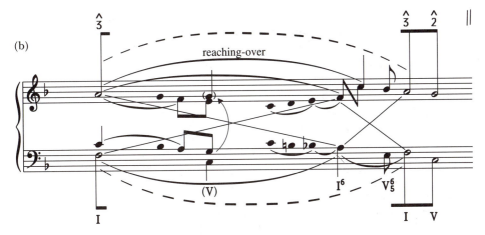

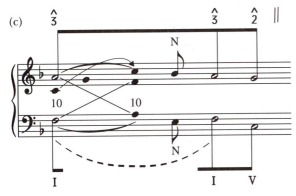

that actually occurs in bar 2 is a leading tone that substitutes for the G, which has been transferred to the tenor voice. As we have learned from our study of linear techniques, the leading tone frequently substitutes for $\hat{2}$. Thus we can understand an implied passing tone g^1 between a^1 and f^1; this third-progression prolongs the primary tone $\hat{3}$ and is embedded within the more elaborate surface motions supported by the progression from I to I^6.

For the consequent phrase, we will limit our discussion primarily to those aspects that represent recomposition or varied repetition of events in the antecedent. Example 7.11 presents an analysis of bars 5–8.

The first difference can be seen in the anacrusis to the consequent phrase. Instead of the simple leap of a sixth that precedes bar 1, the sixth is now filled in with half and whole steps (compare the motivic brackets, marked with an *x*, in Examples 7.10a and 7.11). The anacrusis to the second phrase is elaborated to form a smooth transition, a "link," between the phrases; structurally, however, it is important to bear in mind that the link belongs to the second phrase. After bar 5, the remaining part of the second phrase may seem different at first, but a closer examination reveals similarities that are perceived by delving beneath the surface of the music. In fact, we can understand much of the second phrase as a recomposition of the first. The reductions of Example 7.11 show that the tonic is once again prolonged through a voice exchange within the motion $I–I^6$. The voice exchange of the second phrase, however, is realized in a different way, meaning that Beethoven has incorporated a type of variation procedure to unify the antecedent and consequent phrases, one that does not derive exclusively from exact or slightly varied repetition.

Specifically, note first the expanded use of register. In bar 6, f^2, the last tone of the voice exchange in the upper voice, is now realized in the two-line octave, *marking the climax of the phrase*. Now consider the way in which the voice exchange is worked out so that the higher register becomes prominent (Example 7.11b). The prolonged a^1 ($\hat{3}$) leaps up to d^2, which continues through e^2 to f^2. Notice that the leap effectively separates the primary tone from this stepwise tone succession in different registers. How, then, can one explain the meaning of the tones D-E-F; in what way and on what level do they relate to the primary tone a^1?

Example 7.11b shows that the pitches d^2–e^2–f^2 are in fact the final three pitches of a fourth-progression—C–D–E–F. The first tone is expressed as c^1, that is, it is stated *below* the primary tone $\hat{3}$, before the final three pitches are transferred (through superposition) *above* the primary tone.[11] By referring back to Example 7.10a, you will see this tone succession stated at the surface in bars 2–3, concluding the voice exchange in the first phrase; there the complete line occurred in the lower register. (In both examples, we identify this motive with a *y*). The conclusion we may draw from the recognition of this *motivic parallelism* is that Beethoven has used an element of the first phrase as the basis for a "variation" in the second phrase. The two phrases thus share more in common than the opening theme of bar 1: the voice exchanges and the different versions of motive *y* unify these phrases at different structural levels.

EXAMPLE 7.11:

Beethoven, Piano Sonata, Op. 2, No. 1, II, bars 5–8: (a) and (b) foreground reductions; (c) middleground reduction

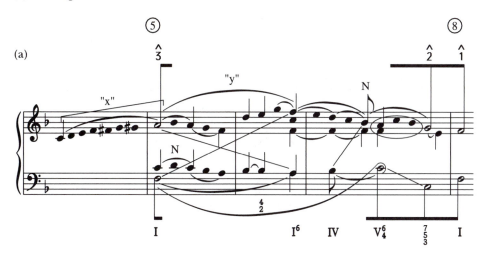

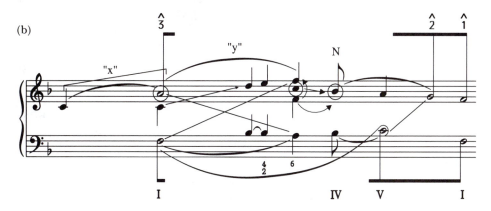

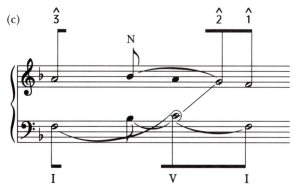

We now turn our attention to the motion that leads to the structural cadence in bars 7–8. Unlike the first phrase, which prolongs tonic harmony for three bars, tonic harmony lasts for only two bars in the consequent phrase. The reason for the change in harmonic rhythm relates to the way in which the different cadential goals are achieved in each phrase. Because Beethoven answers the antecedent phrase with a consequent of equal length (and because the consequent phrase culminates in a perfect authentic cadence that includes a subdominant chord), he introduces the V of the cadence one bar earlier than in the antecedent phrase so that the tonic appears in the eighth bar of the phrase. Thus the harmonic motion bypasses a return to a root-position I (as in phrase 1, bar 3) and proceeds directly to the intermediate IV. Accordingly, the upper voice descends quickly from f^2 in the higher register, enabling the upper voice to descend to the tonic ($\hat{2}$–$\hat{1}$).

A comparison of Examples 7.11a and b will clarify the structure of the upper voice in the final part of the consequent phrase. We have already remarked that F (bar 6) is placed in the two-line octave as the climax of the phrase, and that it is conceptually an inner-voice tone superposed above the primary tone a^1. (Remember that in phrase 1, the inner-voice status of F is made clear through register: it occurs in the one-line octave, serving as the boundary of the voice exchange that prolongs tonic harmony.) Thus, when a rapid descent occurs from f^2 to $b\flat^1$ over IV, the motion paradoxically represents *descending* motion from an inner-voice pitch to one belonging to the structural upper voice of the phrase (compare levels *a* and *b*).

The circled notes in Example 7.11b, a^1–c^2–$b\flat^1$, are the tones of the original reaching-over motion in the first phrase (Example 7.10c). They recur in the voice leading of the second phrase, but are "covered" by the *y* motive and climactic motion to f^2. This point helps to clarify the larger relationship that exists between the primary tone A in bar 5 and its upper neighbor B♭ in bar 7.

We have observed several recurring patterns of tones, most notably the reaching-over motive A–C–B♭–A that unfolds in bar 1. This motive recurs in expanded form to shape bars 1–3, and is covered but still influential in the voice leading of the second phrase. These motivic interrelationships represent types of procedures composers often use—consciously or otherwise—to form the character and unity of a musical work. One important goal of analysis is to perceive the ways in which such individual features may give life to structural patterns that are shared by other pieces. Examples 7.10c and 7.11c, for instance, represent respectively the two branches of an interrupted *Urlinie* from $\hat{3}$, a structural pattern virtually identical to that illustrated in Example 7.7.

Our discussion of this passage will conclude with a beautiful facet of the final two bars that summarizes the primary motivic elements we have examined (Example 7.12).

Example 7.12 shows the beginning of the first phrase and the conclusion of the second, indicating the most significant motivic elements (remember that bars 1 and 5 are virtually identical). Note particularly the succession of tones in the upper voice in bar 7. The upper neighbor B♭ approaches the A,

EXAMPLE 7.12:

Beethoven, Piano Sonata, Op. 2, No. 1, II: motivic summary of first
and second phrases

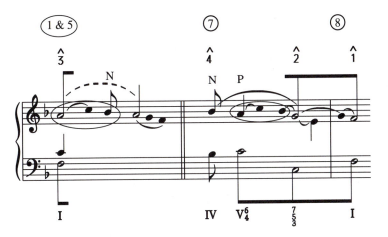

which is a passing tone (over the cadential $^6_4$) that occupies one full beat. The
usual voice-leading implication for the progression V^{6-5}_{4-3} is for the sixth of the
cadential $^6_4$ to progress to the fifth of dominant harmony. Beethoven, however,
delays this motion at the surface of the music with the leap to c^2 followed by
$b^{\flat 1}$, thereby recalling the upper voice in bars 1 and 5, the reaching-over motive we have observed at work in this phrase (even the turn is present!). Thus,
at the very moment closure is about to occur ($\hat{2}$–$\hat{1}$ over V–I), Beethoven in-
serts a motivic recollection that reminds us of one of the ways in which both
phrases began and were developed.

BEETHOVEN, PIANO SONATA, OP. 10, NO. 1, II, BARS 1–16

Example 7.13, from another slow movement by Beethoven, also illustrates an
interrupted fundamental structure. Its phrase structure, however, is somewhat
more complex than the previous passages that we have analyzed in this chapter. A preliminary examination of the phrase organization, one that considers
the broader harmonic structure, will help us to identify important intermediate goals and will enable us at a later time to make some observations about
the rhythmic organization of the phrase.

   The 16-bar passage divides into two eight-bar phrases, with each phrase
composed of two four-bar subphrases. These groupings result in part from
intermediate harmonic goals: dominant harmonies articulate the music in
bars 4, 8, and 12; tonic harmony concludes the passage (as part of a perfect
authentic cadence) in bar 16.

EXAMPLE 7.13:

Beethoven, Piano Sonata, Op. 10, No. 1, II, bars 1–16

Adagio molto

Another factor contributing to the way in which we hear the organization of groups of bars is the tempo: the piece is to be played very slowly. (Features such as tempo are fundamental to the character of the music, and should not be overlooked or considered secondary for analytical interpretation.) Thus the antecedent pair is articulated as a larger unit by the half cadence in bar 8; this cadence serves as the goal of the phrase and signals the interruption of the harmonic and melodic motions. The consequent phrase then "answers" in parallel fashion with the third and fourth subphrases as varied repetitions of the first and second, respectively. This time, however, completion and fulfillment are achieved. In other words, the expectations established in the first phrase are fulfilled in the second as the harmonic and melodic motions begin again and subsequently attain closure in the authentic cadence of bars 15–16.

Example 7.14 presents a voice-leading graph of the antecedent phrase (bars 1–8). Because we have now seen many examples of voice-leading graphs, the discussion will address in most detail those aspects of the music that introduce new techniques or are especially complex.[12]

Consider bars 1–4 in Examples 7.14a and b, and in particular the line A♭–B♭–C (filled in by the chromatic passing tones A♮ and B♮) over I–V–I. (As we have learned, such a stepwise line that ascends to the primary tone is called an *initial ascent.*) Note the resemblance between the openings of this phrase and the previous example by Beethoven (Example 7.9). Both employ virtually identical turn figures (both are cases of reaching over to an upper neighbor); even the letter names of the figures are identical. This is a good example of how similar details of the musical surface can acquire different meanings owing to the differences in the tonal contexts in which they appear. In Example 7.9, the reaching-over figure decorates $\hat{3}$ in F major; here, the same figure decorates $\hat{1}$ in A♭ major.

An additional point concerns the chord on the second beat of bar 3. While technically a tonic chord, it does not represent a return to tonic harmony. One clue to this interpretation lies in the upper voice. The "tonic" supports C, which is clearly an upper neighbor to the prolonged B♭; thus this chord is subordinate to the V_5^6 and V that fall on the downbeats of bars 3 and 4, respectively. In short, bars 1–2 express tonic harmony, and bars 3–4 dominant harmony; the chord on the second beat of bar 3 is an apparent tonic that occurs within prolonged dominant harmony. (A chord of this type is sometimes called a "false" tonic, because it occurs within the prolongation—that is, the harmonic space—of a different harmony.)

We see that Beethoven has composed groups of two bars in the opening of this phrase, which combine—on a different level of rhythmic structure—to form the larger groups of four and eight bars mentioned above. Notice also the resolution of V to I in bars 4–5. Beethoven fashions the broader harmonic motion so that the boundary of the prolonged tonic "cuts across" the end of one four-bar unit and the beginning of the second. This procedure unifies the subphrases and contributes to our overall impression of a larger, eight-bar antecedent phrase.

In the second subphrase (bars 5–8), the tonal motions become more complex. The upper voice becomes disjunct and wide ranging, reaching A♭ as a

EXAMPLE 7.14:

Beethoven, Piano Sonata, Op. 10, No. 1, II, bars 1–8: (a) foreground reduction; (b) and (c) middleground reductions

(a)

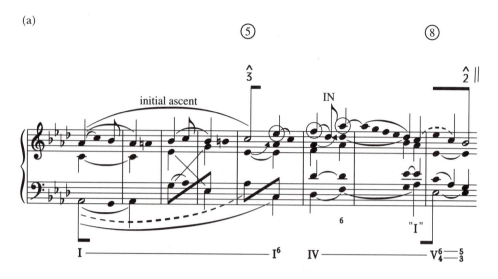

(b)

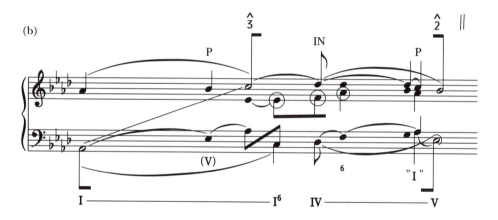

(c)

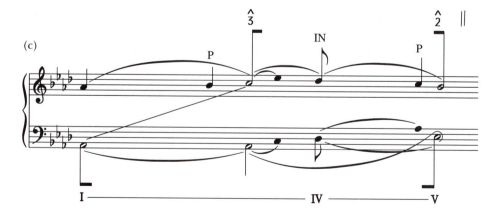

melodic goal in the higher two-line octave (accentuated by the *fp*) in the brief space of two bars. In light of the active top-voice motion in these bars, we might ask the following questions:

1. What are our reasons for understanding the C (3̂) on the downbeat of bar 5 as the primary tone?
2. Could E♭ on beat 2 of bar 5 possibly qualify as a structural 5̂?
3. Considering the disjunct, *rising* upper voice, how is it possible to perceive a deeper motion that leads the upper voice *down* from 3̂ to the 2̂ over V, the half cadence in bar 8?

That E♭ is the primary tone of the *Urlinie* seems an unlikely interpretation: it is in the midst of a motion that begins with C—firmly established by the initial ascent—and ends with high A♭. Note in the reduction that we have circled the tones E♭–F–A♭; comparing the reduction with the music you will see that Beethoven has composed the passage so that these tones are played as octaves in the right hand, enriching the texture. The right-hand doubling provides an important clue for the interpretation of the disjunct and initially rising upper voice.

The curved arrow in Example 7.14a (bar 5) indicates that, after the primary tone C is achieved through the initial ascent, E♭ from the inner voice of tonic harmony is superposed above the C. This superposed E♭ initiates a line in the two-line octave that belongs conceptually to an inner voice (we have seen inner-voice tones occurring above the "main" upper voice in previous examples). E♭ moves to F, which then leaps to the A♭ over the sustained IV chord (IV–IV⁶), in effect answering the first leap (C to E♭) that set this process in motion.

Example 7.14b clarifies the underlying structural relationship between the inner-voice tones just described (shown here in the alto register) and the upper-voice tones in the register above. Notice, for example, how clear and straightforward the alto line appears as represented in Example 7.14b; the circled notes—E♭–F–A♭—are precisely the circled notes in Example 7.14a, which retains the disjunct leaps and register transfer of the actual music.

Observe also in Example 7.14b a simpler, stepwise continuation from the C on the downbeat of bar 5, which supports our impression that C is the primary tone 3̂ of the fundamental line: C moves to D♭, which remains active in the voice leading through the second half of bar 7 (before it descends to B♭ at the cadence). The stepwise motion from C to D♭ has been elaborated or *covered* by the two superpositions, a technique that allows Beethoven to expand the musical space and content in a way that is musically richer and more complex than moving directly from C to D♭ in the upper voice.[13]

We can now see the remainder of the deeper stepwise line that leads to the half cadence in bar 8 and, consequently, the complete structural upper voice from bar 5: C–D♭–C–B♭.[14] Consider the C and the tonic chord on the last eighth of bar 7: does this C over A♭ represent a real return to the tonic, which would mean that D♭ is a *complete* upper neighbor? Locally, as the seventh of the V^6_5 chord, the D♭ does of course resolve to C. But evaluate the larger context. We have noted that the embedded upper neighbor D♭ is present in the voice leading for three and a half beats; notice also that the following C over I lasts for only one eighth (the weakest eighth of the bar). These observations support the interpretation of C as a passing tone between the D♭ and the B♭ at the cadence (Example 7.14c). Because the C to which it returns is not stable, the upper neighbor is incomplete (see Example 7.14b; "IN" means "incomplete neighbor"). What significance, therefore, does this interpretation have for the harmonic structure?

We have seen that motions between the primary harmonies of a phrase— in this instance, IV to V—may be composed out with a variety of intervening motions and chords. The relationships among the chords in this passage are illustrated in a series of stages in Example 7.15. Stage *a* shows the essential motion from the subdominant chord of bar 6 to the dominant chord of bar 8, expanded by the cadential six-four that occurs on the downbeat of the bar. In stage *b*, the soprano enters as a passing tone and is held over the bar as a suspension, creating a more active and varied line. In stage *c* the bass moves up a fifth to A♭, supporting and making consonant the soprano C: since the new bass tone A♭ was already present in the tenor as the fifth of the subdominant chord, this type of harmonic expansion is often described as a motion to the *upper fifth* of the previous chord. (That is, the fifth of the subdominant chord becomes the root of the tonic chord, creating a strong link between the two chords.) The tonic in bar 7 thus does not represent a structural return to

EXAMPLE 7.15:

Expansion of structural motion from IV to V

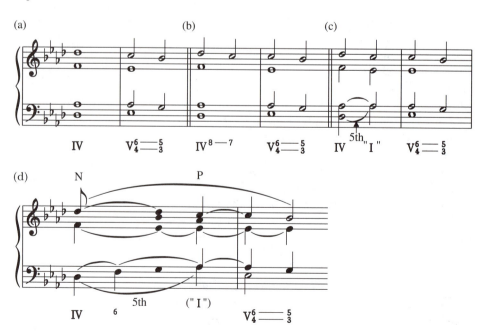

A♭ harmony (and a negation of the IV–V cadential motion), but serves instead as an expansion of subdominant harmony, much as dominant chords may frequently serve to expand and prolong tonics.

The final stage of elaboration (d) is similar to Example 7.14b: it includes the IV^6 in the second half of bar 6 which further expands subdominant harmony, and completes the arpeggiation of subdominant harmony in the bass line (D♭–F–A♭). Note that the melodic leap from F to A♭ in the bass line is filled in with G as the bass note of a V$^6_5$ chord. The resolution of this inverted dominant chord does not change the larger contextual meaning of the I as apparent tonic. The V$^6_5$ (arising from a passing tone in the bass) serves simply to create a more stepwise bass counterpoint, which rises in contrary motion to the descending upper voice. On a slightly higher level the upper note of this chord, D♭, can be understood as retained from the preceding subdominant harmony (compare Examples 7.14a and b with Example 7.15d).

In conjunction with our interpretation of the A♭ chord in bar 7 as an apparent tonic that expands the motion from IV to V, we interpret the C it supports on a comparable level of structure: as a passing tone that leads from the incomplete neighbor D♭ to B♭ (over IV–V). The interplay of levels involved in the incomplete neighbor-note figure is a fascinating aspect of the tonal system that appears in a variety of compositional styles.[15]

Except for some changes in figuration, bars 8–12 are essentially the same as bars 1–4. In closing, we will focus primarily on significant differences (re-composition) in the latter portion of the consequent phrase (Example 7.16).

Consider what appears to be an insignificant change by comparing bars 5–6 to bars 13–14. In the first phrase, we noted that Beethoven doubled the superposed tones in the right hand (the E♭ and F that cover the primary tone C and upper neighbor D♭). In the second phrase, Beethoven more clearly highlights the inner-voice status of these tones by composing them first as grace notes that precede the statements in the higher register. Another change has more far-reaching significance. Because Beethoven has composed the consequent phrase to achieve completion and to be equal in length to the antecedent, the intermediate subdominant cannot be prolonged for two bars as it was in the antecedent phrase. He abbreviates the subdominant to one bar, omitting the elaboration achieved in the first phrase by the arpeggiation to the upper third and fifth. As a result, the line in the upper voice rises only as far as high F before it reverses direction and descends toward $\hat{2}$–$\hat{1}$ at the cadence.

Subdominant harmony is transformed in bar 14, prior to the entrance of the dominant in bar 15. An embedded motion A♭–B♭ in the left-hand scale passage transforms the IV into a II^6 through the 5–6 contrapuntal technique (compare Examples 7.16a and b), a common procedure that is particularly frequent at cadences. Since the II^6 grows out of the IV chord, it is best to regard the entire motion IV–II^6 as an expanded expression of subdominant harmony. Thus the subdominant undergoes expansion, as in the antecedent phrase, but in a much more limited fashion.

A final point concerns the tones of figuration in the next to last bar, before $\hat{2}$ resolves to $\hat{1}$ over the structural cadence. We expect the C on the

EXAMPLE 7.16:

Beethoven, Piano Sonata, Op. 10, No. 1, II, bars 9–16: (a) foreground and (b) middleground reductions

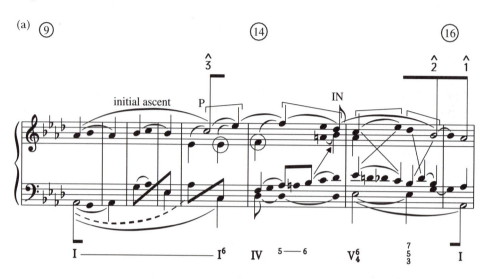

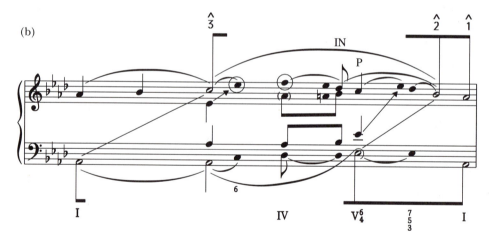

downbeat of bar 15 to descend to B♭; 3̂ moving to 2̂ would be the normal motion as the cadential six-four moves to the dominant seventh. However, composers very often decorate the upper voice at a cadence: here the underlying motion C to B♭ is decorated by the tones E♭ and D♭, tones superposed from the inner voice. As represented in Example 7.16b, the incomplete upper neighbor D♭ passes through C (over the cadential six-four) to B♭ (over the dominant seventh), a motion decorated with tones that recall the upper-voice motion in bar 1 (Example 7.17). As in the Adagio from Op. 2, No. 1 (Exam-

EXAMPLE 7.17:

Beethoven, Piano Sonata, Op. 10, No. 1, II, motivic detail

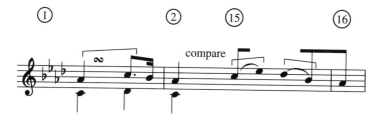

ple 7.12), Beethoven recalls important motivic detail from the beginning of the antecedent phrase as he brings the consequent phrase to a close.

MOZART, PIANO CONCERTO, K. 488, II, BARS 1–12

The beautiful and poignant opening of the second movement from Mozart's A-major Piano Concerto presents subtle complexities very different from the elaborations of fundamental structures that we have examined thus far (Example 7.18). In the previous three examples, we learned how the technique of interruption can divide a fundamental structure: the first branch leads from the tonic to $\hat{2}$ over V (typically a half cadence); the second branch begins again, retraces the path of the first, and achieves closure through a perfect authentic cadence ($\hat{1}$ over I). Such a combination of two harmonic motions (one leading to V, the other to I) does not *necessarily* create interruption, however. The structure of a composition may be articulated or divided into sections without actually being divided through interruption.[16] We will consider this point as we examine the details of this passage. Let us now turn to Example 7.19, which shows the harmonic and melodic framework of the four-bar antecedent phrase.[17]

The upper voice of this phrase is relatively angular and disjunct (Example 7.19a). A careful examination, however, will reveal three distinct lines above the bass. One is in the tenor and requires no further comment. The other two are intertwined in the right hand. To understand the structure of the top voice, it will again be helpful to "normalize" the registers of the intertwined lines, which will clearly reveal the continuity of associated pitches. This process can be observed by comparing Examples 7.19a and b.

These graphs show that the line in the higher register, A–G#–F# in bars 1–3 (see the circled notes) consists of superposed tones from the inner voice; the register transfer of the A and F# is associated with voice exchanges. The example also shows the primary stepwise line that occurs in the middle register, a motion from the primary tone C# ($\hat{5}$) over I to the E# over V at the

EXAMPLE 7.18:

Mozart, Piano Concerto, K. 488, II, bars 1–12

end of the phrase. Example 7.19b simplifies the voice leading and places the transferred inner-voice notes in the alto register. Note first how the initial tonic of the phrase is prolonged by a lower neighbor E♯ in the bass, which supports a neighbor chord. (The first sonority of bar 2 is a II$^4_2$; the A in the right hand is a suspension.) The harmonic structure of the phrase then follows a familiar bass-line pattern: an initial prolonged tonic leads to the half cadence through an intermediate II^6.

One note in the upper voice has not been accounted for in the interpretation of the two lines shown in Example 7.19a: d^2 in bar 3. In other words, D does not appear to have a voice-leading connection either with the upper-voice descent from C♯ to E♯, which forms the underlying continuity of the right hand, or with the inner-voice line A–G♯–F♯ that accompanies the upper voice in the prolongation of the initial tonic (Example 7.19a). As the reductions of Examples 7.19b and c indicate, d^2 is a part of another tone succession on a deeper level of structure. As the line from C♯ descends toward E♯ at the cadence, d^2 returns, recalling the upper neighbor established in the opening

EXAMPLE 7.19:

Mozart, Piano Concerto, K. 488, II, bars 1–4: (a) and (b) foreground reductions; (c) middleground reduction

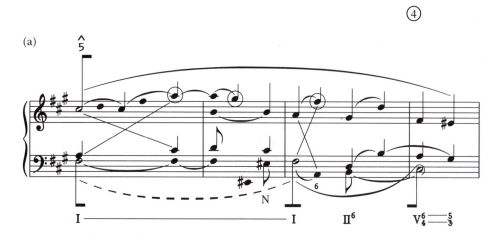

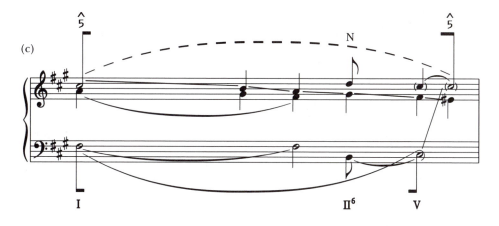

motive of the piece (C♯–D–C♯ on beat 1). Because Mozart has established this strong association between the primary tone C♯ and its upper neighbor, the recollection in bar 3 suggests a connection back to the opening C♯; thus, understood in the context of the complete phrase, the line from C♯ to E♯ represents a motion into an inner voice from a prolonged primary tone $\hat{5}$ (see Example 7.19c). The cadence, of course, literally concludes with E♯ in the upper voice. However, the voice leading at a deeper level implies a motion from D (over the II^6) to C♯ (over V, indicated in parentheses). The deeper

EXAMPLE 7.20:

Mozart, Piano Concerto, K. 488, II, bars 1–12: (a) foreground and (b) middleground reductions

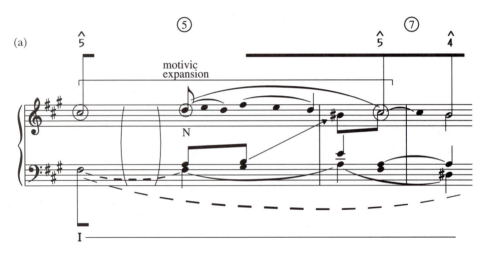

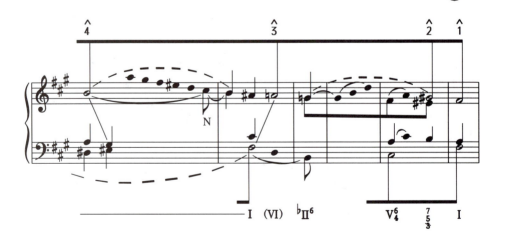

EXAMPLE 7.20 (*continued*)

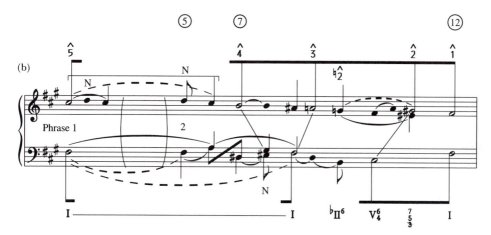

line C#–D–(C#) delineates the phrase and is an expanded motivic reference to the opening motive of the piece. This reading of the upper voice is also related to the consequent phrase, which we shall now consider (Example 7.20).[18]

Notice the different manner in which Mozart begins his consequent phrase: the phrase begins with the opening neighbor-note motion of the first phrase, but the motive is transposed a step higher to begin with D, rather than the primary tone C#. The D, however, returns almost immediately to C# in the next bar.[19] In this varied beginning of the second phrase, the D in the upper voice may be understood as a *displacement* of the expected C#. The inspiration for the displacement (another instance of recomposition) can be understood in terms of the motivic structure of the passage: the D in bar 5 is part of an enlarged expansion of the neighbor-note figure C#–D–C# in bar 1 (Example 7.20a). Since the beginnings of the two phrases are thus associated through a motivic connection over a longer span, the initial tonic and primary tone $\hat{5}$ may be understood as prolonged across the boundary of the antecedent phrase.

We can now understand why the structure is not divided through an interruption, even though two harmonic motions—the first leading to V, the other to I—define the phrase structure and articulate the passage. A comparison of Examples 7.19 and 7.20 reveals that the motivic process described above keeps the primary tone $\hat{5}$ active well into the second phrase, before the *Urlinie* begins to descend in the consequent phrase. The motive C#–D–C#, which first occurs in bar 1, shapes the upper voice in expanded form in bars 1–4 (Example 7.19c), and then recurs in an even more greatly enlarged form across the phrase boundary as we have seen (Example 7.20a); Example 7.21 presents a synopsis of this motivic procedure.[20] Because the C# is prolonged and the

EXAMPLE 7.21:

Mozart, Piano Concerto, K. 488, II, bars 1–6: middleground reduction

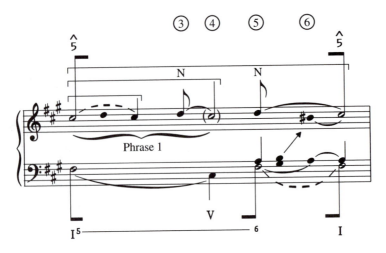

Urlinie is therefore undivided, the structure is correspondingly undivided. The dominant in bar 4, though not divisive for the structure, nonetheless articulates this span of music into an antecedent/consequent pair.

We shall now consider the larger structure of the second phrase. Referring back to Example 7.20b, we see how Mozart leads the upper voice from the primary tone C# through B to A# and then to A♮ in bar 8. Notice that A# appears over the tonic in bar 8: this tone, which, of course, is not diatonic in F# minor, is a chromatic passing tone connecting B with A♮. Because $\hat{4}$ is initially suspended over I (bar 8), the surface line is rhythmically displaced and the A♮ appears *after* the bass has moved from the I to VI. In Example 7.20a and b we show (with a connecting line) that A♮, the real $\hat{3}$ of the *Urlinie,* belongs conceptually over the tonic, which we regard as the boundary of a larger tonic prolongation. In bar 9, the *Urlinie* finally arrives at $\hat{2}$ over the intermediate harmony of the structure. The form of $\hat{2}$, however, is the *Phrygian* or *flat* $\hat{2}$, which we introduced in Chapter 6.

The Neapolitan sixth chord frequently occurs as a chromatically altered intermediate harmony in the tonal language. However, the flat $\hat{2}$ that often appears in the upper voice is a transformation of natural $\hat{2}$ and does not function as the second step of the fundamental line. The reason is that the *Urlinie* is a melodic expression within the diatonic system. In composition, the lowered $\hat{2}$ is normally "corrected" in some fashion to natural $\hat{2}$ at the cadence. Mozart's consequent phrase shows one important possibility (Example 7.20b). The lowered $\hat{2}$ moves into an inner voice, to $\hat{7}$ over V; natural $\hat{2}$ simultaneously covers this motion and appears in the upper voice over the cadential dominant. In other words, both forms of $\hat{2}$ appear in the upper voice. In a later chapter we will discuss another situation in which the inflection occurs in a more indirect manner in two different voices.

MENDELSSOHN, SONG WITHOUT WORDS, OP. 85, NO. 1, BARS 1–17

In our previous examples we have examined fairly brief passages that resemble complete *Ursatz* patterns, that is, tonal structures in which the main upper-voice line and bass arpeggiation unfold completely and attain closure: Î over I. Such passages are often referred to as *Ursatz parallelisms*, because they represent in microcosm the structure of entire pieces. Indeed, they may be considered small-scale "reflections" of *Ursatz* patterns, and in them we have become acquainted with many of Schenker's essential ideas about tonal structure.

Not all small-scale passages, of course, resemble complete fundamental structures with melodic and harmonic closure. Spans of music may also be "open-ended": in other words, they may modulate, end on half or tonicized half cadences, or conclude in any number of ways that do not involve a concluding tonic. Closure will then occur later in the piece, possibly in the next phrase or section, and possibly (depending on the level of structure that is involved) only in the tonic that concludes the composition. The next example prepares us for the analysis of full-scale compositions in subsequent chapters, for its tonal structure is complete at only one level of musical development; in a larger sense the structure remains open and in need of continuation and ultimate conclusion. Example 7.22 presents bars 1–17 from Mendelssohn's F-major *Song Without Words*; Example 7.23 shows a corresponding voice-leading graph of the two phrases, which comprise an antecedent/consequent pair.

As a first step, begin to trace the path of the upper-voice line from C that lies just beneath the surface of the music. The line clearly moves through B♭ in bar 4 to A in bar 5, which is sustained across the bar as the harmonic progression moves from I to VI. Thus far, the upper voice has apparently moved 5̂–4̂–3̂. However, we have seen that not all descents from the primary tone indicate the path of the *Urlinie*. Here, we do not read the motion 5̂–4̂–3̂ in bars 2–5 as part of the fundamental line, but as motion into an inner voice.

One reason for this interpretation is that we regard the primary tone C as being recalled on the second beat of bar 8. In other words, the upper voice has made an "attempt" to descend, but the sixteenth-note C over the intermediate harmony signals that the primary tone 5̂ has been kept active at a deeper level by the lower-level motion C–B♭–A in bars 2–5.[21] In the graph we show the return of C in bar 8 as a (conceptually) suspended tone, a 9–8 suspension that resolves to B♭ over the intermediate harmony of the bass progression. The 4̂–3̂–2̂ descends very quickly, over the cadence in bars 8–9. In general, in lines from 5̂, intermediate harmonies tend to provide the strongest support for scale degree 4̂.[22]

The dominant in bar 9 (supporting 2̂) articulates this 17-bar passage into two phrases; furthermore, after the dominant, the second phrase begins like the first. However a compositional process occurs in the consequent phrase that is very different from the examples we have seen previously in this chapter. Because its opening bars are almost identical to bars 2–5 of the anteced-

EXAMPLE 7.22:

Mendelssohn, *Song Without Words,* Op. 85, No. 1, bars 1–17

EXAMPLE 7.22 (*continued*)

EXAMPLE 7.23:

Mendelssohn, *Song Without Words,* Op. 85, No. 1, foreground reductions: (a) bars 1–9; (b) bars 10–17

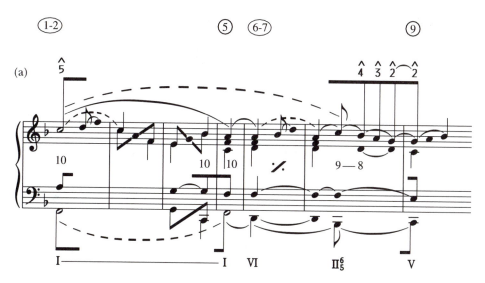

EXAMPLE 7.23 (*continued*)

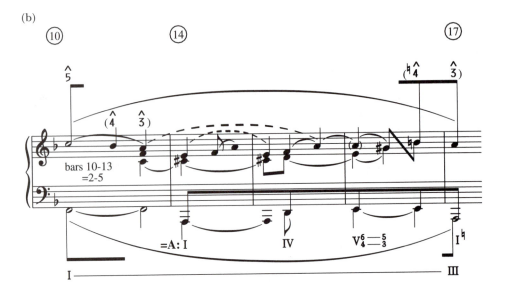

ent, our discussion focuses on the final four bars of the passage (Example 7.23b).[23]

A brief examination reveals that the final four bars modulate. In bars 16–17 a strong perfect authentic cadence in the mediant key area (A minor) establishes a distinct formal section in the piece. Now consider the path of the right-hand melody. An initial motion leads from c^2 to a^1, paralleling the similar descent in the first phrase. From this point, the tone e^1 is prolonged with f as a neighbor tone (compare bars 14–15 with bars 6–7) before a^1 is recalled, which leads to B♮ through a reaching-over figure (Example 7.23b).[24] As the example illustrates, we interpret b^1–a^1 in the upper voice of the cadence (bars 16–17) as tones residing at a deeper level; they relate back to the primary tone c^2 at the beginning of the phrase. Therefore, the graph indicates two descents from the primary tone c^2: the first, C–B♭–A in bars 10–13, is motion into an inner voice (a^1 is conceptually retained through bar 16); the second, C–B♮–A, spans the entire phrase. This last observation means that the structure remains "open," incomplete, and in need of continuation.

Thus, in Example 7.24 we have depicted the second $\hat{5}$ with two beams. The first indicates the larger third-progression C–B♮–A that spans the second phrase. The second beam is left open and is placed higher than the first; it points ahead to the $\hat{4}$–$\hat{3}$–$\hat{2}$–$\hat{1}$ of the *Urlinie* that will eventually emerge as the composition moves toward its conclusion.

Two additional points should be mentioned before we begin to examine entire compositions. First, we have observed that the tonicized mediant in bars 16–17 is a local or secondary goal in the larger motion from the tonic to the structural dominant, which occurs later in the piece. One frequent means through which composers create musical content and form on a larger

EXAMPLE 7.24:

Mendelssohn, *Song Without Words,* Op. 85, No. 1, bars 1–17: middleground reduction

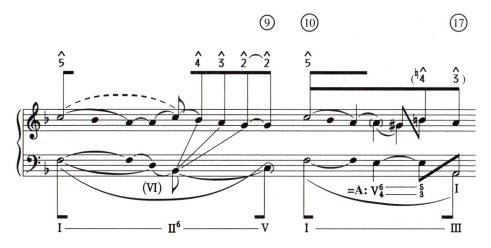

scale—beyond a small group of phrases—is through modulation, the tonicization of secondary key areas that expand the "tonal space" from tonic to dominant.

Second, the discussion in this chapter has been limited to the small number of phrases in each excerpt. Because the broad outer-voice structure in these excerpts achieved closure (except for that in the last example), we were able to explore some elaborations of fundamental structures in very clear and concise contexts. The processes of musical development, of course, continue in these pieces; we have examined only beginnings. For a broader perspective, we need to ascertain the structure of higher levels and, ultimately, of an entire composition.

SOME POINTS FOR REVIEW

We have begun to discover some basic ways in which fundamental structures may be elaborated. For now we have used the term *fundamental structure* in a restricted sense, in the context of a limited number of phrases; ultimately, of course, the term will apply to the structure of entire pieces. But these lower-level replications of fundamental structures, *Ursatz* parallelisms, are revealing for us at this stage because, over a limited span, they exhibit all of the properties of an *Ursatz*. In other words, the techniques of prolonged harmony and counterpoint work in comparable ways at all levels. We will come to understand this characteristic of the tonal system more fully as we examine extended compositions.

We have also seen the most fundamental elaboration of an *Ursatz:* a tonal structure divided through interruption. This procedure causes the "singular"

Ursatz to be expressed in two parts or branches: in the first branch, the tonal motion leads toward V and is interrupted, at $\hat{2}$ over V. The motion begins again at the beginning of the second branch, with the resumption of the primary tone and tonic harmony, and finally achieves closure (completion) at the structural cadence (V-I). Bear in mind that the *entire second branch* resolves the harmonic and melodic instability created by the interruption at $\hat{2}$ over V at the end of the first branch. We saw also (in Mozart's piano concerto) how a structure may exist in two parts even though it is not, strictly speaking, divided through interruption. This means that other procedures bring about the impression of formal divisions; we will see comparable procedures when we examine larger, multisectional forms.

In our final example, the opening bars from a Mendelssohn *Song Without Words,* we saw a passage that did not achieve closure. Subsequent music will complete the motion begun in such passages. In the remaining parts of this book we will see how composers created larger tonal structures by continuing from beginnings that are both "open" and "closed."

Through examination of these excerpts we have considered many essential issues of Schenker's conception of tonal structure and some of the compositional techniques that create breadth and variety in a fundamental structure. We have also begun to recognize that some features of a composition are shared by many pieces, while other characteristics are unique to the piece under consideration. Although it reveals many commonalities among pieces in the tonal repertory, the first concern of analysis is the individuality of a musical creation. We shall now examine complete pieces, to discover how the principles of harmony and counterpoint interact at different levels, and how formal patterns emerge through the articulation at different levels of fundamental structures.

Exercises

Evaluate these passages in a manner similar to the approach used in this chapter. Before you begin your work, review the techniques discussed in Chapter 6, including *initial ascent, superposition, substitution,* and so forth. Then consider the questions listed below.

There is no single correct way to approach a piece of music. You may find that it is best to obtain first a broad overview of the bass-line structure; on the other hand, a study of the upper voice may prove to be the best point of departure. The composition itself often suggests the best place to begin.

a. Examine the contour of the upper voice: is there a tone (or tones) serving as a high point or *climax?* Is one of the tones of the tonic triad a focal point? Is there a descent to the tonic at the cadence, and if so, how is it related to the rest of the melody?

b. How long does initial tonic harmony last (assuming that the passage begins with tonic harmony)? After you discover where the bass-line motion begins to move away from initial tonic harmony, consider the possibility of an intermediate harmony that leads to V (either as a half cadence or part of an authentic cadence).

c. Construct a rough sketch, coordinating your evaluation of the bass-line structure with that of the upper voice. At this stage, coincidence of the components of the outer-voice framework is important.

d. Now consider the surface details (for both upper and lower voices) that give life to the tonal "skeleton" you have found in your preliminary analysis. Do any tone successions become motivic? That is, are they repeated in literal or varied form? At this time you should be considering all voices; motivic details (and sometimes structural elements) are not restricted to the outer voices.

e. Does the passage employ an interruption? What kinds of recompositions become necessary when the technique of interruption divides a tonal structure? (Think here in terms of the cadences involved in antecedent/consequent pairs of phrases.) Be alert for recompositions of all kinds—particularly in repeated phrases—whether or not they are related to the technique of interruption.

f. Create a final graph consisting of at least two levels. One level should show the *middleground* structure, the essential elaboration of the fundamental structure. The other *foreground* level should show as much detail as is necessary to highlight motivic associations and, in particular, the connections and prolongations that *led* you to your deeper, middleground interpretation. When in doubt, refer to the examples in this chapter.

1. Mozart, Piano Sonata, K. 333, III, bars 1–16
2. Mozart, Piano Concerto, K. 467, second theme, bars 128–143
3. Mozart, Rondo in D major, K. 485, bars 1–16
4. Haydn, Symphony No. 104, Hob. I: 104, II, bars 1–8
5. Schubert, *Schwanengesang,* No. 12, "Am Meer," bars 1–11
6. Mozart, Piano Sonata, K. 333, I, bars 1–10
7. Chopin, Nocturne in F minor, Op. 55, No. 1, bars 1–16
8. Mendelssohn, *Song Without Words,* Op. 30, No. 3, bars 3–11
9. Chopin, Prelude in D♭ major, Op. 28, No. 15, bars 1–8
10. Beethoven, Piano Sonata, Op. 31, No. 1, II, bars 1–8
11. Chopin, Nocturne in B major, Op. 32, No. 1, bars 1–8
12. Mozart, Piano Concerto, K. 453, I, bars 1–16

PART

2

Analytical Applications

In Part II we shall focus on complete compositions. Because of the greater length of the examples, discussion of the graphs will emphasize the higher levels of structure, but without neglecting the more important or unusual aspects of the foreground.

We also introduce some conventions not used in Part I. In Chapters 5–7 we discuss only excerpts or short passages and indicate the tones of the "main" line with numerals and the circumflex sign (ˆ). In other words, we often indicate an *Urlinie* of a self-contained segment. Because Schenker in his later writings used the term *Urlinie* for the structural line of an entire composition (see our discussion at the conclusion of Chapter 5), we will use **boldface** in Part II to highlight those tones that belong to the *Urlinie* of a complete piece or tones associated with the highest-level line, such as first-level neighbor notes (**3̂–4̂–3̂** and **5̂–6̂–5̂**). We also use boldface for the tones of both the first and second branches of a divided fundamental structure at the *first level of the middleground*. As we discuss below, we regard the individual branches as essentially representing a singular *Ursatz* pattern.

Numerals not set in boldface, therefore, indicate upper-voice tones of lines at lower levels. In a line shown as $\hat{5}$–$\hat{4}$–$\hat{3}$, for example, the $\hat{5}$ is higher ranking; its continuation to a structural $\hat{4}$ will occur later in the piece. The initial $\hat{4}$–$\hat{3}$ motion prolongs the $\hat{5}$ and unfolds on a lower level (motion into an inner voice). In the examples we place the tones of lower-level lines in *parentheses*. This approach should help you to distinguish visually among structural levels as you read the discussion of the following analyses.

As Schenker's ideas about the structure of tonal music developed, he began to realize that the recognition of form and design by itself provided an inadequate view of a piece. In *Free Composition,* Schenker appears to adopt the extreme position that certain aspects of traditional formal analysis might, in fact, be a misleading way of exploring tonal compositions.[1] For this reason he included a chapter on form in *Free Composition,* which he calls an "Essay on a New Theory of Form," the intent of which is to "derive the forms from the background and middleground."[2] Thus Schenker desired to integrate the dimension of form with his newly developed principles of tonal structure—in essence, to provide a theory of form with a broader foundation.

Schenkerian scholars now recognize that Chapter 5 of *Free Composition* is an interesting but incomplete attempt at such an integration. This recognition has led to research on form from a Schenkerian perspective, which might be considered a continuation of work that Schenker only initiated.[3]

Form may be defined as the articulation of a piece into sections of various dimensions and the relation of these sections to each other and to the whole (based partly on repetition, contrast, and variation). In general terms, structure and design are the two largest articulative forces in producing form. As we shall see in the following chapters of this book, however, prolongations and other aspects of structure do not always coincide with formal boundaries.

One question that arises from recent scholarship, therefore, is whether a true integration of musical form (as conventionally conceived) and tonal structure is either necessary or possible. These are certainly two interrelated domains of tonal compositions, but is it necessary to define one in terms of the other?

Some scholars indeed believe that such a goal is attainable. In this book, however, the primary purpose of which is to introduce and explain Schenker's principles of tonal structure, we have adopted the following position: design, tonal structure, and musical form are discrete but interrelated dimensions of tonal compositions. Though each has its own life and characteristics, these domains are unified in a common ground of tonal principles. We will not attempt to elaborate this common ground systematically; such work is ongoing in the field of music theory and lies outside the scope of a textbook. Instead, we will illustrate informally some ways in which form relates to tonal structure, but not necessarily how it derives from it (or vice versa).

The remainder of this book is organized by formal classifications commonly accepted in music pedagogy. We begin with one-part forms in Chapter 8, proceed through binary and ternary forms, and finally conclude with the sonata principle in Chapter 11 (Chapter 12 is devoted to theoretical issues). The forms themselves, therefore, are accepted in conventional ways and serve as a means of organization by which longer and more complex tonal structures (in the Schenkerian sense) may be elaborated. In the remainder of this book we shall examine in detail some of the relationships between form and structure.

One-Part Forms

In Schenkerian terminology, a *one-part form* is usually a structure that has no high-ranking internal division (such as that produced by an interruption). Normally this term is used to describe a complete composition, but it can also be used in relation to an independent section.[1]

BACH, PRELUDE IN C MAJOR (WTC I)

Our first example of one-part form is Bach's well-known Prelude in C major from the first book of his *Well-Tempered Clavier.* We explored aspects of the bass line and harmonic structure of this prelude in Chapter 3; now we shall consider the complete work.

Compare Example 8.1 with the score of Bach's Prelude and, particularly, with Example 3.15. The arpeggiated figuration of the music has been consolidated into block chords in the graph, revealing a consistent rate of harmonic change (or *harmonic rhythm*). Because the music is fairly uniform in texture, articulation, and rhythm, the form is primarily established by the harmonic and voice-leading structure. (However, since the design is relatively consistent, any changes that do occur take on particular importance.)

In bars 1–4 the tonic is established (and prolonged) with a progression of remarkable simplicity, economy, and beauty ($I–II_2^4–V_5^6–I$). Only common tones or stepwise (neighbor) motion occur between the tonic chords that frame the progression in bars 1 and 4.

Although the tonic note continues in the bass in bars 5 and 6, tonic harmony is destabilized by the 5–6 motion and by the leap to A in the top voice of bar 5 (see Example 8.1). This ascending fourth is an especially dynamic

EXAMPLE 8.1:

J. S. Bach, Prelude in C major (*WTC* I) (sketch after Schenker, *Five Graphic Music Analyses*)

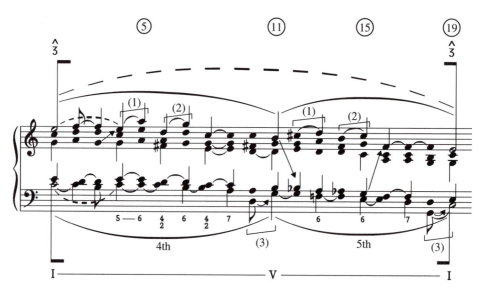

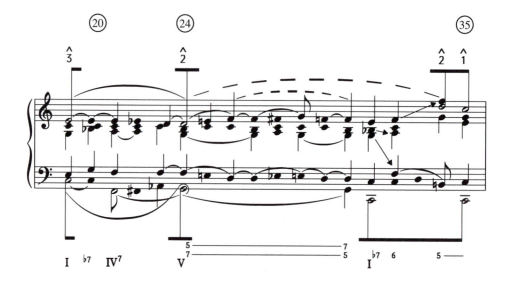

gesture in the context of the passage, since it is the first melodic leap that has occurred. A $^4_2$ chord follows in bar 6, establishing a sequential pattern that leads to the tonicized dominant in bar 11; a similar but more chromatic sequence leads to a return to the tonic in bar 19.

As shown in Example 8.1, the overall motion in bars 1–19 is an octave descent in both bass and top voice. The bass descends essentially in stepwise motion; the leaps in bars 10–11 and 18–19 are cadential patterns that highlight V and I as important goals in the progression, but do not fundamentally alter its linear character. The descent of the top voice is somewhat more elaborate. Following the prolongation of e^2 (bars 1–4), the leap of an ascending fourth in bars 4–5 is echoed in bars 6–7. In the segment defined by the motion from V to I (bars 11–19), the top voice continues its descent to f^1 and then to e^1, an octave below the starting note e^2. However, a complete linear descent fills in the melodic space between b^1 and f^1 (bars 12–15), a motion intensified by the chromatic passing tones of the diminished seventh chords. Note that this line begins in the upper voice but is transferred to the tenor (see the arrows in Example 8.1).[2] Overall, therefore, the structural top voice descends an octave from e^2 to e^1, and, like the bass, is essentially stepwise in character.

The underlying outer-voice structure of bars 1–19, as shown in Example 8.2a, consists of descending parallel tenths between the outer voices (spanning an octave) that unfold within a large-scale prolongation of tonic har-

EXAMPLE 8.2:

J. S. Bach, Prelude in C major (*WTC* I), structural analyses of bars 1–19

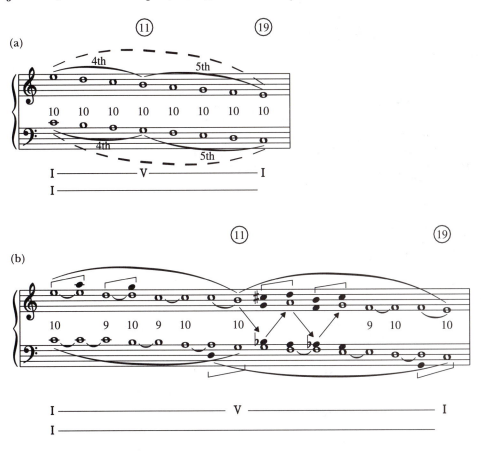

mony; Example 8.2b shows how this series of tenths is further elaborated. As indicated by slurs, the arrival on V in bar 11 subdivides the octave descent into a fourth and a fifth (compare to Example 8.1).

In progressions of parallel tenths or sixths, Schenker believed that one voice typically "leads" while the other "follows." The leading voice will be that whose structure is more intimately linked to the harmony being prolonged. In this case it is the bass that leads because its structural course, C–G–C (the roots of the I–V–I progression), outlines the larger tonic harmony embracing the entire passage, whereas the soprano's parallel E–B–E does not. Thus Schenker says of this passage: "We must consider the bass as the leading voice since it is subdivided at *g*. The upper voice e^2–e^1 does prolong the primary tone of the fundamental line, but we cannot assume a [structural] subdivision at b^1 since this tone is foreign to the *C* harmony."[3]

We have seen that the dominant chord of bar 11 is an interim goal within the extended tonic prolongation of bars 1–19. Following this prolongation, a brief but extraordinary passage leads to the structural dominant, which is established in bar 24. To understand the complex harmonic structure of bars 19–24, compare the stages shown in Example 8.3 with Example 8.1 and the music itself. Example 8.3a shows a characteristic diatonic progression, IV^7–V. The intervening chord (II^6_5) expands the intermediate subdominant seventh chord; furthermore, the motion E to D in the upper voice anticipates the soprano of the dominant (D) and breaks up the parallel fifths that would otherwise occur in the motion IV^7–V.[4] In Example 8.3b, A♭ is added to the tenor as a chromatic passing tone, changing the quality of the II^6_5 chord to half diminished. In the third stage the intervening chord is shifted to $^4_3$ position, so that A♭ occurs in the bass as an upper neighbor to G.

The final stage (Example 8.3d) represents bars 21–24 as they actually occur in the music. A new chord has been introduced, shown in parentheses: a diminished seventh chord is interpolated between the subdominant and supertonic seventh chords (see bar 22 in the score). This chord functions both as a passing chord and as an applied VII^{o7} of V, for its bass note F♯

EXAMPLE 8.3:

J. S. Bach, Prelude in C major (*WTC* I): motion from IV^7 to V

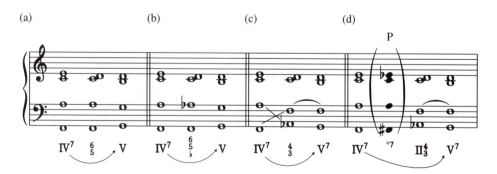

passes from F to G and serves as a leading tone to V. Thus, both the diminished seventh and II$_3^4$ chords serve as interpolations between IV^7 and V, each having its own direct relationship to the dominant. This astonishing progression has baffled more than a few musicians; in fact, many nineteenth-century editors followed the example of one Christian Schwenke (1767–1822), who inserted an extra chord that Bach never wrote, a $^6_4$ (G–C–E♭) following the diminished seventh chord. This anomaly is still perpetuated in some editions today.[5]

Thus, in the span of only four bars (including the altered I chord in bar 20 that functions locally as an applied dominant to IV^7) Bach achieves an exceptionally striking progression to the dominant. Probably the most expressive moment occurs in bars 23–24, where the intense dissonance of bar 23 (notice that B, C, and D sound simultaneously in the figuration!) finds resolution in the dominant seventh chord of bar 24.

During the prolongation of dominant harmony that follows, the top voice, which has reached d^1 (structural $\hat{2}$), begins to climb upward again, supported by a series of contrapuntal chords over the bass pedal tone (Example 8.1). In a voice exchange with the tenor, the upper voice leads first to f^1, the seventh of V^7, which is then decorated with a motion to its upper neighbor, g^1, before the line regains the seventh, f^1, in bar 31. Dominant harmony finally resolves to the tonic in bar 32, but in a way that does not produce closure, for the chord of resolution contains a B♭. Thus, the expected tonic chord is destabilized (compare with bars 5 and 20): the altered tonic, functioning also as V^7 of IV, resolves to a subdominant chord (over the tonic pedal) and initiates a cadential extension (bars 32–35).[6] This extension avoids the stability that an immediate tonic triad would have created and maintains harmonic and contrapuntal tension until the final bar of the piece.

In bars 33 and 34 the regular arpeggiated pattern gives way to a freer type of figuration not unlike an improvisatory passage in a cadenza. The right hand first descends into the left-hand register in bar 33, then regains its opening register in bar 34, reaching f^2 (a superposed inner-voice tone) before structural closure occurs with the motion $\hat{2}$–$\hat{1}$ (d^2-c^2). Example 8.4 illustrates a remarkable feature of this work: embedded in the figuration of the last four bars is a recomposition of the upper neighbor figure from bars 1–4 (E–F–F–E). In effect, the cadential extension is a disguised repetition of the opening; together these motions serve as a frame for the composition.

Another aspect of the prelude's structure is illustrated in Example 8.5a. As we saw in Example 8.1, the top voice descends from e^2 to e^1 over the span of the initial tonic prolongation. During the remainder of the piece, a corresponding motion rises from d^1 to d^2. The stages in Example 8.5c show more precisely how structural $\hat{2}$ is transferred from the one-line to the two-line octave.[7]

These complementary ascending and descending motions represent the technique of *coupling*, discussed in Chapter 6. The motions between the coupled registers, and the various ways in which those motions are expanded and varied, are essential features of the composition.[8] The coupling takes place on the first level of the middleground (Example 8.5a). The background,

EXAMPLE 8.4:

J. S. Bach, Prelude in C major (*WTC* I), comparison of bars 1–4 and 32–35

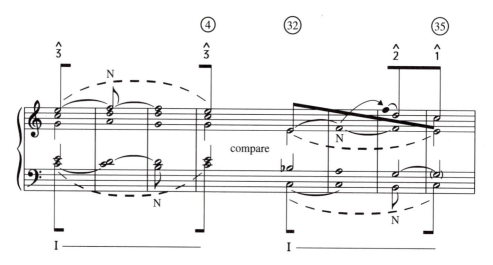

EXAMPLE 8.5:

J. S. Bach, Prelude in C major (*WTC* I): (a) middleground and (b) background reductions; (c) octave transfer of $\hat{2}$

EXAMPLE 8.5 (*continued*)

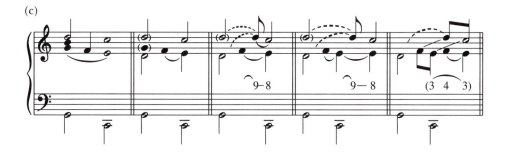

shown in Example 8.5b, consists of the top-voice descent in the principal, or *obligatory*, register. (Schenker's concept of obligatory register will be discussed more fully in a later example.) Because the descent is undivided (even though elaborated through coupling), the work may be said to be in one-part form. The consistency of the figuration and lack of marked internal divisions strongly reinforce this conception of the form.

Now that we have completed the discussion of our first complete piece, a few comments about the "direction" of analysis warrant reflection. You can see that we have proceeded from lower to higher levels, eventually arriving at the background level shown in Example 8.5b. This is only one aspect of Schenker's approach however. Much can be gained from viewing the piece the other way. Thus, one can trace the analysis from *background to foreground,* understanding each successive and more elaborate lower level as an *outgrowth* of the preceding higher level. In this way one can fully appreciate how a composition represents a unique and diverse elaboration of tonal structure.

SCHUBERT, "WANDRERS NACHTLIED"

Our next example is a song composed by Schubert to a text by Goethe, "Wandrers Nachtlied" ("Wanderer's Night Song"), Op. 96, No. 3. Any analysis of a vocal work should begin by considering the text—not only its meaning but also its mood, style, and structure. And, as we shall see, many aspects of the music reflect the spirit of the poem.

The text of Goethe's poem and a translation are given below:

> *Über allen Gipfeln*
> *Ist Ruh,*
> *In allen Wipfeln*
> *Spürest du*
> *Kaum einen Hauch;*

Die Vöglein schweigen im Walde.
Warte nur, balde
Ruhest du auch.

Over all the mountain peaks
is peace,
in all the tree tops
you feel
hardly a breath;
the birds are silent in the forest.
Only wait, soon
You too shall rest.[9]

The general mood of the poem is pastoral, even idyllic. Yet another, deeper (and more somber) level of meaning pervades its character. The description of the air's stillness, "in all the tree tops you feel hardly a breath," and the reference to the silence of the birds invoke a picture of a silent moment that seems to stretch into eternity. And the closing words "only wait, soon you too shall rest" are not a mere promise of physical rest for a weary traveler, but a premonition of death. Yet death, in this context, has nothing sinister or gloomy about it. It is a promise of peace, an end to "wandering" and a union with the peace and beauty of Nature that the Wanderer (who is Everyman) envisions at the start of the poem. Thus the song is religious in a pantheistic, nonsectarian way.

This kind of dramatic contrast between two different levels of meaning— a picturesque depiction of a peaceful night in the forest, and a depiction of death—is characteristic of many German Romantic poems written during the late eighteenth and early nineteenth centuries. In his songs Schubert portrayed such layers of apparently contradictory meanings in musical terms with extraordinary skill. We should also note the striking metrical freedom of Goethe's poem. He did not write it in conventional lines of equal length, but in free verse. Schubert also captures this aspect of the poem in his through-composed setting with its sensitively balanced phrases of unequal length.

The piano introduction in bars 1–2, though short, establishes the mood and character of the song. As shown at the beginning of Example 8.6, it embraces a local, self-contained structure in B♭ major (an *Ursatz* parallelism); its upper voice descends D–C–B♭ ($\hat{3}$–$\hat{2}$–$\hat{1}$), foreshadowing the *Urlinie* of the entire song. (The scale degree numbers are given in parentheses in the graph to show that the *Urlinie* of the complete song is anticipated at a lower level in the introduction.) It might seem appropriate to regard the primary tone $\hat{3}$ (D) as already fully established in the piano introduction (bar 1). To do so, however, would overlook the broader role of the introduction in the song. An introduction precedes, and prepares for, the main body of a work. When the vocal part enters, it sounds like a beginning in psychological and artistic terms, since in performance the singer is seen as the "protagonist" by the audience. Hence, from a structural perspective, it is generally appropriate to associate the entrance of the vocal part with the true beginning of musical development.

A second, related issue concerns the interpretation of the structural top voice. Why does the graph show B♭ as the main note in bar 3, when the piano

EXAMPLE 8.6:

Schubert, "Wandrers Nachtlied," Op. 96, No. 3: (a) foreground reduction; (b) and (c) middleground reductions

EXAMPLE 8.6 (*continued*)

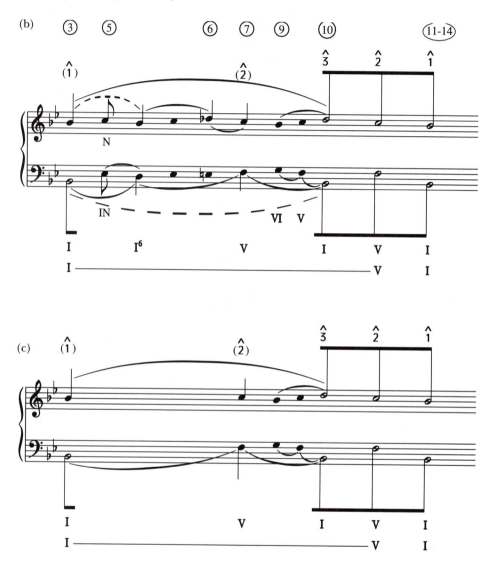

part has apparently established D ($\hat{3}$)? Here the answer is similar: all other things being equal, we generally perceive the vocal line as the leading (upper) voice in a song even if it is lower in register than some notes in the accompaniment. Imagine "Wandrers Nachtlied" performed first by a soprano, then by a tenor: would the lower range of the male voice make the vocal part sound less like the leading melodic line? Certainly not.

Having considered the structural relationship between the piano and vocal parts in the song, we will now focus on its internal shape and articulations. In Bach's C-major Prelude, the one-part form is expressed and patterned through a series of middleground prolongations and motions—the initial tonic prolongation, the motion to the dominant, the dominant prolongation, and the final tonic prolongation. Each section has its own structural character. Similarly, bars 3–11 of "Wandrers Nachtlied" comprise several groups of measures that unite to form a larger, essentially continuous musical idea or structure.

The first integral passage after the introduction (bars 3–6) contains two such groups of measures. The first is the tonic prolongation in bars 3–5, where B♭ is prolonged and elaborated with two versions of the upper neighbor figure B♭–C–B♭. Notice that the first version (bar 3) in particular sounds like an echo of the D–E♭–D motive from the right hand of the introduction; the neighbor C initiates a descending third-motion into an inner voice before resolving across the bar to B♭ (see the Ns in Example 8.6). In bar 4, the upper voice reaches higher, but falls back to B♭ in bar 5 through the second statement of the upper neighbor C.[10]

Turning to the harmonic structure, we see the tonic prolonged with a motion from I to I^6. The bass tones B♭–D are expressed, not as an ascending third, but as a descending sixth. (Compare this passage in Example 8.6a with the reduction in Example 8.6b.) The descending sixth is in turn partly filled in with a combination of arpeggiated and stepwise motion. (Like the corresponding statement of C in the upper voice, the bass tone E♭ in bar 5 functions as a neighbor note at a slightly deeper level of structure than the c^2 in bar 3; compare Examples 8.6a and 8.6b.)

So far the stable harmonic structure, balanced and consistent texture, and steady rhythm seem to portray the pastoral mood of the text. But in bars 5–6, as the harmonies slowly progress from I^6 to V, we sense a change in character: the mood becomes more somber, reflecting the pensive and solemn aspects of the poem. This quality is created by the modal mixture and chromaticism that begins in bar 5 with the introduction of G♭, the lowered sixth scale degree from the parallel minor mode. The modal mixture continues through bar 5 and into bar 6, where D♭ (the third scale degree of B♭ minor) appears as the seventh of VII^{o7} of V.[11]

Some of the chromaticism of this passage results from leading-tone chromaticism (the VII^{o7} of V), which was prepared earlier in a subtle but remarkable way.[12] In bar 2, the inner-voice tones F–E♮–E♭–D introduce a chromatic motion into an otherwise diatonic context. This figure now recurs, in expanded form and in retrograde, as the supporting bass line for the motion from I^6 to V in bars 5–6 (D–E♭–E♮–F). In effect, the figure in bar 2 is a kind of seed for the chromaticism that follows.

As V and $\hat{2}$ are reached in bars 6–7, the diatonicism and relative calm of the opening return. But the greater tension of bars 5–6—and the poem's other meaning—also continue to be felt. Notice, for example, that in bar 5 the chordal texture of the accompaniment changes to a more active and agitated rhythmic pattern that continues in bars 7–8. The beginning of this gentle increase in pulse suggests the faintest rustling (or motion) of the leaves. We feel *hardly* a breath—just a tiny one.

Another, more subtle kind of tension is created throughout the first part of the song by the extraordinarily slow initial ascent of the upper voice, which begins on $\hat{1}$. It remains there—despite two ascending elaborations—through the conclusion of the tonic prolongation in bar 5. The prolongation of this $\hat{1}$ for such a relatively long period is more characteristic of endings than beginnings, because of the stability normally associated with the final tonic. Occurring as it does at the beginning of the song, this stability helps to create the calm, serene mood depicted in the text. Yet, it also carries with it a static quality; as the melody repeatedly moves upward only to fall back to $\hat{1}$, the stillness of the air and silence described in the poem are vividly portrayed in musical terms.

The large-scale initial ascent to $\hat{3}$ (d^2) is finally completed in bars 9–10, where the final climactic line of the poem begins ("Only wait, soon You too shall rest").[13] Notice that just before $\hat{3}$ is attained, a version of the initial ascent B♭–C–D occurs in contracted form (bars 9–10); in other words, the upper voice quickly retraces its long path before the structural goal is reached. This illustrates a motivic technique called *nesting*: a statement of a motive is enclosed within a larger statement of the same motive, and shares one or more common tones.[14] Notice also that the interval of the third, which has been important throughout the song, permeates this passage. The tones B♭ and D of the nested repetition, for instance, initiate falling thirds in bar 9, while the motion in bar 10 continues up a third to the climactic note f^2. Thirds also figure prominently in the piano accompaniment.

The contracted repetition of the initial ascent ($\hat{1}$–$\hat{2}$–$\hat{3}$) in bars 9–10 is supported by the chord succession VI–V–I, forming what Schenker termed an *auxiliary cadence,* a harmonic progression that contains a V–I motion, but lacks an opening tonic (see Examples 8.6a and 8.6b).[15] Like the rising third in the top voice, the supporting chords VI–V–I form a complementary cadential pattern that "points ahead" and resolves to I. In other words, this local cadential pattern relates to the forthcoming tonic, even though it occurs in the "space" of the dominant established and prolonged in bars 6–8. For this reason, we indicate in the graph only local significance for the V (bar 9) that occurs *within* this pattern. (Example 8.6c clearly shows the partially independent character of the auxiliary cadence, and its relation to the nested third B♭–C–D.)

Almost as remarkable as the expansiveness of the initial ascent is the rapidity with which the structural descent and final cadence occur. An extended initial ascent followed by a rapid cadence and structural descent is a most unusual compositional plan; this aspect of the work, like many others that we have discussed, is related to the poem and its expression in the music. In bars 3–5, the prolonged tonic in the upper voice contributes to the stable and serene mood of the opening. As the piece proceeds, the slowly ascending structural line conveys the still and rather confined atmosphere, despite the vast open spaces suggested by the poem, as well as the sense of yearning and foreboding implied by the final words.

The restatement of the auxiliary cadence and structural cadence in bars 11–13 reiterates, but does not supersede, the structural role of the cadence in bars 9–11 (the shift in metrical position will be discussed below). Finally, a one-bar piano postlude recalls the second bar of the introduction and the structural descent of the *Urlinie*. In each of the cadential progressions (bars 10–11, and 13), the inner voice of the right hand echoes the poignant chromatic motive first heard in the "tenor" in bar 2.

Relations between rhythm, meter, and musical structure have been extensively studied by Schenkerian scholars.[16] While it is beyond the scope of an introductory text on Schenkerian analysis to examine this complex and multifaceted subject at length, a thorough analysis should include consideration of rhythm and meter. Rhythmic factors very often influence the decisions analysts make about specific characteristics of structure, as we have seen in discussions of previous examples. Because aspects of rhythm are closely related to the meaning of the text, Schubert's song provides a clear context in which to address informally some of the issues involved in considering the rhythmic dimension of tonal music.

Sometimes conflicts arise between the notated meter and groupings of beats and measures that are fundamental to the compositional plan. In "Wandrers Nachtlied," such conflicts play an essential role in the song's character and expression. Example 8.7 illustrates its rhythmic and metrical framework. The outer-voice framework serves as a basis for our discussion of groupings of beats and measures on various levels.[17]

The piano introduction (bars 1–2) establishes the meter and rhythm with a two-bar grouping (or 4 + 4 beats) in common $\frac{4}{4}$ time. The passage that follows, however, consists of variable groupings of beats and measures that do not always correspond to the characteristic metrical framework of common time. Bars 3–6, for example, span 16 beats, or four measures (Example 8.7a). Yet, as indicated in the example, the groupings in the music form a 6 + 4 + 6 beat pattern. A regular group of measures recurs in the dominant prolongation of bars 7–8. The auxiliary cadence and final structural cadence, however, return again to the irregularity, comprising a six-beat and a four-beat grouping, respectively, within a ten–beat span. Moreover, because it is ten beats long, the passage ends midway through bar 11. The repetition (bars 11–12) ends with a complete bar, allowing the piano postlude to begin on a downbeat.

Schubert employs these varied groupings for expressive purposes. After the introduction establishes the meter and mood of the song, the subtle shifts between regular and irregular groupings of measures—like the chromaticism—reflect the multiple levels of meaning of the poem. For example, in bars 7–8, the pivotal dominant prolongation temporarily establishes stability, where the "birds are silent in the forest." But this only prepares the most climactic and irregular passage of the song. For here it is promised that "rest" is soon coming, the most ambiguous and uncertain image of the text.

Example 8.7 schematically represents these groupings in "Wandrers Nachtlied" in relation to its essential sections and tonal features. Following the piano introduction, the song consists of 48 bars that fall into two equal sections. Thus, despite the irregularities that Schubert employs for expressive purposes at more immediate levels, the song's overall groupings are balanced.

EXAMPLE 8.7:

Schubert, "Wandrers Nachtlied," Op. 96, No. 3: rhythmic and metrical frameworks

SCHUMANN, "LIEB' LIEBCHEN"

We saw that many special and unusual features in "Wandrers Nachtlied" are related to the text. Such a close association of text and music is typical of German lieder. Our next work, a song by Robert Schumann entitled "Lieb' Liebchen" (composed to a poem by Heinrich Heine), also expresses the words in remarkable ways. Following are Heine's poem and a translation:

> *Lieb' Liebchen, leg's Händchen auf's Herze mein;*
> *ach, hörst du, wie's pochet im Kämmerlein?*
> *da hauset ein Zimmermann schlimm und arg,*
> *der zimmert mir einen Todtensarg.*

> *Es hämmert und klopfet bei Tag und bei Nacht;*
> *es hat mich schon längst um den Schlaf gebracht.*
> *Ach, sputet euch, Meister Zimmermann,*
> *damit ich balde schlafen kann.*

> *Dear love, place your hand upon my heart;*
> *Ah! Do you hear how it pounds in its little chamber?*
> *Within lives a grim and evil carpenter,*
> *Who is building me a coffin.*

> *He hammers and pounds by day and by night;*
> *And long has robbed me of my rightful slumber.*
> *Oh, hurry up, Mister Carpenter,*
> *So that soon I can fall asleep.*[18]

Here the subject matter is sardonic and even macabre.[19] Yet beneath the literal meaning of the words this poem also conveys a second, implied level of meaning. Who is the "dear love" to whom the poem (and song) is addressed? It seems evident that the bizarre image of a carpenter building a coffin expresses the bitter feelings of a disappointed lover. The vivid imagery and underlying sarcasm in Heine's poem offer rich possibilities to the composer. For example, as the song begins, we notice a curious musical texture: the melody is accompanied only by offbeat chords in the pianist's right hand. With no bass support for these chords, which portray the hammering inside the chest of the protagonist, they sound eerie and disembodied against the solo voice.

Example 8.8 presents a graph of "Lieb' Liebchen." Despite the absence of the bass, tonic harmony is clearly stated by the right-hand and vocal part and prolonged in bars 1–7. One of the many ways in which analysis can illuminate our understanding of a work is by revealing features implied by the context, but not literally present in the music, as we have frequently seen. The bass part, for instance, seems to acquire even greater significance through its very absence at the beginning of the song. Notice its impact when it finally enters

EXAMPLE 8.8:

Schumann, "Lieb' Liebchen," bars 1–17: foreground reduction

in bar 10: the first appearance of the tonic note in the bass is on the syllable "Todt" ("dead"). Schumann could hardly have found a more effective way to convey the strangeness of the text's imagery in musical terms.

Perhaps the most dramatic moment in the poem occurs when the carpenter is first mentioned: "Da hauset ein Zimmermann schlimm und arg, der zimmert mir einen Todtensarg." ("Within lives a grim and evil carpenter, Who is building me a coffin.") Schumann's setting of this line (beginning in bars 8/9) is equally dramatic. Following arrival on the dominant in bar 8, chromatic notation in flats is unexpectedly introduced, first with the bass tone C♭ in bar 10 (notated as B in Example 8.8), followed by an E♭ minor chord in bars 11–12. This chord is remote indeed from the home key of E minor.

Enharmonic notation sometimes occurs for reasons of notation rather than harmonic function. For example, if a piece in A♭ major modulates to

♭VI (F♭ major, the VI of the parallel minor), it would probably be notated enharmonically in E major to avoid awkward accidentals and to facilitate reading. In other cases enharmonic notation reflects a truly functional change. A common example of this type of enharmonic equivalence is the reinterpretation of a diminished seventh chord in a modulation: for example, in the VII[7] of G minor, changing the root from F♯ to G♭ would transform the chord into the VII[7] of B♭ minor (A–C–E♭–G♭).[20]

To understand whether the use of flats instead of sharps for the chromaticism in this passage is notational or functional, we need to consider the nature of the tones involved. As Example 8.8 shows, the chromaticism occurs within a prolonged dominant region. Example 8.9 interprets the chromaticism of this passage in a series of stages in which the notation in flats has been replaced with enharmonic notation in sharps. Stage 1 shows motion to and from chromatic lower neighbor notes, first in the upper voices, then in the bass. (If all neighbor notes were indicated simultaneously, parallel fifths would result between the soprano and bass voices.) In stage 2 the bass neighbor A♯(B♭) has been moved ahead by one quarter note, so that it now forms an apparent $^6_4$ chord with the upper voices (even though its essential function as a neighbor is unchanged).

The progression is further elaborated in stage 3: the motion from A♯ to B in the bass is inverted to a descending seventh, and filled in with an arpeggiation. While lower neighbor motion is still the basis of the progression in the bass, the resolution of A♯ to B in one register is elided: A♯ moves directly to A natural (in the tenor), the seventh of the prolonged dominant. From a functional point of view, A♯, C×, and E♯ serve as lower neighbors to B, D♯, and F♯ respectively. The notation in flats, therefore, is not necessary for functional reasons. Why, then, does Schumann use flats?

As was mentioned above, one reason for employing notational (as opposed to functional) enharmonic notation is to facilitate reading (such as substituting the notation of E major for F♭ major). This is a possible explanation here, but notating the passage with sharps would probably not present the performer with any special difficulties. After all, accidentals in the form of sharps (and occasional double sharps) are common in the key of E minor, and the D♯ minor triad would not be out of the ordinary.

EXAMPLE 8.9:

Schumann, "Lieb' Liebchen": simplifications of dominant prolongation

Another reason why purely notational enharmonic changes may occur is for expressive purposes, or to indicate a moment of special tension or importance in the music. This may seem odd, since an audience will not be following the score and consequently will not be aware of this kind of enharmonicism. Yet such changes can affect the sound of the music in another way—through their influence on the performers.

When C♭ enters in bar 10, the listener would probably hear it as B, which has been implied as the root of dominant harmony since bar 8. Yet, because of its "flat" notation, the pianist sees it as an unstable tone likely to resolve downward, and will probably play it more intensely and dramatically than if it had been written as B. (In any case, the note is inherently dramatic because it is the first bass note heard in the piece so far, and because it is marked with an accent.) Similarly, the notation in bars 10–11 conveys a visual impression that a remote region has suddenly been entered, a feeling that Schumann surely wanted the artists to convey in performance. Throughout the history of notated music, unusual notation has sometimes been used by composers for such musical and psychological purposes.[21]

Another unusual feature of "Lieb' Liebchen" is the cadence in bars 15–17. In bar 14 the voice concludes on a^1 ($\hat{4}$), the seventh of dominant harmony. The resolution of this note is heard first in the piano alone (bar 15), then a bar later in the voice, whose descending third overlaps the same figure in the piano. This striking disjunction of voice and accompaniment conveys the eerie, poignant mood of the song just as effectively as did the unusual texture at the beginning. It also poses intriguing questions for the analyst regarding which descent should be understood as structurally definitive. Does the voice echo a descent that has already occurred in the piano? Does the piano anticipate the descent, which is delayed until bars 16–17? Or is the descent actually repeated—that is, should both descents be understood as representing the same structural event?

In considering these questions various factors should be weighed, including the particulars of the harmonic support, the rhythm, and the effect of the second voice/piano overlap in bars 16/17 as the piano begins the next phrase. The analysis presented in Example 8.8 interprets the piano descent as preliminary, and the vocal descent as structurally definitive. This decision is based on the following considerations: first, as we have seen in our previous example, in songs the singer is usually perceived as the dramatic protagonist and consequently as being primary in musical terms. Second, the piano descent in this case sounds anticipatory, because (1) it begins over a passing six-four (over a stationary bass), and (2) the seventh of V^7 in the voice (a^1 in bar 14) is not fully resolved until the tonic chord returns, at which point it resolves to the g^1 in bar 16.

In some situations, more than one analytical interpretation may be viable. An analyst then weighs the various factors and makes a judgment as to which interpretation seems best. The analysis presented here offers what is perhaps the most convincing explanation of the passage; however, because of the ambiguity of the double melodic descent, either of the alternative readings mentioned above might be feasible. At the very least, the analytical process of considering multiple possibilities can enrich our appreciation of the subtlety of music, which sometimes does not readily yield to our attempts to conceptualize it.

An additional question is pertinent here: why is the structural descent shown in bars 14–17, rather than in the varied repetition of bars 34–37? (You have undoubtedly noticed that Example 8.8 illustrates only bars 1–17 of the song.) As we have seen with earlier examples in this book, the structural meaning of musical repetition can vary according to the circumstances and the context. Following the piano interlude of bars 16/17–20, the setting of the remainder of the text in bars 20/21–37 repeats bars 1–17 with some alterations. A notable change, for instance, occurs in bars 21–23: the piano accompaniment temporarily has a left-hand part, which had been so notably absent in bars 1–3. Important though this new feature of design may be, the bass line enriches (but does not change) the structure of the opening bars. From bar 23 to the end, the music remains as before (except, of course, for the absence of the piano/voice overlap that occurred in bars 16/17).

Since bars 1–17 represent a complete structure, a listener's impression of the last portion of the song is that of a slightly varied strophic repetition. The structure essentially "happens again," as if the music were unchanged and Schumann used repeat signs, writing the last portion of the text under the first. (Notice that we are speaking of the essential structure as represented in the graph. Some minor changes do occur in the strophic repetition.) Therefore, the graph in Example 8.8 and the depiction of the fundamental structure in Example 8.10 (with some middleground detail) may be understood to represent the last portion of the song no less than the first. The form is one-part (corresponding to the undivided structure) followed by a strophic repetition.

In summary, a one-part form may be thought of in structural terms as a single cadential progression that serves as the basis for a complete work. This structure will be expanded and embellished in the compositional process, but

EXAMPLE 8.10:

Schumann, "Lieb' Liebchen," bars 1–17: deep middleground structure

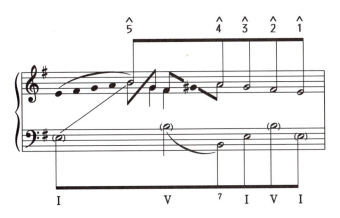

remains essentially undivided. Fundamental structures that are divided, leading to binary and ternary forms, are discussed in Chapters 9 and 10.

Exercises

1. Bach, Little Prelude in F major BWV 927

   a.   Consider bars 1–4 and 5–8 as two four-bar units. How is the opening four-bar unit typical of Bach's preludes?

   b.   I and V harmonies occur throughout bars 10–15. Use register in the upper voice to help you determine the main structural harmonies.

   c.   The bass line in bars 12–13 becomes disjunct. Consider the possibility of a (deeper) rising stepwise line in those bars (to beat 2 of bar 13).

   d.   Create foreground, middleground, and background graphs for this prelude.

   e.   Compare its structure with that of the C-major Prelude given in the chapter. What are their similarities and differences?

   f.   Analyze the B♭-major Prelude from Book I of the *Well-Tempered Clavier,* and compare it with the above works.

2. Bach, Prelude No. 2 in C minor (*Well-Tempered Clavier I*)

   a.   Create a bar-by-bar chordal reduction. Pay careful attention to the figuration patterns in order to distinguish chord tones (especially in bar 12).

   b.   Determine the large-scale prolongations and motions.

   c.   Create foreground, middleground, and background graphs. What is the significance of the figuration in bars 28–33 and bars 34-end?

3. Schubert, *Die schöne Müllerin,* No. 1, "Das Wandern"

   a.   Study the verses of this strophic song. Does Schubert use any obvious musical devices to convey the basic tone and meaning of the poem?

   b.   Create foreground, middleground, and background graphs for this song. Do you think that the voice carries the *Urlinie* by itself, or does the piano introduction form part of the background structure?

   c.   Describe any motivic associations you may find in the vocal melody, and between the voice and the piano parts.

4. Chopin, Prelude in G major, Op. 28

   a.   This Prelude, like some of the shorter passages presented in the previous chapter, comprises an antecedent/consequent construction.

Despite this phrase division, the impression of a single, extended gesture is created. How do rhythmic factors (in the consequent phrase) contribute to this impression? (You may wish to consult the discussion of *metrical expansion* in Chapter 12.)

b. Create foreground, middleground, and background graphs of the Prelude.

c. The figuration pattern in bar 1 is not simply introductory, but includes a motivic figure that is prominent in the work. Trace its manifestations throughout the Prelude and indicate these in your voice-leading graph.

d. A brief coda concludes the piece. What aspects of the Prelude does it summarize?

5. Chopin, Prelude in E minor, Op. 28

a. Construct a figured-bass continuo realization of bars 1–12.

b. This piece contains clear examples of the distinction between *chord* and *harmony*. The first sonority is a I^6, which in this case is a harmony. The last chord of the first phrase is a V^7 chord (bar 12), which is also a harmony. How many of the intervening sonorities, however, are truly harmonies? Does the progression contain a structural intermediate harmony?

c. Create foreground, middleground, and background graphs for this work. (There are two plausible readings of the upper voice. Each has different ramifications for the interpretation of the first level of the middleground.)

d. Compare bar 12 with the initial upbeat figure of the Prelude. How are they related?

e. How does a motivic element in the upper voice of the first phrase shape (and foreshadow) the harmonic progression of the expanded consequent phrase?

f. What is the chord in bar 23? Can you explain its spelling?

Binary Forms

Sectional divisions can arise in a multitude of ways in a composition, with various consequences for the form and for the structure. In Chapter 8 we examined works that are essentially undivided in form and structure, despite articulations created by phrases, harmonic progressions, and changes in design. More often than not, however, tonal compositions incorporate stronger divisions that create formal sections. In this chapter and throughout the remainder of this book we will continue to explore various ways in which compositions may be organized. In so doing we will consider ways in which tonal structures can relate to different types of form.

The perspectives embodied in conventional views of form are practical and reflect the kinds of issues that composers often consider in practice. Many terms associated with forms—such as *binary* and *rounded binary*—refer to basic "ground plans" that occur frequently throughout the tonal literature. Specific genres, the minuet and trio for example, are frequently associated with particular forms, and reflect accepted norms. Such traditions and concepts are vital to the understanding of form.[1]

In our view, form and structure are distinct aspects of compositions, though they are inextricably related and arise through similar musical processes. Moreover, though structural divisions and articulations frequently coincide with major divisions in the form, they do not necessarily do so. Such diversity of compositional possibilities testifies to the richness and complexity of music and to the flexibility of the tonal system itself. In this chapter we will explore a number of works composed in binary form, with our primary concern focusing on middleground elaborations of fundamental structures.

HAYDN, PIANO SONATA, HOB. XVI/43, MINUET 2

In Chapter 7 we described the technique of interruption in the context of two (or four) phrases. We noted that the antecedent and consequent phrases of a musical period often embody, on a small scale, the characteristics of the first and second branches respectively of an interrupted structure. We will now begin to discover how this compositional technique may shape an entire composition. Example 9.1 illustrates bars 1–12 of a minuet by Haydn, the first branch of an interrupted fundamental structure. We will first consider the harmonic structure before turning our attention to details of the upper voice.

As the graph shows, tonic harmony is sustained throughout bars 1–4; in bar 5, the D♮ in the "tenor" voice signals the destabilization of the tonic and the emergence of E♭ major (V), which is tonicized in bars 6–8. Notice that we connect the bass notes of the opening tonic chord and the seventh chord in bar 5 with a slur, indicating that they are related through the common bass tone A♭. In other words, even though the D natural begins to destabilize the tonic, the broader influence of tonic harmony also extends to and includes elements of the chromatic chord. This opening passage (bars 1–5) is a good example of what can be called a *prolongational span:* that is, an "area" of music shaped by a single harmony, linear progression, or some other single voice-leading pattern. In Chapter 12, we will discuss this concept in greater detail.[2] For now, simply be aware that the boundary of a prolongational span may be a chord that is not spelled exactly like the underlying harmony. Both the beginning and end of such a span, however, will necessarily share at least one common tone.

In bars 6–8 the dominant of the first branch is tonicized with the progression (in E♭) I⁶–II⁶–V–I. After we have discussed some aspects of the upper voice, we will return to this passage and put the modulatory progression into a broader perspective.

Following the double bar, the left hand ascends into the higher register of the alto and tenor voices, articulating the sectional division through registral contrast. When F appears in the lower octave (bar 11), the structural bass register is reestablished just before the interruption. Example 9.1a clarifies the broader connections of the bass in bars 8–12: the dominant note is prolonged with the upper neighbor figure E♭–F–E♭.

The upper voice is characterized by consonant skips and linear progressions at different structural levels, figuration that acquires motivic significance and integrates the musical fabric of the Minuet. Considering the opening eight bars as four two-bar groups, notice first the foreground ascending thirds (indicated by brackets) that serve as upbeats to three of the four two-measure groups. On a higher structural level, the primary tone $\hat{3}$ is transferred from the two- to the three-line octave. This upward motion establishes two distinct registers, each with its own melodic activity.[3] As the graph indicates, e♭² in the "alto" register is twice decorated by its lower neighbor D♮ over the course of

EXAMPLE 9.1:

Haydn, Piano Sonata, Hob. XVI/43, Minuet 2, bars 1–12: (a) foreground reduction;
(b) motivic detail

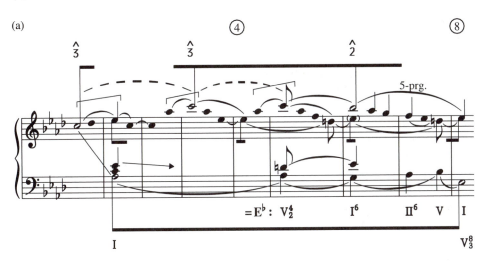

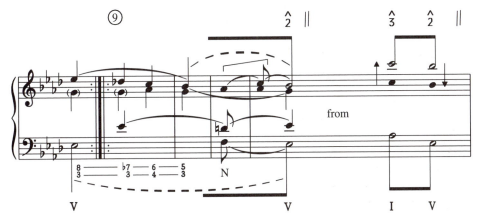

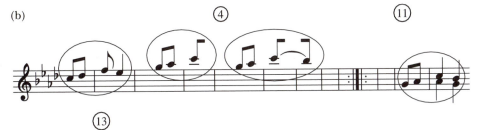

bars 1–8 (notice the doubling of the first lower neighbor figure in the tenor). In the higher register, the primary tone c^3 recurs in bar 5 as a consonant *suspension* (at a deeper level) over the dissonant $^4_2$ we have identified as an outgrowth of the prolonged tonic. The primary tone $\hat{3}$ then moves to $\hat{2}$ (bar 6) which is prolonged as a structural tone of the fundamental line by a lower-level fifth-progression that descends into an inner voice.

In Example 9.1a the motivic brackets indicate third-motions that recur in bars 1–12. In Example 9.1b the circles show motives associated with these thirds: in the anacrusis and bar 1, the motive involves a step, a leap to an appoggiatura, followed by a descending second. In other words, the third from C to E♭—an interval from the underlying tonic triad—becomes a four-note motive with an appoggiatura: C–D♭–F–E♭. In several other places a step followed by a rising third appears prominently in the musical fabric. Notice that in some cases the first note of the figure does not belong to the underlying chord; we refer to these as *nonstructural* motives.[4]

The last circled figure in Example 9.1b actually belongs to the beginning of the reprise (bars 12–13). We show it here because it follows immediately from the similar figure that concludes the first branch in bars 11–12. This procedure of unification is known as *linkage technique:* "A new phrase takes as its initial idea the end of the immediately preceding one and then continues independently, either within the same formal unit or to initiate a new section."[5] This type of motivic repetition can be a compelling means by which composers achieve musical cohesion.

Following the double bar, the foreground top-voice line continues to descend from e♭². It leads to b♭¹, which is prolonged by motion into an inner voice and by its upper neighbor C.[6] Consequently the motion through an octave from b♭² to b♭¹ prolongs $\hat{2}$ from bar 6, and transfers it to the lower register in which the Minuet begins.

Example 9.2 is a graph of the reprise, the abbreviated return of the opening that concludes the second formal section of the piece. Following our discussion of the first part of the Minuet, the structure and motivic detail of this passage should be clear. Two points are of interest. First, the principal difference in harmonic structure between bars 1–8 and 13–18 occurs in bar 15: because no modulation will occur in this section, I⁶ in the tonic replaces the I⁶ in E♭ major (bar 6) of the first part of the Minuet. Otherwise, the progression leading to the final cadence (I⁶–II⁶–V–I) is a transposed version of that in bars 6–8. Second, notice that e♭² plays an important role in this section, just as it does in bars 1–8. Instead of participating in a neighbor figure, however, this tone now initiates the fifth-progression E♭–A♭ that corresponds to the fifth B♭–E♭ before the double bar. As the graph indicates, the line is on a lower structural level than the descent of the fundamental line from $\hat{3}$.[7]

Refer to Example 9.3 as we summarize some key issues of this piece. We have seen that the primary tone $\hat{3}$ is first heard as c^2 in the opening bars. It is then transferred to the three-line octave (bar 3) before leading to structural $\hat{2}$ in this higher register (bar 6). Haydn subsequently transfers structural $\hat{2}$ down an octave to the original register of the piece, three bars before the point of interruption in bar 12. Although the higher register of bar 3 is re-

EXAMPLE 9.2:

Haydn, Piano Sonata, Hob. XVI/43, Minuet 2, bars 13–18: foreground reduction

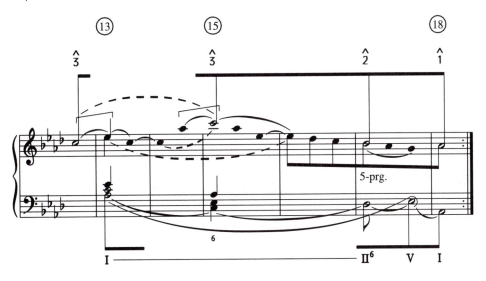

called in the final phrase (bar 15), all of the tones of the fundamental line in the second branch appear in the lower register (c^2–$b\flat^1$–$a\flat^1$).

In *Free Composition,* Schenker defined an aspect of tonal composition that he referred to as the principle of obligatory register. His definition is revealing of the manner in which he thought about the unity of tonal music:

> No matter how far the composing-out [of the structure] may depart from its basic register in ascending or descending linear progressions, arpeggiations, or couplings, it nevertheless retains an urge to return to that register. Such departure and return creates content, displays the instrument, and lends coherence to the whole. . . . In the upper voice it is usually the register of the first tone of the fundamental line which is later confirmed as the true register.[8]

Schenker's concept of obligatory register clarifies and illuminates the structural importance of register in this piece. At the beginning of the Minuet, Haydn composes an interplay of contrasting registers through the initial statements of $\hat{3}$ and $\hat{2}$ of the fundamental line in contrasting registers (see Example 9.3). In this manner he utilizes the registral resources of the piano. In the final phrase, all the tones of the fundamental line appear in the lower register, a compositional strategy that draws together the structural associations of bars 1–12.

The next point that we shall consider is the relation between form and structure. This composition illustrates what is commonly referred to as a "rounded" binary form. The main formal division coincides with the double bar, and the second section of the piece concludes with the abbreviated return of the opening.[9] The structural division, however, does not coincide with

EXAMPLE 9.3:

Haydn, Piano Sonata, Hob. XVI/43, Minuet 2: structural synopsis

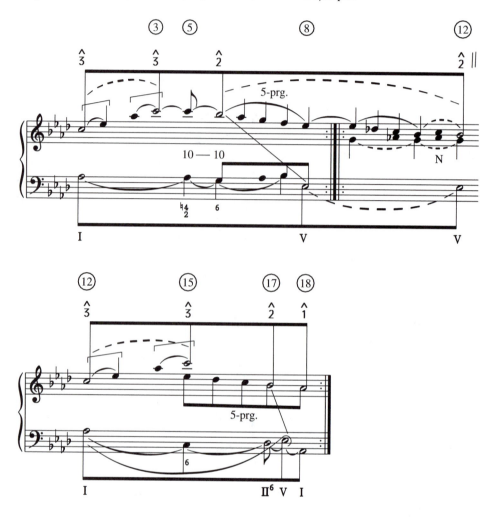

the formal division. The first branch of the interrupted structure goes beyond the double bar and the perfect authentic cadence in the dominant; the interruption occurs just before the return of the opening material. From this perspective we can say that the beginning of the second formal division (bars 9–12) arises through a *prolongation* of the V of the first branch of the structure. This curious relationship between form and structure holds a wealth of compositional possibilities. We will see it again in major-mode sonata movements.

The final issue that we will consider in the discussion of this piece is the modulation associated with the expansion of $\hat{2}$ over V within the first branch. If you review the harmonic progression in bars 6–8 and the upper voice it supports, you will discover an *Ursatz* pattern in E♭ major with incomplete harmonic support: $\hat{5}$–$\hat{4}$–$\hat{3}$–$\hat{2}$–$\hat{1}$ unfolds over I⁶–II⁶–V–I. We are, of course, familiar with lower-level replications of fundamental structures from Chapter 7; the examples there (except the last) are complete structures in the tonic within one or more phrases. The situation in Haydn's Minuet is different from the examples in Chapter 7 for two reasons. First, the transferred *Ursatz* pattern establishes a key other than the tonic. Schenker referred to this compositional technique as "the transference of the forms [or "patterns"] of the fundamental structure to individual harmonies."[10] Second, as we mentioned, the pattern is incomplete because the harmonic progression in the dominant does not begin with an E♭-major chord in root position. This incomplete form of the fundamental structure represents an *auxiliary cadence*. We will see this procedure again in Example 9.11 and will elaborate the concept more completely as a theoretical issue in Chapter 12.[11]

MOZART, SYMPHONY NO. 35, K. 385, TRIO

The Trio from Mozart's Symphony No. 35 ("Haffner") presents us with another rounded binary form, though with a somewhat different structure than that of Haydn's Minuet. Example 9.4 presents a graphic analysis of bars 1–20.[12] The Trio is written in the style of an Austrian Ländler, which is a folk dance in moderately slow 3/4 time. It is not surprising, therefore, that the Trio often alternates between tonic and dominant harmonies in a lilting, relaxed manner, and that the entire first section of this binary form (before the double bar) remains in the tonic.

Another characteristic of folk music can be recognized in the Trio's rhythmic regularity. It is easy to hear the opening eight bars in terms of two four-measure groups (bars 1–4, 5–8) as well as in terms of four two-measure segments. (Overall, the four-bar groups are probably heard as the primary unit of rhythmic organization.) We shall see that a disturbance in this symmetry helps us to make certain analytical decisions about the structure in the second part.

The graph indicates the prevalence of ascending and descending thirds in the upper voice of bars 1–8: the ascending thirds are indicated by motivic brackets, and the descending thirds are circled. This interval is so pervasive in the musical fabric that it becomes the primary motivic feature of the Trio. In the first bar primary tone $\hat{3}$ is expanded by a rising third, which is answered by a falling third in bar 2. These thirds embellish a descent by step to $\hat{1}$ (C♯–B–A, bars 1–3) in an enlarged version of the third-motive. The primary tone $\hat{3}$ is then regained (bar 5) in an expanded version of the third motive. Bars 5–8 are similar to bars 1–4, except that an intermediate II[6] and cadential $^6_4$ intensify the cadence, bringing this section to a close.

You may wonder why scale degree $\hat{3}$ is indicated as the primary tone rather than $\hat{5}$. One reason is the overall melodic continuity, including the large-scale C♯–B–A descent in bars 1–3 (defined partly through the harmonic rhythm) and the motion A–B–C♯ in bars 3–5. This motion from the inner

EXAMPLE 9.4:

Mozart, Symphony No. 35, K. 385, III (Trio): foreground reduction

voice, leading Î to $\hat{3}$, resembles an initial ascent, and strongly emphasizes C♯ as the melodic beginning of the second four-bar group.

Example 9.5 shows how scale degree $\hat{5}$ serves in the elaboration of the underlying $\hat{3}$–$\hat{2}$–Î motion in bars 1–3. The E is superposed above the primary tone C♯, creating a consonant skip in the upper voice (C♯–E) that is filled in with a passing tone. In a broader sense, the primary tone c♯² leads to its neighbor d² (bar 2), which descends a third to $\hat{2}$. (The neighbor is an incomplete neighbor, because the second C♯ is a passing tone, not a stable recurrence of $\hat{3}$.) This is a good example of tones of figuration that reside at different structural levels. The principal embellishing tone is the upper neighbor d² in bar 2. On the surface level, this upper neighbor is approached from

EXAMPLE 9.5:

Mozart, Symphony No. 35, K. 385, III (Trio), bars 1–8: surface and foreground motivic detail

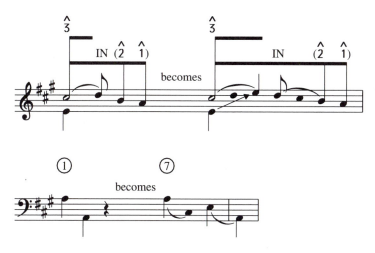

above, following a consonant skip that decorates the primary tone C♯. The second part of the example shows that the cadence is an elaboration of the initial octave leap in the bass.

You will notice that the section concludes with a perfect authentic cadence, with 2̂–1̂ occurring over V⁷–I. The final A section (bars 21–28) is identical to the first and concludes in exactly the same fashion. Since this is the case, it is reasonable to wonder why an *Urlinie* descent does not take place in the first A section as well as the last. In purely melodic terms, the descents are the same. However the meaning of an *Urlinie* descent goes beyond the melodic descent itself. When the *Urlinie* reaches the tonic, the dynamic forward motion of the structure of the section or work under consideration is fulfilled. While a prolongation or coda may follow, the *Urlinie* descent by definition signifies the completion of the main structure. Parallel earlier descents, therefore, do not have the same meaning for the section or piece as a whole. In addition, closure after a single phrase (or section) is not as definitive as closure after a contrasting section and return.

We now return to Example 9.4 and discuss the beginning of the B section of the form (bars 9–20). In Haydn's Minuet, structural 2̂ over V appeared *before* the double bar. The technique of interruption also divides the fundamental structure in Mozart's Trio, but the appearance of 2̂ over V coincides with the beginning of the second formal section. It is also notable that the bass and harmonic structure preceding the return of the opening material in the Trio are slightly more complex than in the corresponding passage of the Minuet. The bass retains its principal register, and more harmonic activity occurs with motions to chords other than the prolonged dominant harmony (bars 11–12 and 15).

Example 9.4 shows the continuation of ascending and descending thirds that characterize bars 1–8 of the Trio. As we have seen, motivic connections can integrate not only different levels of structure, but also different sections of a composition. One particularly striking motivic relationship occurs in bars 16–18.[13] The descending third E–C♯ is stated in a dotted rhythm on beat 3 of each bar (compare the graph and the music); these figures are contracted forms of the descending motives from bars 12 and 15 (Example 9.4). In each case the C♯ is a neighbor (approached from above) to the main tone B ($\hat{2}$). Hence the upper voice of bars 16–18 summarizes, in contracted form, the deeper neighbor figure (B–C♯–B) that unfolds twice over the span of the dominant prolongation after the double bar.

Example 9.4 also indicates that we interpret the A-major triads in the B section not as structural representations of tonic harmony, but as "apparent" tonics—chords that in this context support upper neighbors (C♯) to structural $\hat{2}$. In other words, because the C♯s function contrapuntally in the upper voice, the supporting chords are also contrapuntal in function, even though they are in root position.

You may wonder whether it is possible to interpret the tonic chords in bars 11–12 and 15 as structural; that is, could $\hat{3}$ over I recur after the double bar, with structural $\hat{2}$ (over V) of the first branch of the structure occurring in bar 16? Such an interpretation is, in fact, plausible. Chords in tonal music may often be interpreted in more than one way. Analysts must continually make decisions about aspects of a passage or piece based on the available criteria. This often means considering two (or more) analytical "paths," each of which might be possible.

The difficulty in analyzing this passage arises from the simple, folklike character of this Trio, with its frequent alternation of root-position I and V chords. This limited harmonic vocabulary results in a relatively undifferentiated harmonic structure in which alternative readings can arise. On the other hand, the folklike dance character of the Trio provides a clear metrical framework in which rhythmic features can be evaluated. While there is no absolute relationship between meter and harmony, rhythmic features can nevertheless contribute a great deal to the analysis as a whole.

As in bars 1–8, it is possible to hear the beginning of the passage after the double bar in two- and four-bar groups. Consider for a moment the first subphrase (bars 9–12) as a four-bar unit: $\hat{2}$ and V appear in the position of greatest metrical stress in the first bar of the group (bar 9).[14] A second subphrase begins similarly in bars 13–14, but is reduced from four bars to three because only one bar of tonic harmony appears (bar 15). A final subphrase (bars 16–21) compensates for this truncation through phrase extension: a single chromatic passing tone adds a fifth bar (bar 20). Thus dominant harmony occurs in the first (strong) bar of each group, a feature we use (collectively with aspects of harmony and voice leading) to substantiate our interpretation that a prolonged structural dominant underlies bars 9–20. In this explanation, the tonic chords function contrapuntally—supporting neighbor notes—within the dominant prolongation.

Example 9.6 is a middleground summary of the Minuet. Only the essential voice leading is shown; most repetitions of the rhythmic groups have been omitted. Because the concluding reprise (bars 21–28) is identical to the sec-

EXAMPLE 9.6:

Mozart, Symphony No. 35, K. 385, III (Trio): middleground summary

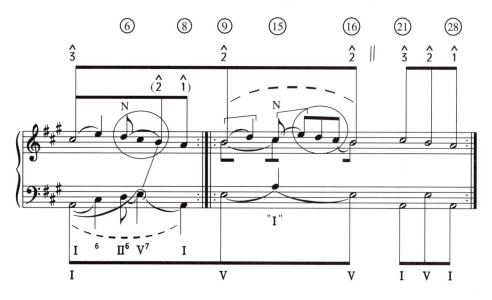

tion before the double bar, we show only the structural tones of the second branch. Compare this graph to Example 9.3, noting in each case how the appearance of dominant harmony (in the first branch) relates to the beginning of the second formal section (highlighted by the double bar). At the end of this chapter we will review these common middleground tonal plans.

BACH, FLUTE SONATA NO. 2, MINUET 1

The first Minuet from Bach's C-major Flute Sonata, another rounded binary form, shares common structural features with the Trio from Mozart's Symphony No. 35. Structural analysis provides a way to understand these similarities, and at the same time to fully appreciate the unique aspects of each composition. As is the case in many rounded binary forms, the fundamental structure of Bach's Minuet is divided through the technique of interruption. Example 9.7 is a graphic analysis of the first and beginning of the second formal sections (the graph represents the primary tone and structural harmony at the beginning of the reprise, which begins after the interruption).

We interpret e^2 as the primary tone of a $\hat{3}$–line, even though the line ascends to g^2 before returning to e^2 in bar 4. A similar situation, where scale degree $\hat{5}$ emerges above the primary tone $\hat{3}$, occurs at the beginning of Mozart's Trio (Example 9.4). Such an interpretation always depends upon the particular characteristics of a piece. Here, the tonic prolongation in bars 1–4 is framed by root-position tonic chords where E ($\hat{3}$) is the principal top-voice

EXAMPLE 9.7:

J. S. Bach, Flute Sonata No. 1, Minuet 1, bars 1–12: foreground reduction

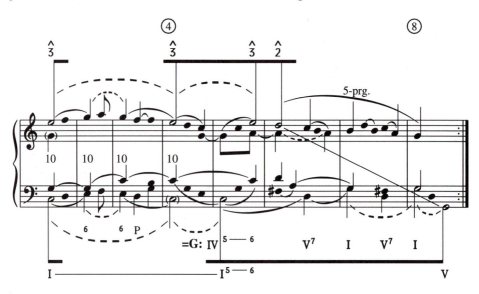

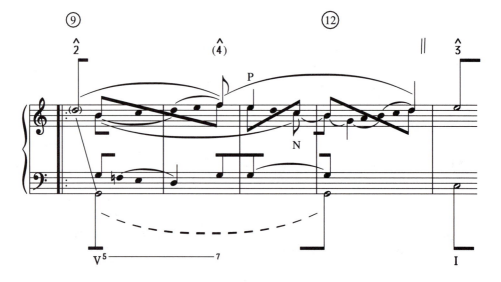

tone. As Example 9.7 indicates, tonic harmony is prolonged by a series of parallel tenths. In the course of this contrapuntal motion, g^2 appears supported by I^6 in bars 2 and 3. The structural correspondence of the outer voices may generally be assumed in contrapuntal patterns of this kind, unless other aspects of the piece suggest differently. Because g^2 is supported by I^6, and both occur within a series of parallel tenths that prolong a root-position tonic chord, the fundamental structure begins with I and $\hat{3}$.

In bar 5 the tonic is destabilized through a 5–6 motion, which initiates the modulation to the dominant: I^{5-6} becomes IV^{5-6} in G major. Two cadential bass motions in bars 6–8 establish the dominant and support a fifth-progression from structural $\hat{2}$ in the upper voice (structural $\hat{2}$ appears in the keyboard part, not the flute). As in Haydn's Minuet (Example 9.1), the secondary fifth-progression prolongs $\hat{2}$ of the background tonic as it delineates a pattern of the fundamental structure in the "new" key (= G: $\hat{5}$–$\hat{4}$–$\hat{3}$–$\hat{2}$–$\hat{1}$). Notice that, as in Example 9.3, structural $\hat{2}$ of the fundamental line appears before the perfect authentic cadence in the dominant; in both cases, the most conclusive statement of the cadence coincides with the end of the secondary fifth-progression in the upper voice.

The dominant of the interrupted first branch is prolonged after the double bar, though the specific technique of its prolongation is different from that in Haydn's Minuet. In the earlier example, a descending stepwise line (through an octave) connects two statements of structural $\hat{2}$ in different registers; the dominant remains throughout the prolongation as a *triad* (Example 9.1). In Bach's Minuet, the upper voice reverses direction and ascends after the double bar. This motion forms a parallel with the path of the upper voice in bars 1–2, an association that unifies the beginnings of the two formal sections. The ascent also serves to introduce the seventh of the dominant seventh chord in bar 10. To summarize, the structural dominant of the first branch is tonicized before the double bar. Before the interruption the seventh destabilizes the dominant as a key area, transforming it into the the dominant seventh chord that prepares the tonic of the second branch.

Example 9.8 shows the return of opening material at the conclusion of the Minuet, a truncated and slightly varied recomposition of the A section. Notice that g^2 is now decorated by upper and lower neighbors, in contrast to bar 2 where only an upper neighbor appears. The motion to the cadence (from I^6) is also changed to accommodate the close of the structure in the tonic. The example shows that we regard e^2 in the figuration of bar 15 as a middleground suspension (a seventh decorating II^6), a fleeting recollection of the primary tone $\hat{3}$ from the beginning of the second branch (bar 13).

In Example 9.9 we show the essential background and middleground features of this Minuet. (Only the structural tones of the reprise are indicated.) Consider in particular the prolongation of dominant harmony after the double bar. The process of transforming V into V^7 is one that leads to formal sections in many rounded binary and sonata forms. Schenker found this to be such a common situation that in *Free Composition* he provides several diagrams showing how the seventh of the dominant may emerge within the prolongation. In Chapter 12 we will examine a variety of such middleground patterns.

In Example 9.9, the designation = n.n. ("equals neighbor note") means that scale degree $\hat{4}$, the seventh of V^7, *appears to be* an upper neighbor to the primary tone $\hat{3}$ of the second branch. At levels very close to the background, the voice leading of the first branch does not carry over to the second branch. At levels closer to the surface, however, the figuration often suggests continued motion into the second branch. For instance, the d^2 on the last eighth of bar 12 is heard as part of a continuous sweep that leads to e^2 in the next bar, even though in a structural sense the presence of the D is implied on

EXAMPLE 9.8:

J. S. Bach, Flute Sonata No. 1, Minuet 1, bars 13–16: foreground reduction

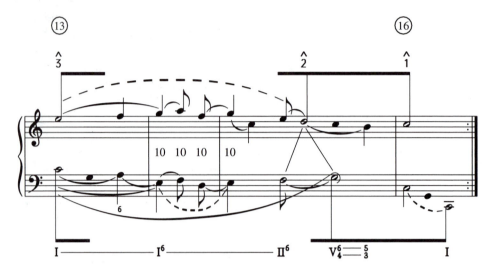

beat 1.[15] That the meaning of a tone may change from the perspective of different structural levels is one of the intriguing features of the tonal system.

CORELLI, VIOLIN SONATA, OP. 5, NO. 10, GAVOTTE

All of the pieces we have studied in this chapter so far are "rounded" in quality, meaning that at least a portion of the material from the beginning of the composition returns in literal or varied (sometimes abbreviated) form near its conclusion. Not all binary forms, however, involve a return of initial thematic material. Those that do not are sometimes referred to as a "simple" binary form. Before we examine another piece by Bach, which is a hybrid of both types of binary forms, we will examine a brief movement by Corelli (Example 9.10). This Gavotte—a clear example of a simple binary form—does not pose any special analytical problems. We will, therefore, concentrate on two salient features. Consider first the overall structure, which shows that an interruption can occur without literal or obvious thematic restatement.

You will notice that many third-motions (indicated by motivic brackets) characterize the musical fabric of this Gavotte. In the final bar, the bracketed tones A–G–F echo the earlier third-motions, but do not constitute an integral linear progression of a third: particularly when a motive is repeated frequently in a work, such "nonstructural" motivic repetitions sometimes occur.

EXAMPLE 9.9:

J. S. Bach, Flute Sonata No. 1, Minuet 1: structural synopsis

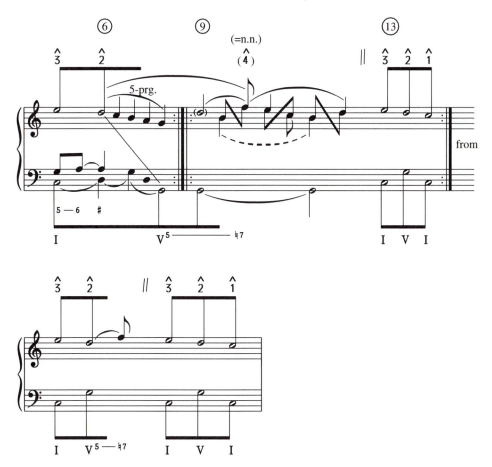

One certainly perceives these tones as a unit, but the A, over a broader span, is a brief restatement of the primary tone and, at the surface, functions as an appoggiatura to G (structural $\hat{2}$) over II$^6_5$. Because a continuo player would realize the second beat as a C-major triad, confirming that G is still active as structural $\hat{2}$, we interpret the F on the second part of beat 2 as an anticipation of structural $\hat{1}$.

Now consider the conclusion of the first section and the development of the second. In bars 3–4 we find an auxiliary cadence supporting a fifth-progression from structural $\hat{2}$ of the first branch. Even though the fundamental structure is divided by an interruption, at the surface the c^2 of bar 4 is restated as the anacrusis to the B section. Tracing the voice leading, you will discover the line C–D–E–F in the intertwined thirds of the violin part (these tones are circled in Example 9.10a). In bar 7, another line, C–B♭–A, overlaps

EXAMPLE 9.10:

Corelli, Violin Sonata Op. 5, No. 10, Gavotte: (a) foreground reduction;
(b) foreground reduction, bars 5–7

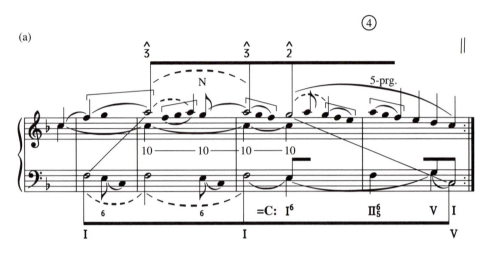

(a)

the conclusion of the fourth-progression and reestablishes the primary tone
$\hat{3}$. Finally, notice a striking recomposition of bars 1–2: the soprano ascent F–
G–A is an enlarged form of the initial ascent from the A section (see the
bracket in the example).

Example 9.10b shows how two strands of the polyphonically conceived violin part are realized consecutively, though unfolding. Consider also that from a deeper perspective one must understand the primary tone $\hat{3}$ as being literally delayed, but conceptually present from the beginning of the B section in bar 5. As an exercise, you may wish to construct your own middleground graph, showing how the tones and harmonies of the two branches align at deeper structural levels.

BACH, FRENCH SUITE NO. 6, MINUET

The E-major Minuet from Bach's French Suite No. 6 presents a remarkable interplay of form, structure, and melodic design. In particular, it employs the structural use of register in ways that recall aspects of previous examples, but are also unique to this work.

The analysis of Bach's music can be challenging. One reason is that his surface textures are often multilinear in character, with polyphonic melodic lines representing two or more implied voices. It can therefore be difficult to define the succession of chords at the surface, a necessary step toward understanding the harmonic structure of a piece. Accordingly, one strategy we suggest for the analysis of Bach's music is to develop first a figured-bass realization of the chords implied by the polyphonic lines. It will then be easier to follow the web of harmony and counterpoint.

The Minuet begins with a straightforward expression of tonic harmony (Example 9.11, bars 1–5). The octave leaps in the left hand (not shown in the graph) emphasize the tonic in two registers; notice also in the music that rests occur regularly in the left hand, except (notably) at points of harmonic arrival.

The E-major tonic triad in bar 5 is a pivot chord, functioning simultaneously as the boundary of the initial prolonged tonic and as IV in the key of B major. In bar 6, the E in the bass supports V_2^4 of B major: this chord introduces A♯ into the tonal fabric, and points ahead to the tonicization of the dominant at the cadence. Thus, what we hear is a modulation that develops gradually, almost imperceptibly, from the initial tonic prolongation.

From this point a direct motion to the cadence occurs, and the bass line outlines the dominant triad: D♯–F♯–B supports I^6–V–I in B major (Example 9.11b). Notice that the dominant does not become fully developed as a secondary key area until the perfect authentic cadence in bars 7–8. This "incomplete" bass progression is an auxiliary cadence.

During the tonic prolongation of bars 1–5, the upper voice gradually ascends from g♯^{1} to g♯^{2}. As Example 9.11 shows, the beautiful and varied figuration in these bars is diminution that expands and elaborates this motion through an octave. Figuration—in the form of motion into an inner voice— also expands the descent from g♯^{2} to f♯^{2} in bars 5–6. Notice that f♯^{2} (structural $\hat{2}$) appears in the upper voice *before* the bass motion has fully established B major.

As the bass continues toward the cadence, f♯^{2} (like g♯^{2} in the previous

EXAMPLE 9.11:

J. S. Bach, French Suite No. 6, Minuet, bars 1–8: (a) foreground and (b) middleground reductions

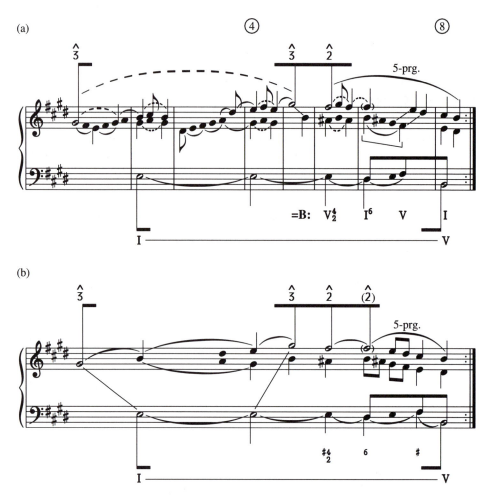

bar) is followed by motion into an inner voice: F♯–E–D♯–C♯–B. The fifth-progression may be difficult to perceive at first glance; as you follow the music, compare this passage with the two levels shown in Example 9.11. They illustrate that the step from f♯² to e² is delayed by the appearance of four notes in the alto register, B–A♯–G♯–F♯ (see the bracket in Example 9.11a). Thus, while the first tone of the fifth progression (F♯) appears prematurely, the second through fifth tones are delayed.[16]

The prolongation of structural $\hat{2}$ through a fifth progression in this Minuet resembles the first sections of Examples 9.1 and 9.7. In all of these cases a lower-level version of a fundamental line (a fifth progression) horizontalizes the dominant harmony and helps to establish, locally, the dominant key. As we mentioned previously, Schenker described this technique as an "incomplete transference of the forms of the fundamental structure [to individual harmonies]" or as an auxiliary cadence.[17] Remember, the transference is incomplete because the harmonic progression that tonicizes the dominant does not begin with a root-position tonic in the new key. The transition from one harmony to another, in these cases from I to V, is made "smoother" (as Schenker puts it) by omitting I in favor of the less stable I^6. We now continue our discussion of this analysis; Chapter 12 contains a more thorough explanation of auxiliary cadences.[18]

Because the remainder of the Minuet is rather complex, we discuss the graphs in some detail (Example 9.12a). In the two measures immediately following the double bar, dominant harmony continues to be active, and f♯^{2} (structural $\hat{2}$) is regained as the prominent tone in the upper voice.

At this point the harmonic progression becomes more difficult to distinguish; we have to rely on the polyphonic melody of the right hand to help us determine the flow of harmony (especially because silence punctuates every other bar of the left hand throughout most of the piece). In the upper voice of bars 11–12, a^2 emerges as a superposed tone and descends to b♯^{1}, here the lowest pitch in the polyphonic melody of the right hand. Because of the silence in the left hand, b♯^{1} is literally the lowest tone of the musical fabric. (In this particular case, the B♯ momentarily represents the bass.) This tone, which supports a diminished seventh chord, is related to the previous bass note B as a chromatic passing tone and implies a resolution to C♯ (see the arrows in Example 9.12a). However, an extraordinary juxtaposition takes place: the diminished seventh chord outlined by the right hand remains active throughout bar 12, despite the C♯ in the bass. The expected resolution to a C♯-minor chord does not actually occur until bar 13. From a broader perspective, therefore, the bass has moved from V to VI through a chromatic passing motion in different registers: B–B♯–C♯ (Example 9.12b).

Once we begin to understand the compound melody of the right hand, viewing it in relation to the direct statements of roots in the left hand, it becomes clear that the interpretation of the harmonic flow depends upon recognizing the verticalities outlined (or horizontalized) in the upper voice. For example, in bar 13, where the C♯-minor triad appears as the resolution of the diminished seventh chord, the lowest tone of the right hand is g♯^{1}, which is followed by a stepwise ascending motion to D♮, regaining the upper voice of the polyphonic melody. This diminished fifth (G♯–D♮) provides us with the clue we need: we interpret it as part of an applied $\frac{4}{3}$ over B that leads to an A-major triad (IV) on the second beat of bar 14 (Example 9.12a). Notice also that, as the A-major triad leads to V in bar 16 (Example 9.12b), an "apparent" tonic (a chord built on the upper fifth of the A-major triad) develops through a voice exchange in bar 15. Example 9.12c further clarifies the function of the apparent tonic and shows that its base tone E supports the passing tone G♯ in the alto voice. The E is a good example of what Schenker called a leaping passing tone. The base leaps from A to E, which supports a literal passing tone in another voice (review Chapter 6, note 16).

We can now put bars 9–16 into a broader perspective. By comparing both levels in Example 9.12, you can see that the dominant is prolonged through

EXAMPLE 9.12:

J. S. Bach, French Suite No. 6, Minuet, bars 9–16: (a) foreground and (b) middleground reduction; (c) function of apparent tonic

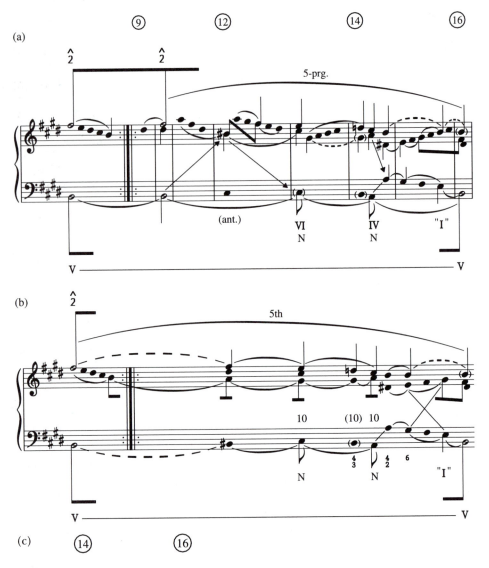

EXAMPLE 9.13:

J. S. Bach, French Suite No. 6, Minuet, bars 16–24: (a) foreground and (b) middleground reductions

brief tonicizations of its upper and lower neighbors (VI and IV). You might think of such tonicizations as "waypoints" within a prolongational span (in this case, within the span of the dominant). Later in this book we will discover that, especially in longer works, such tonicizations can sustain greater emphasis and duration as secondary key areas; nonetheless, the ways in which they can function within a larger prolongation are usually comparable to those we have seen here.

Let us now consider the large-scale motion of the upper voice in relation to the bass up to bar 16 (Example 9.12b). Structural $\hat{2}$ (f#^{2}) is reestablished in bar 10 and at the foreground initiates a descending stepwise motion to b^1 in bars 14–16 (b^1 is stated in bars 14–15, and is implied over the inner-voice tone f#^{1} in bar 16). Thus the upper voice outlines the boundary interval of the dominant triad (F#–B) as the dominant is prolonged in the bass progression with chords built on its upper and lower neighbor notes.

Before examining Example 9.13, which illustrates the remainder of the Minuet, notice in the music that the right hand (after bar 16) initially plays the exact melodic content of bars 1–2, apparently signaling the beginning of a reprise in the form—a return to the thematic content of the beginning. Now focus especially on the bass in bars 18 and 20. Unlike bars 2 and 4, where the initial structural tonic is clearly reinforced, here the left hand emphasizes the dominant note in the manner of a pedal point.

Thus the melodic reprise at bar 17 does not express a reinstated tonic harmony, but rather represents a six-four chord that functions within the ongoing prolongation of dominant harmony. This is possible because of the nature of the six-four chord, in which the "tonic" tones above the bass (E–G#) are unstable, and in need of resolution.[19] Now compare the music to Example 9.13, which will clarify how bars 1–2 are recomposed within the dominant prolongation that continues until the penultimate bar of the Minuet. Notice that b^1 (bar 18) is a prominent element of the melodic reprise, and is a continuation of the lower-level stepwise line that transfers structural $\hat{2}$ from the two-line to the one-line octave (f#^{2} in bars 6 and 10 to f#^{1} in bar 23; compare Examples 9.12 and 9.13).[20]

Example 9.14 presents a structural synopsis of the Minuet. It places Examples 9.11–9.13 into perspective, and clarifies in particular how the recomposition of the opening theme functions within the structural harmonic plan of the movement.

Because the opening theme is literally restated in bars 17–18, it provides a melodic association with the opening that creates a rounded pattern in the melodic design (A^1–B–A^2). Because, however, it is not associated with a return to structural tonic harmony, this passage embodies an entirely different harmonic meaning from that of the opening bars, where we heard the same melody in the sphere of the tonic. The return of the opening theme is associated with a contrapuntal $\frac{6}{4}$ chord within a prolonged dominant harmony, and the passage is thus a "false reprise." That is, it does not involve the kind of structural event that typically occurs in rounded binary forms—namely, the beginning of the second branch of a divided fundamental structure. As Bach's minuet illustrates, melodic (thematic) and harmonic processes will not always coincide and reinforce one another in tonal compositions. Rather, they may stand in an "out-of-phase" relationship in various ways and circumstances.[21]

This has been our most striking example so far of a piece in which elements of form and structure seem to be out of phase with one another, yet function interactively in a unified and integrated whole. The fundamental structure of the Minuet is undivided in the broadest sense, although the auxiliary cadence in the dominant before the double bar articulates the structure into two parts at a lower level. (The tonicization of the dominant at the double bar is a typical procedure in Bach's major-key dance movements.) In another way, Bach also incorporates characteristics of the rounded binary, though not through the technique of interruption that often underlies such forms. Instead, through the expansive and diverse dominant prolongation in

EXAMPLE 9.14:

J. S. Bach, French Suite No. 6, Minuet: structural synopsis

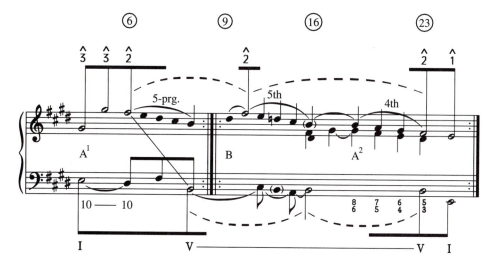

bars 8–23, Bach creates both diversity and unity in a work of startling originality and beauty.

SOME CHARACTERISTIC TONAL PATTERNS

We have seen a variety of ways in which form and structure can interact in works composed in binary form. As a summary and review, Example 9.15 presents in schematic form some characteristic middleground tonal patterns, all notated in C major or A minor to facilitate comparison.

In some cases an undivided structure may embrace a simple binary form. The structure in diagram (a) corresponds to Bach's E-major Minuet. In such undivided structures an auxiliary cadence in the dominant will often establish and prolong $\hat{2}$ over V before the double bar.

Diagram (b), after an analysis by Schenker, shows the middleground (minor-mode) tonal pattern that underlies Bach's Aria Variata, BWV 989.[22] This analysis illustrates one way in which an undivided structure from $\hat{5}$ can span a binary form. The bass structure of this example (I–III–IV–V–I) is commonly found in minor keys (in both divided and undivided structures).[23]

In other types of binary form, most notably rounded binary, the structure is often divided through the technique of interruption (Example 9.15d and e). Here the structure and design divisions do not coincide: the passage immediately following the double bar typically does not signify a beginning in a structural sense, but rather a continuation and prolongation of the dominant

EXAMPLE 9.15:

Binary forms and middleground tonal patterns

(a)

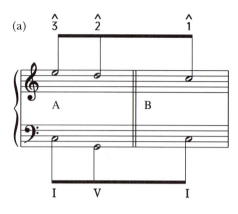

(b)

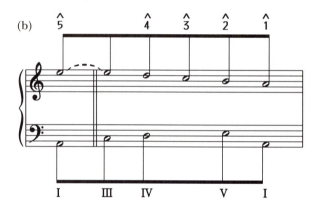

(c)

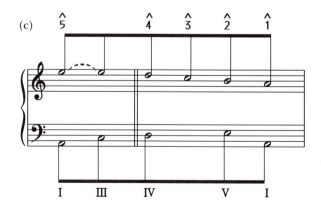

EXAMPLE 9.15 (*continued*)

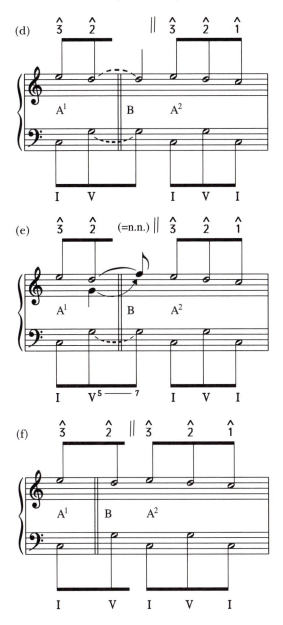

established just before the double bar. Thus, the dominant remains active until the point of interruption. The reprise (indicated by A^2) then arises through the composing-out of the second branch of the structure following the interruption. Mozart's Trio from the "Haffner" Symphony, corresponding to diagram (f), is different from the other examples in this chapter in that the dominant of the first branch does not appear until *after* the double bar.

One might wonder whether viewing the formal patterning of the music in terms of the structure overlooks some features of balance and symmetry, as in cases where the first branch of the interruption extends beyond the cadence at the double bar. Consider further that the repeat signs (an aspect of formal convention) often lead to repetitions of sections that may not coincide with the division in the interrupted structure. To interpret a structural continuation that extends beyond such a repetition, it might be argued, runs counter to a "music as heard" description. Higher levels of structure, however, establish a basis of long-range continuity and motion that is essential in a compositional plan, even if intervening events may divert our attention or awareness along the way. One might say that higher levels of structure are often not so much consciously heard as felt; they involve the articulation and shaping of musical space in the broadest dimensions of a composition.

Much of the dynamic quality of tonal compositions results from the interplay of various tensions on various levels—not only of structure and form, but also of harmony, rhythm, and other aspects of design. That so many diverse and sometimes contradictory elements can be embraced within the ultimately unified structures characteristic of tonal works is truly remarkable, and undoubtedly contributes to the greatness of many tonal compositions.[24]

Exercises

1. Mozart, Variations on "La belle Française", K. 353, Theme

a. Analyze the first phrase. Think carefully about the A♭ in bar 3.

b. Analyze the remainder of the theme. What is the first melodic goal of the line after the double bar? How is this tone related to the first phrase?

c. Explain the voice leading of the A♭ in bar 8.

d. Identify and illustrate in your graph all of the third-motions in the theme. Use motivic brackets where applicable.

2. Jeremiah Clarke, Trumpet Voluntary ("Prince of Denmark's March")

Prepare foreground, middleground, and background graphs of this theme. Is there interruption?

3. Mozart, Variations on "Lison dormait", K. 264, Theme

a. The opening of this piece was presented in Examples 4.2 and 6.11. Complete the analysis, preparing foreground, middleground, and background graphs. What kind of linear progression spans bars 9–16?

b. The reprise in bars 17–32 is longer than the initial section before the double bar and consists of two phrases. Compare the two passages.

c. Does the structure of the piece involve interruption?

4. Haydn, Six Easy Variations in C major, Hob. XVII/5, Theme

a. Identify the number of phrases and the cadences that conclude each phrase. Notice the similarities between the first and third phrases. Does the piece involve an interruption?

b. Sketch a foreground graph of the first phrase. Three common compositional techniques occur in bars 1–2, 2–4, and 5. How are these techniques related to the overall structure of the top voice?

c. Describe the technique that accounts for C in the three-line octave in bars 2 and 12. Also, be able to explain the function of g^2 and f^2 in bar 3.

d. Sketch a graph of the second part of the piece. In the final phrase, how does the change of register in the left hand help you to determine the large bass motion?

e. In bar 7, f^2 is the main tone; it is prolonged through beat 2 of the next bar. To what tone does it then lead? (In the upper voice, the tone in question is implied; the tenor line, however, will help you here.)

f. In bar 10, g^2 is placed on top, but it does not here represent the primary tone $\hat{5}$. In a prolonged dominant region, $\hat{5}$ frequently occurs over structural $\hat{2}$ before an interruption.

  Examine Figures 23b and 25 in *Free Composition*. In this case the harmony in bar 10 is only V, not V^7. How do the last four tones in bar 10 parallel a similar line before the double bar?

g. In bar 15, is the function of the cadential $^6_4$ chord typical in terms of the structural tone it supports? (In Chapter 12, read about the *unsupported stretch* from $\hat{5}$.)

h. Prepare foreground, middleground, and background graphs for this work.

5. Mozart, Variations on a Minuet by Duport,
K. 573, Theme; Variations 1 and 2

a. Prepare foreground, middleground, and background graphs for this theme. In the second section, where does the reprise begin? Is there interruption preceding it?

b. Analyze Variations 1 and 2. Comment on similarities and differences between their structures and that of the theme.

6. Handel, Theme and Variations in B♭ major (from
No. 1 of the second set of keyboard suites, 1733)

   a.   Create foreground, middleground, and background graphs for this
   brief binary form. There are two plausible interpretations (in terms
   of deep middleground structure): try to identify both middleground
   patterns and be able to discuss their differences.

   b.   Consider the role of the f^2 in bar 6 in relation to the preceding $e^{\flat 2}$.
   In view of the elaboration of the latter tone, do we retain a sense of
   it as a "seventh" over A in the bass (a kind of V $^6_5$) that is decorated
   by F, then resolves to d^2 and I in bar 7?

   c.   Study the relationship of the subsequent variations to the theme.
   How is the structure varied, and what kinds of variation procedures
   are used?

7. Haydn, String Quartet Op. 3, No. 3, Minuet

   a.   Prepare an analytical sketch of the Minuet, notated on the grand
   (piano) staff.

   b.   Determine the main prolongations and motions. Structurally, what is
   the relationship between the key area that is prolonged in bars 9–12
   with that prolonged in bars 13–16?

   c.   Prepare complete foreground, middleground, and background
   graphs.

10

Ternary Forms and Rondo

The formal pattern statement–digression–restatement (A^1–B–A^2) is a means of organization by which composers shaped musical compositions for hundreds of years. In the previous chapter we saw that the rounded binary exemplifies this principle to a considerable extent; the rounded part (the restatement), because it is often abbreviated, belongs to the second large formal section of a two-part form (often after a double bar). In other kinds of compositions, however, the A^2 section may proportionately balance the A^1 part (in either literal or varied form). Furthermore, the B section may be distinctly contrasting to the A sections and may be set apart as an autonomous section by double bars, notated key changes, and marked changes in design. Such conspicuous sectional differentiation, though, is not a requirement for a ternary form; many pieces of an apparently consistent nature are based on the principle of statement–digression–restatement. In this chapter we will see some of the ways in which ternary forms develop within fundamental structures.

The relationship between form and structure is complex, and is still being investigated by scholars. A thorough treatment of this subject lies beyond the scope of this book, as does a comprehensive survey of musical forms. However, our investigation of some characteristic compositional types and procedures will serve to illustrate the kinds of analytical issues that are involved.

BEETHOVEN, BAGATELLE, OP. 119, NO. 1

Beethoven's G-minor Bagatelle, Op. 119, No. 1, represents our first example of a ternary form (A[1]–B–A[2]) in which the sections are distinctly set apart. Strong cadences, and changes in thematic design and in tonal center, clearly delineate the B section (bars 17–32) as a separate formal unit that nevertheless forms part of a unified whole.

At our present level of study, bars 1–16 should offer no particular problems. After you listen to or play through the Bagatelle, you will notice that the A[1] section consists of an antecedent/consequent construction that clearly shows the technique of interruption. The section recurs with added figuration in bars 37–52, but it is virtually identical to bars 1–16. For this reason, Example 10.1 represents both the A[1] and A[2] sections.

As you study the graph, consider several features of the A[1] section that play important roles throughout the composition:

1. The primary tone $\hat{5}$ is decorated from the very outset by its upper neighbor $\hat{6}$. This $\hat{5}$–$\hat{6}$–$\hat{5}$ figure (D–E♭–D) is a recurring motive with great significance for the Bagatelle.

2. The right-hand part in bars 1–4 is segmented in such a way as to produce "apparent" fourths at the musical surface. The fourths are apparent (rather than true, structural fourths) because in each case the four stepwise tones comprise a third plus a step, as clarified by the harmonic structure. Notice also the motivic association between these apparent fourths (marked with brackets in the graph) and the linear motion D–A in bars 1–5 (also bracketed): the motive thus occurs at two different structural levels.

3. A very distinctive feature of this composition is the contrapuntal nature of bars 1–5. The outer voices move to a large extent in parallel tenths, a motion prepared by the outer voices of the I[6] chord that begins the piece. It is not unusual, especially in compositions of the nineteenth century, to begin with chords other than harmonically stable, root-position tonic triads. In this case I[6] leads to the I in bar 6, creating a five-bar prolongation of the tonic.

4. Refer now to Example 10.2, which represents the structure of the consequent phrase and clarifies the role of the prolonged tonic. Notice that $\hat{5}$–$\hat{4}$–$\hat{3}$ of the upper-voice descent is harmonized with the progression I[6]–V$_3^4$–I, meaning that parallel tenths shape different levels of the composition: not only the surface of the music (Example 10.1), but also the middleground of the A sections. This contrapuntal and harmonic structure also means that scale degree $\hat{4}$ is not fully supported, as it would be by an intermediate harmony or a root-position dominant seventh chord.[1] Throughout the Bagatelle, however, various kinds of motions occur that, in effect, compensate for this "weak" support. In bar 7 of the antecedent phrase, for instance, notice the motion from C after $\hat{2}$ is reached, in effect retracing the descent at the surface just before the dominant appears (see the circled portion of Example 10.1a).

EXAMPLE 10.1:

Beethoven, Bagatelle, Op. 119, No. 1: foreground reductions of (a) bars 1–8 and (b) 9–16

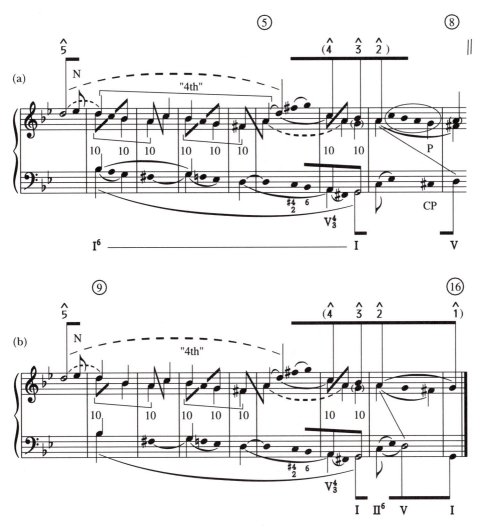

As we turn our attention to the B section, bear in mind that the A^1 section is a tonally self-contained unit within a larger piece, punctuated by a perfect authentic cadence in G minor ($\hat{1}$ over I). When we consider the relation of this section to the entire composition, we will see that the first descent from the primary tone $\hat{5}$ is a motion into an inner voice and, consequently, that the background structure of the A^1 section represents a lower-level form of the fundamental structure.

Listen again to the Bagatelle. This time, focus in particular on the B section, thinking in terms of E♭ major. Ultimately we will integrate our analytical observations into a larger framework in the tonic key of G minor, but this

EXAMPLE 10.2:

Beethoven, Bagatelle, Op. 119, No. 1: structural analysis of bars 9–16

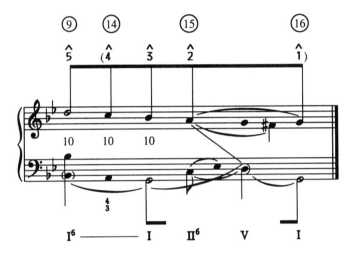

approach often serves well as a first step in analyzing forms with sharply contrasting sections. As you listen, notice the difference in the function of the scale degrees: the tone G, for example, does not sound as stable as it does in the A^1 section (where it is the tonic), and E♭, the active upper neighbor to the dominant in G minor, is now the (temporary) stable tonic.

Example 10.3 presents a voice-leading graph of the first part of the B section.[2] In the first four-bar grouping (bars 17–20), g^1 ($\hat{3}$ in E♭, the local primary tone) is prolonged with the double neighbor figure G–F–A♭–G. This figure is elaborated at the surface of the music with a motion from c^2 (bars 18–19). The c^2, as Example 10.3a indicates, is a tone superposed from the inner voice. If you compare (in the music) the upper voice in bars 18–20 and bars 7–8, you will discover a close parallelism: both passages contain stepwise descents leading from C. The second descent, which is preceded and highlighted by a leap, is a reminiscence (in E♭ major) of the first. In both cases the motions emphasize C, the tone "weakly supported" in the fundamental line of the A^1 section (compare the circled portions in Examples 10.1a and 10.3b).

The second four-bar unit of the B section (bars 21–24) is essentially a disguised recomposition of the first. First study level *b* of Example 10.3, then level *a*. The primary tone $\hat{3}$ of this section is followed again by the upper neighbor A♭ in bar 22 before the cadential motion to $\hat{2}$–$\hat{1}$ occurs. But the resemblance goes further. Example 10.3a shows that the alto line in bars 17–18, B♭–B♮–C, recurs an octave higher in bars 21–22, where it serves as an elaboration (superposed from an inner voice) of the higher-ranking $\hat{3}$–$\hat{2}$–$\hat{1}$ (compare the brackets in Example 10.3a).

Notice also that the repeated upper neighbor $a♭^1$ is approached both times from c^2, a superposed inner-voice tone. The second covering motion begins in bar 20, when the upper voice leaps up to $e♭^2$. This note does not

EXAMPLE 10.3:

Beethoven, Bagatelle, Op. 119, No. 1, B section, bars 17–24: (a) foreground and (b) middleground reductions

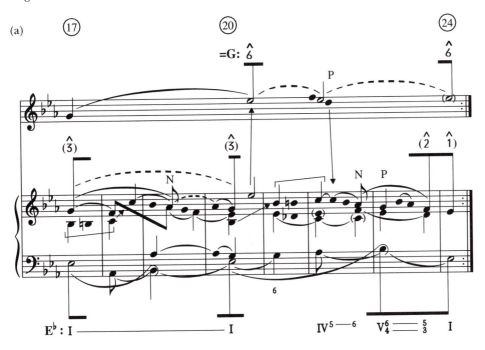

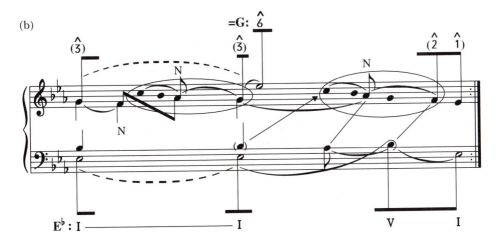

participate in most of the foreground structural motion, but assumes a different and more prominent aspect from a middleground perspective. As the graphs indicate, the top voice descends from E♭ to the C of the second covering motion, but at another level e♭^{2} remains as a tone prolonged by a separate voice-leading strand. The significance of this subtle point will become clearer as we complete our analysis of the B section.[3]

Example 10.4 shows the remaining part of the B section, a portion of

EXAMPLE 10.4:

Beethoven, Bagetelle, Op. 119, No. 1, B section, bars 24–32: (a) foreground and (b) middleground reductions

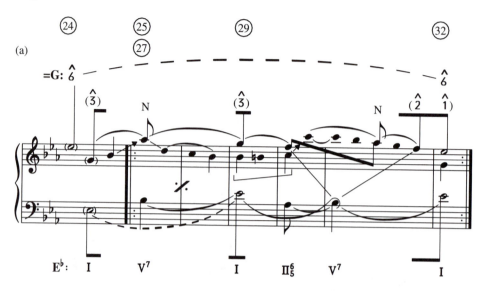

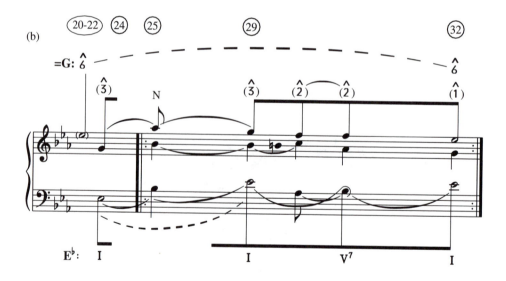

which we also discussed in Chapter 4 (Example 4.9). As you may recall, we used bars 25–29 to illustrate the expansion of a single chord through a linear progression that delineates a dissonant interval—the seventh of the dominant seventh chord. Now we are able to place this brief passage into the perspective of the complete work. (We have shown g^1 in bar 24 of Example 10.4 because it is conceptually prolonged from the beginning of the B section; from a broader perspective the descent before the double bar is motion into an inner voice.)

EXAMPLE 10.5:

Beethoven, Bagatelle, Op. 119, No. 1, retransition, bars 32–36: foreground reduction

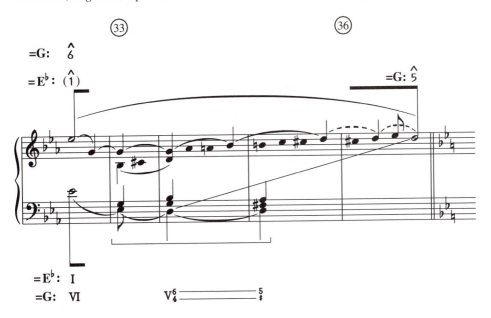

The sole harmony in bars 25–28 is V^7 in E♭ major, which supports A♭, another version of the upper neighbor $\hat{4}$ we have seen in this section. Notice that the neighbor tone is now highlighted, occurring prominently in the two-line octave through a transfer of register. This registral shift is significant: after A♭ resolves back to G (bar 29), a brief reprise of the beginning of the section occurs in the higher register and closes on $e♭^2$. For this reason we have indicated a connection between the E♭s in bars 20–22 and in bar 32 (compare Examples 10.3 and 10.4). This tone, of course, is locally the goal of motion for the lower-level fundamental line in E♭ major ($\hat{3}$–$\hat{2}$–$\hat{1}$); we shall soon discover, however, that it is also motivically significant at a high middleground level of the entire Bagatelle.

Because the B section closes in E♭ major with $\hat{1}$ over I (note also the cessation of rhythmic motion in the repeat of bar 32), a retransition is needed to prepare the return of the tonic that begins the A^2 section. Example 10.5 presents the last bar of the B section and the voice leading of this modulatory passage.

The modulation is based on a pivot chord. The I in E♭ (on the downbeat of bar 32) also functions as VI in G minor. In the alto voice, the subsequent motion from B♭ to C♯ (on beat 3) transforms the sonority into an augmented sixth chord, which resolves to the dominant of G minor (intensified through a cadential $^6_4$ chord); the dominant is prolonged in the remainder of the retransition. Although one might consider this harmonic progression to be a common type of modulation, it also has a particular motivic association. Notice that the bass notes which support this motion are E♭–D. When C♯ enters

EXAMPLE 10.6:

Beethoven, Bagatelle, Op. 119, No. 1: middleground synopsis

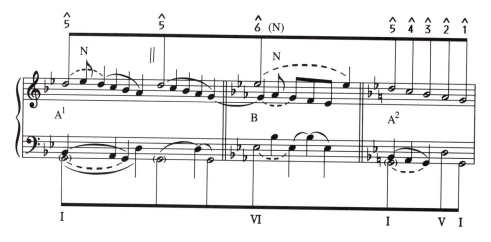

in the alto, the bass note of E♭ is destabilized, and becomes an *upper neighbor* to D, the dominant of G minor.[4] The bass tones E♭–D of the retransition recall the upper neighbor figure from the very beginning of the piece, just before the A² section commences, as if to anticipate the return of the opening theme. This special motivic feature integrates the retransition section into the structural and motivic fabric of the work as a whole.

The upper voice of the retransition begins on g¹; the e♭² shown in Example 10.5, bar 32, is the last note of the B section and is provided for perspective. This perspective is revealing, for we see that the rising line from g¹ to d² represents motion from an inner voice that reestablishes the primary tone $\hat{5}$. In other words, G, the local $\hat{3}$ of the lower-level fundamental line in E♭, must ultimately be understood as a tone belonging to the inner voice of the Bagatelle's G-minor fundamental structure. Example 10.6 is a synopsis that clarifies this subtle relationship among levels, and also reveals a remarkable motivic feature of the middleground.

The three-part form of the Bagatelle is established by a large-scale I–VI–I motion. At a lower level, the I and VI are composed-out through their own *Ursatz* patterns (Example 10.6). This is another good example of Schenker's principle of the "transference of the forms of the fundamental structure to individual harmonies": an *Ursatz* parallelism in G minor (the A¹ section) is followed by one in E♭ major (the B section).[5]

Prolonging motions such as I–VI–I (and I–III–I), which often serve as foundations for three-part sectional forms, can be referred to as *contrapuntal progressions* because the voice leading typically involves common-tone and neighbor motion.[6] Indeed, the $\hat{5}$–$\hat{6}$–$\hat{5}$ motion associated with the I–VI–I progression is a figure with far-reaching ramifications for this piece. We have seen that the first descent from $\hat{5}$ is an *Urlinie* parallelism (from a middleground perspective, a motion to an inner voice). We have also seen that g¹, the final melodic goal of the A^1 section and the local primary tone ($\hat{3}$) of the B section, belongs to an inner voice of the Bagatelle's fundamental structure. What happens, however, to the work's primary tone ($\hat{5}$) as VI prolongs I? If you imagine the I–VI–I progression in four voices, your studies of harmony and voice leading will help to clarify the answer. As the prolonged I of the A^1 section moves to VI of the B section, the primary tone $\hat{5}$ (d^2) moves to $\hat{6}$ (e♭^{2}) in a voice-leading motion on a high level of the middleground. In other words, as Example 10.6 illustrates, the lower-level motion $\hat{3}$–$\hat{2}$–$\hat{1}$ in E♭ occurs conceptually "beneath" the higher-level neighbor note $\hat{6}$ (E♭).[7] This tone is not literally present in the foreground at first, but it emerges in bars 20–22 and at the conclusion of the B section. Here it appears prominently in the two-line octave, establishing a large-scale relationship between the neighbor note e♭^{2} and the primary tone d^2 ($\hat{5}$) of the A^1 section. This connection, in its relatively high register, suggests to listeners that e♭^{2} is a prominent tone in the overall structure, while the local fundamental line $\hat{3}$–$\hat{2}$–$\hat{1}$ shapes the B section. During the retransition, the upper neighbor $\hat{6}$ moves back to $\hat{5}$ (Example 10.5). The A^2 section then retraces the motion $\hat{5}$–$\hat{1}$, which now serves as the descent of the fundamental line and the completion of the fundamental structure.

Our comparative analysis of voice-leading strands at different structural levels now reveals a remarkable motivic association: as indicated in Example 10.6, D–E♭–D, the opening motto of the Bagatelle, is expanded over much of the composition on the first level of the middleground! Such motivic interrelationships often integrate different levels of structure in a composition. Thus, in the middleground expression of the D–E♭–D motive, the neighbor note $\hat{6}$ is associated with the submediant chord whose expansion forms the B section.

Schenker believed that a neighbor note—an aspect of voice leading—could be directly associated with the development of a three-part form: "The neighboring note of the fundamental line is in most cases form-generative; . . . [it] can be expanded at the foreground level to become the middle part of a three-part form."[8] This is what occurs in Beethoven's Bagatelle. The upper neighbor $\hat{6}$ expands the composition and delays the descent of the fundamental line. The neighbor is in turn expanded by the *Ursatz* parallelism in E♭, which defines the B section of the work's ternary form.

Examples 10.7 and 10.8 show the voice leading of the coda, which comprises three segments; as with the A sections, we will limit our discussion to a few features as you study the graphs on your own.

The first issue we shall consider is how the coda relates to the whole; this is indicated in the graphs by the open noteheads in bars 52 and 73–74, signifying that the fundamental line has completed its descent and that $\hat{1}$ over I is prolonged over the remaining span of the composition. Schenker, in fact, seems to define the function of codas in terms of the completion of the structure. In his discussion of sonata form in *Free Composition*, for example, he says that "once the $\hat{1}$ has been reached, a coda section may follow, and there may be a harking-back to the position of the primary tone."[9]

In addressing such aspects of Schenker's work, it is important to bear in mind that his ideas about form are not fully developed. And, as we have seen

EXAMPLE 10.7:

Beethoven, Bagatelle, Op. 119, No. 1, coda, bars 52–65: foreground reduction

in other examples, relationships between form and structure are often complex; it is therefore difficult to make generalizations about the function of codas. In this piece, however, the coda does follow the descent of the fundamental line. Furthermore, explicit in Schenker's comments is the idea of recollection (the "harking-back" to the primary tone). This notion is similar to traditional ways of understanding codas, which often recall important motives and themes, and resolve "unfinished" musical issues. Although the recollection of the primary tone $\hat{5}$ is not a prominent feature of this coda, a musical issue from the very beginning of the Bagatelle is finally brought to fruition. Our final remarks address this intriguing aspect of the composition's "tonal plot."[10]

EXAMPLE 10.8:

Beethoven, Batatelle, Op. 119, No. 1, coda, bars 65–74: foreground reduction

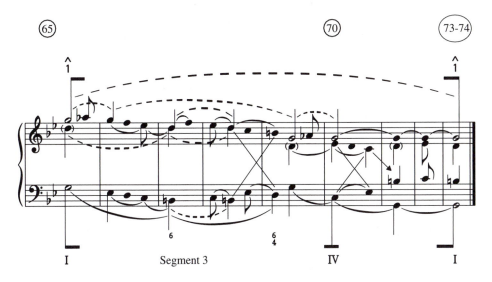

In our earlier discussion of the A^1 section, we commented that scale degree $\hat{4}$ is not strongly supported in the descent from $\hat{5}$ to $\hat{1}$ (compare again Examples 10.1 and 10.2). This situation recurs in the A^2 section, in the descent of the fundamental line (Example 10.6). But now, in the coda, full structural support is given to this tone, as if to balance the unsupported stretch $\hat{5}$–$\hat{4}$–$\hat{3}$ in the A^1 and A^2 sections. We pointed out a motion from C in bar 7, and the varied repetitions that occur in bars 18–19 and bars 30–31. Compare now the upper voice of segments 1 and 2 in the coda (Example 10.7) and you will discover two versions of $\hat{4}$–$\hat{3}$–$\hat{2}$–$\hat{1}$. The first begins with c^2 (bar 53) and through register transfer concludes in the higher position. The second version descends completely by step in the higher register, after a broad rising motion from $\hat{6}$, a consonant recollection (over IV) of the upper neighbor E♭.

Notice two significant features associated with scale degree $\hat{4}$ in bar 62. First, it occurs in the three-line octave. This register is prefigured in the statement of c^3 in bars 30–31 of the B section. The use of c^3 (the highest note in the piece) in these two passages establishes an association through register, so that bars 62–64 may be understood to recall the earlier passage in this way.[11] Second, scale degree $\hat{4}$ is now harmonized by a V^7 chord which, as we pointed out, now "balances" the contrapuntal setting of which it is a part in the A sections. At the climactic point of the Bagatelle, therefore, the recollection of scale-degree $\hat{4}$ of the fundamental line is given its final and most conclusive support.

Example 10.8 illustrates bars 65–74, the third segment of the coda. You will notice that the upper voice transfers $\hat{1}$ from the two-line octave, where it has been stated prominently in the previous segments of the coda, to the one-line octave, the obligatory structural register of the Bagatelle.[12] Because the line begins on G in bar 65, the recollection of the upper neighbor figure from the beginning is transposed and emerges as G–A♭–G (bars 65–66 and 69–70); as we saw, this figure is an integral voice-leading component of the B section (Example 10.3). Notice also that the coda's final bars employ a plagal motion, which in tonal music can produce a sense of serenity and repose at the conclusion of a composition. In this Bagatelle, however, it also serves a motivic purpose. The voice leading of the I–IV–I progression in G minor contains the tone succession E♭–D, a motive that has played a most significant role in the shaping of this piece at various structural levels. In the final bars, as the dynamic level diminishes from piano to pianissimo, this motive is suggested one final time in the inner voice of the right hand as the work quietly reaches its close.

MENDELSSOHN, SONG WITHOUT WORDS, OP. 62, NO. 1

Our next work, a *Song Without Words* by Felix Mendelssohn (Op. 62, No. 1), is very different in style from Beethoven's Bagatelle. With its songlike melody suggested by the title, this *character piece* for piano creates a distinct atmosphere or mood that results, at least in part, from a number of unusual structural features. We shall concentrate on these features, and related aspects of design and form in this expressive piece.

One notable aspect of the compositional style in this work is the consistent arpeggiation pattern that accompanies the right-hand melody. Because of this relative consistency in texture, as well as in other aspects of design, the shape and form of the work may be recognized most distinctly through the composing-out of the melodic and harmonic structure, which is realized in a rich polyphonic framework.

The polyphony is evident as the work begins: the lyrical right-hand melody consists of two voices that are intertwined through unfolding and passing motions (Example 10.9). As the example shows, the upper strand of the melody traces the descending third D–C–B, while the inner voice ascends chromatically A–A♯–B; thus, both voices converge on the primary tone $\hat{3}$. In bars 2–4 the bass tones C–C♯–D in bars 2–4 continue the preceding chromatic motion. These motions—the descending third, and the chromatic ascent through two semitones—are prominent motives throughout the work. Another important motive is the plaintive falling fourth (D–A) with which the melody begins.

A striking feature is the inverted dominant chord that begins the work. (In our interpretation of the figuration pattern in the lefthand, C is a neighbor to D, embellishing the V^6 chord indicated in Example 10.9.) Beginning on a chord other than the tonic is not unusual, especially in nineteenth-century music. Nevertheless, such a compositional decision often has ramifications for the rest of the work, and should be carefully evaluated by the analyst. If we consider bars 1–4, which may be designated an antecedent phrase, it is evident that the only tonic chord occurs at the end of the first subphrase (on the downbeat of bar 2). By emphasizing dominant harmony at the beginning and end of the antecedent phrase, Mendelssohn creates an unstable, restless quality. This quality is poetically enhanced by the falling motive (D–A), which is restated in varied form as a seventh (G–A) in bar 2 and a fifth (E–A) in bar three. These figures invoke a feeling of yearning, as does the suspension of the A♯ from bar 1 to the downbeat of bar 2.

Also remarkable is the relationship between the rhythmic position of the phrase and the underlying meter. Listen to a performance or a recording of the opening bars of the work without the music, and consider where the first downbeat appears. You will probably hear the beginning as a downbeat, even though (as you will see when you check the music) it is notated as an upbeat. Moreover, the first notated downbeat is "suppressed" because it occurs, with no special emphasis, in the midst of what has already begun. This rhythmic displacement continues throughout the opening of the composition; as notated, the rhythm and phrasing of the music do not correspond to the normal metrical framework suggested by the time signature. This conflict between the metrical downbeats and phrasing of the music creates a subtle kind of tension that contributes to the expressive quality of this piece.[13]

The consequent phrase (end of bar 4 to bar 10) concludes, not with an authentic cadence in the tonic, but with a cadence in the mediant. Motivically, the "seed" of this modulation may be found with the A♯–B melodic figure in bars 1–2 and 5–6. Especially with F♯ in the bass, the B minor seems almost foretold. Notice, also, that the consequent phrase is extended from four to six bars; in terms of melodic structure, the extension results from the upper-voice motions that occur within the span D–B. As shown in the graph, the initial motion D–C–B is transformed into D–C♯–B as a result of the tonicization of the mediant.

Certain features of the harmonic structure also contribute to the expansion of the consequent phrase. The progression that tonicizes III appears to begin as early as bar 7 with B minor's cadential $^6_4$. The cadence, however, is evaded through the progression V^6_4–V^4_2–I^6. Notice, furthermore, that following F♯ the bass line tones E–D of this motion are transferred to the *inner voice* of the left hand. This transfer of register highlights B minor's French sixth, which is built on G in the lower register of the left hand. Example 10.9 shows that we regard the French sixth, at a deeper level, as a *chromatic boundary* of the consequent phrases's prolonged tonic harmony.[14] Notice also that this interpretation highlights a continued relationship between F♯ and G in the lower register; these tones, of course, are the initial bass tones of the piece.

We commented above that sectional divisions are not obvious in this work, because of the consistency in texture. However a number of subtle changes establish the phrase that begins in bars 10–11 as the start of the B section (Example 10.10). Beginning with the tonicized E minor chord in bar 11, an ascending 5–6 sequence creates considerably faster harmonic rhythm and a different melodic pattern. The fourth-motive, which was previously a descending figure, is now inverted to a rising fourth in bars 11, 13, and 14. The rising chromatic motive of the opening (A–A♯–B) also appears in new guises, in the alto (bars 10–11), the soprano (11–12 and 14–15), and sequentially repeated in the chromatic rising bass.

Another important change establishing bar 10 as a significant point of

EXAMPLE 10.9:

Mendelssohn, *Song Without Words,* Op. 62, No. 1, bars 1–10: (a) foreground and (b) middleground reductions

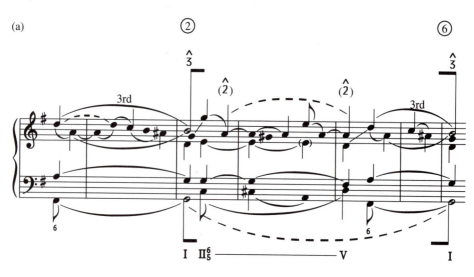

(a)

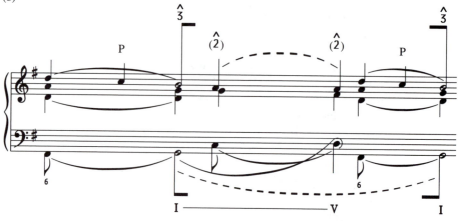

(b)

articulation in the form is that in the ensuing passage (bars 10–18) the phrase rhythm is now in accord with the meter. These changes create a marked contrast to the displaced phrase rhythm and broader harmonic gestures of the preceding A section.

In bar 15 the sequence concludes as the bass reaches B (supporting V^6 of IV), which is further highlighted through repetition in bars 16–18; remember that this bass tone supports the tonicized mediant that marks the end of the first section (bar 10). We therefore relate the main chords in bars 10 and 15–18: the mediant of bar 10 is transformed, through a 5–6 motion at a deeper level, into a G-major $^6_3$ (bar 15), which ultimately leads to IV in bar 18 (Exam-

EXAMPLE 10.9 (*continued*)

ple 10.10b). The ascending 5–6 sequence in bars 11–15 is the means by which this transformation is expanded.

We can now begin to understand the meaning of the G-major $^6_3$ that serves as the goal of the sequence; note that the upper voice moves in parallel tenths with the bass and leads to d^2 in bar 15. After this sonority is prolonged with neighbor motions (bars 15–16), it leads to IV in the same fashion as the V^6 at the beginning of the piece leads to I in bar 2. This similarity in harmonic progressions enables Mendelssohn to bring back the initial theme at the climax of the piece in the subdominant, as a kind of "false return." (Note in Example 10.10b the G–F♮–E motion, which corresponds to the D–C–B motive of the opening.)

EXAMPLE 10.10:

Mendelssohn, *Song Without Words,* Op. 62, No. 1, bars 10–24: (a) foreground and (b) middleground reductions

Having reached the subdominant chord so dramatically, we expect the structural harmonic progression to continue to the dominant. But we soon realize that this is not going to happen. In a moment of extraordinary pathos and beauty, the opening thematic figure is repeated a third lower in bars 19–20; notice that the final two notes of the figure, which had previously ascended by semitone (A♯–B in bar 2, D♯–E in bar 18) now descend (B–A, bar 20). In conjunction with this altered thematic restatement, the subdominant of bar 18 is transformed by the chromatic motive G–G♯–A (in the tenor voice) into the II⁶ of bar 20 (through yet another 5–6 motion).

Thus the passage assumes a quasi-programmatic character: after the considerable time and "effort" that was devoted to the melodic ascent and the

EXAMPLE 10.10 (*continued*)

attainment of IV, the sudden drop in melodic register and the chromaticized 5–6 motion create a profoundly expressive moment as the expected continuation of the harmonic structure to the dominant is abandoned. (This can be clearly seen in Example 10.12, a middleground graph of the complete work.)

A beautiful motivic relationship at the conclusion of the passage is bracketed in Example 10.10a: the descending fifth-motion E–A in the soprano (bar 20) is echoed in longer note values by the descending fifth C–F♯ in the bass (bars 20–22), which leads to V^6. We can now see clearly Mendelssohn's compositional plan. By descending from IV to V^6 (instead of ascending from IV to root-position V), he can realize a possibility inherent in the nontonic beginning of the piece. The V^6 represents a harmonically reasonable continuation

EXAMPLE 10.11:

Mendelssohn, *Song Without Words,* Op. 62, No. 1, bars 24–41: (a) foreground and (b) middleground reductions

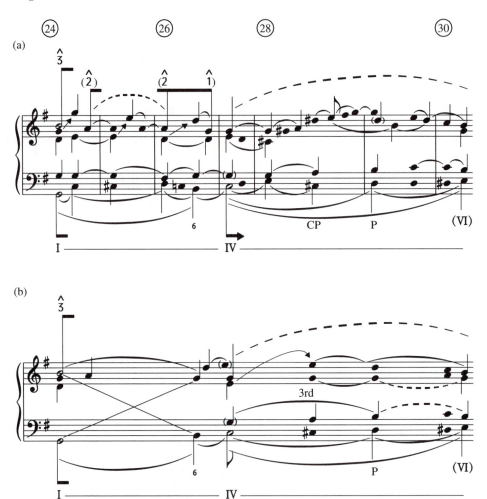

from the IV of bar 18; but it is also the sonority with which the piece begins. Hence the V^6 serves both as the goal of the initial large-scale harmonic progression and also as the beginning of the A^2 section. In this way Mendelssohn leads into the reprise in an almost imperceptible fashion.

The antecedent phrase in bars 22–26 is identical to that of bars 1–4, establishing a return to the opening material (Example 10.11). The following phrase, however, is different from the modulating consequent (bars 4–10) of the A^1 section. It begins with a I^6 in bar 26, becoming the first phrase in the piece to begin with a tonic chord. The phrase then moves directly to IV: significantly, its bass note (C) supported IV and II^6 at the end of the B section, bars 18–20. In the upper voice, the opening thematic motive has also

EXAMPLE 10.11 (*continued*)

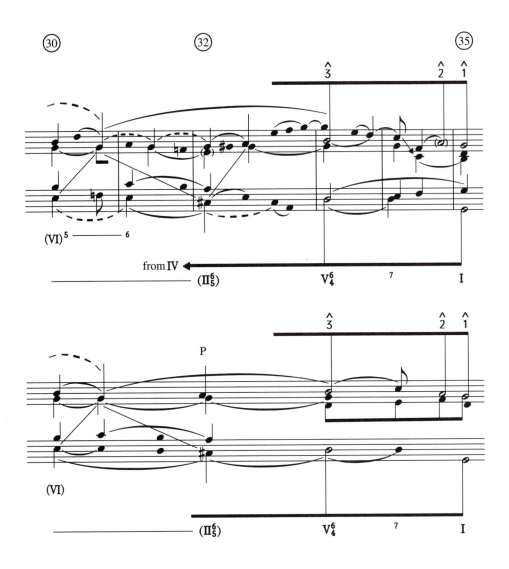

been transformed: the fourth D–A is now replaced by the descending fifth D–G (bar 26), giving a different character to the theme. Not only has the interval of the fourth been replaced by the more stable interval of the fifth, but the supertonic note in the upper voice has also been replaced by the tonic note, a more stable tone (as supported by the I⁶ chord).

The remainder of the theme (and of the phrase) is also transformed: following the motion to IV, the top voice ascends once again to g^2, the climactic high note associated with the earlier motion to IV (in bars 17–18). The chord supporting g^2 (bar 29) appears to function initially as a cadential $^6_4$; because it moves unexpectedly to VI, however, it can therefore be interpreted

EXAMPLE 10.11 (*continued*)

as a passing six-four in a motion that delays the appearance of the structural dominant. The delay is further intensified by a varied repetition of the same phrase in bars 30–33.

The VI (of the deceptive motion) is best understood as the upper third of the preceding IV (Example 10.12). From a broader perspective, the bass note C of IV (bar 27) moves through the chromatic passing tone C♯ (bar 32) to the true cadential $^6_4$ (as noted above, the $^6_4$ of bar 29 is a passing chord). The $^6_4$ (bar 33) signals the beginning of the cadence that supports the descent of the fundamental line. The polyphonic richness and complexity of the upper voice is evident at this cadence, where three voices are suggested (as has often been the case throughout the piece).

Now study the coda in relation to the last part of Example 10.11. Two significant motivic issues should be mentioned. First, the descending fourth D–A in the melody is echoed by the tonally stable fourth G–D in the bass. Second, the coda concludes with a recitativelike passage in which two final statements of the third-motive occur in the upper voice: A–B–C and E–F♯–G (bars 38–39). Here these disparate motives resolve in the concluding tonic chord, as shown in Example 10.11a: the C in bar 38 is transferred into the inner voice, where it resolves to B in the following bar. The tones E–F♯–G are perhaps best described as an "apparent" third; the line originates from the inner-voice tone D and thus belongs to a structural fourth (from $\hat{5}$ to $\hat{8}$).[15] This sense of resolution is underscored by a final poetic touch: in bar 39 the appoggiatura (the second tone of the E–F♯–G motive) is lengthened to a half note, creating a composed ritard that brings the rhythmic momentum fully to rest as the upper voice finally resolves to the tonic note. The motion from F♯ to G has, of course, already been stated in long note values, in the bass at the beginning of the piece!

Our final comments address the issue of form as it relates to the development of tonal structure in this *Song Without Words.* In Beethoven's Bagatelle we encountered a ternary form (A^1–B–A^2) that develops within an undivided (uninterrupted) structure and that is clearly differentiated as a three-part form by several factors: a change in tonal center, strong concluding cadences in the tonic of each tonal region, a contrasting theme in the B section, and so forth.

In Mendelssohn's composition, the structure is also undivided, but this feature by itself does not mean that the three-part forms of the two pieces are similar. In this piece we must rely on broad harmonic motions and somewhat more subtle changes in design than in the Bagatelle to make determinations about the form (Example 10.12). The greater continuity of the *Song Without Words* (relative to the Bagatelle) does not arise merely through the more uniform texture, rhythm, and accompaniment figure. The harmonic progression from I–III, which in part defines the A section (bars 1–10), means that the piece remains "open" and requires continuation and completion much more urgently than in the Bagatelle. In other words, Mendelssohn's composition is a continuous form through its middleground plan as well as through the surface features of its design, whereas Beethoven's Bagatelle is a segmented (or "closed") form for corresponding though opposite reasons—middleground layout as well as surface contrast.

The texture of the B section helps to preserve the continuous nature of the piece, but we can recognize significant changes in design; consider the normalization of rhythmic conflicts discussed above, as well as the contrasting upper-voice motions and the "false" return. The harmonic motion that supports these features and delineates the B section is III–IV–V^6.[16] The harmonic goal of this second motion, of course, is also the beginning of the next section, which can readily be identified as the A^2 section in the form. In considering the formal patterns in the preceding and following examples in this chapter, remember that various techniques may articulate the structure and lead to multisectional forms.

EXAMPLE 10.12:

Mendelssohn, *Song Without Words,* Op. 62, No. 1: middleground synopsis

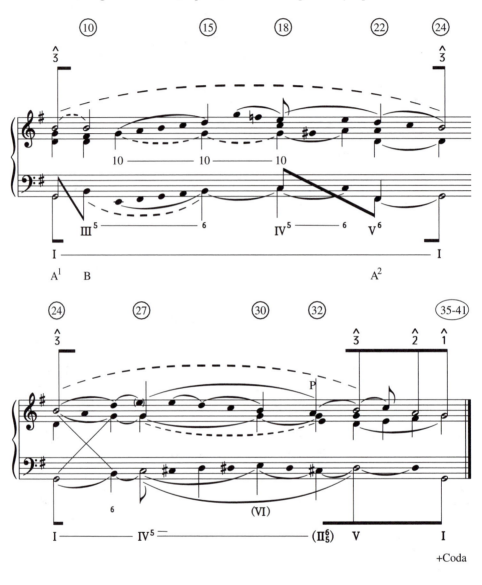

SCHUBERT, MOMENT MUSICAL, OP. 94, NO. 2

Schubert's Moment Musical in A♭ major, like Mendelssohn's *Song Without Words,* is a type of composition often described as a character piece because it expresses a particular mood or atmosphere. Because we are limiting our discussion of specific compositional techniques at this stage (and do not need to treat each section of the composition exhaustively), let us begin with an overview of the form, to which you can refer back as you study the examples. The piece embodies an A–B–A–B–A organization, a three-part form that expands to five parts through the varied restatements of the B and A sections. (The second A section contains a codalike section, which gives a surprising effect to the resumption of B.)[17]

Consider also two motivations for the twofold reprise scheme. The initial A section is tonally open; the second is closed, but it does not resolve the modulatory passage at the end of the first A section. It is the final A section that provides the needed resolution: it contains a cadence in the tonic corresponding to the earlier cadence in the subdominant.

The second motivation concerns the symmetry and balance of phrase groups. The first A section has two large phrase groups, a kind of antecedent and modulating consequent. The second A section contains only one corresponding phrase, so that it seems truncated despite the coda-like section that follows. In other words, without the twofold reprise scheme, the piece would seem unbalanced, in need of further content and stronger completion.

The opening of the work suggests a serene atmosphere of balance and repose. This is achieved through a number of different musical elements: (1) the repeated neighbor-note motions, in conjunction with the compound meter (9/8) and dotted rhythms, create a rocking motion (in both melody and rhythm) that suggests the character of a barcarolle; (2) the prevalence of tonic harmony, prolonged with neighboring dominant chords, establishes a stable harmonic framework; and (3) the repeated E♭ in the tenor (the dominant note of the key, common to both tonic and dominant chords) reinforces the stability of the opening through its constant presence. It forms a consistent element of texture and voice leading, and serves as a stable point about which the other notes move.

The distinction among different structural levels can be difficult in this piece, because of the many repetitions of the neighbor figures. As shown in Example 10.13, the first neighboring motion (on the upbeat) essentially prolongs the initial A♭-major triad. The neighbor chord on the first downbeat, by contrast, receives greater emphasis through its metrical position, longer duration, and its position as the goal of the first subphrase. This passage illustrates how carefully the context must be evaluated in making analytical judgments: although the two neighbor chords are technically the same sonority, the neighbor chord on the downbeat resides at a higher level than that on the upbeat, a consideration that should be reflected in performance. If you play or listen to the opening you will undoubtedly hear that the two neighbor chords do not sound the same in context, because of the different structural levels on which they function.

Consideration of the prolonged tonic chord on the third beat of bar 1 raises an interesting analytical question: does it represent a structural return to I, or does it serve to connect the preceding and following chords? Example 10.13 presents the latter interpretation: the top-voice note c^2 is integrated within the span of a third as a passing tone between $d♭^2$ and $b♭^1$. The tonic chord on beat 3 thus functions as a passing chord, expanding dominant harmony as it connects V_3^4 with V.

The prolonged dominant in bars 1–2 is answered in bars 2–4 with a com-

EXAMPLE 10.13:

Schubert, Moment Musical, Op. 94, No. 2, bars 1–8: (a) foreground and (b) middleground reductions

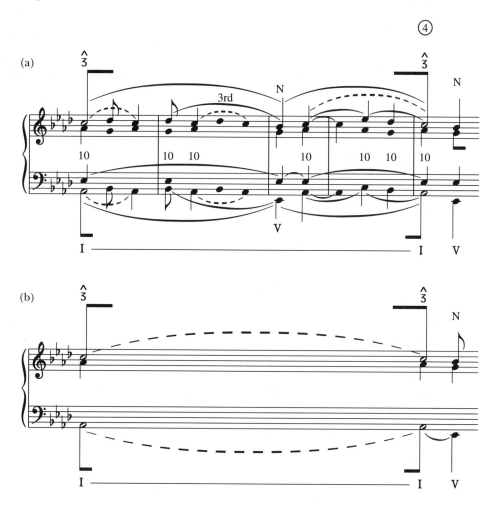

plementary motion that reaffirms the tonic. Notice that the descending top-voice third db^2–c^2–bb^1 is answered by the descending third eb^2–db^2–c^2 in bars 3–4, which is accompanied by lower tenths in the bass.[18]

The neighbor and other motions just discussed (including the brief dominant prolongation in bars 1–2) occur within a prolonged tonic that spans bars 1–4 (Example 10.13). This tonic prolongation is balanced on a higher structural level by a four-bar prolongation of the dominant in bars 4–8. (The symmetry of the tonic and dominant prolongations is prefigured in the complementary subphrases in bars 1–4). Notice the C♭ (bars 4–6), the neighbor tone that embellishes the fifth (B♭) of the dominant chord. This use of modal mixture (C♭ is the natural-sixth degree of E♭ minor) creates a half-step relationship (between B♭ and C♭), which parallels the half step between C and D♭ in the first phrase. The modal mixture continues and is intensified in bars 6–

EXAMPLE 10.13 (*continued*)

7, where the dominant triad itself becomes minor with the addition of G♭. At the end of the phrase (bars 7–8) the dominant chord becomes major again in preparation for the return to the tonic.

Another notable characteristic at the beginning of this Moment Musical is the limited range of the top voice. In the opening phrase the top voice is essentially restricted to the tones c^2, $d♭^2$, and $b♭^1$; the motion to $e♭^2$ in bar 3, therefore, represents a significant motion upward in register. The subsequent rise to $g♭^2$ (bar 7) produces an even more dramatic extension of the upper register. This tone will acquire increased significance as the piece unfolds.

One other important feature should be mentioned: the relation between rhythm and meter. Listen to the opening without looking at the music, and try to determine the location of the downbeats. It is likely that you will hear the upbeat neighbor figures at least partly as downbeats; the phrase rhythm is

EXAMPLE 10.14:

Schubert, Moment Musical, Op. 94, No. 2, bars 8–18: (a) foreground and (b) middleground reductions

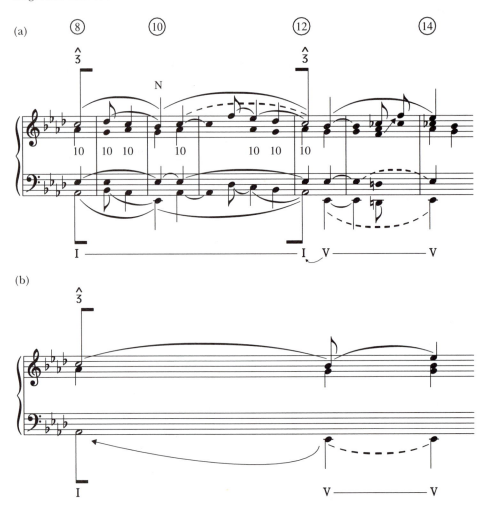

therefore displaced in relation to the notated meter. Yet the upbeats do not simply become downbeats: they retain some of their upbeat character as well, creating a metrical ambiguity that invites a subtle and expressive interpretation of the rhythm and phrasing in performance. This aspect of the work is central to the character of the piece and to its compositional plan.[19]

This piece, like many works by Schubert, makes extensive use of repetition in various ways. These include the repeated neighbor figures and associated chordal repetitions, the repeated dotted rhythms, and the repetitions of composite motivic figures (as in bars 2–3). At the phrase level, the dominant prolongation in bars 4–8 repeats many elements of bars 1–4 in varied form. The following phrase in bars 8–12 is an almost literal restatement of the opening tonic prolongation (Example 10.14). On a middleground level,

EXAMPLE 10.14 (*continued*)

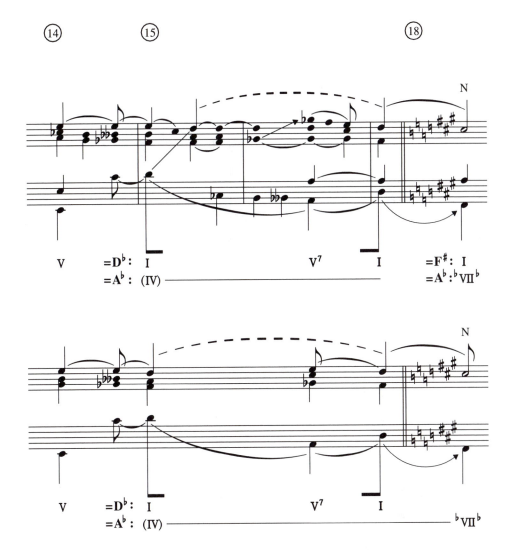

the alternation of tonic-dominant-tonic prolongations echoes the oscillating tonic-dominant harmony motions of the foreground, establishing a highly consistent character in the domain of harmony, similar to that of rhythm and motive (compare Examples 10.14a and b).

The next phrase, beginning in bar 12, gives every indication that it will echo the dominant prolongation of bars 4–8. The course of the phrase, however, is altered by a dramatic event that occurs in the brief passage set off by rests (bars 14–15). Notice the sudden change of register in the left hand and the drop in dynamic level to pianissimo, changes in design that highlight this interruption in the continuity of harmony and rhythm: the passage leads away

EXAMPLE 10.15:

Schubert, Moment Musical, Op. 94, No. 2, bars 18–31: (a) foreground and (b) middleground reductions

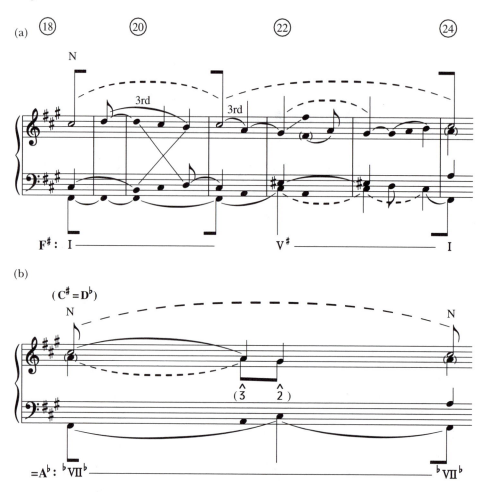

from the dominant toward the subdominant D♭, which is tonicized. Schubert clearly intends that we be surprised, and at first the larger meaning of the unexpected motion to IV is unclear.

This initial motion toward the subdominant (bars 14–15) is inconclusive, but is soon followed by a full structural cadence in D♭ that concludes the opening section of the work (Example 10.14). Notice how the passing motion in the bass (bars 15–16)— which leads from I to V^7 (in D♭)—is divided between two contrasting registers.[20]

The mood and character of the piece change entirely as the B section begins (Example 10.15). We are now in the harmonically remote key of F♯ minor. (In retrospect, we can see that the recently tonicized D♭ triad is reinterpreted as C♯, the dominant of F♯ minor. Moreover, F♯ minor derives not only from the D♭ neighbor note, but also from the prominence of G♭ in the

EXAMPLE 10.15 (*continued*)

opening of the piece, beginning in bar 6.) The dotted rhythms give way to more evenly spaced notes. The displaced, metrically ambiguous phrase rhythm is replaced by metrically regular rhythmic groupings. In contrast to the chordal texture of the first section, an arpeggiated pattern in the left hand accompanies the right-hand melody.

Despite these marked contrasts between the two sections, there are subtle but equally important similarities. Example 10.16a illustrates a beautiful transformation of melody and rhythm in the opening figure: in bar 18, the figure becomes three shorter tones followed by a longer, upper neighbor tone. Thus the neighbor relationship continues to be a primarily melodic element in the B section. Motions through the interval of the third, also motivically prominent in the A section, likewise recur frequently in the voice leading of this

EXAMPLE 10.16:

Schubert, Moment Musical, Op. 94, No. 2, bars 1–22: (a) rhythmic and (b) melodic transformations

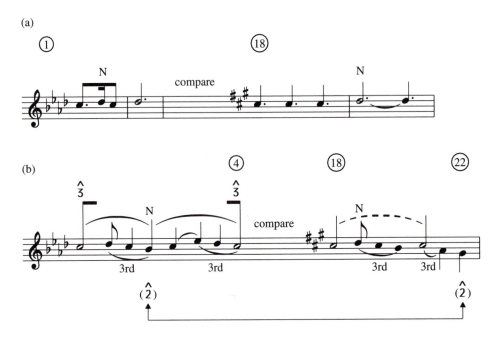

section. In fact, the similarity of melodic character between bars 1–4 and 18–22 is astonishing, as shown in Example 10.16b.

The overall phrase and harmonic structure is also more straightforward in this section than in the first (Example 10.15). In both the antecedent and the consequent phrase, notice that the structural top voice leaps from C♯ to A, so that a complete linear descent does not occur. In such a case the leap from $\hat{5}$ to $\hat{3}$ is typically regarded as a motion into the inner voice, so that $\hat{5}$ (C♯) remains active as the structural upper-voice tone. This interpretation is confirmed by the return of C♯ at the end of the section (bar 32) that prepares the return to the tonic and the primary tone C♮ ($\hat{3}$).

The A² section begins with a literal restatement of the opening of the first section (Example 10.17). The initial tonic prolongation is heard as before; partway through the dominant prolongation, however, an unexpected digression occurs (bar 41). A 5–6 motion (B♭–C♭) initiates a striking harmonic progression that suggests a possible resolution to C♭ major, both because of the accidentals employed, and the implications of the half cadence at the beginning of bar 43 and 44.

What are we to make of this passage in analytical terms? A careful examination of the bass line (Example 10.17b) reveals a broad expansion of dominant harmony in bars 39–44: V to V⁶₅. The interval of a third between V and V⁶₅ (E♭ to G♮) is filled in with diatonic and chromatic passing tones, which produces the line E♭–F♭–G♭–G♮. Compare part of this motion with the bass structure of bars 31–34 in the B section: the rising motion from E♭ to G♭ in bars 41–45 inverts the previous falling motion from F♯ to D♯ (the enharmonic equivalents of E♭ and G♭)!

The explanation of this passage solely in terms of a dominant prolongation, however, does not tell the entire story. If you play the passage slowly, beginning with the anacrusis to bar 42, you will certainly hear a succession of chords that function in the remote key of C♭ major; the implication of this key is further strengthened by the two cadential $^6_4$–$^5_3$ motions over G♭ in the bass (bars 43–44). It would seem that Schubert, in characteristically Romantic fashion, has embarked on an excursion from the "reality" of the home tonic, for this entire passage seems to suggest a dreamlike quality, like the vision of another world (C♭ major). It is set apart from the preceding and following music, not only by the rests in bars 41 and 44, but also by the relatively high left-hand register. The implication of C♭ major, however, is never fully confirmed with an authentic cadence. Following the apparent half cadences in C♭, V$^6_5$ of A♭ suddenly appears in bar 44. Notice that the lower register (from bar 41) is regained with G♮ in the left hand; the connection between V and V$^6_5$ is thus established through the association of bass tones in a common register.[21]

Schubert makes extraordinary use of register as a compositional element in this work. Following the limited range of the opening, the top voice rises to g♭^{2} (bar 7). This tone, respelled as F♯, is the highpoint of the B section (bars 22, 26, and 29). Thus far Schubert has carefully shaped and controlled the registral contour, but with minimal registral contrast. This registral upper limit is exceeded for the first time, as the upper line rises to a♭^{2} in bar 42 (echoed in bar 43). Like the G♭ in bar 16, it is emphasized through a crescendo and decrescendo when it is first heard in bar 42; it subsequently returns as the final note of the section in bars 54–55 (Example 10.18).[22] Because the limit of the upper voice is carefully shaped in this fashion, the ascent to other upper-voice tones becomes very significant in the composition. Schubert clearly intends for us to believe that, at bar 55, the piece is over. (Notice in Example 10.18a the repeated echoing of the $\hat{3}$–$\hat{2}$–$\hat{1}$ descent.) Nevertheless, the reestablishment of a♭^{2} in the second A section subtly prepares for a further extension in the upper register.

Following the double bar in measure 55 such an extension does occur, dramatically reinforced by the rise in dynamic level to forte (from pianissimo) and the accents. In fact the right-hand tessitura seems to break free of its previous constraints, reaching as high as f♯^{3} in bar 60. The thematic material, while based on that of the first B section, is also more impassioned (notice especially the jagged rhythms in bar 58). As shown in Example 10.18, the top voice now prolongs A, the third of the F♯ minor chord, that had been an inner voice in the earlier B section.

These changes are short-lived; the consequent phrase that begins in bar 62 reverts to the character and mood of the first B section (Example 10.19). The neighbor tone C♯ is once again prolonged in the upper voice, and the first portion of the phrase proceeds as before. However, a striking change takes place in bar 67: A♮ is replaced by A♯, so that the F♯-minor chord becomes major. The phrase then proceeds to cadence in F♯ major, which is more closely related to the home key of A♭ major than is F♯ minor. The return to

EXAMPLE 10.17:

Schubert, Moment Musical, Op. 94, No. 2, bars 31–47: (a) foreground and (b) middleground reductions

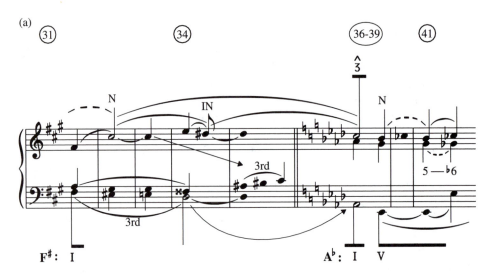

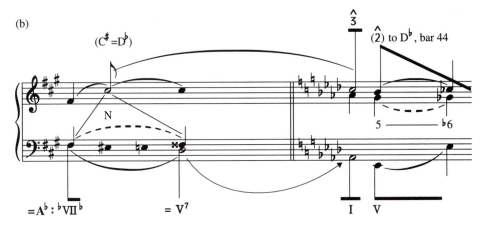

the A section follows this dramatic transformation and the following, brief modulatory progression.[23]

The last section of the work begins exactly like the previous A sections; however, once again Schubert surprises us. The interpolation of bars 14–15 recurs in bars 79–80, suggesting that yet another modulation to ♭VII may occur. But this possibility is decisively negated by the passage that follows, which consists of a motion to the dominant in bars 80–81, and the cadence that concludes the phrase. Notice the bass motion G♭–F–F♭–E♭ in bars 80–81: this is the same motion that led back to the tonic in the retransition at the end of each B section (in F♯), and that occurred in inverted form in bars 41–43. In the final bars of the piece, therefore, this bass motion—using G♭, not F♯—reconciles the "conflict" that has been so essential to the drama of this

EXAMPLE 10.17 (*continued*)

work.[24] It is especially striking that these events take place at the point of structural cadence, so that a comprehensive sense of resolution is achieved.

Our final comments are directed toward issues of the middleground, specifically toward large-scale motivic features and the role of mixture as they relate to the basic elaboration of the fundamental structure. We have already noted some local occurrences of mixture, as in bars 4–8 and 41–44. Mixture also influences the middleground tonal plan: remember that the B sections are in F♯ minor, which is the enharmonic equivalent of G♭ minor (the function of G♭ minor will be clarified below). Why did Schubert choose to notate the sections in the distant key area of F♯ minor?

One answer is certainly that, like many Romantic composers, Schubert

EXAMPLE 10.18:

Schubert, Moment Musical, Op. 94, No. 2, bars 47–62: (a) foreground and (b) middleground reductions

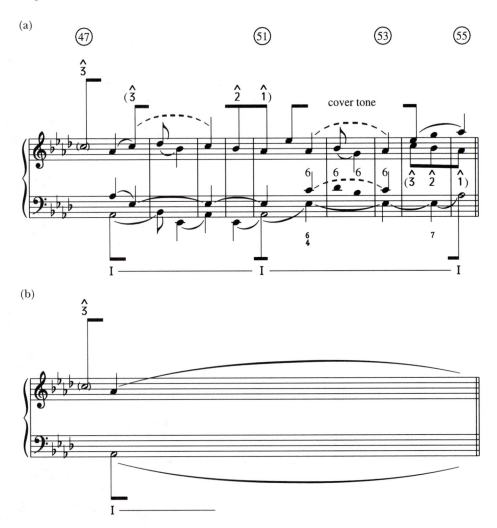

employed remote key relationships for expressive reasons. The contrast in notation itself—from four flats to three sharps—presents a visual impression that invokes a personal response by the performer, highlighting the contrast of keys and modes. Schubert's decision to notate the section in F# minor also serves a practical purpose: it is easier to read than G♭ minor.[25]

To understand the purely tonal function of mixture in the larger context of the structure, it will be helpful to restore diatonic notation and represent the B sections in G♭ minor. A chord built on G♭ would be derived from the parallel minor (A♭ minor), and its quality would be major (representing simple mixture). It is then further altered through double mixture to become a

EXAMPLE 10.18 (*continued*)

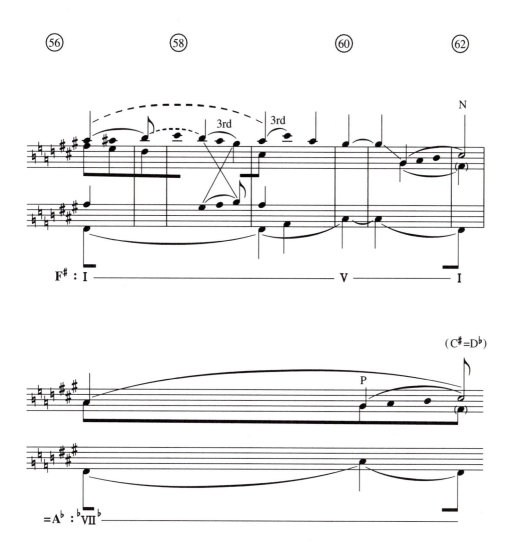

minor triad. Example 10.20b shows the relationship between the G♭-minor chord (representing the F♯-minor sections) and the dominant of the home key to which it leads at the end of each B section. The bass tone of the G♭-minor triad is the upper third of the dominant chord. As Example 10.21 illustrates, this progression (♭VII♭–V⁷) is closely related to the motion V⁶₅–V⁷. The VII triad is frequently used to lead to V in this manner; in major keys chromatic alteration of the chord is necessary, because the diatonic VII chord is diminished. In Chapter 12 we explore this chromatic progression in greater detail.

Example 10.20b shows the upper voice supported by the progression ♭VII♭–V⁷. Notice that the main tone is D♭, which is understood to remain

EXAMPLE 10.19:

Schubert, Moment Musical, Op. 94, No. 2, bars 62–90: (a) foreground and (b) middleground reductions

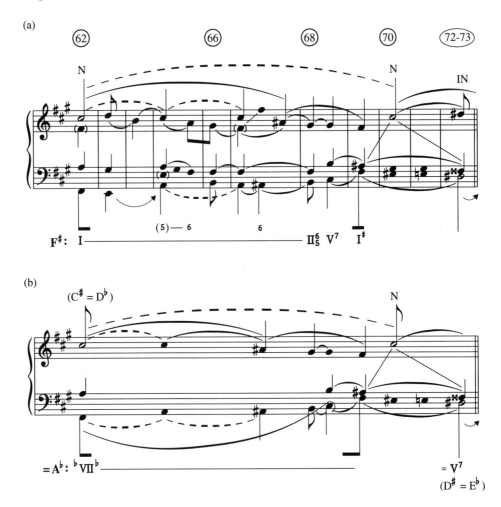

active (at a deeper middleground level) throughout each B section. Because it becomes the seventh of V^7 at the end of those sections, $D\flat$ clearly resolves to the C of the forthcoming A section (and also relates to the primary tone C of the previous section).

What we see here is a remarkable example of an enlarged motivic repetition: the sixteenth-note $D\flat$—a seemingly insignificant neighbor note at the beginning of the piece—becomes the basis for a whole large section of the piece, helping to give the piece a distinctive and most unusual character and shape. An upper neighbor at this structural level can become the point of departure for linear progressions and the basis of separate formal sections.[26] We might, in fact, even speculate that the integration of different structural levels by the neighbor figure "explains" Schubert's choice of $G\flat$ minor as a

EXAMPLE 10.19 (*continued*)

subordinate key area. The key of G♭ (F♯) is the only key that will permit the upper neighbor D♭ (=C♯) to function as a local scale degree $\hat{5}$. The middleground tonal plan, therefore, is in a sense the realization of a "possibility" inherent in the opening surface motive C–D♭–C.

HAYDN, PIANO SONATA, HOB. XVI/37, III

In the previous analyses of this chapter we have seen some of the ways in which ternary patterns arise in the elaboration of tonal structure. Other compositions, however, comprise a number of sections greater than those typically found in binary, rounded binary, or ternary forms. Perhaps the most familiar

EXAMPLE 10.20:

Schubert, Moment Musical, Op. 94, No. 2: structural synopsis

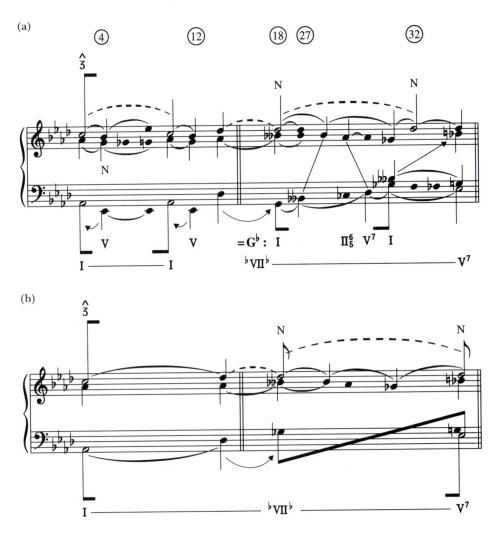

such genre is the rondo, which may consist of five, seven, or even more quasi-independent sections. Thematically, rondos are characterized by the alternation of the *refrain* (also called the *ritornello*) with *episodes* (or *couplets*). The refrain, or A section, begins the composition and usually returns after each intervening episode; in most cases the refrain recurs in exact or slightly varied (perhaps abbreviated) form. Typically rondos have two or more contrasting episodes: A–B–A–C–A or A–B–A–C–A–D–A.

For the final example of this chapter, we examine an A–B–A–C–A rondo, the last movement of Haydn's Piano Sonata No. 50 in D major. This composition is a good example of a rondo form in which each section has a quasi-independent structure. Though not especially long, the movement has many internal divisions that are explicitly indicated by double bars. The five sections

EXAMPLE 10.20 (*continued*)

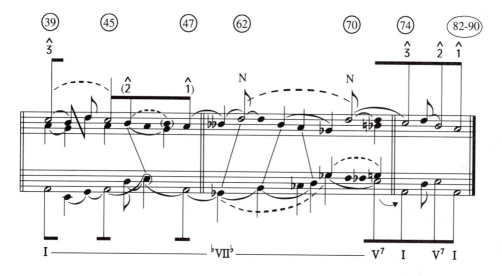

EXAMPLE 10.21:

Function of ♭VII

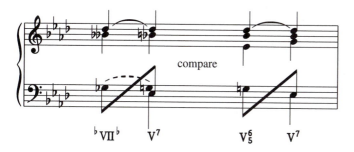

EXAMPLE 10.22:

Haydn, Piano Sonata, Hob. XVI/37, III, A¹ and B sections, bars 1–40: middleground reductions

of this rondo form are clearly distinguished by contrasts in themes and character, yet they form a coherent and unified composition and are related in subtle and remarkable ways through motivic and structural connections.

   Our discussion will proceed somewhat differently than in previous analyses. As you become more familiar with the movement, you will discover that its individual sections present no special problems in analysis; the A section (refrain), for example, is a rounded binary based on the interruption principle, a formal pattern we encountered in Chapter 9. Furthermore, using the middleground analyses as a frame of reference, you should now be able to describe the rich surface and foreground motivic relationships that integrate the tonal fabric within and across the various sections. Therefore, we focus

EXAMPLE 10.22 (*continued*)

primarily on form and structure, on the ways in which a five-part form is articulated within an undivided fundamental structure.

Examples 10.22–10.24 present a detailed middleground synopsis of the entire rondo. As we mentioned above, each of the three A sections or refrains consists of a rounded binary form that is based on an interrupted fifth-progression from $\hat{5}$. The primary tone $\hat{5}$ is prolonged to the double bar, after which $\hat{4}$–$\hat{3}$–$\hat{2}$ of the first branch unfolds over the prolonged, interrupting dominant; the second branch defines the a[2] part of the rounded binary's a[1]– b–a[2] design scheme that occurs in each of the three refrains.[27] As we have seen in other sectional compositions, the main upper-voice lines of the first and second refrains are ultimately interpreted as motions into inner voices

EXAMPLE 10.23:

Haydn, Piano Sonata, Hob. XVI/37, III, A^2 and C sections, bars 41–93: (a) and (b) middleground reductions

(and as *Ursatz* parallelisms in the tonic key). Only in the last refrain does the descent of the fundamental line occur (compare Examples 10.24–10.25).

The B section (bars 21–40) also incorporates an *Ursatz* parallelism, an interrupted 3̂–line in the parallel minor mode.[28] The harmonic plan of the first branch is fairly typical: I–III before the double bar, then III–II^6 before the dominant. The second branch progresses quickly, bringing this section to a close. In a work where each section is self-contained, the larger structural framework may be shaped in unusual ways. This rondo movement is such a case: because 5̂ (A) has already been established as the primary tone in the A^1 section, the B section in the parallel minor could be expected to retain A as its first structural tone. Instead, F♮ is the principal tone of this section.

A fundamental question facing the analyst is how a 3̂–line in D minor

EXAMPLE 10.23 (*continued*)

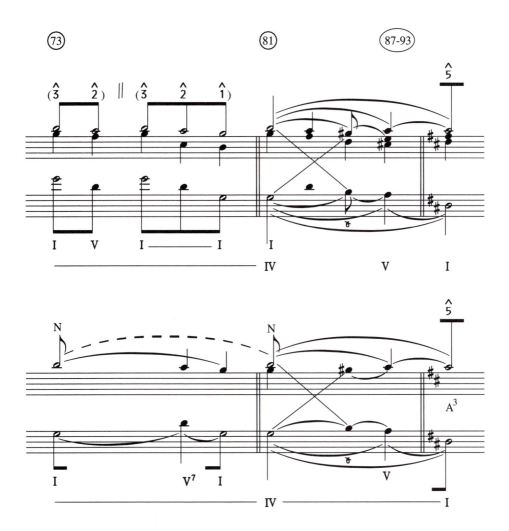

functions in the broader structural framework of a $\hat{5}$–line in D major that is expressed over the span of the entire piece. The answer is that the primary tone of the B section is an inner-voice tone of the fundamental structure from $\hat{5}$ in D major. F♮ is the third of the tonic triad, which has been altered through mixture (Example 10.22); this tone becomes the point of departure for linear progressions (the two branches of the interrupted structure in D minor) that define the B section. Because the tonic has not changed (only the mode), the A ($\hat{5}$), the principal tone of the work as a whole, can be understood conceptually to span this section, and to be picked up again at the beginning of the second A section in bar 41.[29]

The restatement of the A section in bars 41–60 is identical to the beginning and requires no special explanation. As we turn our attention to the C

EXAMPLE 10.24:

Haydn, Piano Sonata in D, Hob. XVI/37, III, A³ section, bars 94–122: (a) and (b) middleground reductions

(a)

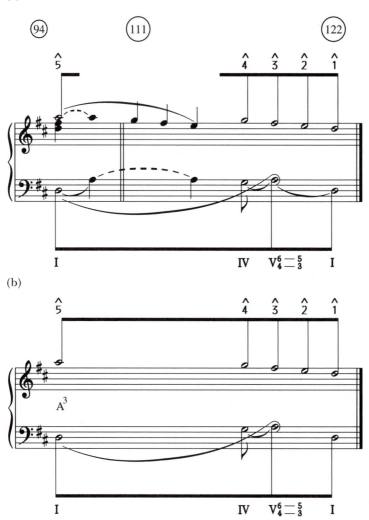

(b)

EXAMPLE 10.25:

Haydn, Piano Sonata, Hob. XVI/37, III: structural synopsis

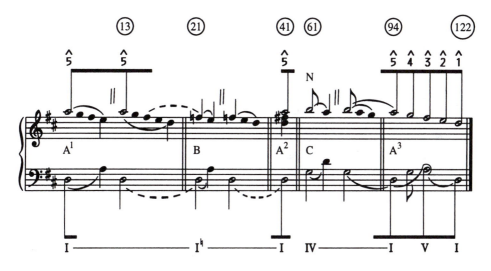

section (the second episode), we can appreciate how contrasting and apparently independent sections may function within and elaborate a broader tonal framework.

The C section presents us with another interrupted structure from $\hat{3}$, now in the key of the subdominant. Example 10.23 shows the two branches of the interruption and how they describe the sections of this rounded binary form. The example reveals that b^2, locally the primary tone of this *Ursatz* parallelism in G major, functions on a larger scale as an upper neighbor to the primary tone a^2 of the rondo's fundamental line. Example 10.23 illustrates the nature of the chromatic voice exchange that shapes the retransition section (bars 81–87). This section provides a smooth return to the tonic of the final refrain; to move directly from I in G major to I in D major would be too abrupt and not in character with the spirit of the rondo. In bar 94, the final refrain commences and brings the structure to a close.[30]

Example 10.25 presents a middleground synopsis of the rondo, which clarifies some of the relationships among form, structure, and large-scale voice leading. As we have observed, the technique of interruption occurs in each section; one way of describing the internal forms of this rondo is in terms of linear progressions, specifically, the first and second branches of each interrupted structure.[31] Recall how the B section arises: the third of tonic harmony is chromatically transformed (F♯ to F♮) and becomes the point of departure for the linear progressions that describe the B section. Notice also the composing-out of the large-scale upper neighbor to the primary tone a^2, a procedure that leads to the C section of the form. Example 10.25 illustrates how a composition of such remarkable diversity (and comprising apparently independent sections) results from the various middleground elaborations of a single, unified fundamental structure.

EXAMPLE 10.26:

Ternary forms and middleground tonal patterns

(a)

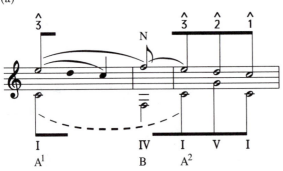

(b)

(c)

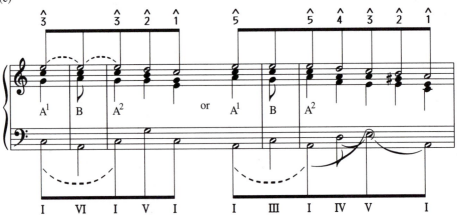

EXAMPLE 10.26 (*continued*)

(d)

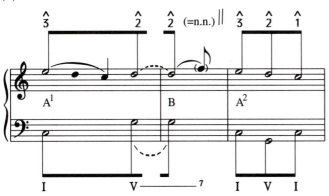

(e)

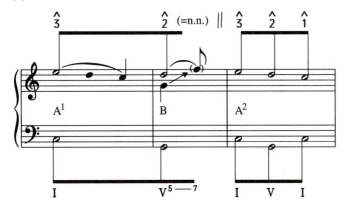

(f)

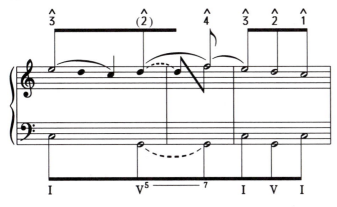

EXAMPLE 10.26 (*continued*)

(g)

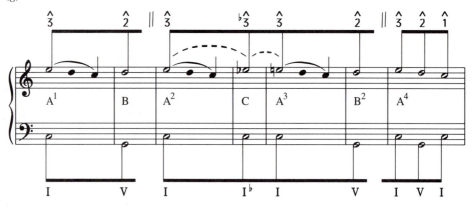

SOME CHARACTERISTIC
TONAL PATTERNS

We now present some additional middleground patterns for ternary forms. This is not indended to be an exhaustive summary, but rather a representation of characteristic possibilities. Only a few of the patterns shown in Example 10.26 require comment; study the rest on your own and refer to them later as you analyze other compositions in ternary form.

The patterns shown in Example 10.26a and b are very common. A formal section arises from the composing-out of a structural neighbor note. The formal ramifications of the neighbor note can be far-reaching. As Schenker observes in *Free Composition:* "the neighboring note of the fundamental line is in most cases form generative; its inherent delaying quality brings organic unity to that which in the foreground is a two- or three-part form."[32]

Schenker's reference to the "delaying quality" of the neighbor note is of interest here. Its meaning can be understood by considering some aspects of strict counterpoint. In third species, the neighbor note—a tone of embellishment—decorates a single pitch; in other words, "it delays or retards ultimate melodic progression without halting local melodic activity."[33]

When a neighbor note appears at the first level of the middleground, it delays the descent of the *Urlinie.*[34] The delay is, in effect, a detour that enlarges the musical space traversed by the *Urlinie.* The neighbor note and its associated harmonic support are often expanded at the foreground to become the B section of a ternary form. The second movement of Mozart's Piano Sonata in A major, K. 331, is a good example of a sectional ternary form (Menuetto-Trio-Menuetto) based on a large-scale neighbor (Example 10.26a).[35] Chopin's Etude, Op. 10, No. 8, also involves a neighbor at the first level of the middleground, though it does not consist of tonally complete and distinct sections as does Mozart's movement.[36] Example 10.26b shows a possibility involving a $\hat{5}$-line.

Example 10.26c shows two contexts in which neighbor motion is related to formal development, but in which a neighbor does not literally embellish the *Urlinie*. In these situations the primary tone is sustained at the first level of the middleground, but also serves more locally as the main tone of a sub-mediant or mediant area, the expansion of which typically leads to a B section. The descent of the *Urlinie* then occurs in the A^2 section. Even though the neighbor motion does not appear in the *Urlinie*, it is nonetheless "form producing" in much the same manner as the pieces cited above; the large-scale neighbor motion simply occurs in one or more inner voices of the structural progression. Several of Brahms's Intermezzi for piano are based upon such plans. See, for example, the Intermezzi in A major, Op. 118, No. 2, and B minor, Op. 119, No. 1.

While the examples we have seen may be considered representative, it is neither possible nor essential to generalize extensively about large-scale neighbor motion and musical form. It can be said, however, that ternary patterns in which the subordinate key areas IV, VI, or III underlie the B section can often be related to the patterns shown in Example 10.26a–c. Contrapuntal structures of this kind are very common, particularly in nineteenth-century music.

Examples 10.26d and e show two possibilities in which a B section arises in conjunction with the prolonged $\hat{2}$ over V of the first branch of an interruption. Note that the B section can begin within the *prolongation* of $\hat{2}$ over V, or with the *appearance* of structural $\hat{2}$ (the A^1 section is tonally closed). The patterns shown in Example 10.26e and f illustrate situations in which scale degree $\hat{4}$ plays a prominent role in the prolongation of a dominant; in some cases, $\hat{4}$ may be the higher-ranking tone, meaning that the structure is not interrupted (Example 10.26f).[37] Finally, Example 10.26g presents another middleground possibility that leads to a rondo form. Notice the use of mixture in the *Urlinie*, a topic we will address more thoroughly in Chapter 12.

Exercises

1. Chopin, Etude in G♭ major, Op. 25 ("Butterfly")

a. Despite the consistency in texture and motivic figuration, this piece can be described as an A-B-A form plus coda. Use broad harmonic motions and prolongations to help you differentiate the sections. (Review our discussion of Mendelssohn's G-major *Song Without Words*, another composition not markedly differentiated into three parts by features of design.)

b. Sequences and linear progressions (ascending and descending) are a hallmark of this piece. (The linear progressions do not necessarily involve tones of the *Urlinie*.) Be sure you can identify the structural function of all sequences and linear progressions.

c. The chord on the downbeat of bar 4 sounds somewhat unexpected, because it is a chromatic variant—appearing very early in the piece— of a more typical diatonic intermediate harmony. Do you think that this chord has motivic significance? Explain.

d. Bars 9–16 are similar in harmonic function to bars 17–24, but in a very different way. The recognition of this difference will help you in determining the parts of the form.

e. The Etude comprises symmetrical pairs of phrases (4 + 4 bars), except for the expansion and recomposition of the consequent phrase in the A^2 section. Explain the expansion of this phrase in terms of harmonic elaboration, and link it to the climax of the composition. How does the climax—usually considered an element of design—relate to the structure of the piece?

f. Prepare foreground, middleground, and background graphs.

g. Describe some possible functions of the coda. Think in terms of structure, register, and motive. Bear in mind that motivic repetition plays an important role throughout the Etude.

2. Mozart, Piano Sonata, K. 545, II *(Andante)*

a. This piece can be described as a composite ternary (the term *composite* means that at least one of the larger sections itself comprises a distinct formal pattern). Consider bars 1–32 as the first A section. What is the form of this section?

b. The B section of this form is defined through a change of mode, not of key. Define first the structural bass motion of the B section. Does Mozart foreshadow this motion in the major-mode context of the A section?

c. How does the G-minor section function in the elaboration of the *Ursatz*? In other words, how does one explain the inflection of B♮ to B♭ (G major to G minor) in terms of the expansion of the background tonic triad? (You may want to review the analysis of Haydn's Rondo in this chapter.)

d. Bars 49–64 are virtually a literal restatement of bars 1–16, which is closed (harmonically and melodically) in the tonic. How would you explain the difference between the respective top-voice descents in purely structural terms?

e. Prepare foreground, middleground, and background graphs of the movement. Identify the coda and explain how it recalls characteristics from earlier parts of the movement.

3. Beethoven, Bagatelle in C major, Op. 33,
No. 2, Scherzo

a. Prepare an analytical sketch of bars 1–16. Notice the interplay of registers in the right hand, particularly in bars 9–16. Which voice-leading strand is the structural upper voice?

b. Prepare a sketch of the minor-mode B section. Be able to explain the significance of the chord on beat 3 of bar 29.

c. Prepare foreground, middleground, and background graphs for the piece. Where does the primary tone recur in the B section, and over what harmony? Think about this in relation to the structure of the flanking A sections.

4. Schumann, *Album for the Young,* Op. 68,
Short Study

a. This piece could be considered either a rounded binary or ternary form, though the harmonic prolongations are sufficiently contrasting to suggest the latter designation. Despite the apparent simplicity of the piece, it is analytically challenging.

b. As a first step, construct a "continuo" realization of the piece, which will help you to make decisions about broader prolongations and upper-voice motions. (Notice the similarity to Bach's C-major Prelude analyzed earlier in this book.)

c. Consider both $\hat{3}$ and $\hat{5}$ as possibilities for the primary tone of the *Urlinie.* In other words, trace the voice leading from both "paths." One will reveal itself as the better choice.

d. Does this piece include an interruption (perhaps more than one)?

e. What is the *structural* bass in bars 1–16? Try to distinguish between tenor and bass voices. The lowest pitch of the left hand is not necessarily a tone of the structural bass. (Large leaps in the bass can often help you make decisions in this regard.)

f. Prepare foreground, middleground, and background graphs of the piece.

5. Chopin, Nocturne in E♭ major, Op. 9, No. 2

a. Consider the work as a whole. What are its large sections, and how are they established?

b. Prepare a sketch of the Nocturne, analyzing the florid melody in relation to the bass line and harmonic structure. Where does the fundamental structure reach its conclusion? What is the function of the section that follows?

c. Prepare foreground, middleground, and background graphs of the work.

6. Mendelssohn, *Song Without Words*, Op. 85, No. 1

   a. Sketch out the work. Like the G-major *Song Without Words* analyzed in the text, this piece has continuous figuration that bridges sectional divisions.

   b. Determine the prolongations and motions. Sketch a middleground graph for the movement, and consider the large-scale harmonic relationships.

   c. Prepare final graphs (foreground, middleground, and background) for the piece.

CHAPTER

Sonata Principle

The sonata principle is one of the most complex tonal compositional procedures. It went through various stages of development from the early eighteenth to the late nineteenth century, and composers during this period created an extraordinarily rich and diverse repertory. Often referred to as a standard formal type, it resists attempts to formulate descriptive generalizations, which can oversimplify rather than accurately represent its multifaceted character. (It is for this reason that we prefer the term *sonata principle* to the more standard "sonata form.") However, certain fundamental characteristics can be identified that distinguish sonata movements from other types such as rondo, rounded binary, and ternary compositions. In this chapter we will limit our discussion to compositions from the high Classical period, a watershed in the development of the sonata. Even so, bear in mind that we are considering only representative examples; composers of the Classical period treated the sonata principle with great flexibility. A comprehensive study of this vast topic would require the scope of several books, not that of a single chapter. The characteristics we explore here, however, will provide a foundation for further study of sonata movements from the eighteenth and nineteenth centuries.[1]

Our first example is a movement from one of Clementi's sonatinas. As the title suggests, this piece is a "little" sonata, displaying on a smaller scale many of the features associated with longer and more complex sonata movements. The second and third examples of this chapter are drawn from the works of Beethoven and Mozart and are more typical of the Classical sonata in terms of breadth and complexity. In accordance with the focus of this book we will concentrate on the structure of each work, but will do so in the context of its form and style.

Sonata movements can easily span hundreds of measures, and we will not discuss all aspects of each piece or graphically illustrate all details of harmony

EXAMPLE 11.1:

Clementi, Sonatina, Op. 36, No. 1, I, bars 1–15: (a) foreground and (b) middleground reductions

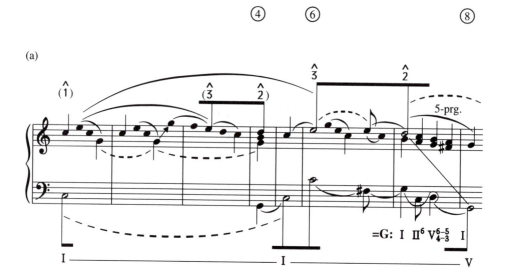

and voice leading. Therefore, we will sometimes present graphs that focus primarily on the harmony and voice leading of middleground levels. You should have no trouble understanding the detail of passages we show only in middleground form; time spent studying the graphs in conjunction with the music will reinforce your understanding of principles presented in earlier chapters.

CLEMENTI, SONATINA, OP. 36, NO. 1, I

Example 11.1 presents a voice-leading graph of bars 1–15. Notice that we interpret a $\hat{3}$–$\hat{2}$ motion in the first phrase, but one that is stated rather indirectly in the diminution of bars 3–4. The primary tone $\hat{3}$ emerges most definitively in the subsequent phrase, on the downbeat of bar 6. In this same bar we also begin to hear harmonic motion away from the tonic toward the key of the dominant: $\sharp\hat{4}$ (F$\sharp$) in the bass is a prominent indicator that a modulation is beginning. In bars 7–8 the emergence of the dominant key is complete: the local upper voice descent $\hat{5}$–$\hat{4}$–$\hat{3}$–$\hat{2}$–$\hat{1}$, in conjunction with an authentic cadence in the key of G, confirms the modulation.

As you know, this first section (bars 1–15) is commonly referred to as the *exposition* of the movement, the essence of which is the juxtaposition of two key areas. You are also probably familiar with other terms such as *first theme* and *second theme* (or *second group*) used to describe the subordinate key area.[2] Schenker's perspective, however, led him to understand an exposition in terms of the processes of composing-out (*Auskomponierung*), involving linear

EXAMPLE 11.1 (*continued*)

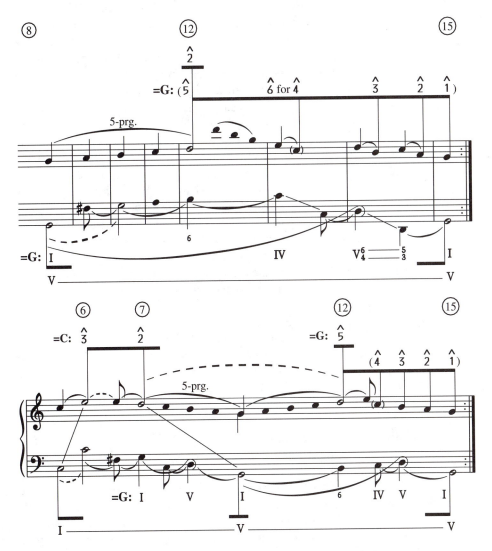

progressions and structural bass motions.[3] In our sonatina he would describe the first part of the exposition in terms of the establishment and prolongation of the primary tone $\hat{3}$ over tonic harmony. The second key area arises from the dominant scale step of the structural bass arpeggiation. The way in which the musical content of the second key area develops is through an *Ursatz* form transferred to a lower level. As Example 11.1 shows, $\hat{5}$–$\hat{4}$–$\hat{3}$–$\hat{2}$–$\hat{1}$ in the key of G over a complete harmonic progression (at the foreground) prolongs the higher-level structural $\hat{2}$ over V in C major ($\hat{2}$ in C = $\hat{5}$ in G). Notice that we depict the arrival of the structural dominant in the bass (with an open note-head) in bar 8. Although a root-position tonic in G appears in bar 7, the modulation is still emerging. Only at the cadence is the secondary key area established conclusively. The upper voice then regains d^2 via an ascending fifth-progression; the exposition concludes with a structural cadence (bars 12–15) in which the upper voice is more elaborated than in bars 7–8. (Notice in Example 11.1b that the covering neighbor tone E in bar 13 substitutes for C in the descent, a common procedure in descents from $\hat{5}$.[4])

The technique of prolonging structural $\hat{2}$ (in the exposition) with subordinate fifth-progressions occurs in a great many sonata movements, but it is by no means the only possible way to prolong $\hat{2}$ over V. The most important points for the analyst to bear in mind are: (1) that the first part of a Classical sonata exposition establishes the primary tone and initial tonic of the structure; (2) that the second part always involves the composing-out of a subordinate key (typically V in major or III in minor) through bass and upper-voice motions in that key (usually involving a transferred form of the *Ursatz*). The particular nature of the *Ursatz* form will vary, however, using any number of the techniques we have explored previously. Analysis will reveal how the basic principles elaborated here are uniquely realized in each case.[5]

The next part (bars 16–23) is the development section of this movement; we will begin by examining the lower voice and harmonic structure (Example 11.2).

As the graph shows, the first notes of the written lower voice are to be understood as a "tenor" line above an implied G bass note, the root of the dominant established before the double bar.[6] In bar 19, the G is reinstated and remains throughout the rest of the section. Notice that the tenor line in bars 16–19, F–E♭–B♮–C, is repeated in the second four-bar segment as well. At this point a brief link (a descending fifth) ushers in the next section (bar 23, beats 3–4).

Let us now consider the upper voice, which begins on b^1, the third of dominant harmony (bar 16), and proceeds upward in a double voice exchange with the apparent bass (actually, the tenor line; see the first part of Example 11.2). Before the voice exchange unfolds completely, G is superposed from an inner voice to the two-line octave (bar 17). As you may recall, voice exchanges often involve outer and inner voices. In this case, the second part of the voice exchange involves the upper voice (F–E♭). We therefore hear a motion G–F–E♭–D that leads to and emphasizes structural $\hat{2}$; the rhythm of this four-bar segment would also suggest that d^2 is the *goal* of the line from G. As Example 11.2a shows, bars 20–23 are structurally identical to bars 16–19, including not only the tenor but also the soprano. Therefore bars 20–23 may be regarded as a recomposition (or variation) of the previous four-bar segment.

One point requiring clarification is that scale degree $\hat{2}$ is understood only through implication in bar 23, while in bar 19 (the corresponding measure) it is stated explicitly. At the end of development sections, it is common to find scale degree $\hat{5}$ occurring prominently in the upper voice, highlighting the dominant of the main key. In bar 23 the g^2 substitutes for d^2, and is melodically related to the previous occurrences of $\hat{5}$ in bars 17 and 20–21.

EXAMPLE 11.2:

Clementi, Sonatina, Op. 36, No. 1, I, bars 16–23: (a) foreground and (b) middleground reductions

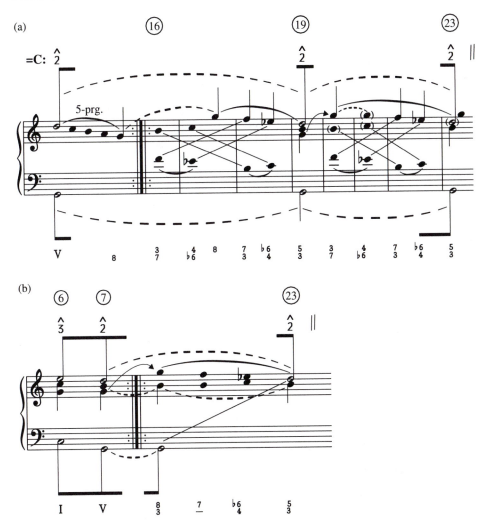

In *Free Composition,* the role of the development section is described in a manner that corresponds to what we have seen in Clementi's sonatina: it serves to "complete the motion to $\hat{2}\over V$ (or in some way to expand that point [in the structure])."[7] Example 11.2b illustrates that this development section expands $\hat{2}\over V$ which was achieved at the end of the exposition. It is important to remember that Schenker thought of sonata principle (and form in general) in terms of the composing-out of the structure. Compositional elements such as modulations and thematic development, important considerations in any analysis, are understood as related aspects of the structure. In this relatively

EXAMPLE 11.3:

Clementi, Sonatina, Op. 36, No. 1, I, bars 24–38: (a) foreground and (b) middleground reductions

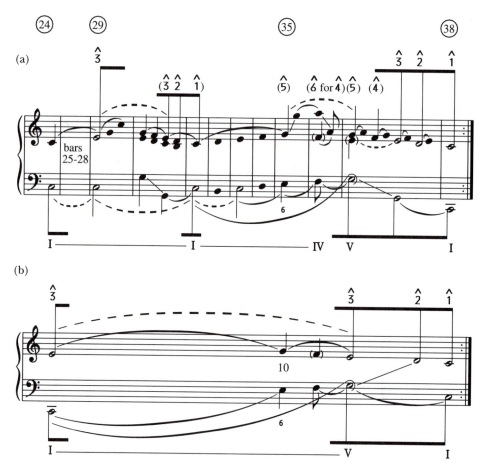

simple and brief development section, for example, the line G–F–E♭–D is an elaboration of $\hat{2}$ (the second note of the *Urlinie*) and of V (the second note in the bass arpeggiation of the *Ursatz*).

Earlier in this chapter we stated that the essence of a Classical sonata exposition is the juxtaposition of two key areas. Another general observation about sonata principle is that, before the movement closes, the two areas must be reconciled in the realm of the tonic. In other words, the material associated with the secondary key area will be recapitulated in the tonic.

Example 11.3 presents the harmonic structure and voice leading of the recapitulation (bars 24–38), most of which requires no comment. It is important, however, to consider those passages that represent compositional modifications. Because one of the functions of a recapitulation is to reinstate and affirm tonic harmony, changes will normally occur when composers transpose modulatory (transition) sections and thematic material associated with the second key area. Particularly in longer and more complex sonata movements, the recapitulation will often reveal the full range of a composer's skill and ingenuity: it can be quite a challenge to write a section that both parallels the exposition and satisfies the harmonic conditions of a recapitulation.

Transposition, therefore, is the essential harmonic procedure of a recapitulation. Because this sonatina is so brief, and the sections so concise, the recapitulation does not involve extensive modification. Except for the change of register of the beginning (bars 24ff.), most of the recomposition simply involves transposing the second tonal area down a perfect fifth. One aspect in particular, however, should be considered. Recall that, in the exposition, a fifth-progression (D–G) delineates the secondary key area of G major (bars 7–8). From a structural perspective, this line prolongs $\hat{2}$ of the *Urlinie*. In the recapitulation, the same line can be expected in the tonic, thereby maintaining a parallel relationship between exposition and recapitulation. Bear in mind, however, that the specific manner in which the fifth is to be interpreted in a recapitulation may differ from piece to piece; each case must be evaluated on its own terms.

In our Clementi example, we can see the tonic versions of the fifth (both descending and ascending) beginning in bar 30 and continuing to the end of the movement. Since the context is different from that of the exposition, how can we interpret their meaning from our structural perspective? As Example 11.3b in particular illustrates, the fifths from g^1 elaborate—at a lower level and by a motion from above—the tones of the *Urlinie*.

Example 11.4 presents a middleground synopsis of the structure of Clementi's movement, which we will use to draw some broad observations about the sonata principle. (Our comments here address tonal processes in the major mode; in the final example of this chapter we will discover the somewhat different structures typical of movements in the minor mode.) You should have no trouble recognizing the two branches of an interrupted fundamental structure, which we saw as the basis for antecedent/consequent pairs in Chapter 7, and as the essential structural principle for some of the longer compositions in Chapters 9 and 10. The relationship between form and structure that is characteristic of sonata principle also frequently occurs in rounded binary forms. The interruption divides the structure into two parts, yet three sections emerge within this articulation of the structure (in the sonata: exposition, development, recapitulation). We can now compare certain aspects of sonata principle, as described in conventional formal terms, with Schenker's view that the sonata is closely linked to the principle of interruption.

The first tonal region embodies the establishment and prolongation of the primary tone and tonic harmony, the first step in the composing-out of the structure. In many movements this section will be highlighted by a distinct first theme. This tonal area, however, need not involve extensive breadth. The listener naturally expects tonic harmony at the beginning of a composition (particularly in the Classical period), and even a brief passage will be sufficient to establish the home key.[8]

EXAMPLE 11.4:

Clementi, Sonatina, Op. 36, No. 1, I: middleground synopsis

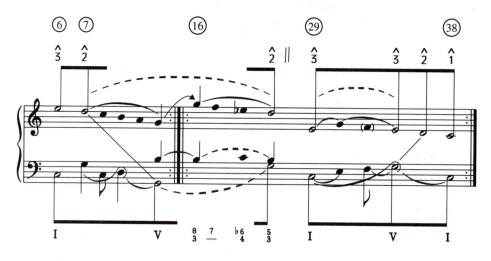

The second part of an exposition (in the major mode) is typically associated with the second step in the structural bass arpeggiation: the motion to (and prolongation of) V, often in conjunction with $\hat{2}$ of the *Urlinie*. As Example 11.4 illustrates, the expansion of this part of the structure very often (but not always) is accomplished in the upper voice through a subordinate fifth-progression. This progression prolongs $\hat{2}$ and articulates the motivic and thematic content of the second tonal area, beginning with the second theme. In longer compositions this part of the exposition may be extensively developed and articulated into additional sections and subsections (such as more "second themes," closing material, codetta, and so forth). Schenker's approach provides us with the means to comprehend the unity of these sections by associating them with an element of the fundamental structure.

As illustrated in Example 11.4, the development section arises within the first branch of the interrupted structure and results from the expansion of the dominant established before the double bar. (Works in minor, however, and some in major, may employ a different structural plan.) The continued prolongation of V, however, is achieved through ways that are different from the motions that tonicize the dominant before the double bar; consequently, we tend to hear the development as a separate section.[9] Finally, the recapitulation consists of the unfolding of the second branch, which completes the structure. Notice that it does so in a lower register, so that Schenker's principle of *obligatory register* does not obtain in this movement. However, the higher register of the first branch is partially recovered in bars 31–36 (Example 11.3), a change from the preceding phrase that reinforces the definitive nature of the final descent.

This leads us to a view of the sonata principle in which a three-part form develops within a two-part structure, a perspective that enables us to understand many of the interrelationships of this rich compositional procedure.[10] In our final examples we will see some of the different ways in which these same basic principles can be realized on much grander scales.

BEETHOVEN, PIANO SONATA, OP. 49, NO. 2, I

Beethoven's G-major Piano Sonata, Op. 49, No. 2, employs procedures that are similar to those in Clementi's sonatina, but are more extensively developed. Consequently, we shall again organize our discussion according to the three sections of the form—exposition, development, and recapitulation. Be sure to examine the portions of the graphs that are not discussed in detail: this will put the discussion into the context of the movement as a whole.

Exposition (bars 1–52)

In the 15–bar exposition of Clementi's sonatina, we saw the essence of the sonata principle but not extensive musical development. Beethoven's exposition, however, is on a larger scale. Within it we can identify several smaller sections, which are conventionally referred to as *first theme, transition (or bridge) section, second theme,* and *closing material.* Important though these terms are, they can be limiting or even misleading at times, since the sonata principle is a complex procedure that can be worked out in an almost limitless number of ways. It is essential for the analyst to discover how each piece expresses the sonata principle in its own terms.

Example 11.5 presents an analysis of the first theme (bars 1–12), the last bar of which overlaps with the beginning of the transition section. Notice the gradual ascent to the primary tone $\hat{3}$ in the one-line octave, followed immediately by a repetition of this ascent in the two-line octave. Note also that a beautiful motivic transformation is already apparent: the descending melodic figure in bar 4 that embellishes the motion to the primary tone $\hat{3}$ emphasizes C (through the trill) so that it takes on the quality of a neighbor tone to B. This figure is then repeated an octave higher. Consequently, the neighbor tone E and its resolution to D that follow in bars 9–10 (Example 11.5) are heard as expanded (and transposed) repetitions of the neighbor figure. The E also recurs (paralleling the earlier repetition) in bar 11, but now in a different context.

Comparison of levels a and b in Example 11.5 will reveal the nature of the melodic motions that cover the primary tone $\hat{3}$ before the one-line octave is reestablished in bars 11–12. Consider, for instance, that the primary tone $\hat{3}$ (bar 8) leads eventually to an incomplete neighbor that resides in a lower register (c^2 in bar 11; see Example 11.5b); tones of figuration do not always appear in the same register as the tone being decorated. As you study the remaining details of the first theme, remember that the first section of a

EXAMPLE 11.5:

Beethoven, Piano Sonata, Op. 49, No. 2, I, first theme, bars 1–12: (a) foreground and (b) middleground reductions

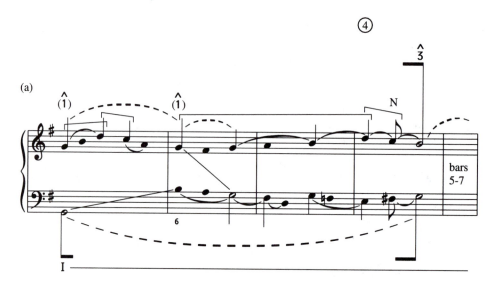

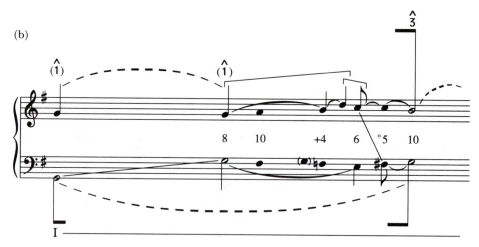

EXAMPLE 11.5 (*continued*)

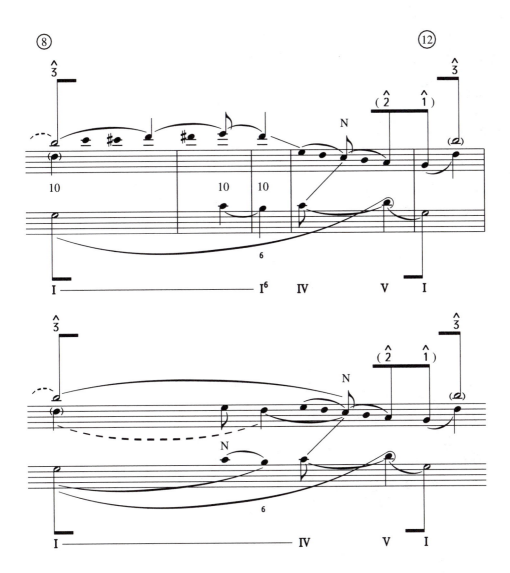

EXAMPLE 11.6:

Beethoven, Piano Sonata, Op. 49, No. 2, I, transition section, bars 12–20: (a) foreground and (b) middleground reductions

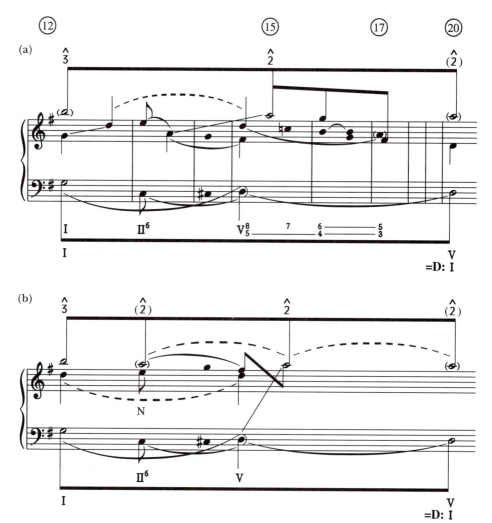

sonata movement establishes the primary tone and initial tonic harmony of the structure; in this respect the Clementi and Beethoven movements are similar.

Example 11.6 represents the transition section, in which the motion begins from the initial tonic toward the dominant. Like many transitions, it begins with a repetition of part of the first theme, and consequently sounds at first like an extension of that theme. Because the harmonic goal is different, however, the progression quickly takes a different course and proceeds, through a chromatic intermediate harmony, to V in bar 15. This V, which lasts through bar 20, is heard as a half cadence in the key of G. But in bar 21, with the onset of the second theme, this chord (in first inversion) suddenly functions as I in D major. Notice how we depict this reinterpretation in Example 11.6.[11]

The upper voice, which is somewhat more complex than the bass, can be clarified by comparing the two levels shown in Example 11.6. (The primary tone $\hat{3}$ is present by implication in bar 12.) As at the end of the first theme, the melodic line rises above $\hat{3}$, but once again we can interpret this line as an inner voice superposed above the structural tone. Example 11.6b simplifies the registral relationships of inner and outer voices, and reveals that $\hat{3}$ moves to $\hat{2}$ over II^6 (and its chromatic alteration). With the arrival on V in bar 15, $\hat{2}$ (A) emerges prominently in the two-line octave. It is then prolonged through motions to inner voices, but remains conceptually present as the transition concludes.

In our discussion of Clementi's sonatina, we saw how the second tonal area of the exposition develops from the expansion of the structural V (in the first branch of the interrupted structure). There, in accordance with the smaller proportions of the movement, the dominant is composed out through very basic means (essentially, the fifth-progression in V). In Beethoven's sonata, on the other hand, the second tonal area is more extended, allowing for considerable musical development. We shall begin with the second theme, which is clearly delineated as a separate section within the broader tonal area (Example 11.7).

As our graphs illustrate, the second theme sounds self-contained because it is itself a small formal unit: a musical period in D major comprising an antecedent and a consequent phrase. Furthermore, as you listen to or play through this passage, you will undoubtedly recognize (bar 28) the technique of interruption so often associated with antecedent/consequent pairs. The second theme, in other words, is a good example of an *Ursatz* pattern transferred to a lower structural level. In a movement of this length, it is important to maintain structural perspective, to keep one's bearings as it were. So as we proceed with a discussion of the second theme, remember that it begins to develop $\hat{2}$ over V of the fundamental structure (which is also $\hat{5}$ in the local key of D).

Example 11.7 shows a foreground analysis of the antecedent and consequent phrases (level a); the entire period is represented by a middleground synopsis (level b). In the first part of the antecedent phrase, the upper voice leads to $\hat{3}$ in D major and is rhythmically articulated into two subphrases (bars 21–22 and 23–24). Notice that the line ($\hat{1}$–$\hat{2}$–$\hat{3}$ in D) is elaborated by reaching-over motions, indicated by the unfolding signs in the graph. In the second part of the phrase (bars 25–28), the large-scale descending motion f$\sharp^2$–e^2 is elaborated by motions into an inner voice. Thus, as often happens at cadences, e^2 remains present by implication as the melody descends to the leading tone at the half cadence (Example 11.7). Our perception of an interruption is confirmed: the antecedent phrase is the first branch of an

EXAMPLE 11.7:

Beethoven, Piano Sonata, Op. 49, No. 2, I, second theme, bars 21–36: (a) foreground and (b) middleground reductions

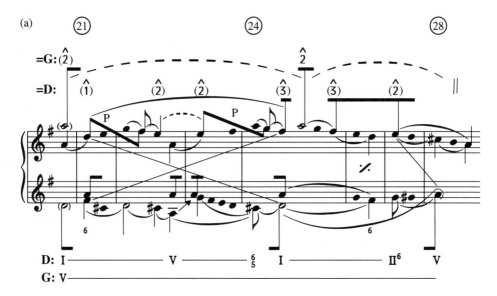

EXAMPLE 11.7 (*continued*)

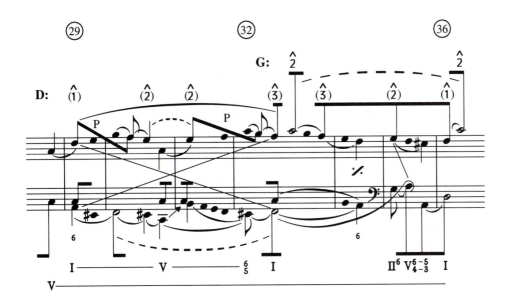

EXAMPLE 11.7 (*continued*)

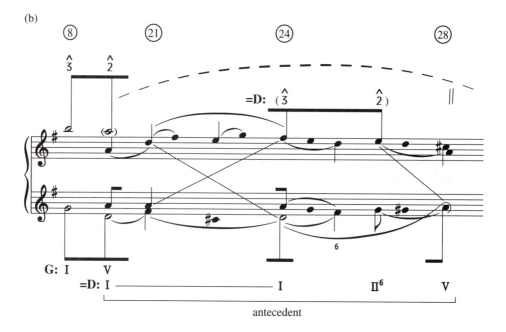

interrupted structure in D major, where $\hat{3}$ moves to $\hat{2}$ over a larger motion from I to V.

We mentioned that the second theme develops from $\hat{\mathbf{2}}$ of the *Ursatz* (a^2 is also $\hat{5}$ in D major). Why, then, do we show a local, interrupted structural line from the more local $\hat{3}$ of the dominant area? In fact, a^2 remains active in the phrase, but it appears only sporadically in bars 24–26. Because of the strong ascent to F♯, both in the antecedent and in the consequent phrases, we interpret the top-voice line in this passage as leading to and from f♯². The structural a^2, $\hat{\mathbf{2}}$ of the *Urlinie*, seems to "hover" in the background, occasionally sounded, but not participating in the local structure.

A practical consideration may have influenced Beethoven's compositional process in this passage. As we have seen, the antecedent phrase consists of two four-bar subphrases. In the first of these (bars 24–28), the ascent of the upper voice in the key of D recalls and parallels the four-bar ascent that establishes the primary tone $\hat{3}$ at the beginning of the movement (compare Examples 11.7b and 11.5a). Thus, through very audible means, Beethoven establishes a close relationship between the first and second themes of the exposition. This similarity will, of course, become all the more apparent in the tonic restatement of the recapitulation, where the second theme will sound almost like a modified repetition of the first.[12] Careful study of Example 11.7b will give you an overall structural perspective of the exposition to this point.

We observed that perfect authentic cadences occur frequently in Classical expositions, articulating smaller segments within a larger section. Since we have identified bars 29–36 as the consequent phrase of the second theme, a

EXAMPLE 11.7 (*continued*)

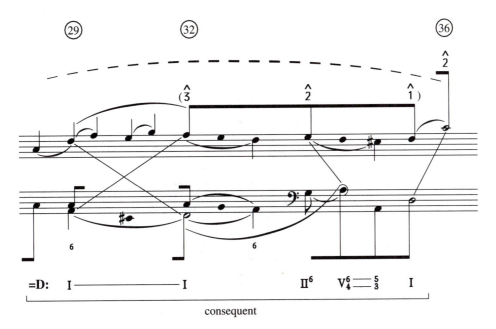

perfect authentic cadence could be expected at its conclusion in bar 36. But, as you may have observed, that is not exactly what happens. Refer to the score and you will see that the upper voice of the second phrase does in fact move to $\hat{1}$, but the d^2 appears as a grace note that is immediately covered by a^2. This is an example of a *phrase elision*: the end of the consequent phrase becomes the beginning of the closing section. Whereas a^2 appeared earlier in the second theme only as fleeting recollections of structural $\hat{2}$, from this point the upper voice clearly emphasizes a^2 and descends a fifth to melodic closure in the concluding bars of the exposition.

Our final observations on the exposition address the closing section and its short codetta (Example 11.8). The graph shows the alternation between the one- and two-line octaves that characterizes the closing section. This interplay of register recalls that of the first theme, which incorporated the initial ascent to the primary tone in both registers. Throughout these sweeping motions in bars 36–43, a^2 is initially prolonged by motion into an inner voice. Finally, the line from a^2 (structural $\hat{2}$, locally $\hat{5}$ in D major) begins its descent toward closure, which occurs with the cadence in bars 42–43.[13] You will notice in the graph that we have beamed the fifth in bars 40–43, indicating it as the primary line from a^2. The descents that follow are in effect extensions of the first, highlighting the two treble registers that have been compositionally juxtaposed throughout the exposition. They provide the cadential "reiterations" that often characterize closing sections, and that frequently confirm the new key through repeated cadential patterns. The final four bars of the exposition are a codetta that parallels the transition section; as there, structural $\hat{2}$ is prominent and is prolonged by the line A–G–F♯.[14]

EXAMPLE 11.8:

Beethoven, Piano Sonata, Op. 49, No. 2, I, closing section, bars 36–52: foreground reduction

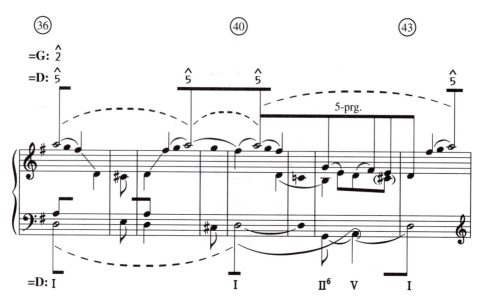

Example 11.9 presents a middleground synopsis of the upper voice of the exposition, indicating some of the motions to inner voices that prolong $\hat{2}$ of the *Urlinie.* You may recall that, in Clementi's sonatina, the second tonal area of the exposition is concisely defined through fifth-progressions from (and to) structural $\hat{2}$, including the perfect authentic cadence in the new key. In Beethoven's exposition, the same fundamental tonal pattern occurs, but the region associated with the fifth-progression in the dominant is greatly expanded. Notice that the first tone, a^2, is prolonged from bar 15 before the descent begins. Consequently, we understand structural $\hat{2}$ and the fifth-progression that prolongs it as governing a span of 38 measures (bars 15–52). Clementi's movement can be considered a "proto-sonata" because of its proportions and limited musical development. Beethoven's movement is more characteristic of sonata expositions, where the prolongation of $\hat{2}$ over V may embrace one or more second themes, followed by closing material and possibly a codetta. Therefore, the analyst should remain open to the manifold possibilities that may occur in the working out of the structure.

Development (bars 53–66)

The nature and scope of development sections in sonata movements will vary according to many factors. These include the length and complexity of the exposition, the style and historical period, the mode, and the genre. In Cle-

EXAMPLE 11.8 (*continued*)

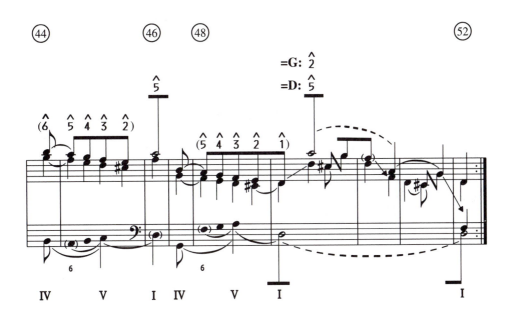

EXAMPLE 11.9:

Beethoven, Piano Sonata, Op. 49, No. 2, I, exposition: middleground synopsis

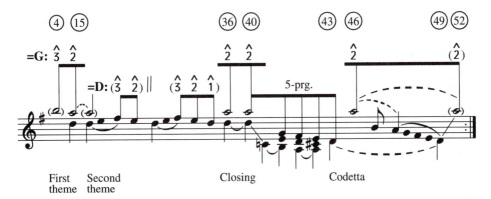

EXAMPLE 11.10:

Beethoven, Piano Sonata, Op. 49, No. 2, I, development: (a) foreground and (b–c) middleground reductions

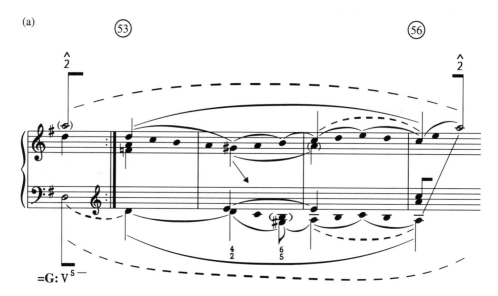

menti's sonatina the development section is brief in accordance with the scale of the movement as a whole; it prolongs the dominant harmony, and prepares for the return to the tonic in the recapitulation. Sonata movements in which the dominant is the secondary key area (usually in major keys) typically employ the same basic structural plan as Clementi's sonatina. But the bass and harmonic motions of more extended movements may be far ranging, involving "modulations" that appear to digress from the dominant. Such procedures can make a development section sound constantly in flux, even unstable. It is important for the analyst to maintain perspective: first, to see the motivic and thematic nature of such local excursions in the broader context; and second, to interpret such diverse compositional processes in relation to the embracing span of dominant harmony from the end of the exposition to the end of the development.

As we have seen throughout this book, strategies for analysis can differ from piece to piece. Sometimes the upper voice may immediately draw one's attention, sometimes it is the bass the analyst may decide to examine first. For this particular development section, we will first consider the bass and harmonic structure.

We shall begin by considering three focal points that appear prominently and articulate the sections. Arriving at preliminary decisions about such reference points will often help to put local motions into broader perspective (Example 11.10). The first is the D-minor triad in bar 53, which represents a continuation of the exposition's dominant. The change to the minor mode

EXAMPLE 11.10 (*continued*)

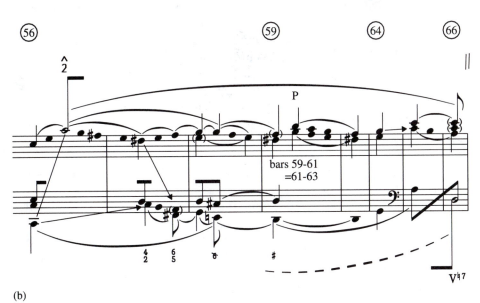

bars 59-61
=61-63

(b)

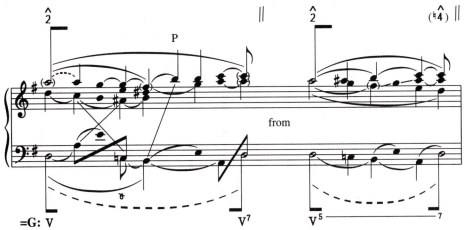

(c)

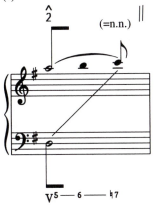

signals the beginning of its destabilization and suggests to the listener that motion away from the dominant is underway. A second prominent point of articulation is the B-major chord in bar 59, marked by the change in design in both hands, particularly in the pattern of the left hand. The repeated pedal (in two registers) emphasizes the tone B as a significant step in the bass line of the section. Notice also the augmented sixth chord in bar 58 that chromatically establishes B as a local goal. Throughout the tonal period, augmented sixth chords frequently mark the boundaries of prolongational spans and signal important points of arrival.[15] Finally, the third point of orientation is the V^7 chord at the end of the development in bar 66. The harmonic motion has returned to the dominant, which no longer functions as a key, but as a chord that prepares the tonic of the recapitulation.

Let us now consider the principal bass motion in relation to these reference points (Example 11.10b). The lower voice initially moves up by fifths, from D minor to A minor and then to E minor, which quickly gives way to the augmented sixth chord. The rapid approach to this dissonant harmony is striking; notice, however, that a broader stepwise motion occurs from the D-minor chord at the beginning of the section through the augmented sixth chord to its resolution in bar 59, as indicated on the graph by a slur. As the graph shows, the motions to A minor and E minor belong to an inner voice above the middleground bass line; the C of the augmented sixth chord reestablishes the true bass voice (albeit in a rather high register) and resolves to B. After a five-bar prolongation of the B-major chord, the bass continues its motion and leads finally to V^7 in bar 66, marking the conclusion of the development section.

Having examined the bass structure, we shall now discover how the upper voice works in relation to the bass motions. The reduction in Example 11.10b shows the role of the ascending fifth-motion in the first part of the development section. On the musical surface, the top line begins from d^2 and develops a melodic figure from the second theme (compare bars 21–23 to bars 53–55). In graph 11.10b, d^2 is interpreted as an inner voice of the dominant harmony—in the light of the overall structure of the development—while a^2 (structural $\hat{2}$) is prolonged on a middleground level from the end of the exposition. As d^2 moves to c^2 over the A-minor chord (Example 11.10a), the line leaps up and regains a^2 in bar 56, which initiates two strands in the voice leading (Example 11.10b). The first (motion into an inner voice) leads through g^2 to $f\sharp^2$; the second simultaneously continues the upward path of the upper voice, reaching b^2 in bar 59.[16] Because of the melodic play of the right-hand part, the A♯ of the augmented sixth chord is present in an inner voice. Structurally, however, the A♯ is the crucial chromatic tone of the chord, resolving to B through the passing motion A–A♯–B (see the second part of Example 11.10b).

From this point the structural top voice continues to rise toward c^3, completing the overarching line A–B–C in the upper voice. Bear in mind that our interpretation of this middleground line is based not only on the harmonic reference points, but also on the large-scale registral association of these principal tones. Owing to the interplay of voices and registers in this section, each tone is not always literally sounding in its primary structural register. By now, however, you are well acquainted with implied tones and motions to and from inner voices, and you should have no trouble interpreting the relationship among the levels shown in Example 11.10.

Previously in our discussion of this development section we mentioned that (in major keys) the development typically transforms, through prolongation, the key of the dominant into the dominant chord that prepares the beginning of the recapitulation. One of the most direct ways in which to transform a tonicized dominant key area back into a dominant chord in the home key is to add the seventh. This procedure completely destabilizes the secondary key, for the dominant (now a seventh chord) will no longer be heard as a local tonic. Furthermore, since the seventh of V^7 is *natural* $\hat{4}$, the leading tone of the secondary key area ($\#\hat{4}$) is canceled and the home key is restored. From your studies of harmony and voice leading, you probably remember the V^{5-7} technique that frequently transforms the dominant triad into a dominant seventh chord. As the synopsis of Example 11.10c shows, this is the procedure at work over the entire span of the development section. Because of the breadth of the section, the third from A to C ($\hat{5}-\hat{7}$ over V) is filled in with a passing tone.

This broad transformational process not only destabilizes the secondary key, but also continues the prolongation of the dominant (of the first branch). This is why, from a structural perspective, the development section can be viewed as a continuation (or outgrowth) of the exposition, where the dominant is first established. In longer developments that entail several smaller sections, the final dominant prolongation preparing for the recapitulation (sometimes over a dominant pedal) is often called a *retransition*. However, as we have noted, developments are enormously varied as to their character and structure.[17]

Recapitulation (bars 67–122)

The recapitulation of a sonata movement can be viewed from various perspectives. Thematically, it combines a statement of the first group and associated material with a transposition of part or all of the second group in the tonic. There may be some deletions or additions; usually, some sort of recomposition occurs. Harmonically, the return of the second group in the tonic requires alteration of the bridge, the first group, or sometimes part of the second group, a challenge that has evoked great skill and imagination from composers.

Interpreting these modifications can be challenging, as well as rewarding, to the analyst. The recapitulation embodies the second branch of the interrupted structure, prolonging the tonic overall (though with the possibility of unexpected harmonic events). Since part or all of the descent of the *Urlinie* normally occurs within the second group (now transposed to the tonic) careful reevaluation of the structure is necessary, including any recomposition that may have occurred.[18] Finally the closing section of the recapitulation

EXAMPLE 11.11:

Beethoven, Piano Sonata, Op. 49, No. 2, I, first theme and transition section of recapitulation, bars 67–87: (a) foreground and (b–c) middleground reductions

(a)

(and the coda, if present) must be considered. Thus, a recapitulation is not simply a restatement of the exposition with the second group transposed; it must be analyzed on its own terms.

Example 11.11 represents the first tonal area and transition section of the recapitulation. The example concludes in bar 82, where $\hat{2}$ over V is conclusively established. (The remaining part of the transition—bars 83–87—is indicated only in the bar numbering since this is identical to bars 15–20 in the

EXAMPLE 11.11 (*continued*)

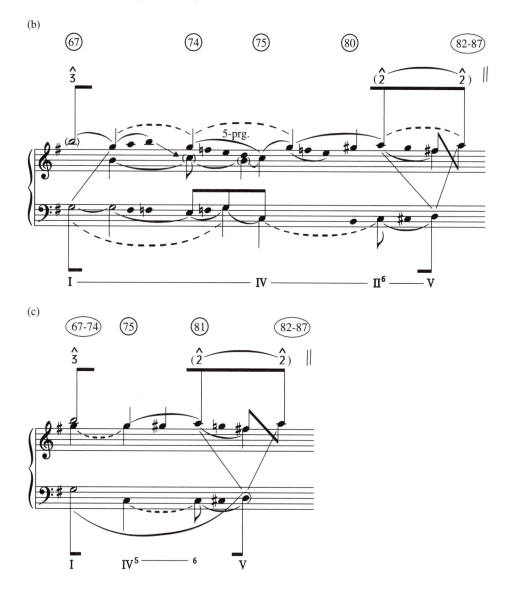

exposition.) Because bars 67–70 are identical to bars 1–4, the graph is abbreviated here to show the primary tone $\hat{3}$ over tonic harmony. Like bars 5ff., the second phrase of the first group (bars 71ff.) leads directly into the transition section.

Here a striking change takes place. In the exposition the transition was brief, leading from I through an intermediate II^6 to a tonicized V that is subsequently reinterpreted as I in the new key of D major (Example 11.6). Now, in the recapitulation, Beethoven has expanded the transition section by incorporating a version of the exposition's closing theme in the subdominant key of C major.

Why did Beethoven make this dramatic compositional change? One answer reflects considerations that were discussed above: some compositional changes are necessary in order for the second-group material to be recapitulated in the tonic rather than the secondary key of the exposition. This must be accomplished in a way that sounds convincing and that recreates the sense of motion and change that occurred in the exposition—even though the second group will now be heard in the tonic.[19] Beethoven accomplishes this not only by introducing thematic material that was previously heard in another section, but also by doing so in the subdominant key. He thereby creates a sense of harmonic change and variety, so that the return of the tonic with the second group sounds fresh. At the conclusion of the subdominant region, a 5–6 shift transforms IV into II^6, which leads to V in the same manner as in the exposition. This is accomplished by the chromatic passing motion G–G♯–A in the upper voice (compare the a and b graphs, bars 79–81), which corresponds to the A–A♯–B motion in the development.

Before we begin to examine the second group and closing section, it will be useful to review their role in the exposition (Examples 11.7 and 11.8). As you may recall, structural $\hat{2}$ (a^2) is active throughout the second part of the exposition, although in the second theme it makes only fleeting appearances, in effect "covering" an interrupted $\hat{3}$-line in D major ($\hat{3}$–$\hat{2}$//$\hat{3}$–$\hat{2}$–$\hat{1}$). At the beginning of the closing section (bar 36), a^2 emerges fully and initiates a fifth-progression that engenders closure in the dominant area of the exposition. Beethoven, therefore, uses two broad linear progressions in the dominant region of the exposition: a third-progression from F♯ followed by a fifth-progression from A. The second is the primary progression, because it leads the upper voice from $\hat{2}$ to the structural close of the exposition.

In the recapitulation, when the second group begins in the tonic we may assume that a straightforward transposition of the rest of the exposition will occur. Two factors, however, should be considered in our analysis: (1) the transposition of the second theme from the dominant to the tonic will change the register, and may thereby alter the compositional fabric; (2) further changes often occur in the working out of the themes, perhaps as a consequence of events stated earlier in the recapitulation or in the development. Therefore, the significance of the transposed material in the recapitulation may require a different structural interpretation than in the context of the exposition.

Example 11.12 presents the second theme and closing section in the tonic key. The graph has been abbreviated; it begins with the consequent phrase of the second theme and concludes in bar 122.

In the exposition, structural tonic harmony spans only 12 bars before the modulation to the dominant, which is prolonged for the last 38 bars of the exposition. Tonal balance is established in the recapitulation, through the large expanse of tonic harmony and the two associated linear progressions: a third-progression from B followed by a fifth-progression from D (see the graphic synopsis in Example 11.12b). The fifth-progression of the closing section parallels the closing section in the exposition, beginning on $\hat{5}$ (in G major) and leading the upper voice to $\hat{1}$. This line reaffirms the tonic key, just as it affirmed the dominant at the end of the exposition.

As Example 11.12 illustrates, the two linear progressions function differently in the structure of the recapitulation. When the second theme is transposed to the home tonic, the third-progression of the middleground now begins on B, which is the primary tone $\hat{3}$ prolonged from the first theme. We interpret, however, the $\hat{3}-\hat{2}//\hat{3}-\hat{2}-\hat{1}$ of the second theme, and in particular the $\hat{3}-\hat{2}-\hat{1}$ of the consequent phrase, as motion into an inner voice. In other words, the primary tone $\hat{3}$ remains active at a higher structural level throughout the recapitulated second theme.[20] This means that the ensuing fifth-progression beginning from d^3 and leading to g^1 (bars 103–110) *elaborates* the descent of the *Urlinie* (see the synoptic graph, Example 11.12b).[21] The multiple lines from D that follow expand and elaborate $\hat{1}$, achieved in bar 110. Example 11.12c summarizes the entire recapitulation.[22]

More on Modulatory Procedures in Major

In the exposition of this sonata we found that the transition section concluded on V (bar 20), one possible goal of the large-scale motion from the initial structural tonic.[23] Other possibilities exist, however, for the modulatory goal of a transition section.

In Beethoven's E♭-major Piano Sonata, Op. 31, No. 3, the tonic of the first theme leads to an F-major triad at the end of the transition. This chord, of course, can be thought of as V of V. From a broader perspective, the V of V can be interpreted also as an altered II that follows from the structural tonic of the first theme (I–II♯–V).[24] Sometimes V of V may be emphasized through its dominant (I–VI♯–II♯–V). This progression further destabilizes the tonic in favor of the emerging dominant, because in VI♯ the tonic note itself is chromatically inflected.[25]

The possibilities for modulations in sonata expositions are too numerous to be listed in their entirety. Those discussed here are among the most common types of modulations in major-mode compositions. The following analysis illustrates a characteristic possibility for the minor mode.

MOZART, PIANO SONATA, K. 457, I

Throughout this book we have recommended different strategies for analysis. Each composition is unique, with its own individual characteristics; sometimes the particular features of a piece may be so striking as to suggest a path for analysis. In this extraordinary sonata movement, the motives and elaborations of the upper voice, particularly of the primary tone, immediately engage one's attention and offer a good point of departure. Our discussion of the structure

EXAMPLE 11.12:

Beethoven, Piano Sonata, Op. 49, No. 2, I, second theme (consequent phrase) and closing section of recapitulation, bars 95–122: (a–b) foreground and (c) middleground reductions

(a)

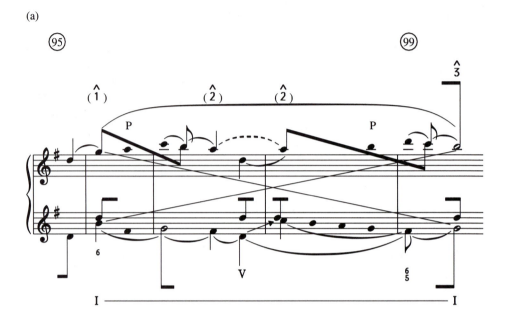

and form will also consider those aspects that are characteristic of the minor mode.

Exposition (bars 1–74)

Before considering aspects of harmony and voice leading, take a few minutes to examine Mozart's use of dynamics and, in particular, of register. The sonic resources of the piano are not as great as those of the orchestra, yet Mozart achieves orchestral qualities through the juxtaposition and isolation of different registers. In bars 1–4, for example, both hands open up a "registral space" from great C in the bass to G and A♭ in the two-line octave of the upper voice. In bars 3–4, the left hand abandons the lower register, only to rejoin it in bar 5. We shall see that the alternation of registers serves a structural function throughout the exposition, highlighting important points of harmonic and melodic arrival.

We shall now turn our attention to the harmonic and motivic structure of the exposition. As a first step, listen to or play through the entire section, noting the salience of G in the upper voice: it appears prominently (through various techniques) in bars 3, 8, 9, 11, 14, 16, 23, and 41, which leads us to make the initial assumption that $\hat{5}$ is the primary tone of the *Urlinie*.

EXAMPLE 11.12 (*continued*)

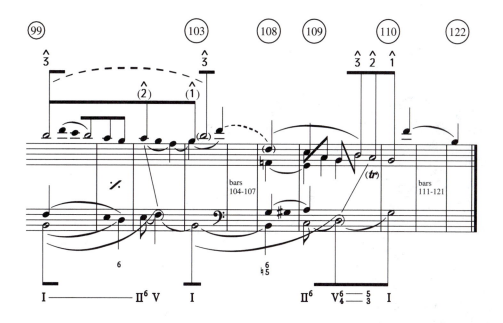

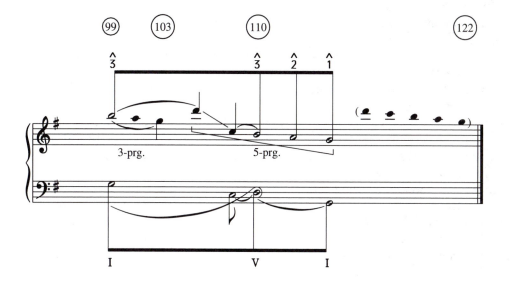

EXAMPLE 11.12 (*continued*)

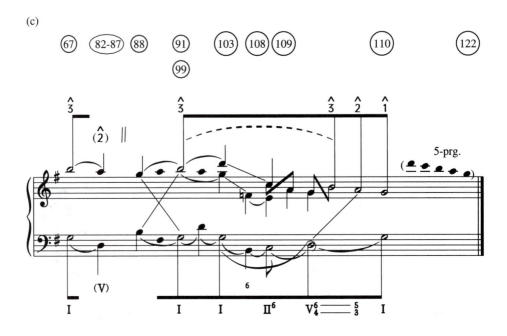

In Example 11.13, which presents a voice-leading graph of bars 1–19 (the first theme), we can see at least two prominent motives associated with $\hat{5}$. The first is the tone succession G–A♭–G, a seminal neighbor figure that elaborates the primary tone and occurs at various levels throughout this movement. Note that the resolution (in the same register) of A♭ in bar 4 is delayed until bar 8; the delayed resolution results in part from the interplay of registers mentioned above. The second motive is a chromatically descending fourth from G to D, which occurs first in bars 9–11 in the alto register.[26] Through inversion of the counterpoint in the right hand, the fourth is shifted to the higher register in bars 11–13, where it prolongs $\hat{5}$ through motion into the inner voice. A careful comparison of graphs a and b of Examples 11.13 will reveal these motives, as well as the harmonic structure, and the local fifth-progression that serves to bring the first theme to a close while retaining the presence of $\hat{5}$ at a deeper level of structure.

Example 11.14 represents the end of the first theme, which through a phrase overlap simultaneously becomes the beginning of the transition. Reflecting the large analytical perspective necessary with complete movements, the graph shows that the primary tone g^2 remains active as the primary tone $\hat{5}$, shown in parentheses over the local $\hat{1}$ in C minor.[27] A comparison of levels in Example 11.14 shows how quickly the upper neighbor A♭ is reestablished over a dominant seventh chord on B♭, which destabilizes the tonic and initiates the motion to the secondary key. The upper neighbor $a♭^2$ is transferred to $a♭^1$ and resolves to g^1 in bar 23.

Mozart's love for opera and his mastery as an opera composer are reflected in the dramatic qualities of many of his instrumental compositions. Not only does this aspect of his work manifest itself in the quasi-orchestral uses of register in this piano sonata, but also in the character of certain themes and sections. In bar 23, we apparently hear a new theme in E♭. Because tonal stability usually follows a transition section, we are likely to interpret this section as the beginning of the second theme, at least at first. Like one of Mozart's operatic characters wearing a disguise, however, this theme turns out to be something different than we initially supposed. First of all, bars 23–30 seem much too short, compositionally out of balance, for a second theme in a movement of this breadth. Further, as early as bar 27, the theme begins to dissolve, quickly leading us back to a B♭ major harmony that is prolonged for six bars—and with a stronger feeling of dominant preparation than that of bars 21–22. In retrospect, we realize that Mozart, in a spirit reminiscent of Haydn, has deceived us: what we initially thought to be the second theme is in fact a *thematic transition.*

Example 11.14 illustrates the harmonic context in which this "tonal deception" occurs. At the surface and foreground of the music, the thematic transition is certainly heard in E♭ major. At a deeper level of structure, however, we regard the E♭-major region as emerging from the upper third of the initial structural tonic.[28] Following this local excursion into E♭, the bass descends by step back to C before B♭, supporting V of III, is achieved in bar 30.

Example 11.14c illustrates the broader voice leading of this passage. The E♭-major transition, represented in the graph as a triad, helps to transform the initial I into a $^6_3$ chord (C–E♭–A♮) before V of III appears (the 5–6 motion avoids the parallels inherent in the progression from I to V of III). The influence of tonic harmony thus extends through bar 29, just before the dominant of the second key area. Notice how much more emphasis is given to this statement of B♭ harmony than to the similar chord in bar 21.

Now that we have a broader understanding of the harmonic context, we can turn our attention to the upper voice. Example 11.14 illustrates that G (5̂) is prolonged and decorated by the upper neighbor A♭ (bar 24), just as it is in the first theme. But, in the new tonal context of the transition section, it is composed-out differently. Instead of proceeding directly to A♭, G first moves to B♭, which decorates the upper neighbor A♭ from above, a reaching-over figure that will itself become motivic.[29] Thus, the seminal motive G–A♭–G from the opening phrase of the sonata returns in a new guise, as a varied motivic repetition, as part of the apparent new theme.

We mentioned that this theme quickly begins to dissolve in bar 27, one reason why the deception becomes apparent as the bass leads emphatically back to the B♭-major harmony. In the upper voice, as shown in Example 11.14b, the principal line from bar 27 essentially consists of the line G–A♮–B♭. The B♭ is then transferred to the two-line octave, where it leads to A♭ before the second theme enters in bar 36. Although not shown in Example 11.14, the A♭ resolves to G in the sixth bar of the second theme. Therefore, the G–B♭–A♭–G motion also spans the end of the transition and the beginning of

EXAMPLE 11.13:

Mozart, Piano Sonata, K. 457, I, first theme, bars 1–19: (a) foreground and (b) middleground reductions

(a)

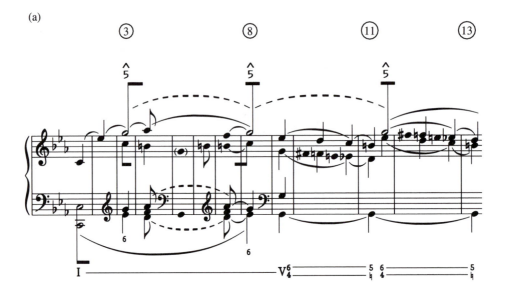

EXAMPLE 11.13 (*continued*)

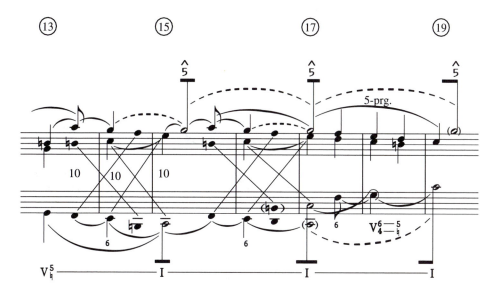

(b)

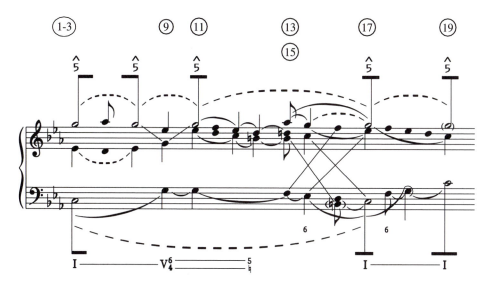

EXAMPLE 11.14:

Mozart, Piano Sonata, K. 457, I, transition, bars 19–35: (a) foreground and (b–c) middleground reductions

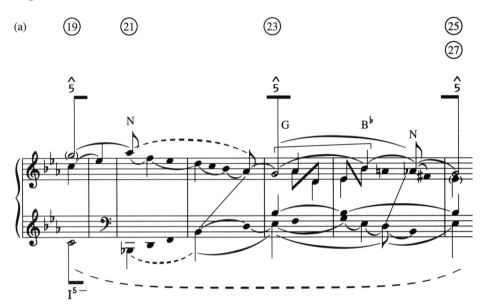

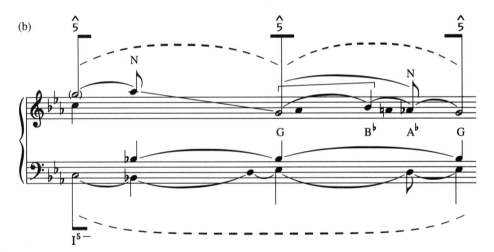

EXAMPLE 11.14 (*continued*)

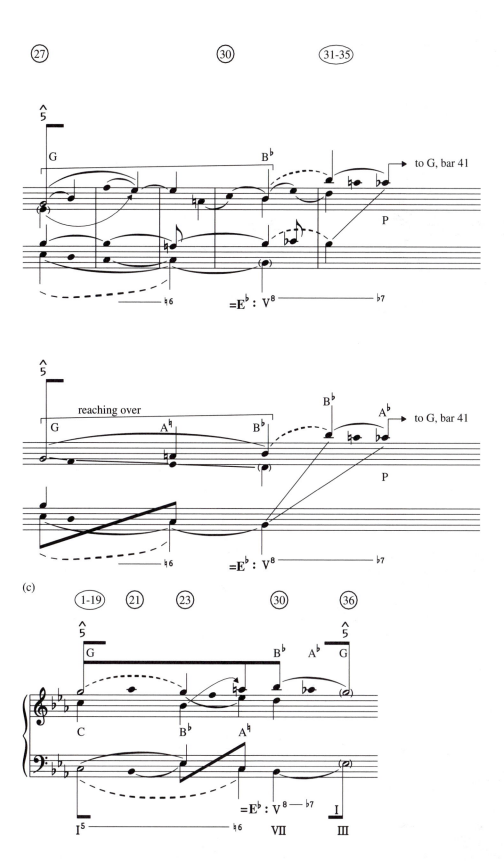

EXAMPLE 11.15:

Mozart, Piano Sonata, K. 457, I, second theme, bars 34–59: (a) foreground and (b–c) middleground reductions

(a)

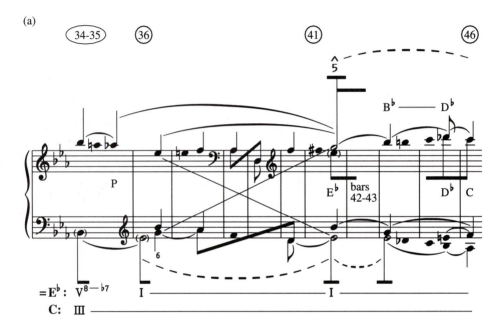

the second theme, but the a♭² in 35 is best interpreted as a passing tone (rather than a neighbor as before). This is an instance of a motivic repetition in which the tones are interpreted in slightly different ways.

Example 11.15a shows the end of the transition and the second theme in E♭ major, which concludes in bar 59. The first part of the section, bars 36–41, is rather straightforward; the upper voice (in a voice exchange with the bass) rises to reestablish the primary tone $\hat{5}$ ($\hat{3}$ in E♭ major) in bar 41. Notice the clef changes and alternation of registers that punctuate this ascent, suggesting a dialogue of high and low instruments in orchestral style, in conjunction with a dialogue of thematic figures. This passage also recalls the opening theme, where a similar technique delays the resolution of the upper neighbor A♭ in the higher register (bar 4 to bar 8). In the opening bars of the second theme, we see another beautiful example of a delayed resolution: the A♭ at the end of the transition, as the seventh of V⁷ in E♭, resolves to G over tonic harmony in bar 41 (Example 11.15a). Hence the motivic A♭ established in the opening bars of the movement again decorates the primary tone G, in a different tonal context and over a longer span of the upper voice.

Our examination of Beethoven's piano sonata revealed that the second theme composes out structural $\hat{2}$ of the *Urlinie*. By contrast, in the minor-mode context of Mozart's sonata, the primary tone $\hat{5}$ (which is common to

EXAMPLE 11.15 (*continued*)

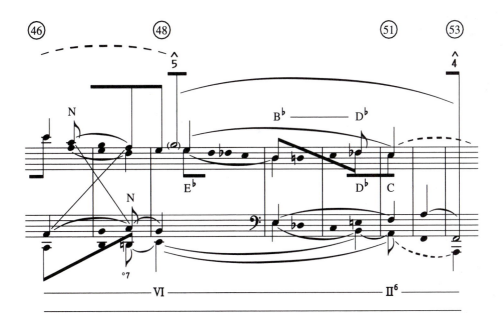

both tonic and mediant harmonies) is still active through the beginning of the second theme. The *Urlinie* begins its descent in the mediant key, representing the second step in the large-scale bass arpeggiation I–III–V. In such cases, $\hat{5}$–$\hat{4}$–$\hat{3}$ of the *Urlinie* is composed out as $\hat{3}$–$\hat{2}$–$\hat{1}$ in the mediant. (The closure produced by this descent usually marks the conclusion of the second theme.) We will begin with an examination of the harmonic structure of bars 41–59, then consider the upper voice.

If the *Urlinie* descent from $\hat{5}$ to $\hat{3}$ happened too quickly, it would leave the second theme sounding too short for the proportions of the movement. And, as we have seen, much of the compositional interest lies in the ways in which a structure is composed out. Consequently, Mozart uses a kind of delaying tactic, one that extends the second theme. He leads the tonic of bars 36–41 to a II^6 (bar 46), suggesting the imminent arrival of an authentic cadence. The II^6, however, is followed by a deceptive cadence in bars 47–48, which delays closure in the mediant key. The motion is repeated, now concluding on a very strong and extended II^6 (bar 51). Because the repetition of the tonic in bar 49 is a merely local event in the context of the section as a whole, the overall motion is best understood as a broad bass arpeggiation from the beginning of the second theme: in E♭, I–VI–II^6 (Example 11.15b).

EXAMPLE 11.15 (*continued*)

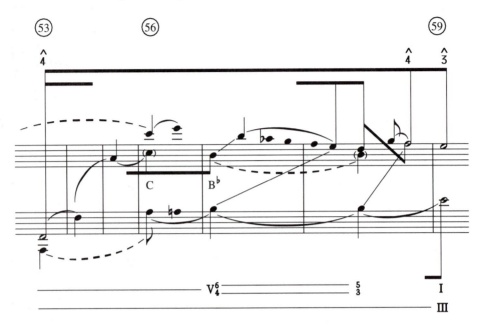

Notice also the character and prominence of the II^6, which leads to the structural cadence and conclusion of the second theme in bars 58–59. It is prolonged from bars 51–56 through cadenzalike figuration similar to bravura passages in concerto cadenzas. With the bass structure clarified, we can now describe the voice-leading strands that elaborate the descent of the *Urlinie* from $\hat{5}$ to $\hat{3}$. The top voice leads upward from E♭ in bar 36 to G in bar 41, with a climactic motion from B♭ to D♭ in bars 44–45 (Example 11.15a). The resolution of D♭ to C is a new statement of the neighbor motive, higher in register than before. A comparison of levels a and b in Example 11.15 reveals this B♭–D♭ motion to be an inner-voice line superposed above the primary tone $\hat{5}$. This observation is confirmed in bars 49–50, where a repetition of the gesture (produced by the delaying effect of the deceptive cadence) occurs in the lower register, beneath the primary tone g^2 (which remains conceptually present). Level b in particular shows that the two motions from B♭ to D♭ serve locally to elaborate a broader "alto" line, which is more easily understood if one considers the e♭^{2} implied beneath the primary tone $\hat{5}$ in bar 41.

The other principal voice-leading strand leads the primary tone G through F to E♭ (bars 41–48). Because of the deceptive cadence, we interpret this line as motion into an inner voice that retains the structural presence of $\hat{5}$. With the arrival of II^6 in bar 51, however, G moves to F, which prepares the descent F–E♭ ($\hat{4}$–$\hat{3}$) at the cadence in bars 58–59.[30] A comparison of all three levels will reveal the ingenious way in which Mozart uses an interplay of registers to work out the inner voices of the tonal fabric as the *Urlinie* leads from $\hat{5}$ to $\hat{3}$.

EXAMPLE 11.15 (*continued*)

Example 11.16a shows the voice-leading structure of the closing section to bar 71.[31] (We shall discuss the final four bars in conjunction with the development section.) As we have seen, closing sections confirm the secondary key area, often through repeated cadential patterns. In Mozart's sonata, the emphasis of $e\flat^2$ ($\hat{3}$) over III throughout this section is easily recognized, both in the music and in the graph. Yet this closing section also involves recollections of previous motivic figures. (For this reason we have provided an additional reduction of part of the second theme in the second level.) Notice in the music, for example, the rising fifths (upper voice) from E♭ to B♭ that unfold

EXAMPLE 11.16:

Mozart, Piano Sonata, K. 457, I: comparison of (a) bars 59–71 and (b) bars 41–59

in bars 59–61 and 63–65, recalling in retrograde form not only the identical line (in the same register!) from the cadence in bars 57–58, but also the fifth in the lower register in bars 42–43 (not shown in the graph).[32] Even more subtle are the recollections that begin on the downbeat of bar 67: the first is from eb^2, structural $\hat{3}$, the second from bb^1, the fifth of the mediant harmony understood through implication (it appears literally in the higher register on beat 2).

By comparing the two graphs in the example, you will discover that the two "alto" strands that appear consecutively in bars 41–59 unfold simultaneously in the closing section from bars 67–71.[33] These presentations, of course, occur twice, for bars 69–71 form a repetition (in the lower register) of bars 67–69. In the closing bars of the exposition, therefore, Mozart summarizes previously heard motivic strands in a continuing interplay of registers, an aspect of this movement established from its very beginning.

Development (bars 75–99)

In our analysis of Beethoven's G-major Piano Sonata, we saw that the development section prolongs structural $\hat{2}$ over V of the structure. In minor-mode compositions, the second key area is typically the mediant. From a structural perspective, if the *Urlinie* begins on $\hat{5}$, it usually descends to $\hat{3}$ at the end of the exposition. In the development section the bass arpeggiation of the first branch of the interrupted structure will continue from III at the end of the exposition to V at the end of the development. In the upper voice, structural $\hat{3}$ will descend to $\hat{2}$ over V.[34]

Example 11.17a includes the final bars of the exposition for perspective (with bars 69 and 71 represented as a single sonority). In bar 71 we can clearly hear $\hat{3}$ over III, the active elements of the fundamental structure. Bear in mind, however, that due to the convention of repeating the exposition, the final bars of the exposition have a dual nature. They must serve both as a *retransition* back to the tonic at the beginning of the movement and as a *transition* into the development. Consequently, this passage moves quickly to a V^9 in C minor, a chord that recalls the motivic upper neighbor A♭ in the two-line octave (the register in which A♭ has appeared numerous times).

When the V^9 chord then leads into the development, in fact it again takes us to C harmony. But another unexpected transformation occurs: unlike the beginning of the movement, we hear C-*major* harmony. As the development progresses, we realize that this is not a real tonic at all, but an applied V of IV that is transformed into an applied VII^{o7} of IV before F minor appears in bar 79. The subdominant is strongly articulated by the return of the theme from the thematic transition (bars 23–26); hence we can consider the arrival of IV as a waypoint in the harmonic plan of the development section. In the upper voice, the A♭ of the V^9 resolves across the double bar to G (bar 76), which then leads to A♭ over the IV in bar 79. After we examine completely the large-scale bass motion, we will return to the upper voice and discover how it functions in the composing-out of the fundamental structure.

As Example 11.17a illustrates, the subdominant is prolonged for five bars. (Because bars 81–82 are a varied repetition of bars 79–80, they are represented by the same two bars on the graph.) In the music you will see that, during this prolongation, the melodic design of the right hand changes from the theme of the transition to the arpeggio of the first theme. In bars 85–87, G minor is preceded and established by its own applied V^7 chord. G minor is another important reference point, signaled as such not by a change in melodic design (since the arpeggio of the first theme continues), but by a

EXAMPLE 11.17:

Mozart, Piano Sonata, K. 457, I, development, bars 71–99: (a) foreground and (b) middleground reductions

(a)

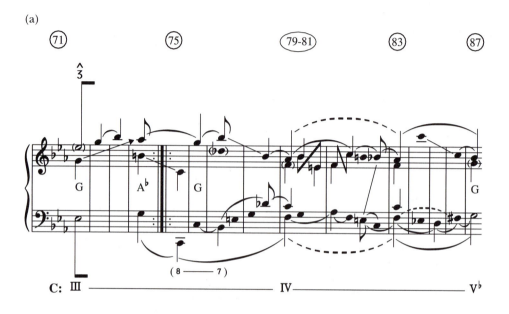

change in direction of the bass. The bass now begins to descend by step, reaching B♮ in bar 93, which is repeated in bar 96 and, finally, in bars 98–99, where it concludes the development section. Notice the register at this point: the left hand recalls the low register of previous points of articulation, such as the opening of the movement, the preparation of the thematic transition (bar 21), and the beginning of the development section.

Example 11.17b puts the broad bass and upper-voice motions into structural perspective. Recall that the IV and minor V, the primary reference points in bars 79 and 87, are each preceded by applied leading-tone chords. The reduction shows that these chords are elaborations of an ascending 5–6 sequence. Consequently, the C-major harmony at the beginning of the development section is, as we mentioned above, not a real tonic but a continuation of III; the 5–6 motion above a chromatic bass transforms the mediant into the applied V and VII$^{\circ 7}$ chords of the forthcoming IV.[35]

Exactly the same contrapuntal process transforms IV into the applied $^6_5$ of minor V. Thus we see a chromatically ascending bass that leads from III to V: E♭–E♮–F–F♯–G. If you take a moment to review the first part of Example 11.15a, you will see that this chromatic tone succession—from E♭ to G♮—is the beginning of the exposition's second theme! The recomposition of this line serves to unify different sections of this movement at different structural levels. From bar 87 the minor V is transformed into the V$^6_5$ (a major-minor seventh chord) of the home tonic. Notice also the decorating diminished seventh chord in bars 95–98 (played very softly in bar 98), which recalls the motivic G–A♭–G as the development section closes.

EXAMPLE 11.17 (*continued*)

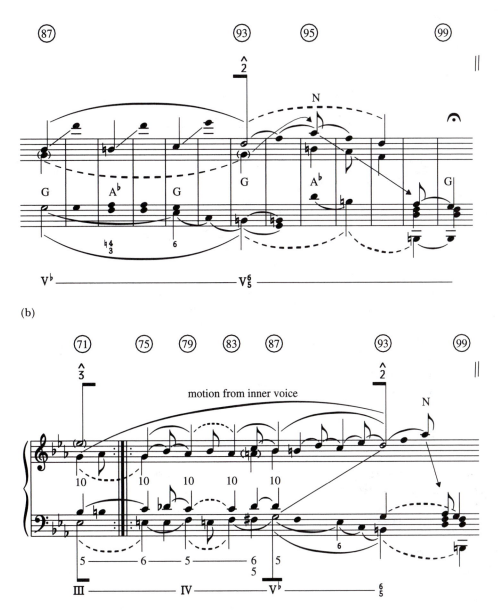

We had left the upper voice at the point where A♭ is established over IV in bar 79. Example 11.17b illustrates that as the bass rises in the 5–6 sequence, the upper voice does as well. (Remember that, in an ascending 5–6 sequence, one voice will move in parallel tenths with the bass.) Hence the upper voice moves from G (at the beginning of the development) to B♭ (over the minor V) through the technique of reaching over; the pattern in this case is the leap of an ascending third followed by a descending step. As the bass changes

EXAMPLE 11.18:

Mozart, Piano Sonata, K. 457, I: middleground synopsis of exposition and development

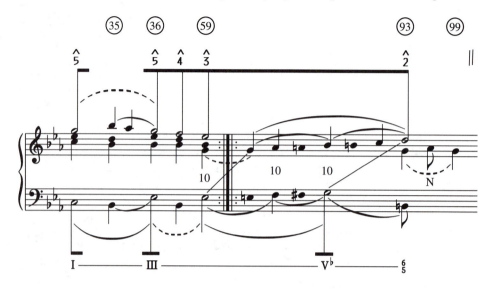

direction and descends to the V_5^6, the upper voice continues its ascent, arriving at d^2 in bar 93, followed by the superposed inner-voice tones F and A♭.[36]

We identify d^2 as a structural goal—the conclusion of a linear progression, for two reasons. First, beginning in bar 87, the upper voice consists rhythmically of two-bar units, corresponding to the span of the arpeggios in the right hand. In other words, the downbeats of bars 87, 89, 91, and 93 define the final part of the stepwise foreground ascent of the upper voice: B♭–B♮–C–D. Second, following bar 94, a change in design occurs: the triplet figuration ends, highlighting bars 93–94 as the final two-bar unit and, consequently, pointing to d^2 as the goal of the ascent. The reduction shows that we interpret this tone as structural $\hat{2}$, following which are local, prolonging motions that, in a grand sweep downward, summarize the important registers of the movement and recall the upper neighbor A♭.

Using Example 11.17b, we can summarize the function of the middleground line that spans the development section, from G over III (bars 71ff.) to D near the end of the development (bar 93). This is motion from an inner voice that, at a lower structural level, connects $\hat{3}$ over III at the end of the exposition with $\hat{2}$ over V at the conclusion of the development section. In other words, this line serves to expand the tonal space between $\hat{3}$ and $\hat{2}$, and to lead the fundamental line (of the first branch) to the point of interruption.

Example 11.18 illustrates some of the large-scale features we have discussed to this point. We see here an exposition in which the primary tone $\hat{5}$ is prolonged in the first theme before it descends to $\hat{3}$ in the mediant region of the second theme. During the course of the development section, structural $\hat{3}$ descends to $\hat{2}$ as the bass arpeggiation continues from III, through a passing IV, to the V at the point of interruption. This upper-voice motion is common in the minor mode and is different from many major-mode movements, where scale degree $\hat{2}$, the goal of the first branch, is reached in the exposition. Also bear in mind that the progression III–IV–V occurs frequently in the development sections of minor-mode compositions; it represents a continuation of the structural bass motion from the end of the exposition to the dominant of the first branch. In the major mode, the development section, on the other hand, typically prolongs the V.[37]

Recapitulation (bars 100–185)

The recapitulation of the first theme, bars 100–117, is identical to the corresponding passage in the exposition. Consequently we will proceed directly to some features of the transition. We recommend that you examine the details of its voice leading on your own; these are illustrated in Example 11.19.

Notice that the transition section is substantially abbreviated by comparison with the exposition. That is, what we have labeled the "thematic transition" of the exposition (bars 23–30) is not recapitulated. Its omission here underscores its transitory quality, providing more analytical evidence that on first hearing it was a deception and not the authentic second theme.

Mozart, however, now misleads us in a different way. We have noted that, in the recapitulations of many Classical sonata movements, the transition section is reworked to prepare the presentation of the second theme in the tonic. Mozart's recomposed transition retains some of its modulatory character, but here it apparently begins to lead to the remote key of D♭ major. It is as if Mozart becomes "lost," in a manner reminiscent of some of the improvisatory passages in his keyboard Fantasies. Yet we soon realize that we have been deceived once again, for the progression quickly corrects itself and leads to V of C minor in bar 126.

As the reductions of Example 11.19 illustrate, Mozart is playing on the dual nature of the German augmented sixth chord. On the one hand, the chord could lead to a major key (paralleling the original transition section) if it functions as a dominant seventh chord (of the Neapolitan). On the other hand, functioning as an augmented sixth chord in the tonic, its resolution yields a recollection, in the bass, of the A♭–G motive from the very beginning of the movement. The motivic reference and the need to affirm the tonic overwhelm the dreamlike possibility of leading to a tonal context as remote as D♭ major. The chord resolves to V of C minor, after which the transition section continues as it did in the exposition.[38]

Our examination of the second theme begins with an important consideration. In major-mode movements in which the second group is in the dominant, the transposition in the recapitulation can be literal, involving a change of register but not of mode. In minor-mode movements, however, the interval of transposition is down a minor third, from the major mediant to the minor

EXAMPLE 11.19:

Mozart, Piano Sonata, K. 457, I, transition section in recapitulation, bars 118–128: (a) foreground and (b) middleground reductions

tonic; because of the different arrangement of whole and half steps in the major and minor modes, direct transposition is generally possible only if the second group is recapitulated in the tonic major, a not infrequently encountered possibility. Composers, therefore, often make adjustments in the recapitulation of the second theme in the minor-mode environment of the recapitulation.[39]

If you return briefly to Example 11.15a and compare it to Example 11.20, you will discover the modifications Mozart makes in the second theme of the recapitulation. In the exposition, the theme spans a major third, beginning

EXAMPLE 11.20:

Mozart, Piano Sonata, K. 457, I, second theme of recapitulation, bars 130–139: (a) foreground and (b) middleground reductions

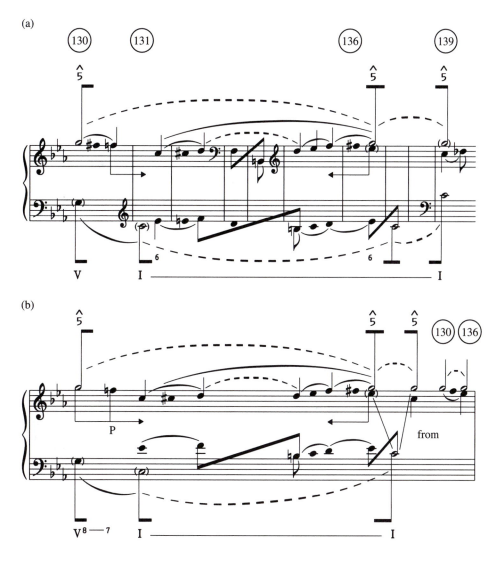

on $e\flat^2$ and ascending chromatically to g^2 (structural $\hat{5}$). In the recapitulation, Mozart recomposes the theme to span a perfect fifth, an adjustment that retains g^2 as the goal of the line. Once again the second theme leads to structural $\hat{5}$, which will descend completely to closure in the remaining part of the second theme.

In the concluding bars of the second theme (bars 139–156), the fundamental line of the structure twice leads to $\hat{1}$ and closure. To clarify the details of each descent, as well as the continuing adjustments Mozart makes in the recomposed second theme, we have provided two graphs for this passage,

EXAMPLE 11.21:

Mozart, Piano Sonata, K. 457, I, second theme of recapitulation, bars 139–145: (a) foreground and (b) middleground reductions

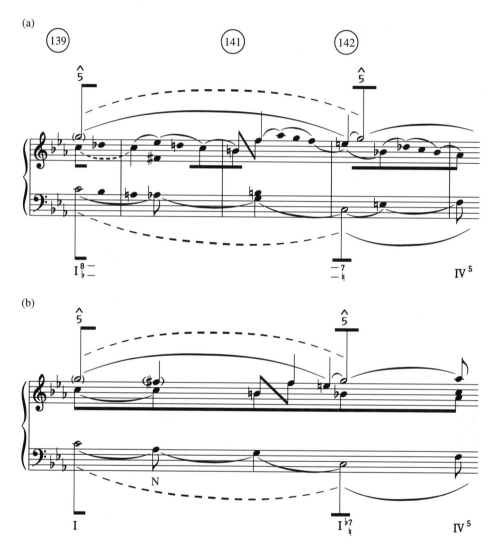

which we ask you to study on your own (Examples 11.21 and 11.22). Bear in mind that we have abbreviated certain repeated passages and normalized register to indicate the function of superposed inner-voice lines. In Example 11.21, for instance, only the lower octave of the right hand is shown for the climactic passage of bars 139–141. As in the exposition, this line elaborates and prolongs the descent of the structural upper voice.

Also notable is a significant difference between the two descents that occur in the latter part of the second theme. In bar 143 of the first descent, the

EXAMPLE 11.21 (*continued*)

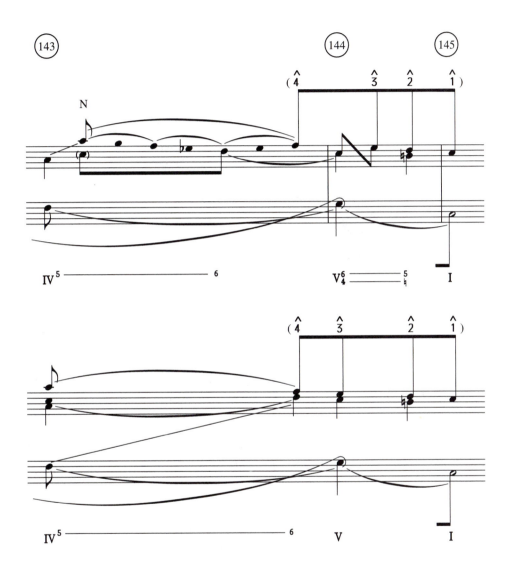

intermediate harmony of the bass progression is transformed from a IV to a II^6 through a 5–6 shift, a common transformation of subdominant harmony at a cadence (Example 11.21). In the upper voice, the primary tone $\hat{5}$ (last stated in bar 136 and touched upon in bar 142) moves again to A♭, which now functions as an incomplete neighbor, moving to $\hat{4}$ over the intermediate harmony.[40]

In the descent of the *Urlinie* (Example 11.22), we hear again the bravura, cadenzalike passage from the exposition that highlights and expands the in-

EXAMPLE 11.22:

Mozart, Piano Sonata, K. 457, I, second theme of recapitulation, bars 145–156: (a) foreground and (b) middleground reductions

(a)

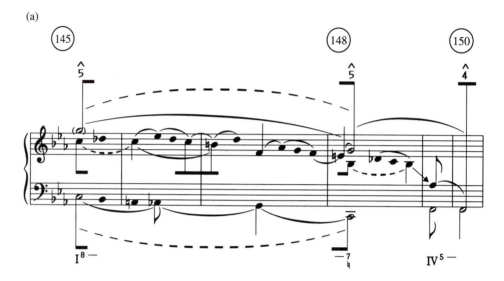

termediate harmony of the structural cadence. As the example illustrates, the incomplete neighbor A♭ appears once more over the subdominant chord and, through a passage that sweeps through three octaves, is transferred to the two-line octave in bar 153, the register in which it appears so prominently throughout the movement. In bar 156, the upper voice leads to structural 1̂.

You will notice that we give structural priority to the descent concluding in bar 156, using open noteheads in Example 11.22 to signify the descent of the fundamental line. The reason for this interpretation lies in the way the intermediate harmony is worked out in bars 149–153. The change of design to triplet figuration and the sweeping motion that summarizes the various registers of the composition produce a drive to the cadence more forceful than the similar passage in bars 142–145. The second perfect authentic cadence is more conclusive and represents the definitive completion of the structural upper voice.

The closing section of the recapitulation (bars 156–176) is very similar to the corresponding section of the exposition, differing only in some details. Example 11.23, an abbreviated voice-leading graph, illustrates some points of interest and the essential structure of the coda that follows in bars 168–185. One point of interest is the descending fifth-progression from G to C, which retraces the path of the fundamental line and contains a recollection of the upper neighbor A♭ resolving to G (bar 163).[41]

The inclusion of a coda is optional in the Classical sonata. Here, the V^9 of bar 167 has a dual function similar to that in the final bar of the exposition: it

EXAMPLE 11.22 (*continued*)

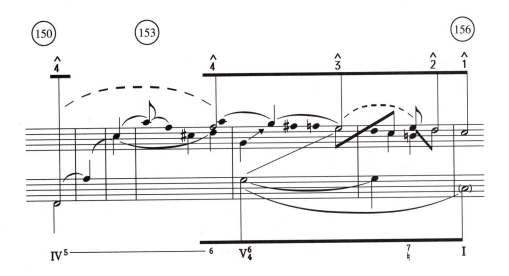

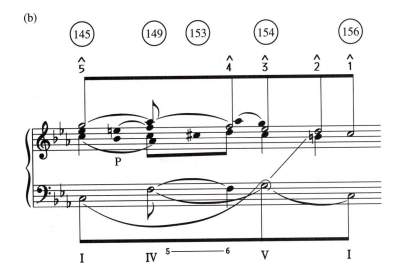

(b)

353

EXAMPLE 11.23:

Mozart, Piano Sonata, K. 457, I, closing section and coda, bars 156–185: foreground reduction

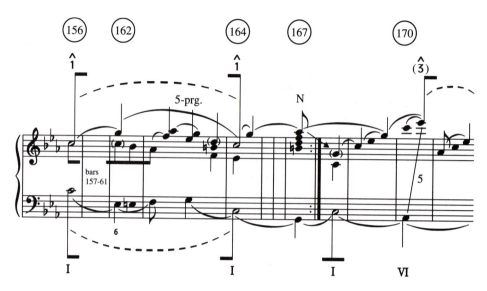

leads into a repetition of the development and recapitulation and, the second time, leads into a coda. You will notice in the graph that we show a lower-level descent from $\hat{3}$, beginning from eb^3 (bar 170). We regard this local emphasis on Eb as the recollection of previous motions to eb^2 (sometimes in conjunction with the third C–Eb): compare bars 17, 20, and 61–62 in the exposition; bars 85 and 92 in the development section; bars 116, 119, and (especially) 140 in the recapitulation. Mozart's periodic motions to this tone create a unifying association in the highest register of the movement.

In addition to summarizing motivic features, the function of many codas is to affirm the tonic of the recapitulation through repeated cadential motions, which is certainly the case here: multiple bass arpeggiations (eventually doubled in the right hand) connect the tonic with cadential dominants. Finally, as shown in the final bars of the graph, Mozart brings his stormy movement to a close with one final recollection of the fundamental line from $\hat{5}$ to $\hat{1}$, played very softly in a low register over I–V–I in the bass.

Example 11.24 presents a synopsis of the structure of this minor-mode movement. As in the major-mode movements by Clementi and Beethoven, the fundamental structure is divided into two parts, yet three formal sections emerge in the composing-out of its two branches. A significant difference exists, however, between the major- and minor-mode schemes. In the major mode, $\hat{2}$ over V (the goal of the first branch) is often established in the second part of the exposition (the second tonal area) and is then prolonged through the development. One might, in fact, associate the techniques of

EXAMPLE 11.23 (*continued*)

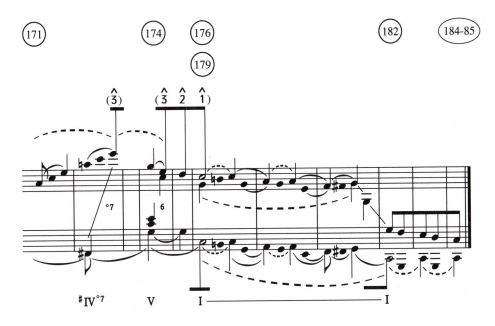

EXAMPLE 11.24:

Mozart, Piano Sonata, K. 457, I: middleground synopsis of form and structure

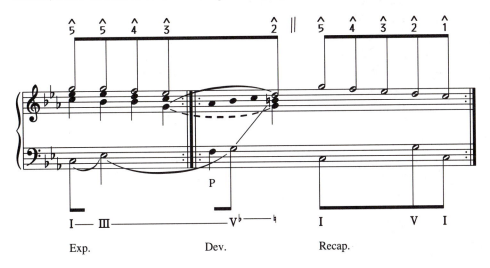

prolongation themselves with the formation of the development section. In minor-mode compositions that progress to the mediant in the exposition, the mediant scale step provides continued support for the primary tone (both $\hat{5}$ and $\hat{3}$ are possibilities); $\hat{2}$ over V in this situation then occurs at the end of the development, representing a continuation of the bass arpeggiation of the first branch. In both contexts, the composing-out of the second branch and ultimate completion of the fundamental structure corresponds with the recapitulation.

With their great variety and marvelous detail, the three sonata movements presented in this chapter may serve as an introduction to this extraordinarily rich compositional genre. In a sense, we have come full circle with our analysis of Mozart's great movement, the last in this introduction to the analysis of tonal music using Schenker's approach. For as we urge you to approach each sonata movement on its own terms, we reiterate our conviction—the guiding philosophy of this book—that analysis must begin with consideration of the individuality of musical compositions, with those characteristics that make each work unique. For example, when one begins to ponder the significance of the A♭ in bar 4 of Mozart's sonata, and then discovers its relationship to the structure and to other aspects of the composition, then one will stand at the threshold of deeper and richer musical understanding.

Exercises

1. Kuhlau, Sonatina, Op. 55, No. 1, I

a. Map out the main harmonic areas of the exposition (bars 1–20) and the corresponding areas of the recapitulation (bars 35–62). Be sure to consider the recomposition that occurs in the recapitulation.

b. In what bar does the primary tone of the *Urlinie* occur? What technique is used to achieve this tone and how is that technique foreshadowed at the surface level in bar 1?

c. What structural tone of the *Urlinie* is active in bar 9? (Where is that tone first stated?)

d. How does g^2 in bar 20 relate to d^3 in bar 9? In other words, what is the structural relationship between the two tones? Show this explicitly in your graph.

e. What harmonic transformation underlies the development section (bars 21–34)?

f. In the recapitulation, where does the *Urlinie* reach $\hat{1}$? To what tone does this correspond in the exposition? (What is the structural status of that tone?)

2. Clementi, Sonatina, Op. 36, No. 2, I

Follow procedures similar to those above.

3. Haydn, Piano Sonata, Hob. XVI/35, II
(Adagio—F major)

a. Sonata principle appears in many eighteenth-century works, such as this brief slow movement. The first theme is not restated in the recapitulation: how does Haydn compensate for this omission earlier in the movement?

b. Is the I^6 in bar 3 a real or "apparent" tonic? (Two interpretations are plausible here.) If you hear the latter, how does the I^6 function?

c. Consider the "delaying tactic" that Haydn composes in bars 15–16 to avoid premature closure of the secondary fifth-progression. How would you explain the two approaches to the cadence in bar 17? In other words, should bar 16 be considered parenthetically, or can it be understood as part of the essential voice leading of the prolongation of structural $\hat{2}$? (Think about the possibility of proceeding directly from bar 15 to bar 17.)

4. Mozart, Piano Sonata, K. 331, II (Menuetto), bars 1–48

a. This minuet employs sonata principle in condensed form. First map out the principal key areas and associated themes. Locate the transitional passages, and determine how the modulations occur.

b. Analyze each section of the form. Determine: (1) the principal goals, motions, and prolongations; (2) the bass-line and harmonic structure; (3) the nature of the top and inner voices in relation to the bass line and harmony.

c. Prepare foreground and middleground graphs, considering the relationships of the various compositional elements (as analyzed in b, above) with one another.

d. Considering the work as a whole, prepare a background graph.

5. Scarlatti, Sonata in C major, K. 159, L. 104

Though they predate the works of Haydn, Mozart and Beethoven, Domenico Scarlatti's keyboard sonatas exemplify the principles of sonata in beautiful and inventive ways. Like many of Haydn's sonatas, this work does not employ contrasting themes.

a. Determine the large-scale harmonic prolongations and motions in relation to the form. Then analyze each section in detail.

b. Particular attention should be paid to two aspects of the piece: (1) Phrases are often elided, so that the beginnings and endings of sections must be determined with care. (2) Because of the thin texture and frequent high register of the left-hand part (which is often linked with the top voice), interpretation of the bass line may be somewhat difficult. You may wish to review Example 8.8, Schumann's song "Lieb' Liebchen," which is comparable in this respect.

   c. Prepare foreground, middleground, and background graphs. Evaluate the harmonic structure and voice leading carefully, and consider the possibility of implied tones or registers.

6. Mozart, Piano Sonata, K. 330, I

   a. Once again, obtain first an overview of the movement. Map out the areas of the exposition (first theme, second theme, closing section, etc.) and the corresponding parts of the recapitulation.

   b. Play through or listen to the development section and concentrate on the bass movement. What is the structural tone in the bass in bars 59–66? Compare to bars 79ff. Consider any brief tonicizations that occur between bars 68–79.

   c. What structural upper-voice tone is prominent in the first tonal area of the exposition? That tone appears sporadically throughout the second tonal area, but is it necessarily of the same structural status as in the first large section of the piece?

   d. Where is closure of the secondary linear progression attained in the second tonal area? Because of the numerous perfect authentic cadences in bars 34–58, there are several possibilities. Be able to justify your answer (verbally and graphically).

7. Mozart, Piano Sonata, K. 310, I

   a. Obtain a broad overview of the exposition. Identify the first tonal area (first theme and transition) and second tonal area (second theme and closing material). Bear in mind that a I^6 initiates the second tonal area, a not uncommon technique in Classical compositions.

   b. Make sure you can identify the *middleground* voice leading that leads (modulates) from I in A minor to V of C major (bars 11–16).

   c. In the second theme, make sure you can identify all deeper upper-voice motions, as well as any sequential or linear-intervallic patterns. Be aware also that stepwise lines unfold in contrasting registers.

   d. A secondary fifth-progression underlies the second theme. Remember, however, that the second theme is in the major mediant. Where does this line end? For what reasons? (There are four perfect authentic cadences in bars 34–49.)

   e. In bars 53–55 of the development section, Mozart notates both D♭ and C♯ as upper neighbors to C in the left hand. After you finish analyzing the development, see if you can think of a reason why C♯ makes its brief appearance.

f. The sequential passage in the development section helps to highlight an important "waypoint" in the structural harmonic progression of the development section.

g. Evaluate carefully the corresponding transition section in the recapitulation. Remember that composers often compose this section to appear as if it may modulate, even though it ultimately "returns" to the home tonic of the recapitulated second tonal area.

For Further Study

Most of the pieces in the following list are more difficult to analyze than the compositions included above. We believe, however, that studying them will provide a transition to more advanced analysis.

Mozart, Symphony No. 41 ("Jupiter"), K. 551, II (exposition only)
Mozart, Piano Sonata, K. 333, I (exposition only)
Beethoven, Piano Sonata, Op. 53 ("Waldstein"), I (exposition only)
Beethoven, Piano Sonata, Op. 10, No. 1, I (complete movement)
Beethoven, Piano Sonata, Op. 31, No. 2, I (complete movement)
Beethoven, Piano Sonata, Op. 81a ("Les Adieux"), I (complete movement)

12

A Theoretical View of Tonal Structure

INTRODUCTION

In this book we have focused both on the principles of structural analysis and on the analytical process itself, allowing Schenker's ideas about tonal structure to emerge through the study of selected compositions. Not only is this the most practical and musical way to learn Schenkerian analysis, but it also parallels the way in which Schenker's own ideas and insights developed. In this final chapter we shall concentrate more specifically on the theoretical aspects of Schenker's work—though the chapter, like the book itself, can be only an introduction.

Two questions may have occurred to you, which we will explore briefly before proceeding:

1. What is the distinction between *theory* and *analysis?*
2. How does an understanding (an awareness) of theoretical matters aid musicians in analysis?

In considering the first question, bear in mind that theory and analysis are closely interrelated facets of musical understanding. For purposes of discussion, however, it is useful to describe each separately. Analysis is the process by which musicians seek to understand the structure and characteristics of *specific* compositions. The focus on explaining the individual attributes of a particular piece (such as motivic interrelationships) is perhaps the most distinguishing aspect of analysis. Theory, on the other hand, seeks to identify what is *general* about musical structures. As such, it involves the explanation of general principles shared by many pieces throughout a repertory (in this case, of course, the tonal repertory). The technique of interruption, for example, can be described through a few *middleground patterns* that appear with great frequency. (We might think of such patterns as "common denominators" shared by many tonal compositions.)[1]

As far as the second question is concerned, consider that as analysts we are continually making decisions. In a given passage, for instance, we often consider which tones or harmonies in the musical fabric are higher ranking, and consequently primary in the structure. Or, given two interpretations, we might need to decide whether one is clearly better, or whether both are feasible (but one may be preferred). Theory can help us here because it provides criteria and guidelines for evaluating a particular context.[2] Our decisions about the specific characteristics of individual pieces can be more informed and focused when we understand the underlying principles of musical structure.

It would not be feasible in this chapter to address every theoretical issue associated with Schenker's work. Our purpose is to summarize certain general aspects of theory encountered in the analyses of previous chapters, but not fully considered there. Most of the examples will be general figures, broad representations of general tonal patterns, some of which are drawn from *Free Composition*. Schematic diagrams represent clearly the structural principles that can shape both small and large spans of music. One final point cannot be emphasized enough: although theory involves generalizations, such generalizations (and their representations) are not models to be discovered in a piece of music, but representative possibilities that musicians may draw upon in the process of analysis to interpret individual works of art.

MORE ON THE *URSATZ*

In Chapter 5 we introduced one of Schenker's central concepts: the *Ursatz* (fundamental structure), which comprises the *Urlinie* (fundamental line), and the *Bassbrechung* (bass arpeggiation). We can now investigate more thoroughly the meaning of these interrelated formations. Example 12.1 shows some of the basic ways in which the bass arpeggiation of the *Ursatz* can be elaborated.[3]

The patterns in *a* and *b* show perhaps the most common intermediate harmonies: II, IV, and II⁶. Notice both the melodic and harmonic relationships embodied in both of these diagrams. In the case of *a*, the supertonic is melodically related to the tonic (the bass moves by step). It is also harmonically related to the forthcoming dominant: the bass moves up a fourth (or down a fifth) to V, simulating the harmonic leap from V to I. In *b* the situation is reversed, with IV or II⁶ related to V melodically as well as harmonically. All of these harmonies, of course, intensify the motion from I to V.

EXAMPLE 12.1:

Elaborations of the bass appeggiation

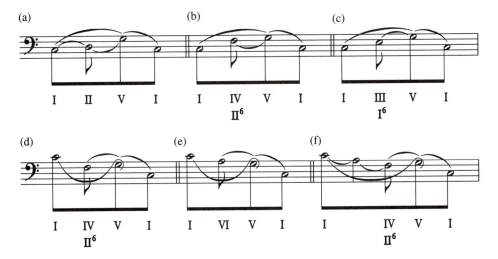

The pattern in *c* is a bit more neutral in character because of the common tones shared by I–III–V. Notice also that the bass on its way to V *completely arpeggiates* the tonic triad: Î–3̂–5̂. This progression becomes more goal-oriented if it is elaborated by one or two additional tones and chords (see Figures 14/2a, 14/3a and 14/4a in *Free Composition*), a procedure that we will discuss later in this chapter. It is more characteristic of minor than of the major mode because the major mediant chord (relative major) offers an effective contrast to the minor tonic.

The patterns we have discussed thus far all involve ascending motion from I to V. A very important point to stress is that, for Schenker, the basic position of the V is *above* the I, as it occurs in the overtone series, and that the most important elaborations of I–V–I result from partially filling in the space between I and the upper V. Motions from the tonic *down* to the dominant, illustrated in the final three diagrams in Example 12.1, are a common variant form of this pattern; conceptually, however, Schenker saw the position of V above I (progressions 12.1a–c) as more fundamental.[4]

Now that we have examined these essential bass patterns, we turn our attention to the structural upper voice. Schenker saw the *Urlinie* as a linear expression of tonic harmony (Example 12.2). It originates in the *vertical* major triad of the overtone series, which is arpeggiated (and consequently horizontalized) and then filled in with one or more passing tones to become the descending stepwise component of the *Ursatz*.

Notice that Example 12.2 shows an *Urlinie* from 3̂, the third of tonic harmony. Relative to the root of tonic harmony (that is, the fundamental of the overtone series of a key), 2̂ is a dissonant passing tone. The bass also expresses tonic harmony through arpeggiation, but it does so through a motion that remains *disjunct*. The resulting bass arpeggiation provides consonant support for the passing 2̂.

EXAMPLE 12.2:

Conceptual origin of the *Urlinie*

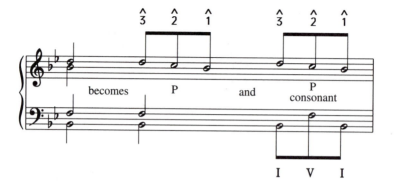

That a dissonant passing tone can be given consonant support is one of the key tenets of Schenker's theory. From strict counterpoint we learn that a dissonant passing tone connects two consonances and is therefore dependent upon them for its meaning; the dissonant passing tone by itself cannot lead to further musical development (that is, diminution or elaboration). In free composition, however, which integrates counterpoint and harmony over various structural levels, the passing tone can be given consonant support and become the point of departure for linear progressions and even subordinate key areas. In Example 12.2, for instance, the $\hat{2}$ over V can develop into a subordinate area (an *Ursatz* parallelism) in the dominant, which ultimately serves to expand the main tonic of a composition. We have seen that second tonal areas in the expositions of major-mode sonata movements are very often associated with this particular expansion of the dominant. The prolongation of $\hat{2}$, made consonant by the dominant tone in the bass, holds far-reaching ramifications for the elaboration of musical structure.

Example 12.3 illustrates the *Ursatz* formation with $\hat{5}$ as the primary tone.[5] This pattern is more problematic than an *Ursatz* beginning on $\hat{3}$, at least from a theoretical perspective, because of scale degree $\hat{4}$, which is dissonant against the fundamental of the tonic.[6] Schenker states that "in this context the first part of the fundamental line $\hat{5}$–$\hat{4}$–$\hat{3}$ has more the effect of a transiently filled space of a third . . . [which] creates a certain void, or unsupported stretch, at the very outset of the fundamental line of a fifth."[7] Even with the support of the dominant, scale degree $\hat{4}$ remains dissonant (a seventh above the bass). As Carl Schachter has explained, however, "The consonant support of each note of the fundamental line is not an overriding issue for Schenker, though it is one that he takes into account in his interpretations of the middleground."[8]

Example 12.4 illustrates in schematic fashion some of the ways in which the segment $\hat{5}$–$\hat{4}$–$\hat{3}$ can be worked out. A very common possibility, shown in *a*, occurs when scale degree $\hat{4}$ is provided the consonant support of the octave, a contrapuntally stable interval (compare to V^7) that yields the intermediate IV

EXAMPLE 12.3:

Ursatz formation from $\hat{5}$

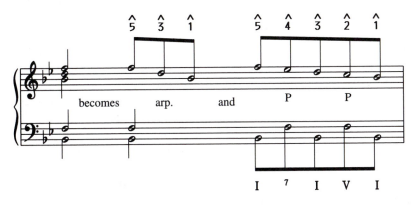

harmony of the bass arpeggiation (a II^6 is also possible here). You will notice in our first scenario that when $\hat{4}$ is given consonant support, another unsupported stretch emerges: $\hat{4}$–$\hat{3}$–$\hat{2}$. The interesting aspect of this situation is that $\hat{3}$, normally the consonant third of tonic harmony, becomes a dissonant passing tone against the fundamental of the IV chord. In composition, it is quite possible to find such fleeting (and even dissonant) support for $\hat{3}$; as Carl Schachter has also stated, at lower levels "the notes of the fundamental line will possibly evolve in different ways. Some may be richly elaborated, others less richly, still others not at all. Yet each is an essential element in the structure."[9] More typically found, however, is the tonal pattern shown in Example 12.4b. Scale degree $\hat{3}$ remains a passing tone, but in this case it enters as a *consonant* sixth above the root of dominant harmony. As you can see from the figured-bass symbols, this coincidence of the structural upper and lower voices

EXAMPLE 12.4:

Ursatz formations from $\hat{5}$

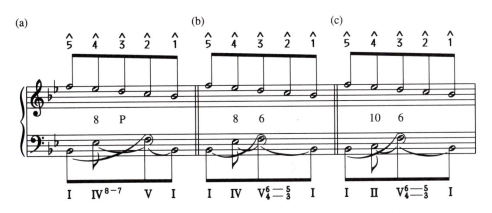

yields the familiar cadential $^6_4$, which very often supports structural $\hat{3}$ in a $\hat{5}$-line. Example 12.4c shows another possibility for the support of $\hat{4}$. In this case, the outer voices form a consonant tenth, which results in an intermediate II harmony; again, $\hat{3}$ is supported by the cadential $^6_4$ that signals the beginning of dominant harmony.

In this brief discussion we have not attempted to list every conceivable possibility. You can see, however, that the "void" of the unsupported stretch can be reduced through various types of consonant support for $\hat{4}$. Bear in mind, however, that *either* $\hat{4}$ or $\hat{3}$ will almost always be accompanied by a dissonant chord, or by no chord at all (that is, it will remain a passing tone in the foreground).[10]

Schenker's theory suggests one more possible *Ursatz* formation, one that begins from $\hat{8}$ (remember that the tonic triad from which the *Urlinie* arises can be expressed with the top note in the position of the third, fifth, or octave). Example 12.5, which presents two diagrams from *Free Composition*, shows this possibility.[11] From the first diagram you can begin to see why an $\hat{8}$-line can be a problematic structure: there are many unsupported tones, even more than in a $\hat{5}$-line. Although consonant support for all *Urlinie* tones is not an overriding issue in the analysis of structure, the situation is different in this more extensive line. The issue is more pressing given the number of unsupported tones, especially *consecutive* unsupported tones. And notice that the second tone of the line is the leading tone, which in the major mode has a marked tendency to move in an ascending, rather than a descending, direction.

EXAMPLE 12.5:

Ursatz formations from $\hat{8}$

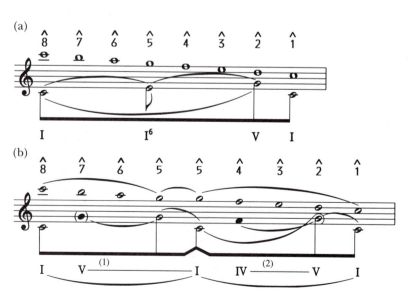

The second part of the example shows that two bass arpeggiations may be necessary to support this structural line. Because of the considerable practical considerations involved, 8̂-lines are very rare in composition, although they do appear to occur more frequently at structural levels below the background. This aspect of Schenker's theory, while theoretically consistent with its basic principles, is still being considered by those involved with his work.

TONAL EXPANSION AND MUSICAL FORM

In Chapters 7–11 we have seen that compositional procedures that expand and elaborate the fundamental structure are often associated with recurring formal patterns. In this section we examine some of the general tonal patterns—characteristic possibilities of the middleground—and briefly discuss their roles in the expansion of structure and the evolution of musical form.

As a point of departure consider Example 12.6, another of the diagrams in *Free Composition* (Figure 34,c). This general pattern illustrates an essential characteristic of tonal expansion: linear progressions give "life" (content) to the *Ursatz* by expanding its tones and harmonies.[12] In this case we find two linear progressions: the first expands 3̂ and the initial tonic, while the second expands 2̂ and the dominant of the *Ursatz*. Schenker refers to these lines as *linear progressions of the first order*, because they represent the first elaborations of the *Ursatz* (they might be considered the initial "offshoots" of the fundamental line, residing at the first level of the middleground).[13] Although patterns such as this appear at all structural levels (including the musical surface), we will concern ourselves in this section with how they shape the structure at levels just below the background. In this way we can gain profound insights into the ways in which form and structure develop over the spans of entire compositions.

Example 12.7 shows a common elaboration of the first branch of an inter-

EXAMPLE 12.6:

First elaborations of the *Ursatz*

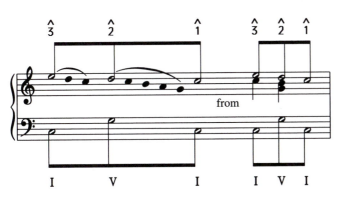

EXAMPLE 12.7:

Middleground elaboration of first branch (major mode)

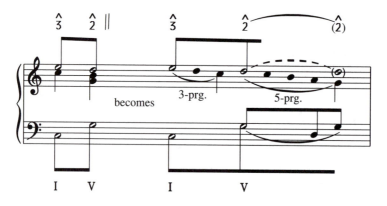

rupted fundamental structure: a third-progression followed by a fifth-progression. This pattern often underlies the initial sections of ternary and rounded binary forms, and the first and second themes of sonata movements in the major mode (review the analysis of Beethoven's G-major Piano Sonata in Chapter 11). The fifth-progression from $\hat{2}$, in particular, is an aspect not only of sonata movements, but of various other forms in which an expansion of the dominant shapes the initial section of the piece. Schenker explicitly states that such linear progressions "lead the way to two- or three-part forms."[14]

Example 12.8 illustrates the corresponding situation in the recapitulation of a Classical sonata movement. The linear progression that delineates the tonic area and first theme remains the same, but the function of the secondary fifth-progression is different. The line is transposed, leading toward structural $\hat{1}$ (instead of prolonging and leading away from $\hat{2}$). Considered together, Examples 12.7 and 12.8 depict one of the essential characteristics of the sonata principle: a contrasting tonal region in the first part of a movement is balanced, in the final section, by a recapitulated version of that region in the

EXAMPLE 12.8:

Middleground elaborations of second branch (major mode)

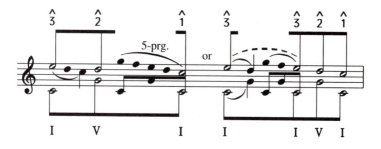

tonic (compare the fifth-progressions in the examples). The second part of Example 12.8 shows another possibility for the interpretation of the secondary fifth-progression in the second branch of an interrupted structure.

The patterns in Example 12.9 illustrate characteristic possibilities for $\hat{5}$-lines in the major mode (most typically found in sonata movements). The first is similar to Example 12.7 in that structural $\hat{2}$ and the supporting dominant are composed out in the same manner. Notice in the $\hat{5}$–line shown in Example 12.9, however, that the initial tonic region must support a larger segment of the *Urlinie* ($\hat{5}$–$\hat{3}$). This is the unsupported stretch discussed previously: the analyst must sometimes determine whether a structural $\hat{4}$–$\hat{3}$ motion represents an *Urlinie* descent from $\hat{5}$. Particularly in pieces in which the first theme involves a prominent $\hat{5}$, appearances of $\hat{4}$ may be fleeting and function only at more local levels, meaning that a *structural* descent to $\hat{3}$ does not actually occur. In such cases the structure may follow the pattern shown in the second part of Example 12.9. Here the elaboration of scale degree $\hat{2}$ (the subordinate fifth-progression) still expands the dominant area of the form; scale degree $\hat{2}$, however, is understood as emerging from $\hat{3}$ in an inner voice. In other words, the motion $\hat{3}$–$\hat{2}$ takes place beneath the higher-ranking $\hat{5}$, which is prolonged into subsequent sections. This means that the piece is not based on an interruption in the usual sense. The primary tone $\hat{5}$ is prolonged from the beginning until the final section (recapitulation), where it descends to $\hat{1}$ in the transposed fifth-progression that now represents the descent of the *Urlinie*.[15]

Example 12.10 is similar to Example 12.7, with one significant difference. This pattern illustrates in concise form how the structural $\hat{2}$ and the dominant may be further expanded and elaborated *after* the secondary fifth-progression initially defines the dominant region of the form. This helps us

EXAMPLE 12.9:

Elaborations of an *Ursatz* from $\hat{5}$ in major

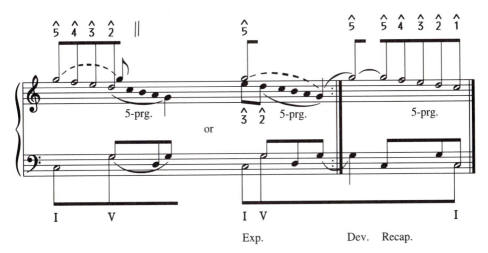

EXAMPLE 12.10:

Further expansion of the first branch

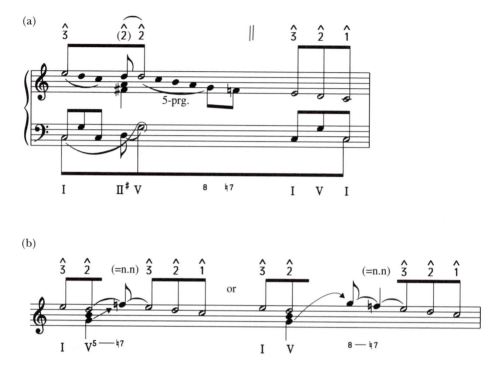

to understand in broad terms how middle sections in rounded binary forms and development sections in sonata movements arise in the major mode. Note the II♯ (V of V) and the associated chromatic element (the new leading tone) that prepares the dominant area. After establishing the dominant as a key area, the composer must subsequently prepare for the return of the tonic (in the second branch of the structure), returning the dominant to its original function as V.

The most direct way to do so is to replace sharp $\hat{4}$ (the temporary leading tone of the tonicized dominant) by natural $\hat{4}$ as the seventh of V^7 in the home key (V^{8-7}). With the chromatic element sharp $\hat{4}$ no longer a part of the musical fabric, the aural impression of the dominant as a secondary key area is very much weakened. You have no doubt encountered development sections that lead to a prominent and elaborated V^7, marking the beginning of a retransition and leading you to anticipate the return of the tonic.

Although the V^7 now functions as a chord in preparation of the forthcoming tonic, it is nonetheless an outgrowth of the dominant tonicized at the end of the first section. Play the direct chord succession V^8–V^7 at the piano: your ear will perceive the transformation of a *single* harmony. It is a remarkable feature of the tonal system that such a simple contrapuntal procedure, V^{8-7}, can shape extensive passages of music and lead to a separate section in the form of a composition. In these situations the V^7 serves as the boundary of the prolongational span of the dominant.[16]

Example 12.10b indicates that the transformation of V^8 into V^7 does not necessarily occur in the same register, as a continuous motion over the dominant tone in the bass. Through register transfer the seventh may be transferred up an octave, where it will appear as an upper neighbor to the primary tone $\hat{3}$ of the second branch; this technique allows the second branch to begin in the original register.[17] Note also that in relation to structural $\hat{2}$ in the soprano, the seventh appears as a 5–7 motion above the dominant (V^{5-7} is a common variant of V^{8-7}).

One final possibility is also shown in the last part of Example 12.10b. Here the complete 8–7 motion is transferred up an octave, preserving its stepwise continuity. Schenker indicates that the seventh remains the primary element in the transferred line; at the surface, however, the seventh is decorated from above by the root of dominant harmony.[18]

In cases where the V^{8-7} motion shapes large spans of a composition (such as a development section), dominant harmony may not always be literally present at the surface and foreground levels. In simple rounded binary forms and brief development sections, however, it may be present throughout. Example 12.11 illustrates some specific ways in which musical content may develop from within the prolongational span of a dominant. For ease of discussion we will focus primarily on the bass structure; the indicated upper voices are elaborations of those discussed in Example 12.10.

Examples 12.11a and b show common situations in which the underlying dominant scale step is expanded by upper and lower neighbor notes. Such prolonging neighbors can support triads, which, in turn, can be expanded into local "key areas" at surface and foreground levels. Temporary key areas of this kind are often best understood in terms of contrapuntal elements that expand a more fundamental harmonic region.

Our next few examples show possibilities for the minor mode (Example 12.12). (While especially characteristic of sonata procedures, they may occur in various other formal types as well.) Because of the position of the tritone in the natural minor scale (between $\hat{2}$ and $\hat{6}$), and the traditional desire of composers to balance the minor key with a section in major, the first sections of pieces in the minor mode frequently employ III as the second key area ($\hat{2}$ and $\hat{6}$ resolve to $\hat{3}$ and $\hat{5}$, as the root and third of III). Notice in Example 12.12a the lower-level *Ursatz* parallelism (= III: $\hat{3}$–$\hat{2}$–$\hat{1}$ over I–V–I) that contributes to the development of musical content in the mediant region (another example of Schenker's principle of the "transference of the forms of the fundamental structure to lower levels").

Example 12.12b shows a situation often encountered in minor-mode compositions with $\hat{5}$-lines (up to the double bar). Two points are of particular interest here: the first involves the issue of the unsupported stretch $\hat{5}$–$\hat{4}$–$\hat{3}$. We have already discussed the nature of scale degree $\hat{4}$ in the *Urlinie*, and noted that it may be integrated into a musical fabric in various ways. In this case, the V–I cadential motion used to establish the mediant area (which often

EXAMPLE 12.11:

Middleground elaborations of a prolonged dominant

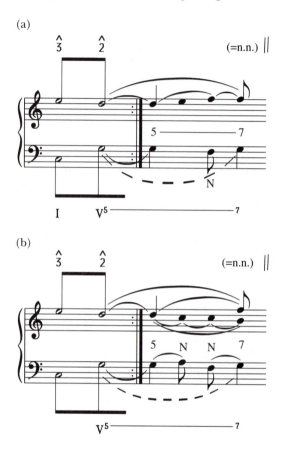

occurs in a transition) may support the descent $\hat{4}$–$\hat{3}$ ($\hat{2}$–$\hat{1}$ in the mediant). Note that parallel fifths arise between I and the beginning of the cadential pattern in III. In compositions the motion from I to V of III would be elaborated, and the fifths would not appear in direct succession at the surface of the music.

Notice also the secondary fifth-progression that begins on natural $\hat{7}$. This is the minor-mode equivalent of the fifth-progression that expands the dominant in the major mode, but note that the final tone of this line is the principal structural tone $\hat{3}$. The reason for this elaborating line can be explained in practical terms. If scale degree $\hat{3}$ is reached at the beginning of the mediant region, and does not receive further elaboration, the structural upper voice could become static (see the second part of Example 12.12b). Example 12.12d shows a possibility from $\hat{3}$.

Thus a lower-level replica of a fundamental line often occurs within the mediant region, providing the foundation for thematic and motivic develop-

EXAMPLE 12.12:

Middleground elaborations of first branch (minor mode)

(a)

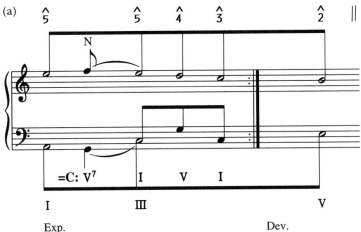

Exp.   Dev.

(b)

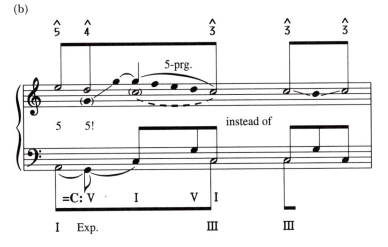

(c)

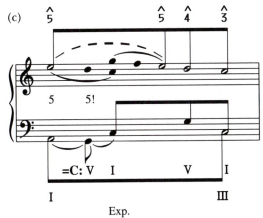

Exp.

EXAMPLE 12.12 (*continued*)

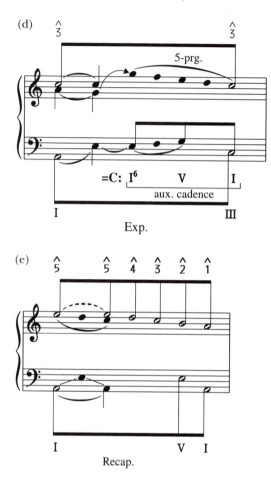

ment in the upper voice (typically before the double bar).[19] When this line returns transposed in the recapitulation, it represents the descent of the *Urlinie* (compare Examples 12.12b and e).

Example 12.12c shows one additional possibility; the voice leading is similar to the pattern shown in Example 12.12b. The main difference involves the interpretation of scale degree $\hat{4}$, which, as we have seen, is often the most difficult tone to evaluate in $\hat{5}$–lines. In cases where an initial motion $\hat{5}$–$\hat{3}$ appears to be composed-out in an inconclusive manner (some analysts refer to $\hat{4}$ being "weakly" supported), it is possible to regard the final three notes of the secondary fifth-progression as the structural descent $\hat{5}$–$\hat{4}$–$\hat{3}$. (As a result the fifth is articulated into two overlapping thirds.) Because $\hat{5}$–$\hat{4}$–$\hat{3}$ appears locally as $\hat{3}$–$\hat{2}$–$\hat{1}$ in the mediant (over I–V–I), $\hat{4}$ receives locally consonant support in the cadence that is more defined than some other patterns involving $\hat{4}$.[20]

Example 12.13a illustrates one way in which the process of tonal expansion may continue in the minor mode. We noted that, in major-mode compositions, sections after the double bar (in binary, rounded binary, and sonata forms) usually develop through the prolongation of the structural dominant, the goal of the first branch of an interrupted fundamental structure. In the minor mode, these middle sections often arise through the continuation of the structural harmonic motion toward the dominant: III–V♯. The tonal space between III and V is frequently filled in with a passing tone (not shown in the figure) that may be expanded into a subdominant region. For example, in the first movement of Beethoven's Piano Sonata in C minor, Op. 10, No. 1, an expansive F-minor area (beginning in bar 118) connects the mediant of the exposition to the dominant that serves as the harmonic goal of the devel-

EXAMPLE 12.13:

Tonal expansion and form in the minor mode

opment section (bars 158–167). The large-scale plan of the exposition and development, therefore, is I–III–IV–V. As Example 12.13a indicates, the upper voice may lead to a recurrence of scale degree $\hat{5}$ at lower levels (covering structural $\hat{2}$). This procedure allows $\hat{5}$ to be prepared before its return as the primary tone of the second branch.[21]

Although the pattern I–III–IV–V is common in Classical minor-mode movements (to the point of the recapitulation), composers in the early nineteenth century also used this progression in the major mode. The first movement of Beethoven's "Waldstein" sonata is a particularly good example. In the exposition, III♯ (E major) emerges through secondary mixture as the second tonal area (instead of V). Perhaps the emergence of harmonic plans involving third-relationships in the early nineteenth century can be explained in part as the incorporation (and alteration) of diatonic minor-mode procedures developed by seventeenth- and eighteenth-century composers.

It is very often the case that movements in minor keys tend to modulate first to the mediant, but this is not the only possibility. Example 11.13b shows that the dominant may appear before the double bar, the same place in the form as in the major mode. In this situation, however, the key area employed is the minor dominant (compare fugal expositions in minor). The middle section of the form (such as a development section) can therefore be explained in terms of the expansion of the dominant and its transformation from minor to major (the leading tone must be added in preparation for the tonic of the second branch). The first part (a rounded binary) of Mozart's Alla Turca movement from the Piano Sonata, K. 331, illustrates this harmonic procedure.

AUXILIARY CADENCES

In the preceding sections of this chapter we have explored the fundamental structure in greater detail and have discussed some common middleground formal patterns. It is an appropriate next step to return to Schenker's notion of the *auxiliary cadence* (introduced in Chapter 8), because auxiliary cadences can be understood in terms of the fundamental structure.

Not all of Schenker's mature ideas are explained as fully in *Free Composition* as one might like. His discussion of auxiliary cadences is brief and, consequently, can be somewhat puzzling. This section is not intended to be an exhaustive treatment of this subject, but a general explanation that sheds additional light on examples that we have analyzed in this book.

You will frequently encounter harmonic progressions in the midst of compositions that do not begin with a root-position tonic chord. The simplest pattern is V–I, though an intermediate chord will often precede the V; we can represent this possibility generally as X–V–I, with "X" representing II, III, IV, VI or I^6 (I^6 is often similar in function to III). A very clear instance of an

EXAMPLE 12.14:

Brahms, Intermezzo, Op. 118, No. 1: basic pattern and auxiliary cadence as fundamental structure

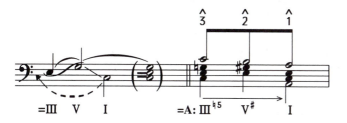

auxiliary cadence occurs in Schubert's "Wandrers Nachtlied": VI–V–I (review Examples 8.6 and 8.7).

If you take a moment to examine Figure 110, a–e in *Free Composition,* you will see the basic patterns for auxiliary cadences and discover that they are essentially incomplete bass arpeggiations.[22] Example 12.14 reproduces Figures 110,d and 110,d3. The first shows how III–V–I arpeggiates and hence defines the "tonal space" represented by the concluding triad in root position. The second shows a piece in which an auxiliary cadence serves as the underlying structure for an entire composition, Brahms's Intermezzo in A minor, Op. 118, No. 1.[23]

Auxiliary cadences more typically occur at lower structural levels and are related to Schenker's discovery that forms or replicas of the fundamental structure are often transferred to levels below the background. This is reflected in the heading of the section in *Free Composition* in which auxiliary cadences are discussed: "Incomplete Transference of the Forms of the Fundamental Structure; Auxiliary Cadences."[24] And because transferred forms of the *Ursatz* are often applied to scale steps other than the tonic, auxiliary cadences may be considered *agents of modulation.*

As we mentioned, the harmonic progression of the transferred form may begin with an intermediate chord or with an inversion (I^6) of the "new" tonic. According to Schenker, "The transition from harmony to harmony is made smoother by the omission of the I, the first tone of the bass arpeggiation [of the transferred form]."[25] Refer now to Example 12.15, which is a structural analysis of Haydn's A♭-major Minuet, analyzed in Example 9.1.

In level *a* we see the essence of the progression that leads from A♭ to E♭. The initial I of the fundamental structure is related to V_2^4 of the dominant (the C in the upper voice is a suspension of the primary tone $\hat{3}$). In other words, the A♭ in the bass continues, at a higher structural level, the influence of the tonic as the tones above the bass begin to express, at a lower level, the scale system of the emerging dominant (D♮, altered $\hat{4}$, signals the destabilization of A♭). The subsequent harmonic progression and the fifth-progression, an offshoot of structural $\hat{2}$, establish the emerging key area of E♭ major. The auxiliary cadence concludes with a V–I motion in the bass.[26]

In Example 12.15 we use special details of graphing to convey precisely the relationships and subtle meaning in Schenker's description of auxiliary cadences. Schenker would say that the voice leading that defines E♭ is "closed off" from what precedes; the chords of the auxiliary cadence "point ahead" to the forthcoming root-position I. Schenker makes the comment that "the space up to its actual entrance [of the new root-position tonic] belongs conceptually to the preceding harmony [in this case, to the initial tonic]. In a sense, the territory of the previous harmony provides a base for the preparation of the following one."[27] Bear in mind that the "closing off" of the voice leading pertains to the middleground and does not preclude a link at a lower structural level, such as the V_2^4 shown in Example 12.15.

In Example 12.15b, we use upward beamed stems in the bass to show that the chords of the auxiliary cadence relate to the forthcoming I in E♭; notice

EXAMPLE 12.15:

Haydn, Piano Sonata, Hob. XVI/43, Minuet 2: structural analyses

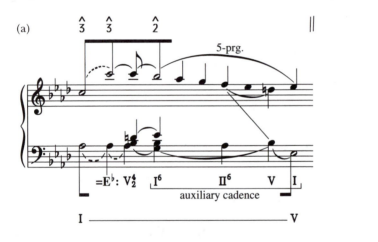

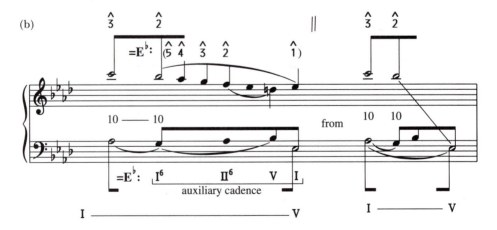

the incomplete bass arpeggiation of the dominant triad, G–B♭–E♭, revealed by this notation. To indicate the harmonic progression of the middleground, we use downward beamed stems connecting half notes (I–V) in the bass. This shows that the scale system of E♭ is gradually developing at a lower level. But when viewed from the middleground, the dominant arrives in a structural sense only at the completion of the auxiliary cadence. This is what Schenker means when he says that the "space" of the emerging new key (defined by the auxiliary cadence) belongs conceptually to the preceding harmony. The progression in E♭ develops in the foreground under the influence of the initial structural tonic, because that is the last structural harmony we have heard. The tonic, therefore, remains active at a deeper level until the authentic cadence has established the root of the dominant.

MORE ON THE PRINCIPLE OF INTERRUPTION

We have seen in many examples throughout this book how the technique of interruption elaborates the *Ursatz* and can serve as a source of form (particularly of rounded binary and sonata forms).[28] Schenker's discussion of interruption, like that of the auxiliary cadence, can seem puzzling and perhaps a bit inconsistent at times, particularly when one examines the most abstract examples of interruption in *Free Composition*.

We will now consider several issues associated with this far-reaching compositional technique. (This discussion is based on Figures 21–26 in *Free Composition*.) Though it is assumed here that the *Urlinie* begins on $\hat{3}$, these observations will not change when $\hat{5}$ is the primary tone. Consider now the two branches of the interrupted *Ursatz* as shown in Figure 21, a of *Free Composition*.

First, bear in mind what is being interrupted: the descent (or "journey") of the *Urlinie* on its way to $\hat{1}$. When $\hat{2}$ over V is reached in an interruption, all melodic and harmonic progressions cease—at least on the level at which the interruption occurs. This means that the $\hat{2}$ is not a lower neighbor to the $\hat{3}$ of the second branch, and V does not resolve to the following I.

Consider, for example, a parallel period in which a half cadence is the goal of the antecedent phrase (Chapter 7 has several such examples). The V does not resolve to I at the beginning of the consequent phrase; if it did, there would be no half cadence but an authentic cadence.[29] There is, of course, considerable tension produced by an interruption, for $\hat{2}$ over V carries definite expectations. This tension is resolved only at the conclusion of the second branch, with $\hat{1}$ over I (in a parallel period, at the end of the consequent phrase).

Schenker conveys this meaning in a specific fashion. Notice in Figure 21, b of *Free Composition* that most of the second branch (the retracing of the *Urlinie*) is placed in parentheses, and the final $\hat{1}$ over I is beamed to the first branch. Even in Figures 24–26, where Schenker does not use parentheses, this interpretation of the relationship between the two branches is retained, for the I–V–I of the second branch is connected with a beamed upward stem; only the final $\hat{1}$ over I is connected to the first branch. Perhaps Schenker subordinates most of the elements of the second branch to the first because he ultimately feels compelled to relate the two-part interrupted structure to the unitary *Ursatz*.[30]

METRICAL EXPANSION

Schenker has sometimes been criticized for not addressing rhythm and meter, perhaps because he appears to concentrate on harmony and counterpoint and their roles in shaping tonal structure. This view, however, is unfortunate and misleading. Chapter 4 in *Free Composition* is devoted exclusively to issues of meter and rhythm, and many of his graphic analyses highlight rhythmic features of a composition. Furthermore, in many of his earlier published writings (which are not as well known as *Free Composition*), one can find many revealing discussions of rhythm and meter.[31]

During the past three decades, scholars have been exploring rhythm from a Schenkerian perspective and have, in a sense, created a new field of musical inquiry.[32] Our discussion here, consequently, can provide only a brief glimpse into a vast and complex topic. We will focus on one specific technique discussed by Schenker, what he calls an *expansion* (*Dehnung*).[33] In Chapter 9, we analyzed the Trio from Mozart's Symphony No. 35 ("Haffner") and discussed some aspects of rhythm in the B section. We will now return to this piece and examine the first branch of the interrupted structure somewhat differently, in terms of *metrical* expansion (refer back to the voice-leading graph presented in Example 9.4).

In the A section (bars 1–8), we pointed out the two prominent four-bar units (an eight-bar unit is also evident). If you think in terms of weak and strong (of an "accent" pattern), you will find that each four-bar unit comprises individual measures in a strong-weak-strong-weak organization. In other words, the accent pattern of the entire unit resembles the internal metrical organization of a single 4/4 bar. A group of measures whose accent pattern resembles that of a single bar is termed a *hypermeasure*.[34]

The B section (bars 9–20) commences with another four-bar hypermeasure. By this time, of course, we are accustomed to the regularity of four-bar units. We are soon surprised, however, for the final hypermeasure of the B section is "stretched" to eight bars (bars 13–20). This metrical expansion occurs because the fourth measure of this four-bar hypermeasure (bar 16—a "weak" bar in the hypermeasure) is expanded to five bars (through repetition and the addition of the chromatic passing tone B♯ that forms the link to the second branch). The overall result is that the four-bar unit is expanded to eight bars. Schenker refers to such a pattern as the *metric prototype* and to the varied form as the *expansion*.[35] You will find that metrical expansions result from varying techniques and are common in the consequent phrases of ante-cedent/consequent units.

CHROMATIC ELEMENTS

As represented in the *Ursatz*, the fundamental nature of tonal structure is diatonic. Nevertheless, chromaticism—the use of tones foreign to a composi-tion's tonic scale—offers possibilities that are of the utmost importance for compositional development. Chromatic elements, for instance, can create new sonorous possibilities through mixture or intensify the directed motion of diatonic procedures through applied (secondary) dominant chords. The role of chromaticism in tonal music is an enormous, complex subject that is beyond the scope of this book. We will, however, consider some representative possibilities that pertain to broader spans of tonal structure. As in earlier sections of this chapter, we will begin with levels very close to the back-ground.[36]

Mixture in the Fundamental Line

Example 12.16 shows two situations involving mixture of $\hat{3}$ in the *Urlinie*. The first part of the example is a general diagram showing one way in which mix-ture may develop at the first level of the middleground; the second part is Schenker's middleground representation of Chopin's Mazurka in A♭ major, Op. 17, No. 3. If you consult the score of this piece, you will discover that the B section is written in E major, not F♭ major: Chopin uses notational enhar-monic equivalence, so that the performer does not have to read a passage in eight flats. Nonetheless, Schenker shows the tonality of the passage in relation to the background tonic: the graph in Example 12.16 indicates an extended area in ♭VI, the composing-out of which creates the B section in the ternary

EXAMPLE 12.16:

Mixture in the fundamental line

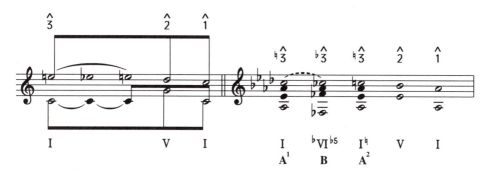

form. Notice that the main upper-voice tone of the section, b^1 ($c\flat^1$), is not a lower neighbor to the primary tone C of the background tonic (because it is the same scale degree, $\hat{3}$): it represents a chromatic inflection of the primary tone from C to C$\flat$. The inflection creates a delay, for the diatonic primary tone $\hat{3}$ will usually be reestablished before the *Urlinie* of the structure descends (this occurs in the A^2 section). Moreover, the composing out of a B section will typically involve a linear progression at a lower level. Progressions such as I–$\flat$VI–I are contrapuntal progressions (note the motion E$\flat$–F$\flat$–E$\flat$ in the inner voice of the example) which often serve to expand the initial tonic of the fundamental structure in ternary forms.

Chromaticism and Prolongational Spans

Chromatic elements frequently mark the boundaries of prolongational spans. In Chapter 4, for instance, we saw sequential patterns and linear intervallic patterns creating unified areas. In Chapter 7, we discovered that bars 1–20 of Bach's C-major Prelude represent a broad expansion of the initial tonic of the structure. Example 12.17a shows one of the simplest representations of such a span. The chord succession I–I^6 may occur as adjacent sonorities at the surface of the music, or may be expanded to unify (as nonadjacent sonorities) much larger areas of music. We have seen many examples of such proce-

EXAMPLE 12.17:

Prolongational spans

(a)

(b)

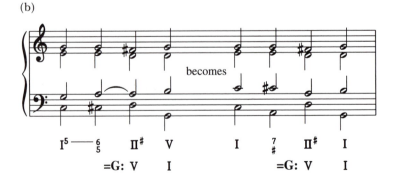

dures. In this case, the I^6 is the conclusion, or boundary, of the span, so that the boundary is harmonically identical to the chord that initiates the span.

Example 12.17b shows a different situation. This voice-leading pattern occurs frequently in movements, such as sonata expositions, in which a modulation to the dominant plays a significant role. The motion II♯–V, which may occur over a considerable number of measures, is also the V–I that establishes the key of the dominant. Were the tonic to progress directly to II♯, parallel fifths would result at a foreground (if not surface) level. The intervening $^6_5$, produced by a 5–6 motion over a chromatic step in the bass, intervenes. The chromatic motion also serves to produce the leading tone of II♯, a procedure that helps to destabilize the home tonic. As shown in the example, the intervening chord can also be expressed in root position. This bass strongly establishes the dominant and often appears, for instance, in the transition sections of sonata expositions.

In terms of prolongational spans, we can consider the scope of the initial tonic to encompass the chromatically altered $^6_5$ (or its root-position variant, shown in the second part of *b*). The boundary of the span in this case is not a literal version of the tonic, but a chromatic transformation of that harmony.[37] Notice the two (or three) common tones with the tonic, one of which is chromatically inflected (C♯). In the example, the A-major-minor seventh chord, an applied dominant, is actually a continuation—an outgrowth—of the diatonic origin of the span, the tonic triad.

Example 12.18, a simplified version of Schenker's graph of Chopin's Etude, Op. 25, No. 1, shows another way in which chromatic elements can affect a prolongational span.[38] The piece begins in A♭ major and modulates, in the B section, to C major (bar 14). Schenker shows that the C-major region represents the expansion of a chord built on the upper third of the A♭-major

EXAMPLE 12.18:

Chopin, Etude, Op. 25, No. 1: prolongational span

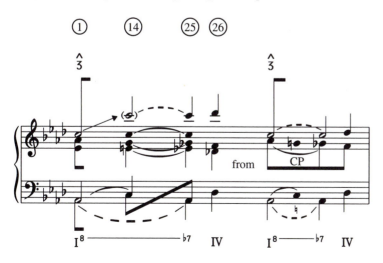

tonic. The bass progression subsequently returns to A♭ (bar 25), which now supports a V^7 of IV. The applied chord, as Schenker indicates, is the boundary of tonic harmony from the beginning of the piece, transformed through the 8–♭7 technique. The C-major harmony, which functions as a subsidiary goal within the overall span, is also derived from the tonic; notice again the three common tones, one of which is inflected (E♭ to E♮). The synoptic graph shows the broader function of C major. In a deeper sense, the transformation of the initial tonic into V^7 of IV has produced the descent of the inner-voice chromatic passing tone G♮ to G♭: this inner-voice tone transforms the initial tonic into V^7 of IV.

Applied dominant chords are by no means the only sonorities that may represent a transformation of a diatonic harmony and serve as the boundary of a prolongational span. Diminished seventh chords and, particularly, augmented sixth chords frequently serve in this capacity. The harmonic function of augmented sixth chords is very often determined by the diatonic harmonies from which they develop. In Example 12.19a, the Italian sixth chord develops from and expands subdominant harmony; note the chromatic voice exchange, a common feature of prolongational spans involving augmented sixths.

Example 12.19b shows the modulatory plan for bars 1–10 of Mendelssohn's G-major *Song Without Words*, which we examined in Chapter 10. The French sixth in bar 8, perhaps the most distinctive sonority of the piece thus far, is a kind of chromatic pivot chord. It functions as a chromatic transformation of the initial tonic (note the common tones), and it resolves as an augmented sixth chord in B minor. In the large-scale harmonic progression from I to III in bars 1–10, the prolongational span of the initial tonic ends with the French sixth.

Example 12.19c shows a prolongational span that governs a much larger passage of music in the first movement of Mozart's Piano Concerto in C, K. 467. After a lengthy orchestral tutti and first theme, Mozart leads to a passage in G minor, which one might initially regard as the beginning of the dominant area of the exposition.[39] This restless and unstable passage in the minor mode, however, quickly leads (through an augmented sixth chord) to D major harmony. After a six-bar flourish, the lyrical and tonally stable second theme begins in G major.

In retrospect, we realize that we have been fooled by the motion to the minor dominant. It does not signal the beginning of the dominant key area, but rather the beginning of a thematic transition to the second theme. In terms of the large-scale voice leading, the G-minor harmony supports a passing tone within an immensely expanded voice exchange that prolongs tonic harmony for 121 bars. The augmented sixth, the boundary of this enormous prolongational span, resolves to II♯, the dominant of the forthcoming dominant region. The large-scale harmonic progression of the first part of the exposition is therefore I–II♯–V, a characteristic modulatory procedure that we have already discussed.[40] There are, of course, many other ways in which augmented sixth chords may function. As you continue to analyze compositions, bear in mind that they often serve as the boundaries of prolongational spans,

EXAMPLE 12.19:

Prolongational spans and augmented sixth chords

(a)

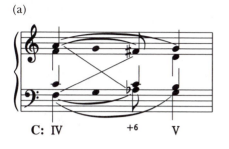

C: IV   +6   V

(b)

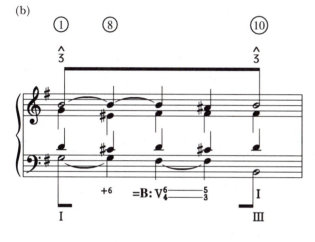

(c)

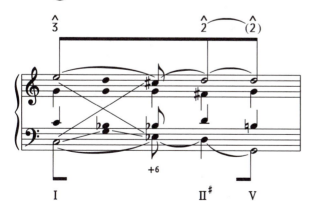

and consequently signal important points of articulation in the form and structure.

The first part of Example 12.20, which is Schenker's sketch of the Scherzo from Beethoven's String Quartet, Op. 135 (bars 1–32), shows a characteristic situation in which the chromatic element serves as the beginning of a prolongational span that is fundamentally diatonic in origin.[41] It is not uncommon for ♭VII—a major triad built on the subtonic—to emerge as a local key area. It is, of course, possible to explain this phenomenon in terms of simple mixture: the subtonic triad is borrowed from the minor mode and expanded through tonicization. But there is more to be said. If you study the second part of the example carefully, you will notice that the tones of the ♭VII triad correspond with the upper three tones of the V^7 chord; the upper third of dominant harmony is chromatically inflected so that a major triad (rather than an unstable diminished triad) results on the seventh scale degree.[42] As this harmonic progression descends from I through ♭VII to V^7, the ♭VII in a sense becomes "absorbed" by the V^7. All the tones of the ♭VII chord are members of the V^7 (with the replacement of E♭ by E♮), and the VII and V chords are closely related in harmonic terms. Consequently the chromaticism is produced by the inflection of the third of dominant seventh harmony. We may describe the bass note of the ♭VII chord as the chromatically transformed "upper third" of the following dominant seventh chord. The ♭VII marks the beginning of a prolongational span that belongs within the realm of the dominant.

Our final example of a prolongational span is taken from the first movement of Beethoven's "Appassionata" Sonata, Op. 57 (Example 12.21). Bars 1–35 of the exposition, the first theme and transition (not shown in the example) comprise a motion from I to III. The second theme begins in A♭ major (bar 35) and the closing theme shifts to A♭ minor (bar 51). From this point a series of brief tonicizations leads back to A♭ major in the midst of the development section (bar 88). As Example 12.21 illustrates, A♭ major is subsequently transformed into the applied dominant of the forthcoming region, D♭ major.

The III of the middleground harmonic progression has been prolonged through motion that divides the octave into a series of major thirds: A♭–E–C–

EXAMPLE 12.20:

Beethoven, String Quartet, Op. 135, II, bars 1–32: chromatic elements in prolongational span

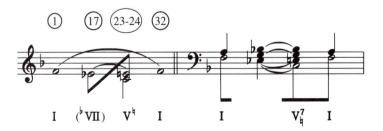

EXAMPLE 12.21:

Beethoven, Piano Sonata, Op. 57, I, bars 35–109: prolongation and transformation of III

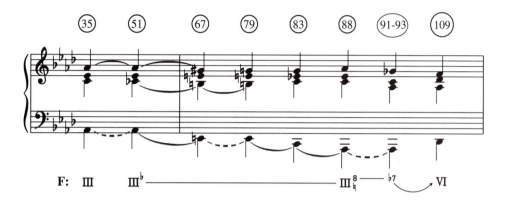

A♭.[43] Of the intervening sonorities, E major is most strongly tonicized: it marks the beginning of the development section and supports a statement of the opening theme. The shift to A♭ minor in the closing section of the exposition helps prepare the arrival of E major (C♭ = B♮); in similar fashion, the transition to C minor is prepared by the shift from E major to E minor (G♯ to G♮, which is the fifth of the forthcoming C-minor harmony).

There are other ways of dividing the octave into equal subdivisions, and such techniques became increasingly important in music of the later nineteenth century.[44] In the repertory addressed by this book, such motions often represent an expansion of a diatonic harmony within the structural progression from I to V. And as can be seen by examining both the reduction in Example 12.21 and the passage from Beethoven's sonata, the working out of the intermediate goals of such a prolongational span can introduce chromatic elements quite distant from the tonic key itself.

Mixture and Large-Scale Tonal Plans

Example 12.22a shows a familiar possibility for minor-mode compositions: I leads to III, which then moves through a passing IV to the structural V (the technique of interruption occurs very often after such a V). Example 12.22b shows a more elaborate variation of this large-scale tonal plan that underlies the exposition and development sections of Beethoven's Piano Sonata in C minor, Op. 13 ("Pathetique").

The exposition closes in E♭ major (III) before the material of the slow introduction returns in G minor (bar 132) and punctuates the beginning of the development (this is not shown in the example).[45] In a sense, the recollection of the slow introduction serves as an introduction to the development; the development proper (Allegro molto) begins in bar 137 in the key of E minor, which supports a restatement of the first theme. The next important

EXAMPLE 12–22:

Beethoven, Piano Sonata, Op. 13, I: harmonic plan of exposition and development sections

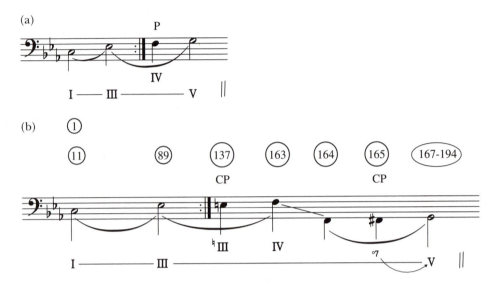

(a)

(b)

goal in the course of the development occurs in bar 163 with the arrival of IV (as a chord, not a key area), which leads through an applied VII^{o7} to the structural V of the first branch of the divided structure. The key of E minor that begins the development section can be interpreted relative to the C minor tonic in terms of simple mixture: E minor belongs to the parallel major mode of the home tonic, C major. The harmonic reduction in Example 12.22b, however, also suggests that E minor, which—as a key—involves chromatic tones quite foreign to C minor, arises through the expansion of a chord built on a chromatic passing tone between III and IV of the diatonic structure: E♭–E♮–F. Both mixture and leading-tone chromaticism help us to understand this passage. While mixture can explain the local significance of the chromaticism produced by E minor, the larger voice-leading function of E♮ as a passing tone (and a leading tone) informs us that this chromatic region intensifies, on a large scale, the motion from III to IV within the characteristic progression from I to V in the minor mode.

Example 12.23 shows a large-scale tonal plan involving secondary mixture in the major mode; the bass diagram indicates the structural plan of the exposition and development sections from Beethoven's Piano Sonata in G major, Op. 79.

The chromaticism in the relatively brief exposition and development (of this sonatina-like movement) is remarkable. Over the span of just 75 bars, four scale systems emerge: G, D, E, and C (all major). In the first part of the development section alone (bars 52–75), the chromatic density of the texture shifts quickly from four sharps to no sharps.[46] The key of E major can, of

EXAMPLE 12.23:

Beethoven, Piano Sonata, Op. 79, I: harmonic plan of exposition and development sections

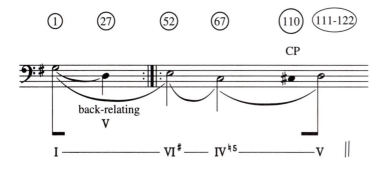

course, be explained in terms of secondary mixture within a familiar progression: in a characteristic bass arpeggiation, VI♯ serves to lead from I to the intermediate IV of the bass structure.[47]

This brief discussion of chromaticism has indicated ways in which chromatic relationships and techniques can be related to a structural context. In particular, we have considered some issues associated with Schenker's late ideas of tonal structure as expressed in *Free Composition*. Much research still remains to be done concerning the role of chromaticism in late nineteenth-century music and in compositions in which the structure itself may be chromatic in nature. Such compositions, and the techniques associated with them, lie for the most part outside the purview of Schenker's primary concerns.

The analytical and theoretical perspectives presented in this book demonstrate the extraordinary richness of Schenker's approach. Ongoing research is further exploring many of these concerns, and (as the Bibliography indicates) work in areas such as rhythm and form is expanding the scope of Schenkerian theory. The tools and insights that you have gained offer a multi-faceted way to approach the magnificent repertoire of tonal music.

Notes

Chapter 1

1. This Bibliography contains full citations of all sources referred to in the text and Notes of this book.

2. *Free Composition* is well known in the English-speaking world because of the excellent English translation by Ernst Oster (1979). Frequent citations to passages in *Free Composition* will be given in the course of this book, so that you can gradually get to know this seminal work and its modes of organization.

3. See for example his study of Beethoven's last sonatas (published 1913–20) which, as Allen Forte has pointed out, "gave a major impetus to the entire modern movement toward better editing practices" (see Yeston, p. 8). Other editions by Schenker include a complete edition of Beethoven's piano sonatas (which has been reprinted by Dover with an introduction by Carl Schachter), selected keyboard works by C. P. E. Bach, and the J. S. Bach *Chromatic Fantasy and Fugue*.

4. For example, the cover of Schenker's first major theoretical work, *Harmony*, says the book is "von einem Künstler" ("by an artist") without giving the author's name.

5. Understanding how we perceive music is complex, and has become a field of research in itself. Perception is a multifaceted process: it includes the physical acts of hearing and cerebral processing of sound, but also mental recognition and interpretation. Like literary comprehension, our ways of hearing music are grounded in our cultural environment, and represent the sum of our experience, training, and preferences.

    Learning to read and to create graphs will develop not only your understanding, but also your ability to hear and recognize—to perceive—many kinds of musical relationships and events.

6. It is assumed that the reader of this book is familiar with the basic types of form. Any reader who needs to study or review musical forms should consult an appropriate text, such as Douglass Green's *Form in Tonal Music*.

7. Our analysis of this piece is a liberal paraphrase of Schenker's analysis in *Der Tonwille*, Vol. 2. This periodical is less well known than *Free Composition*. *Der Tonwille* contains many analyses; it also presents essays on theoretical issues that received fuller explanations in the three volumes of *Das Meisterwerk in der Musik* and eventually in *Free Composition*. See the Bibliography for a listing of available translations.

8. Some scholars prefer the term *group* to *theme* in discussing sonata form, since there may be more than one first or second theme. Both terms are now widely in use, and both will be used in this book depending upon context.

9. Examine the upper voice of bar 21 in the second theme. Here we find yet another version of the falling sixth, a form—appearing within a single bar—of the descent from E♭ to G presented three times during the course of the transition.

10. In a tonicization, a chord temporarily assumes the quality of a tonic, as indicated below bars 69 and 71 of this example. In a modulation, a new key center remains in effect for a longer period of time, and with greater significance for the composition as a whole.

11. The term *harmonic rhythm* is defined in the *Harvard Dictionary of Music* as "the rhythmic pattern provided by the changes in harmony."

12. You may wonder why we isolate these four notes—C, B♭, G, E♮—from the surrounding notes of the right hand. These notes are associated in the right-hand line because of the harmonic support. The D♭ in bar 119 is a dissonant upper neighbor tone that resolves to C, as is the lower D♭ in bar 121. In other words, the tones C, B♭, G, E♮ arpeggiate V⁷ in F minor, the harmony suggested by the octaves in the left hand. For this reason, we can consider the four tones as a unit. (Consider also the downbeat of bar 119, where the *vertical* form of C and E♮ occurs in the right hand before the *linear* form outlined by the four notes of the motive.)

13. In a sense the motive has yearned for closure from the very beginning, because in bar 8 it ends on the leading tone E♮. We will discuss the tendencies of tones in the scale in Chapter 2.

14. This motto, which occurs more than once in Schenker's writings, appears at the beginning of *Free Composition*. The Latin reads *Semper idem sed non eodem modo*.

15. See, for example Kevin Korsyn, pp. 1–58; and William Pastille, in Siegel pp. 29–44.

Chapter 2

1. A nonharmonic passing tone is one that is not a member of the supporting chord. For a review of passing tones, neighboring tones, consonant skips, and suspensions in a harmonic context, read Aldwell and Schachter, pp. 309–45.

2. Victor Zuckerkandl's excellent book *Sound and Symbol,* includes extensive discussion of tonal relations and dynamics in the major scale.

3. The combination of stepwise motion and leaps in a melody is stressed in the study of melodic construction in species counterpoint. See for example the section on cantus firmus writing in Salzer and Schachter, Chapter 1.

4. That is, the V on the second beat of bar 3 and the I on the first beat of bar 4 are one beat each, in contrast to the prevalent length of two beats per chord. This and other facets of phrasing and rhythm in Chopin's Op. 10, No. 3 are discussed in Rothstein, pp. 221ff., and in *Free Composition,* ¶287 and Figure 138/5.

5. The ability to recognize long-range connections is one of the most difficult skills to acquire, and its development depends on experience and musical training. Over the course of this book we will study the nature of different structural levels, how they are related, and how they can be distinguished.

6. The natural seventh degree in minor is often called the *subtonic* because it is a whole step below the tonic, and therefore has no marked tendency to ascend. Therefore, the key-defining property of the leading tone can only be obtained by raising the seventh degree, as with the E♮ at the end of bar 1. Technically, the raising of the seventh and sixth degrees in minor can be regarded as *modal mixture*—that is, tones that have been "borrowed" from the major mode. These alterations are so characteristic, however, that they are considered part of a conceptually expanded minor mode.

7. The various forms of the minor scale illustrate the chromatic alterations that may be needed for chord building (*harmonic minor*) and the composition of melodies (*melodic minor*). Bear in mind, however, that chromatic alterations of scale-degrees $\hat{6}$ and $\hat{7}$ can occur freely in melodies, and will not necessarily take the form represented in a particular scale.

8. In addition to this primary meaning, parentheses can also be used for other purposes: principally, to set off one or more tones that are present in the music, but are not actually part of the structural context in which they occur.

9. For a thorough overview of the principles of two-part counterpoint, read Chapters 1–5 (the first sections only) in Salzer and Schachter.

10. For a listing of this and other works by Schenker, see the Bibliography.

11. Allowable consonances in first species include the perfect unison (in the first and last bars), the perfect octave and fifth, and major and minor thirds and sixths.

12. The term *applied dominant chord* was first used by William Mitchell in his book *Elementary Harmony*. It is used more frequently in Schenkerian literature than the alternative term, *secondary dominant chord*.

13. The figures B–C–B and B–A–B are implied in this double neighbor. Mentally add a fifth note (B–C–[B]–A–B) and you will discover how the apparently incomplete neighbors are heard as complete (the middle note is elided in the four-note span of the measure).

Chapter 3

1. With the freedom characteristic of instrumental idioms, Mozart allows the seventh, C, to return up to D in the top voice, rather than to resolve downward in the customary manner. The resolution is transferred into an inner voice: notice that the C is doubled in the tenor, where it resolves normally.

2. The cadential $^6_4$ defines the beginning of the dominant "space" (signaled by the dominant tone in the bass, which is normally doubled in the cadential $^6_4$), even though the upper notes of the dominant triad or seventh chord are delayed. The two most common ways in which the fourth and sixth enter are either by suspension or accented passing tone (or a combination of both). For example, in the progression IV–V$^6_4$, the fourth may be held over as a suspension while the sixth enters as an accented passing tone.

3. It might seem to make sense to regard the V in bar 8 as resolving to the I in bar 9; after all, V–I is a very common aspect of tonal "grammar." This does not mean, however, that all V to I chord successions should necessarily be understood in this way. One refers to a "half" cadence (or *semicadence*) precisely because the V is the *goal*; if you genuinely hear a V moving to I, with the tonic serving as the goal, then, by definition, you are dealing with an authentic cadence. In Example 3.1, the tonic in bar 9 is not the goal chord of a cadential motion, but the beginning of the second phrase. The tonic that decisively resolves the tensions of the V in bar 8 is the tonic that *concludes* the consequent phrase.

4. From a theoretical point of view, intermediate-harmony chords are not on the same structural level as the fundamental harmonic progression I–V–I. Nevertheless, they often participate in cadential motions. Informally, therefore, they may be regarded as forming an integral part of structural harmonic progressions such as I–IV–V–I, I–II^6–V–I, etc. The role of intermediate-harmony chords on higher levels of structure will be discussed more fully in subsequent chapters.

5. The III chord is a contrapuntal chord that "intervenes" between VI and IV. Its bass note, D, is an incomplete neighbor to E♭, and the median chord supports A as a passing tone in the top voice.

6. The initial motion from I down to III, which prolongs the tonic through the first bar, is subsumed by the avoided cadence and consequently by the I–I^6 that governs bars 1–2. In other words, the broader I–I^6 is structurally "higher ranking" than the I–III of bar 1 that also prolongs tonic harmony on a different, more immediate level.

7. The progression is essentially V$^4_2$–I^6, though at first glance there may appear to be three sonorities supported by the bass motion D♭–C: VII$^{\varnothing 4}_3$–V$^4_2$–I^6. The VII$^4_3$ on the downbeat of bar 5 arises through a remarkable motivic transformation in the soprano. As shown by the motivic brackets in Example 3.9, the ascending second A♭–B♭ of bar 3 is expanded into E♭–F in bars 4–5. It is also filled in chromatically (E♭–E♮–F), echoing the previous D♮–E♭ half-step motion (see the arrow in Example 3.9). For motivic reasons, therefore, f^1 substitutes for e♭^{1} (which momentarily produces the VII$^4_3$ instead of V$^4_2$, the chord that would more customarily occur in this context). The F is an upper neighbor that moves to E♭ by implication in the V$^4_2$ chord on the second beat, and is explicitly resolved in the upper voice by E♭ on the downbeat of bar 6.

8. In a larger sense it would be possible to suggest a I–II–V–I motion, so that the descending seventh from A♭ to B♭ would be seen as the inversion of an ascending second, and the overall bass motion would be A♭–B♭–E♭–A♭. This is a more advanced interpretation, which does not negate the association of bass tones through a descending octave suggested here.

9. The register has been "normalized" in Example 3.10 to show more clearly the essential scalar motion of the bass in bars 1–8. Large leaps are used in counterpoint to change registers. Here, we have expressed large leaps in a single register to highlight stepwise motion (for instance, see bars 3–4, F up to e♭). Bear in mind also that the fifth is the most "natural" dividing point of the major and minor scales, because of the inherently close relationship of the dominant and tonic described earlier in this chapter (see Example 3.4) which has melodic as well as harmonic implications. The E♭ in this case is the upper "boundary" tone of the A♭-major triad.

10. A thorough familiarity with figured-bass symbols is essential for the study of Schenkerian analysis. This is necessary not only for the study of works from the Baroque era that employ figured bass, but also because they are used in many graphs. In fact, the analysis of tonal compositions—regardless of style—benefits from an approach that considers underlying figured-bass "frameworks."

11. The figures "4 ♯" in bar 1 indicate a suspension into the leading tone.

12. Such an anticipation of a later harmony (including the intervening dominant chords) is called an *auxiliary cadence,* a concept that will be discussed later in this book.

13. The 5–6 motion occurs in second species counterpoint (see Chapter 2), and is the basis of the "5–6" sequence that we will discuss in Chapter 4.

14. Bach's C-major Prelude is a piece that has been studied by generations of musicians. Schenker found it a treasure of the tonal literature and used examples in several of his published works. We also feel that it can be used in different contexts in this book. Hence, we present aspects of it here and a more detailed analysis in Chapter 8. See especially Schenker's analyses in *Five Graphic Music Analyses* and *Free Composition*, Figs. 49/1; 62/5; 95/e3; 115/1a; 118/1; 133/2.

15. Compare this 5–6 motion with the chromaticized figure in bars 13–14 of Example 3.11. In both cases the 5–6 motion initiates harmonic change: in Example 3.11 it leads from the mediant key area back to the tonic, while in the present example it begins motion away from the tonic.

16. The leaping bass motions shown in Example 3.16 do not alter the stepwise nature of the bass. They serve to highlight the subdivision of the scalar bass, at V and I, respectively.

17. In principle, a scale step can be any one of the seven triads of the scale. Scale steps need not appear in root position, even though in the purest form of the concept of *Stufen* the representations are root-position triads. Schenker made a distinction between the actual bass of a composition and the progression of scale steps, an ideal or abstract entity consisting of harmonic roots—an entity that sometimes coincides with the structural notes of the sounding bass and sometimes is a kind of imaginary presence underneath the actual bass.

    Special conditions exist with diminished triads in root position: thus the diminished II in minor is used sparingly, but this scale step *can* readily appear as II^6, II$^6_5$, II^7, etc. Similar conditions hold for the VII scale step when it supports a diminished triad, as in the major mode. If chromatically altered to become major or minor triads (♭II, ♭VII, etc.), these chords can of course readily be prolonged. Root movements will frequently proceed by fifth (e.g., I–IV–VII–III–VI–II–V–I), by third (e.g., I–VI–IV–II), and by second (e.g., IV–V, I–II, VI–VI). For more information about scale steps, see Schenker's *Harmony,* Part I, Division II, Section I, "Theory of Scale Steps."

18. The term *imaginary continuo* was first used by William Rothstein. See his article in Cadwallader *Trends in Schenkerian Research*, pp. 87–113.

19. See the discussion of *prolongational spans* in Chapter 12.

20. *Free Composition*, p. 98.

Chapter 4

1. It is as if the music in bar 2 and the first part of bar 3 is an outgrowth of bar 1. This compositional technique is called a "hidden" repetition, and it is a procedure that can unify various spans of music; we will frequently see its influence in other contexts later in this book.

2. The interpretation of linear progressions is a fundamental aspect of Schenkerian analysis. They unite melodic fluency with the linear expression of harmony. The sense of motion they embody is produced in part by the chordal relationship between the first and last tones; the passing tones in between create tension as the line proceeds to its goal.

3. The intervening tones support chords that are referred to as *passing* (or contrapuntal) chords because they are based on passing tones. The series of chords expands the motion from I to II$^6_5$.

4. The shape and pace of the soprano line, which is of course a preexisting chorale melody harmonized by Bach, is somewhat related to the text (though to a limited extent since the same melody is used to sing different stanzas of the chorale text). Notice that special and expressive emphasis is given to the word "Jesu" with the repeated B in the soprano, and to the word "Freude" with the change to half notes; in the second verse the word "lange" is similarly emphasized.

5. *Stufen* are introduced and defined in Chapter 3, p. 67.

6. Many chords are not harmonically significant in this sense: their function is more local in nature. Such chords often arise contrapuntally—that is, through horizontal/melodic elements such as passing motion, neighbor motion, etc.—within a harmonic framework. We saw contrapuntal chords in Example 4.4, which expand the motion from I to II$^6_5$, which are scale steps in the harmonic framework.

7. Schenker, in his own analyses, often uses a broken slur to show the association of a single tone prolonged by *intervening pitches*. (If the pitch is simply repeated or tied, you may use an unbroken tie in your graphs.) Bear in mind also that a broken slur may be used to connect a chromatically altered pitch, such as in a broader motion from C to C♯.

8. For a more complete discussion of the principal graphic symbols, see Chapter 5.

9. In examining the upper voice, it seems sufficient to observe simply that the tones A, B♭, and C receive structural emphasis through metric placement in bars 1–3, since they occur on the downbeats of the bars. Their prominence, however, also depends on the way each is sustained through each measure. Consider the upper voice of bar 1. The A is decorated by its lower neighbor, followed by a consonant skip to F, the root of tonic harmony, in the inner "alto" voice (which doubles the bass at this point); a stepwise motion then leads back to A. Exactly the same process occurs in conjunction with B♭ in the next bar.

10. Two additional points about the example merit brief comment. First, notice in Example 4.5b that the initial B♭ in bar 2 is stemmed, but the B♭ in bar 3 is not (both are passing tones). This nuance of graphic notation reflects the fact that the first B♭ receives independent chordal support, whereas the second B♭ "passes quickly" from the C, *within* the V^6 chord, to the A in the next bar.

11. In graphic notation, square brackets are generally used to indicate parallelisms. For a more thorough discussion of motivic parallelisms, see Burkhart, "Schenker's 'Motivic Parallelisms.'"

12. All movements of this little sonata are brief, hence the name "Sonatina." Our example begins in the dominant area of the exposition.

13. The tonality of this movement is C major. Bars 6–8 represent a modulation to G, the key of the dominant. In terms of the overall tonality, bars 8–12 represent an expansion of V (as a *Stufe*).

14. In Baroque style, bass motions through a descending fourth were frequently associated with sadness and mourning—especially when filled in with chromatic passing tones. See Ellen Rosand's landmark article, "The Descending Tetrachord: An Emblem of Lament," *The Musical Quarterly*, Vol. LXV, No. 3 (July, 1979), pp. 346–59.

15. The first and last notes of the progression, E and B, form an interval of the tonic triad, the first chord of the progression. We have already seen cases (Example 4.3) in which the linear

progression outlines an interval of the *goal* chord. In general, a linear progression will frequently delineate an interval of either the beginning or ending harmony of the underlying harmonic progression. This observation will help you to distinguish between stepwise lines that are genuine linear progressions and those that are not.

16. Notice that, in the third bar of the example, the seventh A♭ is ornamented by the tone B♭ above. The seventh of a seventh chord is often decorated in this manner.

17. Notice the A♭–G motion that occurs in both the "soprano" and the "tenor" strands of voice leading. This is a characteristic feature of keyboard writing analogous to instrumental doubling in concerted music, where apparent parallel octaves are formed through doublings of a single voice-leading strand.

18. Our purpose is not to introduce new terminology or a class of linear techniques, but to make the point that some linear progressions span a dissonance that ultimately must resolve. In Example 4.9, for instance, the four bars of expanded dominant seventh harmony function in a way exactly analogous to a simple V^7–I progression. In this case, the *entire* passage embodies tension that is released when the seventh resolves to the third of the tonic triad. Thus dissonance is not exclusively a local event, but may influence broader spans of music. This observation has far-reaching ramifications for tonal structure and musical form, ramifications we will see in greater detail when we begin to examine prolonged harmony and counterpoint in larger contexts.

19. The term *linear intervallic pattern* was introduced by Forte and Gilbert, *Introduction to Schenkerian Analysis*, pp. 83 ff.

20. Linear progressions and intervallic patterns, however, are not mutually exclusive concepts. Linear intervallic patterns usually involve a linear progression in one or both of the voices.

21. Notice that a $\frac{5}{3}$ chord does not occur on the downbeat of bar 5. (Dowland avoids the diminished VII chord that would otherwise occur in an accented metrical position.) Nevertheless, the continuity of the line has been so strongly established that we may understand a C in the upper voice, even though it does not appear in the tenor (C, of course, is literally present in the previous bar).

22. Although the sequence does connect VI with I^6, it does so only from a limited perspective— considering only the literal succession of adjacent chords from bars 11–15. In Chapter 10, we will discover how this sequence functions over a broader span, as part of the structural harmonic framework of the entire piece.

23. Remember that "chords" and "harmonies" are not mutually exclusive. The I and I^6 chords are harmonic in the sense that they both represent the broader tonic scale step and define the boundaries of its prolongational span. The intervening triads are clearly *only* chords because of their passing function.

24. The beginning and the end of a voice exchange are not necessarily of equal structural status. As the second part of Example 4.17b shows, the tones of the first interval of the pattern, B over G, move into the inner voices of the tonic over the course of its prolongation. The structural upper and lower voices are resumed with the attainment of dominant harmony. Thus the broader structural connections, as shown in the last part of Example 4.17b, are B– A–B in the upper voice (a neighbor figure) over I–V–I in the bass.

25. The neighbor in the figure 3–4–3–2–1 does not always function as an incomplete neighbor. In some of his examples, Schenker shows that $\hat{3}$ returns as a structural tone, which means that the upper neighbor is complete. The subtleties of the incomplete neighbor, however, are not fully explored by Schenker. As a general rule of thumb, you may consider the second $\hat{3}$ a passing tone if $\hat{4}$ is supported by a prominent intermediate harmony (the following $\hat{3}$ is then passing). Because similar formations can have different meanings in different contexts, even this observation is open to exceptions.

Chapter 5

1. Remember that the analytical *process* should include all aspects of the work. Hence, consideration of elements such as rhythm, dynamics, and texture is integral to the analytical process. Features such as these can be addressed in the textual discussion of the music or indicated through special markings on the graphs or in separate examples.

2. See also Mitchell and Salzer, *Music Forum* I: pp. 260–68, upon which the present listing is partly based. They provide an extensive discussion of graphic symbols together with sample graphs.

3. In many of Schenker's later graphs, tones on the highest level of structure had extended stems. An innovation that originated with his student Felix Salzer, varied stem lengths are often used by many Schenkerians to differentiate different structural levels.

4. Schenker also used broken slurs to denote an association between chromatic variants of the same pitch (C to C♯). See Schenker, *Fünf Urlinie-Tafeln*. In the analysis of Haydn's Sonata in E-flat major, p. 43 (Dover ed.), a broken slur connects A with A♭ in the top voice. Bear in mind also that Schenker did not use broken beams to indicate prolonged tones in his graphs. This symbol originated with his student Felix Salzer.

5. The initial E has two stems that represent different aspects of its role in the melody. Because it is the initial note, it is understood as the top voice at first. However as the melody continues C and A emerge as the main upper-voice tones, and E is clearly an inner-voice note. Thus, the descending stem indicates the role that this tone plays in the phrase as a whole.

6. In Schenkerian analysis, a particular analytical interpretation is often referred to as a *reading*.

7. In German music theory, and in Schenker's writings, both tones are referred to as *leading tones*; as noted in Chapter 2, the second scale degree is called the *descending* leading tone.

8. Another common type of implication occurs in the melodic motion $\hat{3}$–$\hat{7}$–$\hat{1}$ (over I–V–I). The distinction is that the implied tone $\hat{2}$ never actually appears; it is substituted for by $\hat{7}$ and is implied solely through its membership in the dominant triad. One assumes here that $\hat{3}$–$(\hat{2})$–$\hat{1}$ is structurally the main upper voice, because it is more direct and melodically fluent than the disjunct $\hat{3}$–$\hat{7}$–$\hat{1}$. Thus, we see that in some cases implied tones can take structural precedence over tones that actually appear and substitute for them. Again, the notion of the imaginary continuo helps us to confirm this observation.

9. The c^2 in bar 2 is a suspension at a deeper level of structure, but it also functions as an appoggiatura at the surface of the music. An important aspect of the tonal system is that the same tone may function differently at different structural levels.

10. Our concern here is with the "space" occupied by a particular harmony, exclusive of such elements as rests and figuration tones that may delay chord tones. For example, in the Schenkerian tradition the cadential $^6_4$ chord is labeled V—even though it contains the tones of tonic harmony—because it prolongs dominant harmony by delaying some of the tones of the dominant chord.

11. Some commentators might see this passage as composed of two phrases; we prefer to regard it as a single phrase composed of two subphrases, for reasons that will become clear as we proceed. Like many concepts in music, it is difficult to define precisely what is meant by *phrase* and *subphrase*, and these terms can be used in a variety of ways. Note also that some graphic symbols have been marked on the music itself; this kind of analytical "overlay" can be a useful companion to a graph.

12. This phrase can be analyzed in one of two possible ways. The first reading was actually published by Schenker in *Der Tonwille*; the second (which is not shown) interprets the upper voice in a slightly different manner and is based on subtle rhythmic features of the phrase. We have followed Schenker's rather early analysis, because of the direct way in which it portrays details of the upper voice and harmonic prolongations.

Also worth considering is that the V of bar 4 does resolve to a tonic in bar 5. Not all half cadences, however, "resolve" immediately to a following tonic, particularly in cases in which an *interruption* divides a structural framework. We will discuss the technique of interruption in subsequent chapters.

13. It is to some extent arbitrary where one begins detailed analysis. We chose the bass structure because, in this phrase at least, it is the most straightforward component of the harmonic/contrapuntal framework. In some pieces one might very well begin with the upper voice to discover the features that lead to a broader interpretation of the structure.

14. Be careful not to be confused by the reference to "upper voice." The right-hand part by itself is the upper voice, but it is another good example of polyphonic melody—a melody consisting of multiple voices. As soon as we begin to see how the tones are grouped and

function in different ways, we can become more specific and further distinguish upper and inner voices of the right-hand part.

15. See Burkhart, "Schenker's 'Motivic Parallelisms.' "

16. It is theoretically possible for an *Urlinie* to begin on $\hat{8}$; however, it is a considerably more problematic construct than the $\hat{3}$- or $\hat{5}$-line. An *Ursatz* from $\hat{8}$ is based on the third possible disposition of the tones of the tonic chord, with a descending scale from $\hat{8}$ to $\hat{1}$ in the top voice. Practically speaking there are considerations— not present in the $\hat{3}$- or $\hat{5}$-lines—that complicate the working out of such a lengthy linear expression of tonic harmony in actual composition, especially over the span of an entire work.

17. They are images in that they are manifestations of naturally occurring overtones that are not usually noticed in listening to a particular tone.

18. Since tonal music characteristically embodies a sense of motion—melodic motion as well as harmonic motion—a top voice structure that consists of the prolongation of a single tone is often incompatible with the dynamic nature of major-minor tonality. In other words, the continued prolongation of a single tone can lead to a static quality that is foreign to the "directed motion" inherent in tonal music of the seventeenth through nineteenth centuries.

19. Schenker, *Free Composition*, p. 26.

20. Many Schenkerians also use the word "deeper" to refer to structural levels that are more or less remote from the musical surface; confusingly enough, a "deeper" level in this usage means exactly the same thing as a "higher" level. The contradiction, however, is more apparent than real, because the notions of deeper and higher both convey, in different ways, the sense of distance from the immediate position of the observer.

21. Burkhart, "Schenker's Motivic Parallelisms."

Chapter 6

1. Jonas, in Rothgeb translation, p. 41.

2. You may notice that our graph does not indicate the flute line, which leads to a higher register at the conclusion of the phrase, while the violins continue downward in the same register (bars 7–8). The motion of the flute to the higher register is an example of a variation in instrumental doubling at a moment of special importance (in this case, the cadence), rather than a true registral shift. And, in Classical orchestral music, the flute(s) often sound above the first violins even if the *violins* are carrying the principal upper voice.

3. Schenker also shows the unfolding of a *single* interval, but the important point to remember is that a change of direction is involved (for instance, C up to E down to C within a C major chord).

4. See *Free Composition*, Fig. 43 and ¶140–41 for illustrations of many other unfolding patterns. In its pure form unfolding involves leaps, as shown in Examples 6.4 and 6.5. These leaps, however, may be filled in at a later level, wholly or in part, by passing tones.

5. The interpolation of a tone before the resolution of a seventh is a common technique, closely related to the embellishment of the resolution of a suspension.

6. This technique should not be confused with an initial ascent, which leads only to the first tone of the *Urlinie*.

7. Here we see that the first chord of the voice exchange is primary, like the first two voice exchanges of the Beethoven example. The reason, in this particular instance, is that we regard the broader motion of the bass as $\hat{4}$ moving to $\hat{5}$ (IV–V), not flat $\hat{6}$ moving to $\hat{5}$.

8. When sung by a male voice, the vocal line will of course sound an octave lower than written. However, it will still be heard as the principal upper voice, regardless of the register in which it is sung.

9. *Free Composition*, p. 51, ¶147. See also Example 2.16 in Chapter 2, which provides a clear illustration of the principle opposite from that shown here, *ascending register transfer*. In bar 75, the tone g^1 (and the lower neighbor $f\sharp^1$) are shifted up an octave, and g^2 is then further embellished by the incomplete-neighbor tone a^2 before the motion to F$\sharp$ (and D) in the next bar.

10. The internal grouping of the passing tones is based on the harmonic support: G up to C is part of the tonic triad; D up to F is part of V_5^6. Always be thinking in terms of the imaginary continuo, which is actually quite explicit here.

11. *Free Composition*, p. 51, ¶149.

12. Scale degree $\hat{3}$ over a cadential $^6_4$ chord would often be interpreted as a passing tone rather than a structural return to $\hat{3}$. In this case, however, both the emphasis of C in bar 23 and the recurrence of the third motion (C–B–A) strongly suggest that C is associated with the earlier primary tone.

13. The term *superposition* is used in *Free Composition* to denote a specific form of reaching over (see below and Ernst Oster's amplification of reaching over on pages 48–49 of *Free Composition*). We use the term in a more general sense to mean the transfer of an inner-voice tone above the main top-voice line.

14. In this case, the octave shifts may also be related to ascending register transfers. Bear in mind that many of the techniques we have been describing incorporate transfer of register; consequently, two or more such related techniques may be relevant to a single example. While register transfers may involve any tone in any voice, superposition refers specifically to one or more inner-voice tones shifted above a structural top-voice line.

15. We read an upper neighbor figure, A♭–B♭–A♭, in bars 1–2, which may seem perplexing at first glance because the B♭ occurs as part of a descending motion. Listen carefully, however, to each tone of the figure in the right hand. The c^2 of the reaching-over figure sounds like an incomplete neighbor—an appoggiatura; in other words, the B♭ is clearly decorated by the C, which means that C is closer to the musical surface than the harmonically supported B♭. The B♭, in turn, decorates the A♭, which is the main tone in bars 1–2. This is a good example of related tones that function on different levels of structure.

16. Thus, in this seemingly simple top-voice line, four different levels of structure may be discerned: (1) the principal motion E–F–G ($\hat{3}$–$\hat{4}$–$\hat{5}$); (2) the lower-neighbor tones D and E supported by the intervening chords of the sequence; (3) the reaching-over tones (g^2 and a^2); and (4) the suspensions on the downbeats of bars 2 and 3. Notice also that the tones g^2 and a^2 do not have stems in graph c, but do have stems in graph b to distinguish them from the nonharmonic suspensions.

17. When a group of at least two descending tones is used to place an inner voice into a higher register, I call the phenomenon a *reaching-over.*" Schenker, *Free Composition*, p. 47. Additional examples of reaching over in different contexts are presented in Fig. 41. See also Ernst Oster's valuable commentary on pages 48–49.

18. The concept of *substitution* is crucial to a full understanding of voice leading in tonal fabrics. We recommend the article "On Implied Tones" by William Rothstein.

19. The name *Phrygian* does not mean that a passage incorporating the Neapolitan sixth is composed in the Phrygian mode. Rather, it refers to the presence of a tone—the lowered second scale degree—that is associated with the Phrygian mode. We will use the more familiar *Neapolitan sixth chord*, though Schenker uses the term *Phrygian* $\hat{2}$.

20. *Free Composition*, p. 41.

Chapter 7

1. In this case the hemiola consists of the three groupings of two beats in bars 8–9, articulated by the rhythm of harmonic change and the associated grouping of the figuration.

2. Remember, our decision to regard D as primary is only a provisional assumption. The first prominent top-voice note may not necessarily be the first tone of the *Urlinie*. Also, a $\hat{5}$ at the beginning of a piece may have to be reevaluated in favor of $\hat{3}$ at a later point in the composition (or vice versa); only the continuing unfolding of the music, that is, the development of a broader tonal context, will enable us to make a more definite analytical decision.

3. The term *design* is used by musicians in different ways, though it is often considered in relation to form. Generally, design refers to the organization of elements such as repetition, contrast, rhythm, meter, figuration, texture, motivic associations, and thematic layout—in

other words, those aspects not directly related to the voice-leading structure. We will discuss the distinction between form and structure more completely in Chapter 8.

4. The c^2 in bar 9—the seventh of V^7—is a doubling of the tenor voice, where C is stated and resolved.

5. It is not always necessary to show all registral associations in a graph; too much detail could becloud the elaboration of structure the graph is intended to convey. Therefore, make a point of consulting the music as you read the discussions; don't rely on the graphic analyses by themselves. If you refer briefly back to Example 7.1, you can readily perceive the relationship of a^2 (bars 2–3) to g^2 (bars 4–6), an association that prepares the attainment of an even higher register (d^3) in bar 8.

6. Bear in mind that Schenkerian graphs are primarily intended to show aspects of harmony and voice leading, as well as some motivic, rhythmic, and other characteristics related to structure. When a literal or slightly varied repetition occurs, the analyst may at times choose to abbreviate a graph, so long as the structure is completely and faithfully represented. In Example 7.3, the main phrase closes in bar 10, and Mozart's extension retraces the latter part of the structure.

7. Schenker believed that repetition was the most fundamental element for the creation of musical form. In hierarchical tonal structures, repetition may appear in different guises and forms. In other words, this compositional procedure is not restricted to the musical surface nor must it occur in exact or "literal" form. In fact, we will discover that very often repetition holds the most far-reaching consequences for a tonal fabric when it appears in varied form and, in particular, when it occurs at different levels of tonal structure.

8. Carl Schachter has written on this movement; our analysis of bars 1–16 follows his in most details. If you wish to consult his study, which examines in more depth issues of motive and rhythm, see his "Rhythm and Linear Analysis: Durational Reduction," pp. 218–22.

9. The seventh of a dominant seventh chord is in principle a passing tone (this observation concerns bar 6, where a V^6 is followed by a V_5^6). Very often the first tone of the passing motion is elided, so that only the seventh would appear over the chord. But in cases such as the one we are examining, the function of the chordal seventh, as a descending passing tone, is made clear by the inclusion of the *beginning* of the passing motion (the B in the upper voice of the V^6 chord). Although the underlying connection must be understood as the primary tone $\hat{3}$ moving to its upper neighbor and back (G–A–G), as shown in Example 7.4c, the surface line B–A–G is significant in that it serves as a kind of motivic "echo," recalling the structural unfolded thirds, E–G, F♯–D♯, that lead the primary tone $\hat{3}$ into the inner voice in bars 1–5. Also salient is the association between E–F♯–G (bar 5) and B–A–G (bar 6), two thirds converging on G ($\hat{3}$). And finally, the tone F♯, structural $\hat{2}$ over the half cadence, is decorated by another third—A–G–F♯, which prolongs F♯. Thus we can see that related third-motives unify this phrase throughout.

10. We have stated that, theoretically, an *Ursatz* can express an $\hat{8}$-line. They are, however, relatively rare; rarer still would be any division of such a structure. Schenker states that an $\hat{8}$-line is not interrupted, but that a segmentation of the line $\hat{8}$–$\hat{5}$,$\hat{5}$–$\hat{1}$ takes the place of interruption.

11. The c^2 is, of course, is actually stated (if only briefly) in the ornament in bar 5.

12. For ease of discussion, many graphs from this point forward will combine sections of varying degrees of detail. For example, in 7.14a we show the basic harmonies and upper-voice line in bars 1–4 and omit some of the tones of figuration. Because bars 5–8 are more complex and raise new issues, the remaining part of the graph shows as much detail as is necessary to clarify the tonal structure.

13. The technique we use in Example 7.14 of *graphic normalization* is a useful way to approach a complex upper voice such as this. After making a preliminary decision about which tones belong to an inner voice and which belong to the main upper voice, we simplify the register. In other words, we sketch the tones in the register in which we believe they function (Beethoven has made it easy for us here, for he has duplicated the line E♭–F–A♭ in the inner voice of the right hand). This strategy will clarify the voice leading and enable us to follow (or "trace") different stepwise melodic strands, even though they may be broken up at the surface by register shifts and other compositional procedures. Here we see the melodically

fluent lines beneath the disjunct motion and transfer of register Beethoven uses to achieve the climax of his phrase.

14. Once again we see a descent from a inner-voice tone to one that belongs to the upper voice. The high A♭ has been superposed from the "alto" register and leads *down* to the D♭ in the upper register. The stepwise descent of a fifth from A♭ down to D♭ stands for the ascent of a fourth from A♭ *up* to D♭. The notes at the surface of the music that connect a♭² with d♭² belong to a lower level than the prolonged upper neighbor d♭² shown in Example 7.14b.

15. We would also point out that one of Schenker's more esoteric ideas is that of the *leaping passing tone,* which he developed through his study of strict counterpoint. A leaping passing tone is a tone that leaps in a lower voice to support a literal, stepwise passing tone in an upper voice; the A♭ that supports the "apparent" tonic in Example 7.14c is a good illustration of a leaping passing tone (the C in the upper voice is the literal passing tone). For more on this phenomenon, see Schenker, *Counterpoint* II, pp. 181–82.

16. Understanding the subtle distinction between *articulation* and *division* (through interruption) is essential in clarifying relationships between traditional concepts of musical form and Schenker's ideas of tonal structure.

17. An analysis showing essentially the compound melodic structure of bars 1–4 is presented by Forte and Gilbert in *Introduction to Schenkerian Analysis,* p. 77.

18. In Example 7.20 we have indicated the beginning of the first phrase to signify its relation to the beginning of the second phrase; the parentheses symbolize the remainder of the first phrase that has been omitted. This type of notation is frequently employed in voice-leading graphs.

19. The B♯ on the downbeat of bar 6 delays the return of C♯ and sounds like an incomplete lower neighbor. Example 7.20a, however, shows that the B♯ can also be described as a chromatic passing tone that arises from a motion in the inner voice that helps to reestablish C♯ from below: A–B–B♯–C♯.

20. The implied and actual repetitions of the 5–6–5 motive (the second and third statements) are not only expanded but somewhat "concealed" because they unfold at deeper structural levels. Schenker sometimes used the terms *concealed motivic repetition* and *expanded repetition* to reer to this compositional procedure.

21. Bear in mind that the retention of $\hat{5}$ is conceptual (i.e., "mental"), rather than literal at the surface of the music. Motion into an inner voice frequently retains a higher-ranking pitch in this fashion. Sometimes, as here, the main tone is literally recalled; sometimes it is not. In any case, the effect of "mental retention" is a form of prolongation: the mentally retained tone is prolonged until the next tone of the structural upper voice becomes active (in this case, until $\hat{4}$ and $\hat{3}$ appear in bar 8).

22. In such cases $\hat{4}$–$\hat{3}$–$\hat{2}$ may occur over a single intermediate harmony. See our discussion of the *unsupported stretch* in chapter 12.

23. Some of you may hear this 17-bar span of music in four phrases instead of the two we have been alluding to. There is certainly nothing incorrect with this interpretation, for one can make a good case for four-bar groups of measures. However, in our view, bars 1–4 sound incomplete as a musical unit and thus function as a *subphrase.*

24. The form of reaching over is somewhat complex. The A is stated explicitly in bar 15 and is retained through implication in bar 16 over the cadential $^6_4$ in A minor. When the $^6_4$ resolves into the V⁷, the A conceptually moves both to G♯ and B. The interval G♯-B, however, is not expressed vertically, but horizontally. Consequently, the A literally moves first to the G♯, which then leads (or "reaches over") to the B♮.

Part 2: Analytical Applications

1. See especially Schenker's comments on sonata from in *Free Composition,* pp. 133–41. Despite the apparently extreme position, however, Schenker continued to incorporate conventional aspects of form in his late work.

   In the article "Form," the *Harvard Dictionary of Music* makes a useful distinction between "form *in* music" and "form(s) *of* music." "The former . . . consists of [compositional] elements arranged in orderly fashion according to numerous obvious principles as well as a still greater number of subtle and hidden relationships. [The latter] refers to the existence of certain schemes that govern the over-all structure of a composition and were traditionally used in various periods of music history, e.g., the fugue or the sonata."

2. *Free Composition*, p. 130.

3. See Cadwallader, "Form and Tonal Process: The Design of Different Structural Levels."

Chapter 8

1. We shall see in later chapters that one-part structures may also embrace binary and ternary forms.

2. The ascending two-note patterns from the sequence parallel the earlier ascending leaps of a fourth. In other words, as indicated with numbered motivic brackets in Example 8.1, the initial leaps of a fourth are echoed in the bass by the cadential motions in bars 10–11 and 18–19 and are repeated in the varied form of a rising second (bars 12–15). These ascending figures elaborate but do not disrupt the downward sweep of the passage. Schenker shows these motivic parallelisms in *Free Composition*, Figure 118, and in *Five Graphic Music Analyses*.

3. *Free Composition*, p. 80. See also Figure 95, e³. Motions in tenths, sixths, and thirds occasionally create harmonic ambiguities. For instance, in Beethoven's Piano Sonata, Op. 110 (Example 6.8, bar 3), the "II$_3^4$" is produced by an inner voice that "follows" the melody at the tenth below, within a prolongation of what is essentially a IV. Without the motion in tenths, the chord would be a IV⁶.

4. Schenker writes "IV⁷–II$_5^6$," then "V." The first two chords, however, express just one function—the subdominant. The II$_5^6$ emerges because the seventh of IV⁷ resolves within the chord, before the bass moves to V. See Schenker, *Five Graphic Music Analyses*.

5. In *Five Graphic Music Analyses*, Schenker includes a separate example next to the graph that reproduces Bach's notation of the bass in the original autograph. Whereas the bass stems generally go down in the autograph, the stems on the F♯ go up, appearing like an inner voice. Schenker felt that by means of this highly unusual stemming, Bach ingeniously conveyed the idea that the IV⁷ and II$_3^4$ are to be heard as more fundamental than the interpolated diminished seventh chord.

6. What occurs here is a contrapuntal elision. Normally the tonic would be stated initially as a triad, with the destabilizing seventh subsequently added through the 8–♭7 or 5–7 technique. In this case, the two-step transformation is contracted into one step; the chord emerges from the outset as a I♭⁷ (V⁷ of IV). Note specifically that B (alto) would normally resolve to C and only then move to a passing B♭. Compare the very similar elision in Beethoven's Op. 14, No. 1 (second movement, bars 3–4), analyzed in Chapter 7 (Examples 7.4–7.7).

7. Example 8.5c is an illustration worked out by Ernst Oster. We are indebted to Charles Burkhart for bringing this to our attention. Compare the unfolding pattern shown in stage 5 with stage 3: the first tone of each pair is stated *before* the second tone.

8. An interesting feature of the structure is that the coupling of the octave from d¹ to d² occurs partially over tonic harmony (Example 8.5a). It is not uncommon for the final statement of a prolonged structural tone to appear locally as a tone of figuration, such as an appoggiatura, or here, as a suspended ninth (Example 8.5b). In either case, the final appearance of the prolonged tone as a dissonance emphasizes the motion *from* the prolonged tone to the next tone of comparable rank. (Review Example 7.23 in Chapter 7.)

9. Translation by Philip L. Miller, *The Ring of Words* (New York: Doubleday, 1963), pp. 88–89.

10. There are two versions of the B♭–C–B♭ motive in bars 3–5 because the second neighbor C in bar 5 also relates to the B♭ prolonged from the beginning of bar 3. Because both versions share the same *initial* pitch, we refer to these as "nested" motivic repetitions (see the alignment of the motivic brackets in Example 8.6). See below for a discussion of this technique.

11. In Example 8.6, we show d♭² as resolving to c² across the bar. In a local sense, of course, D♭ resolves to C in an *inner voice* of dominant harmony in bar 6. However, the resolution of D♭ to C in the *same register* is delayed until the new vocal phrase begins.

12. Two fundamental types of chromaticism heighten the somber quality of this passage. One results from modal mixture, and the other results from the alteration of diatonic tones (for example, chromatically transforming a diatonic tone to create a new leading tone).

13. One might be tempted to understand F, or $\hat{5}$, as the first *Urlinie* tone, because of its prominence. Notice, however, that the motion to and from F is fleeting and unsupported. The F occurs through superposition: the inner voice tone f^1, which occurs frequently in bars 6–8, rises above $\hat{3}$.

14. The term *nesting* was introduced by Charles Burkhart in his article "Schenker's 'Motivic Parallelisms.' "

15. We discuss the concept of the *auxiliary cadence* in more detail in Chapters 9 and 12.

16. In a landmark series of three articles Carl Schachter has developed a new way to analyze and represent rhythmic and metrical relationships on different structural levels: "Rhythm and Linear Analysis: A Preliminary Study," "Rhythm and Linear Analysis: Durational Reduction," and "Rhythm and Linear Analysis: Aspects of Meter." Our discussion of Schubert's song is based in part on Schachter's analysis in the last of these articles, pp. 17–23. Another lucid exploration of rhythm in Schenkerian terms is William Rothstein's *Phrase Rhythm in Tonal Music*.

17. The voice-leading graphs we have studied are primarily devoted to harmony and voice leading; there are, however, ways of representing a work's rhythmic structure. Example 8.7, a simplification of the outer-voice structure with groups of beats aligned above, is one possibility.

18. Translation by the authors.

19. Both poems we have examined use imagery that suggests death as release from the cares of life. The tone of Goethe's poem, however, is one of quiet exaltation, while Heine's tone conveys grim and sardonic humor and fantasy.

20. Aldwell and Schachter (p. 560) describe this distinction as follows. "[One type of enharmonic] is purely notational: a composer uses an enharmonic spelling for ease in reading or to convey some expressive nuance. True enharmonics, on the other hand, are inherent in the musical structure; no change in notation could possibly eliminate them, for they would be heard even if they were not expressed in the notation."

21. The flat notation is also related to the imagery of the poem, which starts in a normal conversational way and then suddenly brings in the weird figure of the carpenter.

Chapter 9

1. Most musicians seem to agree that *rounded binary* form comprises two large sections. The first section is often repeated, and the second includes a return to thematic material stated at the beginning of the composition. This means, of course, that there is a three-part or ternary quality in the form. Some musicians, therefore, may differ in the designation they use: in a particular piece, some may perceive a rounded binary, others a ternary form. For this chapter we have chosen examples that, in the broadest terms, comprise two *distinct* sections, even though they may be of different length.

2. In this prolongational span, the A♭ in the bass is the higher-ranking structural tone; the D natural and B♭ are contrapuntally related to the other tones of the A♭ major triad. Because the A♭ in the bass retains its structural significance, we regard the chord as an outgrowth of the tonic triad. In a sense we see an overlapping of harmonic areas. A primary aspect of modulation is the emergence of a new scale. In this case, the scale of E♭ (signaled by D♮) begins to emerge over the A♭ tonic.

3. The graph indicates that we regard the initial c^2 as the primary tone $\hat{3}$, an interpretation that is not obvious at first glance but develops retrospectively. C in the two-line octave first appears in a weak metrical position, but returns in a stronger position on the downbeat of bar 2. The subsequent octave transfer to c^3 confirms that C is in fact the main top-voice tone supported by the prolonged tonic harmony.

4. Very often the first and last pitches of a motive define an interval of the underlying harmony, but this is not a requirement for a tone succession to become a motive. (Some have objected

to this notion, but no requirement exists in Schenkerian analysis that *all* elements in a composition be interpreted as part of the structure.) Rhythmic and registral characteristics, for example, may lead the ear to perceive a group of tones as a motive, even though it does not completely "fit" within the underlying harmony. We refer to these as *nonstructural* motives because they exist somewhat independently of the underlying voice-leading structure.

5. Jonas, *Introduction*, pp. 7–8.

6. Notice the nonstructural repetition of the motive A♭–C from bars 2–3 in bars 11–12.

7. Bear in mind that both fifth-progressions serve to expand the higher-ranking tones of the fundamental line: the first (B♭–E♭) elaborates and thus prolongs structural $\hat{2}$ of the first branch; the second (E♭–A♭) participates in the composing-out of the descent of the fundamental line ($\hat{3}$–$\hat{1}$) that occurs in the second branch of the interrupted fundamental structure.

8. *Free Composition*, p. 107.

9. Strictly speaking, the dividing element is the *cadence* in E♭, not the double bar and repeat signs. The piece would be a rounded binary form even if the repeats were not observed.

10. *Free Composition*, pp. 87–88.

11. In our discussion of "Wandrers Nachtlied" in the previous chapter, we briefly commented on the notion of an *auxiliary cadence*. In that situation, VI–V–I is an "incomplete" harmonic progression. In Haydn's Minuet, the auxiliary cadence begins with a I⁶, which suggests a tonic without firmly establishing it; this progression is also incomplete, because it does not begin with a root-position chord. See our additional comments on the *auxiliary cadence* in Chapter 12.

12. Examples 9.4 and 9.6 also show only the structural tones of the second branch (the reprise) of the Minuet.

13. These bars are abbreviated in Example 9.4.

14. We are regarding the four-bar unit as analogous to a four-beat measure (like $\frac{4}{4}$), with the first bar strongest, the third bar next strongest, and the second and fourth bars weak. Such a unit is referred to as a *hypermeasure,* a term introduced by Edward T. Cone in *Musical Form and Musical Performance.*

15. Remember that the half cadence occurs on beat 1 of bar 12. The other five eighth notes constitute a lead-in to the reprise. Consider also another perspective on the nature of interruption. At a level just below the background, the interruption after $\hat{2}$ represents a break in the voice leading. Levels closer to the surface, however, can build a bridge over that break, more or less like two separate phrases that are connected at the surface by a linking passage (which is usually an upbeat).

16. One consequence of this delay is the appearance of the sixth c♯²–e¹, belonging to the V⁷ harmony of B major, over the bass B in bar 8. This sixth "belongs" with the preceding bass note F♯ (V).

17. *Free Composition*, pp. 88–89.

18. Schenker describes "complete" transference of forms of the fundamental structure as those that begin with a root-position tonic in the new key. He says that "every transferred form has the effect of a self-contained structure within which the upper and lower voices delimit a single [tonal] space. See *Free Composition*, p. 87. In Chapter 7, which examines self-contained passages at the beginnings of pieces, the transferred *Ursatz* forms appeared in the tonic key, and are therefore most similar to the *Ursatz* of the composition itself. However, as Schenker points out, in tonal music "the tendency to propagate the forms of the fundamental structure . . . goes through all voice-leading levels." Thus, *Ursatz* formations can also be replicated in keys other than the tonic.

19. Strictly speaking, only the fourth is dissonant. The sixth above the bass in a $\frac{6}{4}$ can function as a consonant suspension, passing tone, or neighbor, and thus tends to "resolve."

20. Consider that f♯¹ in bar 16 is a strong *reminder* of structural $\hat{2}$, even though it actually belongs to an inner voice.

21. Among nineteenth-century composers, Mendelssohn and Brahms were especially fond of beginning the thematic reprise away from the structural tonic. For example, in his Inter-

mezzo in F minor, Op. 118, No. 4, Brahms brings back the thematic reprise over the V^6_4 that prepares the final statement of prolonged dominant harmony; the harmonic reprise (beginning with the structural tonic) does not enter until two bars later.

22. *Free Composition*, Figure 152/4. The authors have modified Schenker's figure to show only the most essential structure.

23. Much more typical than diagram b is the context in which the progression I-III occurs before the double bar; see diagram c. Other characteristic patterns for minor-mode compositions are illustrated in Example 12.12.

24. Such structures—in particular, the *Ursatz*—embody these musical forces that lead experienced listeners to feel the need for a tonal composition to end in the key in which it began. This is why a cadence in the dominant at the double bar does not constitute a satisfying ending to a piece.

Chapter 10

1. See our discussion of support for scale degree $\hat{4}$, and its role in the two *unsupported stretches* of the *Urlinie*, in Chapter 12.

2. The B section itself comprises a rounded binary form (a^1–b–a^2). The term *composite* is often applied to compositions whose larger sections are composed of smaller, complete formal patterns. The Bagatelle, therefore, is a composite ternary form.

3. For now we again urge you to consider the B section as a separate (but lower-level) fundamental structure in E♭ major. Because $e♭^2$ plays a relatively limited role in the structure of this section, we have assigned it to its own staff above that which depicts the primary motions of the structure in E♭.

4. Only the E♭ of the augmented sixth chord functions as a *local* neighbor to D. From a broader perspective, the E♭ of the B section is higher ranking than the V in the retransition, as we explain in a subsequent note.

5. In Chapter 9 we discussed the principle of transference in the context of incomplete forms of the fundamental structure (auxiliary cadences). Complete forms may appear within a section (such as the antecedent/consequent constructions in Chapter 7) or may define distinct sections of a multisectional work, as in the A and B sections of this composite ternary form.

6. Character pieces of the nineteenth century often have three-part forms arising from large-scale contrapuntal progressions. Many of Chopin's Nocturnes and Brahms's Intermezzi, for example, are ternary pieces in which the B sections are based on harmonic scale steps (typically VI, III, or IV) that contrapuntally prolong the initial tonic of the *Ursatz*. In Beethoven's Bagatelle, one might consider incorporating the retransition section into the larger reading of the large-scale harmonic progression: I–VI–V–I. Because of the extremely sectionalized form and the motion of the upper voice, in this case we regard the retransition almost parenthetically; hence, the V of the retransition belongs to a lower level than I–VI–I.

7. in Example 10.6 we indicate both the neighbor tone E♭ and the bass note of the prolonged E♭ major harmony with open note heads. Sometimes an upper-voice tone and supporting harmony receive such prominence in the large-scale structure and form of a composition that it becomes for all practical purposes almost as significant as the tones of the *Ursatz* itself. For that reason it is sometimes possible to indicate such a tone in the same way that we indicate the tones of the Ursatz. In a real musical sense, the E♭ receives as much compositional working-out as the initial D. It is for this reason that we are showing these soprano and bass tones with open note heads, thereby indicating their far-reaching significance.

8. Schenker also stipulated that a neighbor note could "delay" the descent of the fundamental line and "reinforce" (prolong) the primary tone; both effects occur at the first level of the middleground in this piece. See *Free Composition*, pp. 42–43. You may also want to read Chapter 5, which is Schenker's essay on form. Although many of the ideas are incomplete, the chapter provides a glimpse into how Schenker viewed the nature of musical form. The role of the neighbor note as an elaboration of the fundamental line is discussed briefly (p. 133); we deal with this issue again in Chapter 12 of this book.

9. *Free Composition*, p. 138.

10. One might regard a piece as working out aspects of a compositional "plot," which can involve special motivic, harmonic, and contrapuntal features. Hence the coda could be described dramatically, like the final scene of a play in which prominent characters are recalled and "unfinished business" is completed. Interpreting music (without words) in dramatic terms can offer valuable insights, so long as the interpretations are developed with care, in conjunction with the purely musical attributes of the composition.

11. See Oster, "Register and the Large-Scale Connection," and Gagné, "The Compositional Use of Register in Three Piano Sonatas by Mozart."

12. An awareness of the obligatory register can often help the analyst to make observations about the structure. In the A^1 section, the obligatory register of the upper voice from d^2 to g^1 is clearly established. As a result, in the B section the statement of E♭ in the two-line octave becomes a reminder, a subtle recollection, of the very same E♭ that decorates the primary tone d^2 at the beginning. As the piece progresses, our recognition of the position of the E♭ in the obligatory register eventually enables us to discover the middleground relationships shown in Example 10.6. Finally, in the last segment of the coda we perceive that the piece is "winding down," seeking completion. This impression arises not only from the descending motion of the upper voice (remember that descending motion suggests completion and a release of tension), but also from the fact that the upper voice is returning to $\hat{1}$ in the one-line octave, where it was stated in bars 16 and 52. In a sense, we now expect a final statement of $\hat{1}$ to appear as g^1.

13. For a more detailed discussion of rhythm and meter in Mendelssohn's Songs without Words, see Rothstein, *Phrase Rhythm in Tonal Music*, pp. 183–213. See also discussions of this piece in Schachter, "The Triad as Place and Action," and in Cadwallader, "Form and Tonal Process."

14. We discuss this particular chromatic extension of tonic harmony in Chapter 12.

15. The span of a fourth can be segmented in various ways. Here, in accordance with the motivic grouping, the line from D to G appears to be a step plus a third (D/E–F♯–G). Harmonically, the subdivision is D–E–F♯/G.

16. Note that, technically, the B section begins with III$^7_\sharp$. Because this chord is an *outgrowth* of the III, at a deeper level of structure one can regard the B section as beginning with mediant harmony.

17. Some musicians regard this type of expanded ternary as a Rondo. In this chapter, we will restrict the term *Rondo* (our final example) to pieces that have least two *different* contrasting sections.

18. The bass accompaniment to D♭–C–B♭ can also be described as lower tenths, with E♭ substituting for G for greater stability. (This situation is common beneath $\hat{4}$–$\hat{3}$–$\hat{2}$.)

19. The "downbeat" quality of the opening chord comes from its being a stable, root-position triad, which, occurring at the very beginning, one assumes to be a tonic. The V$^4_3$ on the downbeat, by contrast, is an unstable chord, and one that would more often occupy a weak beat. Its duration, however, by far the longest up to now, gives it an emphasis compatible with its being a downbeat and thus a metrical accent.

20. The chord on beat 2 of measure 16 is given as $^6_4$ in many editions, with A♭ in the thumb of the right hand, and the same in the corresponding measure of the last section. The graph follows the first edition; the autograph no longer exists. Editors have generally been unsure which version is correct.

21. Schubert's emphasis on G♭ (in the bass progression from V to V$^6_5$) might also be explained in terms of a very specific recollection. G♭ is, of course, the enharmonic equivalent of F♯, the key of the B section. Although G♭ supports a major triad, the prominence of this tone as a local goal harks back to the F♯s of the previous section.

22. Another notable feature in the coda section (bars 47–55) is the emergence of the repeated inner-voice tone E♭ above the structural top voice. In the higher register, this sustained tone becomes a *cover tone* (see Chapter 6, p. 149, and Example 6.16.)

23. G♭ (F♯) major is the subtonic of A♭ minor and is therefore more closely related (through simple mixture) to A♭ major than is an F♯-minor triad.

24. Consider also that the top-voice cadential descent of bars 81–82 returns to the higher register

that occurs in the second B section (bars 56–61), so that this higher register is now integrated with that of the rest of the piece.

25. Such notational enharmonics should not be confused with essential enharmonic changes, such as the reinterpretation of a German augmented sixth chord as a dominant seventh.

26. See Chapter 12 for a discussion of the role of the upper neighbor and musical form.

27. This tonal pattern is one of several possible realizations of interrupted $\hat{5}$-lines in the major mode. Refer to chapter 12 for a more theoretical description of middleground tonal patterns and form.

28. One example of a motivic relationship that integrates sections occurs at the outset: if you compare bars 19–20 with bars 21–22, you will observe that in the final cadence of the A section a D major chord is outlined, while the B section begins with the passing motion A–D through a D minor triad. Though partly disguised by the difference in contextual setting and mode of the chords, the close association of these two figures creates a strong sense of continuity from the A to the B section. Such a use of a specific figure or gesture to link two sections is called the *linkage technique*. See Jonas, pp. 7–9.

29. The structural issues raised here are comparable to those associated with the B section of the Beethoven's Bagatelle discussed earlier in this chapter. In that context, the local fundamental structure of the middle section ends, rather than begins, with a tone (the upper neighbor $\hat{6}$) that participates in the structural top voice on the highest level. In the rondo, the primary tone of the local fundamental structure (in the B section) is not the same as that of the work as a whole, despite the fact that its tonic note is still D. As these two very different compositions suggest, the combination of several quasi-independent sections in a work can result in unusual structures. Nevertheless internal factors within the piece (such as the parallel major-minor relationship in our Haydn Rondo) usually clarify the nature and meaning of these middleground relationships.

30. Despite some changes in chords (which are partly related to new accompaniment patterns), the underlying structure of the final refrain remains largely as before. However, one noteworthy change occurs at the final cadence: whereas the top voice tone G ($\hat{4}$) was supported by IV^6 in the previous top voice descents (bars 18 and 58), it is now supported by a IV chord in the final *Urlinie* descent (bar 119). In making these compositional choices, Haydn surely chose the inverted chords in the earlier passages to avoid overly strong cadences and maintain the momentum of the Presto, and then employed the root-position subdominant chord in order to provide appropriate harmonic weight to the final cadence.

31. In his later thought, Schenker found it more satisfying to think about form in terms of governing linear progressions than in terms of "themes" and "motives." See particularly his comments on sonata form in *Free Composition*, pp. 133–37.

32. *Free Composition*, p. 43. See also the later chapter on form, where he reiterates the importance of the neighbor note in the development of formal patterns (p. 133).

33. Salzer and Schachter, p. 58.

34. Schenker says that "only the upper neighboring note is possible at the first level. If it occurred in the fundamental line, the lower neighboring note would give the impression of an interruption. The upper neighboring note, however, is free from the danger of such misunderstanding." *Free Composition*, p. 42. (Schenker is obviously considering a $\hat{3}$-line here.)

35. Schenker's pattern shows an interruption in the A sections, but this does not change the essential "form producing" role of the neighbor as summarized in Example 10.26a. See *Free Composition*, Fig. 35/1.

36. See Schenker's analyses of these pieces in *Free Composition*, Figs. 35/1 and 42/1. See also his analysis of Chopin's Etude, Op. 10, No. 8, in *Five Graphic Music Analyses*.

37. The distinction between rounded binary and ternary is not always unequivocal and you may find that some of these patterns may occur also in rounded binary forms. Certainly the presence of repeat signs helps to strengthen the two-part nature of a rounded binary. Furthermore, the binary quality is also enhanced if the first part is tonally open. Ternary forms often entail tonally closed A sections and the B sections with markedly contrasting thematic material. Furthermore, the A^2 section often balances the A^1 section in length and a coda may follow.

Chapter 11

1. For more information about the sonata, see Charles Rosen's landmark studies *The Classical Style* and *Sonata Forms*. See also William S. Newman's three-volume survey, *The Sonata in the Baroque Era, The Sonata in the Classic Era, The Sonata Since Beethoven;* various works by Donald Francis Tovey, especially *A Companion to Beethoven's Pianoforte Sonatas;* and Schenker's study "On Organicism in Sonata Form," *The Masterwork in Music: A Yearbook*, Vol. II, pp. 31–54.

2. Other terms used to describe aspects of the second key area include *closing section, closing theme*, and *codetta*.

3. Schenker believed that terms such as *first theme, second theme*, etc., do not adequately express the nature of the sonata principle. For one thing, sonata movements are often too variable. You will discover that this tiny movement really has no second theme (but proceeds directly to a closing theme), even though it does exhibit the expected modulatory plan. Other movements do not have a closing theme, while others have only one principal theme (often in Haydn). Although we will consider the significance of thematic relationships (and will refer to themes in our discussions), in this chapter we will focus on the techniques associated with large-scale harmonic plans and the composing-out of the structure. We believe this provides for a flexible approach to what is perhaps the most varied and flexible of all tonal compositional procedures.

4. This type of substitution is quite common and one may refer to this technique as "$\hat{6}$ for $\hat{4}$."

5. Circumstances can differ in cases where $\hat{5}$ is the primary tone. In the major mode, $\hat{5}$–$\hat{4}$–$\hat{3}$ normally occurs before the working out of structural $\hat{2}$ over V produces the second tonal region. In the minor mode, on the other hand, the primary tone $\hat{5}$ may hold as a common tone over a composed-out mediant area. These represent only some of the middleground possibilities.

6. The figured-bass symbols are to be understood *only* in relation to G, the root of the dominant, which is continually active at a deeper level throughout this brief section. The surface chord progression could carry its own set of symbols, (such as $^4_2$–$^6_3$ for bars 16–17), which would be somewhat misleading from a broader, structural perspective. In other words, one should understand the succession of chords at the surface as occurring over a pedal G, which is sometimes not sounding. Schenker referred to such a higher-level note as a "silent" cantus-firmus tone.

7. *Free Composition*, pp. 136–37. In the minor mode, as we shall see, the development section very often *continues* the motion to the structural V$\hat{2}$.

8. This explains why the listener is deceived upon hearing the beginning of Beethoven's First Symphony. The piece is in C major, although the opening bars begin with V^7–I in F. See Aldwell and Schachter, pp. 405–6, for an explanation of this unusual beginning. Also, compare the first and second tonal areas of Beethoven's first piano sonata, Op. 2, No. 1; the transition to the second tonal area begins very early, at the upbeat to bar 9.

9. In other words, we hear an end to the exposition (highlighted by the repeat signs) and a beginning of the development; this juncture is often highlighted by the return of the first theme (transposed) at the commencement of the development. Bear in mind, however, that both sections arise within the first branch of the interrupted structure.

10. One may encounter sonata movements in which the principle of interruption is not the basis of the structure, at least in the strictest sense. For example, in some pieces with $\hat{5}$ as the primary tone, the $\hat{5}$ may be prolonged through the exposition and development sections, which is possible because $\hat{5}$ is common to both tonic and dominant harmonies. This means that the *Urlinie* does not descend over the initial bass arpeggiation (I–V); hence, no interruption technically occurs. Nevertheless, the harmonic motion of the structure is interrupted and exhibits two branches; one might, therefore, plausibly refer to a "harmonic" interruption.

11. At the end of this analysis we present a brief discussion of other modulatory schemes for transition sections.

12. An interesting way of viewing this thematic relationship is to consider that Beethoven has composed a disguised "monothematic" exposition. Strictly speaking, of course, and unlike

Haydn's true monothematic movements, this is not the case; the second theme has a distinct character of its own. First and second themes, however, are often related in similar fashion. In the first movement of Mozart's Piano Sonata in B♭ major, K. 333, both themes begin with a prominent descending fifth. In the tonic environment of the recapitulation one might also hear the second theme as a varied repetition of the first.

13. Notice that we take g¹ in the figuration of bar 42 as $\hat{4}$ in the descent; the presence of G in the tenor supports this reading. Note also the realization of $\hat{3}$ as an appoggiatura to $\hat{2}$, a cadential figure common to Classical textures we have seen before.

14. In Example 11.8 you will notice, in bars 45 and 48, that we have represented the D-major chords in $^6_3$ position. We regard the root-position "tonics" as substituting for first-inversion chords that function subordinately in the motion from IV to V. This elaboration of the IV-V progression occurs frequently at cadences.

15. See the discussion of prolongational spans in Chapter 12.

16. Note that the f♯² is rhythmically postponed until the end of bar 59, avoiding the parallel fifths that would occur if G were to move to F♯ as the bass moves from C to B.

17. For Schenker, the technique of interruption is "a source of form in the foreground. Interruption . . . opens the way to two- or three-part forms . . . it is even the basis of the extended form of the sonata, with exposition, development, and recapitulation." *Free Composition*, p. 39. Implied in Schenker's statement about the development of form at the foreground is the necessity of *prolonging* the dominant of the first branch. We can now begin to understand more clearly how Schenker conceived of formal matters in structural terms.

18. Clementi's sonatina has no second group per se but, in general, it is true that the descent of the *Urlinie* normally occurs in the second part of a recapitulation.

19. However, as stated above, the structural plans for sonata movements are highly varied, and not all of the second-group material will necessarily recur in the tonic.

20. The g² in bar 103 is written as a grace note and is immediately covered by d³; furthermore, the left hand states the root of tonic harmony in a high "alto" register. Thus, closure of the structure appears postponed until bar 110. (If Beethoven had followed the exposition more closely here, the bass of bars 102–3 would have been an octave lower. Hence the high bass register is clearly deliberate here.)

21. Notice in Example 11.12 that we have not indicated b¹ (bar 109) in parentheses. The trill begins on the upper note and hence b¹ is literally stated. As shown in Example 11.12a, b¹, supported by the cadential $^6_4$, is a recollection of the primary tone. Remember, the sixth of a cadential $^6_4$ often appears as a suspension. At a deeper level, therefore, b¹ is a consonant suspension (the D and C "reduce out" at deeper levels). It is worth repeating that the transposed fifth-progression in a recapitulation may be interpreted in various ways, depending upon the tonal context.

22. It is not uncommon to find several authentic cadences in closing sections; these sections typically reinforce the key through cadential patterns. For a similar example, see the final bars of Mozart's Piano Sonata in A minor, K. 310, first movement, bars 116–29. These bars contain three perfect authentic cadences. Only in the third, however, do the right and left hands play simultaneously on the downbeat of the respective bars. Thus, in this case, the third cadence represents the structural close (bar 129).

23. Because the V is preceded by V⁶ of V, we might refer to this goal as a *tonicized half cadence*. For a similar example, see the first movement of Mozart's Piano Sonata in C major, K. 330. In that exposition, the goal of the transition section is a simple half cadence (the V is not prepared by its leading tone). The second theme commences in G in the following bar; in other words, the V of the half cadence in C major is interpreted immediately as I of the dominant key area.

24. See also the goal of the transition section in the first movement of Mozart's Piano Sonata in F major, K. 332.

25. The progression from I to II♯ carries the risk of faulty voice leading (parallel fifths). Therefore, a 5–6 motion very often transforms the initial tonic into a $^6_3$ chord before II♯ enters. If II♯ is preceded by its own dominant, with raised scale degree $\hat{1}$, VI♯ will often occur in first inversion within a chromatically rising bass. Think in terms of C major: in the bass, C–C♯–D.

A 5–6 shift occurs as the bass moves from C to C♯, transforming the initial tonic into V^6 of II♯.

26. The fourth is subdivided into a third plus a step. This interpretation is based on the $\frac{6}{4}$ resolving to the $\frac{5}{3}$ over V.

27. As is often (though not always) the case in Classical sonata movements, the beginning of the transition is similar to the first theme.

28. See Aldwell and Schachter, pp. 235–36 for a discussion of chords built on the upper third and fifth of triads. The difference here is that the chord built on the upper third of the tonic is expanded locally into a brief key area.

29. As we show in the example with a bracket, G reaches over to B♭, which falls to the neighbor A♭. As we have discussed before, the technique of reaching over often involves multiple figures that decorate the tones in a rising line or arpeggiation: an ascending third followed by a descending second is one such pattern. Nonetheless, it is common to find a *single* step or leap decorated by a motion from above.

30. The F appears fleetingly as f^2 in bar 51, and is transferred up and down through several registers during the prolongation of II^6. Perhaps the most emphatic statement is F in the bass register, which is why we have shown the motion from G to F as such in Example 11.15a. Bear in mind also that low A♭ (bar 53) is not indicated in many editions of this sonata, although the tone does appear in the autograph.

31. The graph basically shows the *second* occurrence of the phrase in the closing section, bars 63–67 (bar 59 "equals" bar 63).

32. Example 11.16a shows only one of the two rising fifths. The special bar numbering, shown as 59–63, indicates the repetition in a concise fashion.

33. The second strand, a descending fourth from E♭ to B♭ (Example 11.16b; bars 48–58) appears as a rising fourth from B♭ to E♭ (embellished with a chromatic passing tone) in bars 67–69 (Example 11.16a).

34. Not as frequently encountered, but a very important possibility, is the situation in which the harmonic progression of the exposition moves from I to minor V (as in Beethoven's Piano Sonata, Op. 31, No. 2, "Tempest," I). Here the structural function of the development section is to transform the *key* of the minor V into the major dominant *chord* of the home tonic. This procedure represents a prolonged V and is similar in this respect to the function of major-mode development sections.

35. In Example 11.17b the chords in bars 75 and 85 are expressed in $\frac{6}{3}$ and $\frac{6}{5}$ position, respectively, even though they appear in root position in the foreground of the music (compare to Example 11.17a). In essence, a deeper contrapuntal progression (III-IV-V with chromatic passing tones) appears within a disjunct bass line at the foreground. This technique is an instance of what Schenker refers to as the *addition of a root*. In *Free Composition* (p. 90) he says, "Voice-leading may also arrive at roots by actually adding [inner-voice] tones that are implicit in the context, that is, by placing them underneath the lowest voice." ("Lowest voice" here means the middleground bass shown in Example 11.17b.) Ernst Oster adds in a footnote, "In this process, then, an original $\frac{6}{3}$, $\frac{5}{5}$, [sic; perhaps Oster means $\frac{6}{5}$] or even a $\frac{6}{4}$ position that results from voice-leading is transformed into a root position." In many cases, the root-position chords produce a cadential effect (V–I); in this passage, IV and minor V are emphasized in this manner.

36. The interplay of register has been simplified in Example 11.17b.

37. Similar structural bass motions appear in the first movements of Beethoven's Piano Sonatas Op. 2, No. 1, and Op. 13 ("Pathetique"). The first is analyzed by Schenker in *Tonwille* II, pp. 25–48 and supplement. Chromatic passing tones often intensify each step in the progression III–IV–V. In the first movement of Op. 13, the mediant E♭ concludes the exposition, as in Mozart's C-minor Sonata; Beethoven's development section, however, begins in E minor. In this case, the chromatic passing tone between III and IV (E♮) is emphasized through tonicization.

38. This momentary excursion makes the eventual return of the tonic sound almost like a newly established goal, even though C minor has been in effect since the beginning of the recapitulation. In other words, Mozart has recomposed the transition to sound as if it may modulate, even though it quickly leads back to tonic harmony. Remember, in purely functional terms,

there is no need for a modulating transition section in a recapitulation; for purposes of symmetry, however, composers often found ingenious ways of "modulating" to the tonic of the second theme.

Consider also the deflection of the bass from A♭ to A natural before resolving to G. In combination with D natural (passing) in the right hand, A natural dispels the "dream" of D♭ major even before V of C minor arrives.

39. Eric Wen ("A Disguised Reminiscence") has written on the differences between sonata- form movements in major and those in minor (including the first movement of K. 457). The discovery of the ways in which composers deal with this compositional issue is a fascinating aspect of the analysis of sonata movements. Beethoven, for example, in the first movement of his Piano Sonata, Op. 2, No. 1, composes the second theme of the exposition (in the mediant) with a good deal of modal mixture (elements belonging to A♭ minor are incorpo- rated into the theme). Consequently, in the recapitulation, very little modification is neces- sary; the theme is transposed rather literally from the mediant to the tonic minor.

40. From a broader perspective the descent in Example 11.21 is motion to an inner voice. For this reason we have indicated $\hat{4}$–$\hat{3}$–$\hat{2}$–$\hat{1}$ in parentheses. The actual descent of the *Urlinie* occurs in the following passage.

Note also the absence of a deceptive cadence in the second group. The VI of bar 48 becomes, here, a perfect authentic cadence (bar 145), so that there are *two* complete fifth- descents. Closure is thus emphasized.

41. Codas and codalike passages *often* contain such lower-level descents. Review Example 11.16a to see how the similar descent works in the codetta of the exposition.

Chapter 12

1. There is unavoidable circularity in describing separately such interrelated ideas as theory and analysis. The analysis of many pieces leads to the recognition of theoretical principles, which are then used to analyze other compositions. This is the approach used by Schenker in the development of his theoretical ideas.

2. You might find it useful to think of theory in terms of general possibilities, broad principles that underlie the tonal system. We can then say that analysis seeks to discover how those possibilities are uniquely realized through the specific details of a composition.

3. Some of these patterns are freely adapted from Figure 14 in *Free Composition*. You should study all of the diagrams in that figure to discover how the bass arpeggiation may be further elaborated. Also consult Figures 15–16 to see how the upper voice works in conjunction with these basic patterns.

4. Schenker does not show descending motion in his Figure 14, but these progressions also represent valuable compositional resources.

5. In a $\hat{5}$-line, it is perhaps clearer that the *Urlinie* is essentially an *arpeggiation* of the tonic triad, with passing tones filling in the motion $\hat{5}$–$\hat{3}$–$\hat{1}$.

6. Scale degree $\hat{2}$, of course, is also dissonant against the fundamental of tonic harmony. The point about the problematic nature of $\hat{5}$-lines is that the dominant can provide consonant support for $\hat{2}$, but not for $\hat{4}$.

7. *Free Composition*, p. 20.

8. Schachter, "A Commentary on Schenker's *Free Composition*," pp. 125–26. We highly recom- mend this article for a lucid explanation of some of Schenker's more difficult theoretical issues.

9. Schachter, "A Commentary," p. 126.

10. For a more thorough discussion of the two unsupported stretches and the support for struc- tural $\hat{3}$ in an *Urlinie* from $\hat{5}$, see Cadwallader, "More on Scale-Degree Three and the Caden- tial Six-Four." One reason why $\hat{4}$ and $\hat{3}$ can be worked out with such flexibility is that, in principle, all of the tones between $\hat{5}$ and $\hat{1}$ are passing. We again direct you to Schachter's commentary: "The conjunct upper voice [the *Urlinie*] fills in the 'tone-space' created by horizontalizing an interval of the tonic triad. All of the notes between the first and the last

are passing; some are dissonant and some consonant [against the fundamental tone of tonic harmony]." Schachter, "A Commentary," p. 126.

11. *Free Composition*, Supplement, Figure 18/1 and Figure 19,b.

12. That Schenker associates living qualities with a composition is a significant aspect of the way he thought about music. For Schenker, the development of musical content reflects, in a metaphorical sense, the organic processes of life: "Every linear progression shows the eternal shape of life . . . [a progression] begins, lives its own existence in the passing tones, ceases when it has reached its goal—all as organic as life itself." *Free Composition*, p. 44.

13. *Free Composition*, pp. 43–46.

14. *Free Composition*, p. 45. While Schenker did not treat musical form in a comprehensive manner, it is clear that he understood the development of formal patterns (in the broadest sense) in terms of linear progressions of the first order. In the chapter on form in *Free Composition*, for example, he relates the composing out of $\hat{2}$ over V to the traditional "second theme" of a sonata exposition. A good example of a first-order linear progression (in a binary form) is the fifth that prolongs structural $\hat{2}$ in Haydn's A♭-major Minuet (Example 9.1).

15. This possibility is not described as such by Schenker, but by Ernst Oster in an important annotation to the English translation of *Free Composition*, pp. 138–41. Bear in mind that Oster is considering sonata forms in his discussion.

16. We discuss *prolongational spans* in a separate section below.

17. The designation " =n.n." in the first part of Example 12.10b means that scale degree $\hat{4}$ (the seventh of V^7) resembles and acts like a neighbor to the primary tone $\hat{3}$ of the second branch, but it derives from a passing motion at a higher level. Bear in mind also that, at the first level of the middleground, the only upper-voice tones are $\hat{3}$–$\hat{2}$//$\hat{3}$–$\hat{2}$–$\hat{1}$, with the $\hat{2}$ of the first branch directed toward the $\hat{1}$ of the second branch. Subsequent elaborations, as in Example 12.10b, do not alter the functions of any of these tones. In other words, the interruption resides solely at the first level of the middleground, which is not active during the composed-out link (for instance, V$^{5-7}$) that connects the two branches.

18. The decoration of the seventh from above by a consonant appoggiatura (the octave above the bass) is a frequent contrapuntal procedure, not just a possible characteristic of retransitions.

19. Similarly to expositions in the major mode, this secondary fifth-progression from natural $\hat{7}$ is frequently the basis of the second theme in the minor mode.

20. The exposition of Mozart's Piano Sonata in A minor, K. 310, exhibits the basic characteristics of this middleground pattern.

21. You will notice that Schenker places the scale degree numbers of the second branch in parentheses. His diagrams of interruption patterns are not always consistent in their notation, raising a theoretical question as to whether the second branch is structurally "equal" to the first branch. There does not seem to be clear consensus among Schenkerian scholars on this point. In our view it is acceptable (at least in practical terms) to regard the second branch as a second descent of the *Urlinie*, one which achieves the closure denied the first by the technique of interruption.

22. It might appear in his discussion and initial diagrams in *Free Composition* (Figure 110) that Schenker believes the first chord of an auxiliary cadence should not be the tonic defined by the cadence (regardless of position). However, a I^6 as a beginning chord would satisfy the notion of an incomplete bass arpeggiation (the first tone of the "complete" bass arpeggiation in this case still does not appear). The patterns in Figure 14 of *Free Composition* explicitly show that I^6 and III can function similarly as first elaborations of the bass arpeggiation. Hence, Figures 110, c and d could read I^6–V–I.

23. This possibility represents an advanced aspect of Schenkerian theory. For the purposes of our discussion, it is sufficient to point out that the tonal system is very flexible, even in some of the ways in which the fundamental structure may appear. See Carl Schachter's discussion of Chopin's E-minor Prelude, Op. 28, No. 4, in "The Triad as Place and Action," pp. 150–53.

24. *Free Composition*, p. 88. We initially saw *complete* forms of the fundamental structure in Chapter 5, where we introduced the characteristics of the fundamental structure in terms of a

single phrase closed in the tonic; in Chapter 8, we examined antecedent/consequent constructions (a musical period) in the tonic. And in Chapter 10, in Beethoven's G-minor Bagatelle, we examined a self-contained B section defined by a replica of a fundamental structure in E♭ major.

25. *Free Composition*, p. 88. The phrase "the transition from harmony to harmony" does not refer to the chords of the auxiliary cadence. Schenker is referring here to the transition from one tonicized scale step to another—in conventional terms, from one key area to another.

26. We indicate the beginning of the auxiliary cadence with the I^6 in E♭, not with the V_2^4. Although the V_2^4 can be heard retrospectively as the very beginning of the area in E♭, it is also, as indicated by the broken slur, an outgrowth of the initial tonic. Strictly speaking, therefore, the auxiliary cadence begins with the I^6. Another reason to consider is that the *Ursatz* pattern (the fifth-progression, the bass ascending toward V) begins in this case with the I^6. (Bear in mind, however, that the influence or "outgrowth" of the initial tonic may be absent.)

27. Schenker's text also reads: "The voice-leading is 'closed off' from what precedes it: that is, the IV, III, and II are related only to the forthcoming I; they point only to it." *Free Composition*, p. 88.

28. The expression "source of form" is Schenker's. See *Free Composition*, p. 40. Bear in mind also that Schenker's discussion of form in *Free Composition* (Chapter 5) relies heavily on the technique of interruption as a basic premise.

29. As we have mentioned previously, a link—at a lower structural level—may connect the two branches of an interruption.

30. In Example 12.9 we show a theoretical possibility in which a primary tone $\hat{5}$ may literally be prolonged until very near the end of a composition. The structure may sound interrupted, however, even though the *Urlinie* is not actually divided. The reason for this is that an interruption necessarily occurs at $\hat{2}$ in an *inner voice*.

31. See Rothstein, "Rhythm and the Theory of Structural Levels" for a lucid presentation of Schenker's ideas on rhythm.

32. See especially the three articles by Carl Schachter in *The Music Forum*. Another landmark contribution to this topic is Rothstein's book *Phrase Rhythm in Tonal Music*.

33. The term *expansion* used here is different from harmonic expansion (or prolongation), as will become clear (we are dealing with metrical expansion). Our discussion is adapted from Schachter's "Rhythm and Linear Analysis: Durational Reduction." See also Schenker's discussion in Chapter 4 of *Free Composition*.

34. See Rothstein, *Phrase Rhythm in Tonal Music*, for a discussion of *hypermeter* and *hypermeasure*; the author also cites the origins of these concepts in the theoretical literature. Bear in mind also that this piece is in *triple* meter at the surface level and *duple* meter at higher levels of metrical organization. This is a common feature of pieces in triple meter.

35. *Free Composition*, p. 124.

36. In a theoretical sense, there is a distinction among techniques that involve modal inflection, chromaticism, and enharmonicism. Our focus here primarily concerns chromaticism in terms of tones that do not occur naturally *in the mode* of the key in question. Examples include chromatic elements that represent *mixture*, those that represent secondary *leading-tone motion*, or procedures incorporating both of these types of chromaticism.

37. The bass of the A-major triad in the first part of Example 12.17 is still scale degree $\hat{1}$ (inflected). In the second part of the example, the root has been added to the $^6_3$, creating a root-position chord.

38. *Free Composition*, Figure 53/4.

39. In Example 12.19c, the aligned bar numbers indicate the beginning of the orchestral tutti and first theme, respectively. In terms of the structure, both beginnings represent $\hat{3}$ over I.

40. The exposition of Beethoven's Piano Sonata, Op. 2, No. 3 (first movement) is similar, although Schenker's sketch in *Free Composition* (Figure 154/2) does not highlight the augmented sixth chord.

41. Schenker, *Free Composition*, Figure 111,a1.

42. Schenker shows only a dominant *triad* in his sketch of the Beethoven passage. Other parts

of Figure 111, however, show the VII belonging conceptually to a dominant seventh chord. The second part of Example 12.20 illustrates this situation.

43. One of the major thirds must be respelled if the motion is to lead back to an A♭. In this case, A♭–F♭ becomes A♭–E (a notated diminished fourth).

44. For discussion of compositional techniques involving equal subdivision of the octave. See Aldwell and Schachter, pp. 542–51.

45. Example 12.22b is constructed to show only the most basic elaboration of the bass arpeggiation, how III progresses by step (at the middleground) to V. A more complete graph would show the function of the G-minor passage in relation to the preceding E♭-major and following E-minor regions. It should not be inferred that foreign keys may be inserted at random into a structure.

46. After C major has been established, the music becomes decidedly flat-key oriented, progressing first to C minor and then to E♭ major, before the structural dominant is achieved. These intermediate goals between major IV and V reside at lower structural levels (they are not indicated in the bass diagram). This harmonic plan and the interpretation we present are drawn from Ernst Oster's discussion in a footnote to Schenker's *Free Composition*, p. 139.

47. In this analysis, the V that ends the exposition (bar 27) is not given the structural weight that would be typical at this point in the movement. It is instead interpreted as a "back-relating" dominant, which relates back to and expands the initial tonic, but does not reside at the same structural level as the other members of the higher-ranking progression I–VI–IV–V.

Selected Bibliography

Works by Heinrich Schenker

1904,   *Ein Beitrag zur Ornamentik.* Vienna: Universal Edition.
rev.   "A Contribution to the Study of Ornamentation," trans. Hedi Siegel. *Music Forum,*
1908   Vol. IV, ed. Felix Salzer and Carl Schachter, pp. 1–139. New York: Columbia
            University Press, 1976.

1906   *Neue Musikalische Theorien und Phantasien,* Part I, *Harmonielehre.* Vienna: Universal
            Edition.

         Harmony, ed. Oswald Jonas, trans. Elizabeth Mann Borgese. Chicago: University
            of Chicago Press, 1954. Reprinted: Cambridge: M.I.T. Press, 1973.

1909   J. S. Bach. *Chromatische Phantasie und Fuge, Erläuterungsausgabe.* Vienna: Universal
            Edition, 1909. Newly revised edition by Oswald Jonas. Vienna: Universal Edi-
            tion, 1970. *J. S. Bach's Chromatic Fantasy and Fugue,* trans. and ed. Hedi Siegel.
            New York: Longman, 1984.

1910   *Neue musikalische Theorien und Phantasien,* Part II, *Kontrapunkt,* Vol. I. Vienna: Uni-
            versal Edition.

         Counterpoint, 2 vols., trans. John Rothgeb and Jürgen Thym. New York: Schirmer,
            1987.

1912   *Beethovens neunte Sinfonie.* Vienna: Universal Edition.

         Beethoven's Ninth Symphony, trans. and ed. John Rothgeb. New Haven: Yale Univer-
            sity Press, 1992.

1921–24 *Der Tonwille.* Ten issues. Vienna: A. Gutmann Verlag. (Reprinted in 3 vols. by
            Universal Edition.)

1922   *Neue musikalische Theorien und Phantasien,* Part 2; *Kontrapunkt,* Vol. II. Vienna: Uni-
            versal Edition.

         Counterpoint (See 1910 above).

1925   *Beethovens fünfte Sinfonie* (reprinted from *Der Tonwille*). Vienna: Universal Edition.

Reprinted: Vienna, Universal Edition, 1969. See also "[Beethoven, Symphony No. 5: Analysis of the First Movement]." Trans. Elliot Forbes and F. John Adams, Jr. In *Beethoven, Symphony No. 5 in C minor*, Norton Critical Scores, pp. 164–82. New York: Norton, 1971.

1925–30   *Das Meisterwerk in der Musik.* Jahrbuch I, 1925; Jahrbuch II, 1926; Jahrbuch III, 1930. Munich: Drei Masken Verlag.

Thirteen Essays from the Three Yearbooks "Das Meisterwerk in der Musik" by Heinrich Schenker: An Annotated Translation, trans. Sylvan Kalib. Ph.D. dissertation, Northwestern University, 1973.

The Masterwork in Music: A Yearbook, Vol. I (1925). Ed. William Drabkin, trans. Ian Bent, William Drabkin, Richard Kramer, John Rothgeb, and Hedi Siegel. Cambridge: Cambridge University Press, 1994.
     Vol. II (1926). Ed. William Drabkin, trans. Ian Bent, William Drabkin, John Rothgeb, and Hedi Siegel. Cambridge: Cambridge University Press, 1996.

"The Largo of J. S. Bach's Sonata No. 3 for Unaccompanied Violin" (Vol. I, pp. 63–73), trans. John Rothgeb in *Music Forum*, Vol. IV, ed. Felix Salzer and Carl Schachter, pp. 141–59. New York: Columbia University Press, 1976.

"The Sarabande of J. S. Bach's Suite No. 3 for Unaccompanied Violoncello" (Vol. II, pp. 977–1004), trans. Hedi Siegel in *Music Forum*, Vol. II, ed. William J. Mitchell and Felix Salzer, pp. 274–82. New York: Columbia University Press, 1970.

"Organic Structure in Sonata Form" (Vol. II, pp. 45–54), trans. Orin Grossman in *Journal of Music Theory* 12:2 (Winter 1968), pp. 164–83. Reprinted in *Readings in Schenker Analysis and Other Approaches*, ed. Maury Yeston, pp. 38–53. New Haven: Yale University Press, 1977.

1932   *Fünf Urlinie-Tafeln.* New York: David Mannes School, and Vienna: Universal Edition. New York: Dover Publications (*Five Graphic Analyses*, with an introduction in English by Felix Salzer), 1969.

1933   *Johannes Brahms, "Oktaven und Quinten" u. A., aus dem Nachlass herausgegeben und erläutert von Heinrich Schenker.* Vienna: Universal Edition.

"Brahms's Study, Octaven u. Quinten u. A., with Schenker's Commentary Translated," trans. Paul Mast, *Music Forum*, Vol. V, ed. Felix Salzer and Carl Schachter, pp. 1–196. New York: Columbia University Press, 1980.

1935   *Neue musikalische Theorien und Phantasien.* Vienna: Universal Edition. Vol. III, *Der freie Satz* (Book 1, text; Book 2, musical figures). Second edition, ed. and rev. Oswald Jonas, 1956.

Free Composition, trans. and ed. Ernst Oster. New York: Longman, 1979 (now published by Schirmer).

Secondary Sources

Books (includes dissertations and collections of articles)

Aldwell, Edward, and Carl Schachter. *Harmony and Voice Leading*, 2nd ed. San Diego: Harcourt Brace Jovanovich, 1989.

Beach, David. *Aspects of Schenkerian Theory.* New Haven: Yale University Press, 1983.

Cadwallader, Allen, ed. *Trends in Schenkerian Research.* New York: Schirmer, 1990.

Cone, Edward. *Musical Form and Musical Performance.* New York: W. W. Norton, 1968.

Forte, Allen, and Steven Gilbert. *Introduction to Schenkerian Analysis.* New York: W. W. Norton, 1982.

Green, Douglass M. *Form in Tonal Music,* 2nd ed. New York: Holt, Rinehart and Winston, 1979.

Jonas, Oswald. *Introduction to the Theory of Heinrich Schenker.* Vienna: Universal Edition, 1934. Trans. and ed. John Rothgeb: New York: Schirmer, 1982.

Laskowski, Larry. *Heinrich Schenker: An Annotated Index to His Analyses of Musical Works.* New York: Pendragon Press, 1978.

Mitchell, William. *Elementary Harmony.* New York: Prentice-Hall, 1939.

Newman, William S. *The Sonata in the Baroque Era,* 4th ed.; *The Sonata in the Classic Era,* 3rd ed.; *The Sonata Since Beethoven,* 3rd ed. New York: W. W. Norton, 1983.

Rosen, Charles. *The Classical Style.* New York: W. W. Norton, 1972.

————. *Sonata Forms.* New York: W. W. Norton, 1980.

Rothstein, William. *Phrase Rhythm in Tonal Music.* New York: Schirmer, 1989.

————. *Rhythm and the Theory of Structural Levels.* Ph.D. diss. Yale University, 1981.

Salzer, Felix, and Carl Schachter. *Counterpoint in Composition.* New York: Columbia University Press (Morningside Edition), 1989.

Salzer, Felix. *Structural Hearing.* New York: C. Boni, 1952 (reprinted by Dover Publications, 1962).

Salzer, Felix, and William Mitchell, eds. *The Music Forum.* New York: Columbia University Press. Vol. I, 1967; Vol. II, 1970; Vol. III, 1973.

Salzer, Felix, ed. *The Music Forum.* New York: Columbia University Press. Vol. IV, 1976; Vol. V, 1980; Vol. VI, Part 1, 1987.

Siegel, Hedi, ed. *Schenker Studies.* Cambridge: Cambridge University Press, 1990.

Tovey, Donald Francis. *A Companion to Beethoven's Pianoforte Sonatas.* London: The Associated Board of the Royal Schools of Music, 1931.

Yeston, Maury, ed. *Readings in Schenker Analysis and Other Approaches.* New Haven: Yale University Press, 1977. (Includes annotated bibliography by David Beach.)

Zuckerkandl, Victor. *Sound and Symbol: Music and the External World.* Princeton: Princeton University Press, 1969.

Journal Articles (General)

Beach, David. "The Current State of Schenkerian Research." *Acta Musicologica,*" Vol. LVII (1985), pp. 275–307. This article contains an extensive bibliography on Schenker and his work.

————. "Schenkerian Theory." *Music Theory Spectrum,* Vol. 11, No. 1 (1989), pp. 3–14. This article contains a brief overview of the current state of Schenkerian theory (to 1989). It also includes a valuable bibliography that extends the one in *Acta Musicologica* above.

Cadwallader, Allen. "More on Scale-Degree Three and the Cadential Six-Four." *Journal of Music Theory,* Vol. 36, No. 1 (1992), pp. 187–98.

Gagné, David. "The Place of Schenkerian Analysis in Undergraduate and Graduate Curricula." *Indiana Theory Review,* Vol. 15, No. 1 (1994), pp. 21–33.

————. "The Compositional Use of Register in Three Piano Sonatas by Mozart," *Trends in Schenkerian Research,* ed. Allen Cadwallader (New York: Schirmer Books, 1990), pp. 23–39.

Korsyn, Kevin. "Schenker and Kantian Epistemology." *Theoria* 3 (1988), pp. 1–58.

Laufer, Edward. Review of *Free Composition* by Heinrich Schenker, *Music Theory Spectrum* 3 (1981), pp. 158–84.

Mitchell, William, and Felix Salzer. "A Glossary of the Elements of Graphic Analysis." *Music Forum,* Vol. I (New York: Columbia University Press, 1967), pp. 260–268.

Oster, Ernst. "Register and the Large-Scale Connection." *Journal of Music Theory,* Vol. 5, No. 1, 1961. Reprinted in Maury Yeston, ed., *Readings in Schenker Analysis and Other Approaches* (Yale University Press, 1977), pp. 54–71.

Pastille, William. "Music and Morphology: Goethe's Influence on Schenker's Thought." *Schenker Studies,* ed. Hedi Siegel (Cambridge: Cambridge University Press, 1990), pp. 29–44.

Rothstein, William. "On Implied Tones." *Music Analysis,* Vol. 10, No. 3 (1991), pp. 289–328.

Schachter, Carl. "A Commentary on Schenker's *Free Composition.*" *Journal of Music Theory,* Vol. 25, No. 1 (1981), pp. 115–42.

Journal Articles (Motivic Relations)

Beach, David. "Motivic Repetition in Beethoven's Piano Sonata Op. 110. Part I: The First Movement." *Integral* 1 (1987), pp. 1–29.

Burkhart, Charles. "Schenker's 'Motivic Parallelisms.' " *Journal of Music Theory,* Vol. 22 (1978), pp. 145–75.

Cadwallader, Allen. "Schenker's Unpublished Graphic Analysis of Brahms's Intermezzo Op. 117, No. 2: Tonal Structure and Concealed Motivic Repetition." *Music Theory Spectrum* 6 (1984): pp. 1–13.

———. "Form and Tonal Process: The Design of Different Structural Levels." *Trends in Schenkerian Research* (New York: Schirmer Books, 1990), pp. 1–21.

Oster, Ernst. "The *Fantaisie-Impromptu:* A Tribute to Beethoven." Reprinted in *Aspects of Schenkerian Theory,* pp. 189–207.

Rothgeb, John. "Thematic Content: A Schenkerian View." *Aspects of Schenkerian Theory,* ed. David Beach (New Haven and London: Yale University Press, 1983), pp. 39–60.

Schachter, Carl. "Motive and Text in Four Schubert Songs." *Aspects of Schenkerian Theory,* pp. 61–76.

———. "The First Movement of Brahms's Second Symphony: The Opening Theme and Its Consequences." *Music Analysis* 2, No. 1 (1983), pp. 55–68.

Wen, Eric. "A Disguised Reminiscence in the First Movement of Mozart's G Minor Symphony." *Music Analysis,* Vol. 1, No. 1 (1982), pp. 55–71.

Journal Articles (Rhythmic Studies)

Rothstein, William. "Rhythmic Displacement and Rhythmic Normalization." *Trends in Schenkerian Research,* ed. Allen Cadwallader (New York: Schirmer Books, 1990), pp. 87–113.

Schachter, Carl. "Rhythm and Linear Analysis." *Music Forum,* ed. Felix Salzer, Vol. IV (1976), pp. 281–334.

———. "Rhythm and Linear Analysis: Durational Reduction." *Music Forum,* ed. Felix Salzer, Vol. V (1980), pp. 197–232.

———. "Rhythm and Linear Analysis: Aspects of Meter." *Music Forum,* ed. Felix Salzer, Vol. VI, Part 1 (1987), pp. 1–59.

———. "The Triad as Place and Action." *Music Theory Spectrum,* Vol. 17, No. 2 (1995), pp. 149–69.

Index of Musical Examples

Subject Index